The Abandonment of the West

Also by Michael Kimmage

*The Conservative Turn: Lionel Trilling, Whittaker Chambers
and the Lessons of Anti-Communism*

In History's Grip: Philip Roth's Newark Trilogy

The Abandonment of the West

THE HISTORY OF AN IDEA IN AMERICAN FOREIGN POLICY

MICHAEL KIMMAGE

BASIC BOOKS
New York

Basic Books
Hachette Book Group
1290 Avenue of the Americas, New York, NY 10104
www.basicbooks.com

Printed in the United States of America

First Edition: April 2020

Published by Basic Books, an imprint of Perseus Books, LLC, a subsidiary of Hachette Book Group, Inc. The Basic Books name and logo is a trademark of the Hachette Book Group.

The publisher is not responsible for websites (or their content) that are not owned by the publisher.

Print book interior design by Trish Wilkinson.

Library of Congress Cataloging-in-Publication Data has been applied for.

ISBNs: 978-0-465-05590-6 (hardcover), 978-1-5416-4604-9 (ebook)

LSC-C

10 9 8 7 6 5 4 3 2 1

to Ema and Maya
the north, south, east and west of my compass

Contents

Look at me, going everywhere! Why, I am a sort of Columbus of those near-at-hand and believe you can come to them in this immediate terra incognita that spreads out in every gaze. I may well be a flop at this line of endeavor. Columbus too thought he was a flop, probably, when they sent him back in chains. Which didn't prove there was no America.

—AUGIE MARCH IN SAUL BELLOW'S
THE ADVENTURES OF AUGIE MARCH, 1953

Introduction

Westward the course of empire takes its way;
The first four acts already past,
A fifth shall close the dawn with the day
Time's noblest offspring is the last.
—GEORGE BERKELEY, "VERSES ON THE PROSPECT OF
PLANTING ARTS AND LEARNING IN AMERICA," 1728

SEPTEMBER 14, A Friday, had been declared the National Day of Prayer and Remembrance. One day later, a council of war met in Camp David's main building, Laurel Lodge. Everyone present knew that Afghanistan would soon be invaded. That evening, George W. Bush's national security advisor Condoleezza Rice sang "His Eye Is on the Sparrow" and "For You, O Lord, Are Faithful to Us" to the piano accompaniment of Attorney General John Ashcroft. Before dinner Rice had voiced the words of a prayer: "We have seen the face of evil but we are not afraid," she promised. That Saturday night, with New York's World Trade Center a hole in the ground, its remains still smoking, the future took on an apocalyptic hue. The face of evil had shown itself just three days earlier when the nation was struck by a phased terrorist attack. Thousands of Americans had been killed at work, on the way to work, at leisure, in uniform, not in uniform, indoors and on the street.

1

Throughout the autumn of 2001, that September attack had the feel of a prelude, the opening salvo of a strenuous and terrible new era.[1]

Landing on the White House lawn on Sunday, September 16, President Bush walked over impromptu to the waiting reporters. "This crusade, this war on terrorism, is going to take a while," he cautioned them. "War on terrorism" would stick as a description of American grand strategy after September 11. The word *crusade* had another effect. Within the White House, the discontent registered immediately. "After advisors explained it to him," journalist Peter Baker wrote about this vivid turn of phrase, "Bush never again used the word [*crusade*] to describe the war on terror, but the onetime unscripted utterance proved a defining moment to many Muslims for years." On September 17, in the apologetic mode, the president visited the Islamic Center of Washington. He assured his audience that the United States was not about to embark on a crusade. Casually and spontaneously spoken, the president's wording had evoked all the wrong historical analogies.[2]

Prior to September 11, however, the United States had amassed a rich history of foreign-policy crusades. Quite possibly, President Bush had been spontaneously alluding to them in his comments to the press. The motif of crusading predates the American republic, recalling the European image of a New World. Christopher Columbus had the zeal of the Crusaders behind him, although he did not point his ships eastward toward Jerusalem or set forth to retake the Holy Land. Columbus went off in the opposite direction—to the West. When he encountered land and people there, he comprehended them through the prism of conversion and conquest. Later, countless paintings, murals and sculptures depicted him with a sword in one hand and a cross in the other. Conquistadors and other explorers followed in his wake, faithful knights making the world's known geography amenable to European dominion. The European settlement of the Americas had many of the hallmarks of a crusade, of a holy war.

Europe's crusades shaded into American ones. If England's Puritans could not physically retake Jerusalem, they could at least plant a new Jerusalem on the Atlantic seaboard. The Puritan experiment in New

England was no pacifist exemption to the bloody rule of crusading, all cross and no sword. Without Muslims to contest for their divine Israel, the Puritans faced Native Americans, Quakers, Catholics and other apostates. Those whom they could not convert they were ready, if necessary, to expel or to kill for the true faith. The eighteenth-century American republic jettisoned many of the old Catholic and Protestant furies, but it did not give up on crusades. According to one of the city's designers, the layout of downtown Washington is meant to depict "a crusader's shield, emblazoned with a cross." The westward thrust of Manifest Destiny was not precisely a crusade, though in its invocation of providence and usurpation of others' land it had echoes. As the Crusades had been for the actual Crusaders, Manifest Destiny was for the geopolitics—the territorial annexation, willed, sanctioned and called for by God.[3]

The twentieth century appealed most directly to Americans' crusading instinct. The enemies were legion, and at the beginning of the century the United States had a world-class economy, a world-class navy and much unrealized world-class potential. In a standard trope, the historian Anthony Hopkins denotes the "crusading foreign policy" shared by Theodore Roosevelt and Woodrow Wilson. Looking back on the event that lifted him from Midwestern obscurity to the front lines of international affairs, Harry Truman called World War I "that first crusade." The president who sent him into war, Woodrow Wilson, would surely have agreed. Righteousness was as much Wilson's cause in entering the war as was a cessation of hostilities or the protection of American commercial interests. The Paris Wilson visited in 1919 might have become a new Jerusalem had it not been so stubborn about remaining Paris. London was similarly stubborn about remaining London. Neither imperial capital was eager to make the world safe for democracy—that was not their preferred crusade. But across the Atlantic, Americans were so fond of crusading that they could even do so in the name of peace. Recalling the horrors of World War I, pacifists launched the wonderfully named No Foreign War Crusade in 1937.[4]

The second crusade for Truman and his generation was the Second World War. A war so brutal had to be fought with the fervor of a crusade. Because of Hitler, millions of midcentury crusaders gathered on the British Isles. With the D-Day invasion, they threw themselves on Hitler's French citadel. The general who made the agonizing decision about when to launch the invasion, Dwight Eisenhower, mostly avoided grandiloquence. Yet he titled his 1948 memoir of the war *Crusade in Europe,* which was made into a twenty-three-part television documentary of the same name. By 1948, the third crusade was the Cold War, with Truman a blunt-spoken crusader against Soviet and Chinese communism. Only by delineating a war of good against evil, a clash of the god-fearing and the godless titans, could Truman convince the parsimonious American taxpayer to fund the struggle against communism. In his 1952 speech to the Republican nominating convention, Eisenhower declared that "I will lead this crusade"—against communism. Between 1947 and 2005, Eisenhower's friend, the Reverend Billy Graham, in whose presence George W. Bush was born again, led 417 complementary religious crusades in 185 countries. In 2001, Billy Graham was also compelled to change his language. His spokesperson, Melany Ethridge, explained that after September 11 "there was increased consciousness other faiths in the U.S. would find the term 'crusader' offensive." Billy Graham repurposed his crusades into missions.[5]

AN AMERICAN CRUSADE is an appropriation of a medieval European motif, however inaccurate, artificial or absurd the appropriation may be. An American crusade presumes Western Europe as the touchstone of history and of American foreign policy. Before the founding of the republic, educated Americans—educated British subjects living in the colonies, that is—studied the European past as the history that was truly history. When Americans first had a country of their own, history meant the history of classical antiquity, the history of Europe's beginnings. After that, it was the history of medieval, Renaissance, Reformation and Enlightenment Europe. For the Founders, the United States was more vividly European before it was ever palpably American.

Even the most blatant American gesture of separation from Europe was a European act. The Revolution was fought and the republic founded in a fit of neoclassicism, which provided the founding generation with an inherited political culture neither exclusively British nor exclusively Protestant. The liberty of Periclean Athens could be combined with Ciceronian virtue and tempered with the restraint of Cincinnatus, the Roman who had given up power to return nobly to his farm. A classical education revealed the forces that had corrupted the Roman Republic and the decadence that had weakened the Roman Empire. Thomas Jefferson, James Madison and John Adams could plausibly be portrayed as Roman statesmen. *Publius,* the Latin word for "the people," was the pseudonymous author of the *Federalist Papers,* and George Washington was celebrated for reflecting the best of the classical spirit, for being the picture of civic virtue, a modern soldier and statesman with an ancient Roman's appetite for restraint and limits. The retired George Washington at Mount Vernon—followed by the retired Eisenhower at his Gettysburg farm— was the American Cincinnatus par excellence. An avatar of ancient philosophy in the revolutionary imagination, Washington governed himself so that his fellow citizens might succeed at the tortuous task of self-government, one of the most powerful myths of origin for the American republic. The Italian sculptor Antonio Canova, selected by Thomas Jefferson, fashioned a statue of George Washington in Roman garb drafting his farewell address. The statue was unveiled in 1821 and destroyed in a fire a decade later, yet Washington as noble Roman is an enduring image.[6]

From the very beginning, an imagined classical past shaped Americans' understanding of international affairs. The eighteenth-century Polish-Lithuanian commonwealth was a cautionary example for the authors of the *Federalist Papers.* It was the wrong republic, deficient in executive power and insufficiently ancient perhaps. Far more thrilling was the French Revolution, which might release republican virtue throughout a monarchical and corrupt Europe. The Franco-American intermediary was the Marquis de Lafayette, a hero of the American Revolution who went on to participate in the French Revolution as well. When the Bastille was stormed in July 1789, the key to the prison, as potent a symbol of liberty as there is in modern history, ended up with Lafayette. He then entrusted the key to another lion of the American Revolution, Thomas Paine, so that it might be transported to George Washington, the first president of France's sister republic. In summer 1790, Washington received the key, which can still be viewed on the first floor of his Mount Vernon home. The timing of Lafayette's gift is important: after 1790, the Terror and the arrival of an Emperor Napoleon tarnished the republican bona fides of the French Revolution for many Americans. The prison of European politics had been unlocked. Classical virtue had been summoned and a French republic proclaimed, but in Europe the house of liberty would be long in the making.

After the loss of France to military despotism, after the French monarchy was restored and then rebelled against, ancient liberty could still stir in Europe. Nineteenth-century Greece's independence from centuries of Ottoman rule described a marvelous horizon for democratic Europe. For many in America, it was a sentimental milestone on the Euro-American path to liberty, a departure and a return, if only the Asiatic overlords on the Bosporus could be cast aside. Just as Americans could be latter-day Greeks, Greeks could be present-day Americans. The Greek Revolution that began in 1821 garnered American support because Greece was Greece, a colony of the American mind and therefore deserving of America's diplomatic support. In an 1824 poem titled "The Vision of Liberty," Henry Ware rhapsodized about a Greece that was coming to life—"Oh Greece, reviving Greece! Thy name / Kindles the scholar's and the patriot's flame." Channeling the "Greek fever" of the American 1820s, Edward Everett, a pastor and politician and secretary of state from 1852 to 1853, contemplated "the great and glorious part which this country [the United States] is to act, in the political regeneration of the world." (It was Edward Everett who, trying to recapture the glories of the Pericles funeral oration, gave the longer, less memorable speech at Gettysburg in November 1863.) What the American scholar knew from Greek letters, the American patriot would defend in the arena of international affairs, regenerating the world. Ideally, the scholar and the patriot were the same person.[7]

For the engaged scholar, an imported Europe was ubiquitous in the antebellum republic. Set-piece American architecture had long been Palladian, based on the works of the Italian architect Andrea Palladio. His 1570 volume, *Four Books on Architecture,* was a popular pattern book in the early republic, and Palladian motifs were especially beloved in the American South. They graced Thomas Jefferson's Monticello. They set the tone for the White House itself, which was designed by a practitioner of Irish Palladianism, James Hoban. From roughly 1820 to 1850, a Greek revival in American architecture—simultaneously elite and popular—spread across New England, upstate New York and the Midwest. In 1830, Asher Benjamin's book *The Practical House Carpenter* showed how Greek architectural styles could be fashioned. John Francis Rague, another architectural star of the Greek revival, helped design the philhellenic campus of the University of Wisconsin at Madison and was responsible for the Old State Capitol in Springfield, Illinois. Not far from the frontier, Rague erected a Greek venue for American politics. In 1858, Abraham Lincoln announced his candidacy in this temple. In 2007, Barack Obama did the same.[8]

The versifying Edward Everett helped to found the Boston Athenaeum in 1807. Everett hoped Boston would be the Athens of America. Perhaps in 1807 it already was. A library and place for learned discussion, the Boston Athenaeum was among the first of many institutions intended to harmonize the European past with the American future. In this vein, several great art collections, much more European than American in content, were made available to the public after the Civil War. They were as much civic statements as aesthetic monuments, and they came to define the cities that built them: the Museum of Fine Arts in Boston (1870), the Metropolitan Museum of Art in New York (1870), the Philadelphia Museum of Art (1876) and the Art Institute of Chicago (1879). Scholarly institutions followed suit: the Archaeological Institute of America (1879) and the American School of Classical Studies at Athens (1891). The ruthlessly neoclassical American School of Architecture was founded in 1894. Meanwhile, on the American stage, Shakespeare was everywhere, his characters speaking easily in the local accent. Shakespeare's plays taught European history to those Americans for whom a college education was inaccessible. Shakespeare did this for the young Abraham Lincoln and many others. History, political philosophy, architecture, theater and music consciously and subconsciously situated the American republic in a preexisting European narrative.[9]

The scholar and the patriot were meant to walk hand in hand. Their partnership was vividly depicted in an 1860 mural in a staircase of the House of Representatives chamber painted by Emanuel Gottlieb Leutze, the child of German liberals who had fled to the United States. Titled *Westward the Course of Empire Takes Its Way*, the painting portrays a motley crew of American types rushing toward California's golden light. (Leutze's iconic 1852 painting *Washington Crosses the Delaware* is also in the US Capitol.) Leutze's 1860 mural, a visualization of a 1728 poem by George Berkeley, philosopher, bishop and British man of letters, came from Berkeley's "Verses on the Prospect of Planting Arts and Learning in America." A year after writing the poem, Berkeley visited the Americas himself, hoping to plant arts and learning there. Berkeley wanted to found a college on St. Kitts in the British Virgin Islands. The college never got off the ground, but the intention behind it yielded some enduring lines of poetry:

> *The rise of empire and arts*
> *Not such as Europe needs in her decay;*
> *Such as she had when fresh and young,*
> *When heavenly flame did animate her clay,*
> *By future poets shall be sung.*
> *Westward the course of empire takes its way;*
> *The first four acts already past,*
> *A fifth shall close the dawn with the day*
> *Time's noblest offspring is the last.*

EMPIRE AND ARTS did not signify military power for Berkeley. Those who attached his name to the University of California in 1866 were not commemorating the soldiers of empire. But there it is: empire running its centuries-long course, from Athens to Rome to Paris to London to the New World. Empire *and* arts were to grace this New World. They were due to arrive in Berkeley, California, in 1866. Not just in learning and arts would the American republic crown itself with the laurels of the West. By the 1860s, Bishop Berkeley's poem was honored on a university campus and in the American legislature. Thus did the scholar and the patriot walk hand in hand.

BERKELEY'S POEM UNITED Europe and the Americas in a single geographical motion. *Westward* the course of empire takes its way. In the English language, *west* is a point on the compass and a signifier of evening. *Vespers* is a related word. In Latin, *occident* also means "setting sun," as does the German word *Abendland,* "land of evening." In Russian, *vostok* and *zapad,* "east" and "west," likewise suggest rising and falling. The sun starts the day in Asia—the East, the Orient, *das Morgenland*—and finishes in Europe or farther to the west. In English, Latin, German and Russian, the decline of the West is foreordained by the sun's oscillations from east to west, by its daily fall into the West. The West is the empire upon which the sun is always setting.

Geopolitical meaning came slowly to the West. Athens saw in itself a West opposed to the despotic Persian East. This was followed by the Western half of the Roman Empire positioned against the empire's eastern half and then the territories that would become Charlemagne's Europe (parts of today's France, Germany, Holland, Belgium and Italy). *The West* could also connote Latin Christianity—the Protestant and Catholic territories—as opposed to those of the Eastern Orthodox churches. After the Eastern half of the Roman Empire and its capital Constantinople fell to the Ottomans in 1453, the West might also have been Christian Europe versus the East of Islam, Christendom in the West and an Islamic Caliphate in the East. In the recurring idea of the West, power, belief and geography have tended to bend in the same direction, linking religion and politics to the four points of the world map.

Over the centuries, the geopolitical West has taken on multiple shapes. The age of exploration broadened many of the original East-West divides, serving to globalize them. Whatever the rivalries among the European empires, whatever their religious and political differences, they could still amalgamate into the West vis-à-vis the foreign domains of Asia, Africa and the Americas. Mention of "our western world" dates back to 1601, and in 1839 a distinction was drawn between "India and the western nations." Symbolically, at least, World War I was fought along an East-West axis, a clash of authoritarian (Prussian) East and liberty-loving (Franco-Anglo-American) West, despite the war's many and shifting European fronts. East and West were to be found within and outside of Europe. In 1914, the Ottoman Empire, the German *Kaiserreich* and the Austro-Hungarian Empire were arrayed, according to the London *Times,* "against the Western Powers and Russia." Presumably for the *Times,* Russia stood outside the Western powers in more than just geography.[10]

World War I, World War II and the Cold War were all wars of East against West. In a 1938 thriller about the worsening international situation, *Cause for Alarm,* Eric Ambler wrote that "the Nazis and the Fascisti . . . agreed to pursue a united front to the Western powers." The Soviet Union was not among the Western powers in 1938, but the United States was, and once again Germany was antagonizing the West from the center of Europe. Between 1941 and 1945, the Soviet Union fell awkwardly alongside the Western powers, replicating the World War I partnerships. The Cold War, however, was in every respect an East-West conflict, synthesizing and combining all the previous conflicts of East and West: Athens versus Persia; Western versus Eastern halves of the Roman Empire; Western Church versus Eastern Church; Christendom versus Islam; the empires of the West versus the Asian East; the democratic Western powers versus their enemies in World War I; and the democratic West versus the Nazis and the Fascisti. When China joined the ranks of the communist countries in 1949, the perfection of the East as a despotic foil to the democratic and anticommunist West was complete.[11]

After many tribulations, the West triumphed in November 1989. It did not so much defeat as overtake the communist East. The bedraggled, denim-clad citizens of East Germany voyaged westward over the Berlin Wall. The force was no longer there to restrain them. They, too, wanted to be in and of the West, as did many of their counterparts in the Soviet Union. When the Soviet Union collapsed in 1991 the West was austerely alone in victory, far better positioned than it had been in 1918 or 1945. In 1918 and 1945, the enemies of the West had not been subdued. Interwar Germany and the Soviet Union were still poised to wreak havoc, whereas both the West and the Western model were victorious in 1991. The political economy and culture of the West were all there was, or so it could seem to Westerners in the rush of victory. The task of the 1990s, then, was to export the winning model across Europe and around the world. One might worry about Western hegemony or Western triumphalism in the 1990s, but the strengths of the Western enterprise were obvious. They had found their confirmation in the objective weaknesses of a humiliated communist East.

The geopolitical West having prevailed, the Cold War crusade was finally over. So why, if the crusading West signaled success, did George W. Bush recoil in embarrassment from using the word *crusade* in September 2001? Why did he not stick with a phrase that had caused no controversy when Eisenhower labeled World War II a crusade in Europe? "I will lead this crusade" against the Soviet Union, Eisenhower had declared to thunderous applause and to no recorded outrage or criticism. If anything, a crusade against an Islamist menace made more historical and ideological sense than a crusade against National Socialism or a crusade against Bolshevism. There is something odd about a crusade *in* Europe, because the original Crusades had taken Europeans to the Middle East. Their wars had been waged to regain Jerusalem for the West and to spread Christianity. Was President Bush not at war with Islamist extremism after September 11? Was this extremism not a threat to the West? These queries lead to another more ironic question about President Bush and crusades. Why, after tactfully retracting the word *crusade*, did he join forces with Great Britain and a handful of other European powers for an invasion of the Middle East—in effect doing what the first Crusaders had done between the eleventh and fourteenth centuries? To its critics in Europe, the United States and the Middle East, the Iraq War was a mad crusade launched by "Chief Crusader Bush," as Osama bin Laden referred to the American president in a September 2001 interview.[12]

There is an answer to the question of why a crusade and, by extension, why a lyrical image of the West did not figure in George W. Bush's response to September 11. Something had changed in American thinking about the world, in American society and in American foreign policy since the days of Eisenhower. Put differently, George W. Bush did not respond to the provocation of September 11 as his own father might have. A World War II veteran, George Bush Sr. had been educated at a Western-oriented Yale, class of '40. After college, he enlisted in the Cold War contest of East against West. In 2001, George Bush Sr. might have been more at ease with the us–them rhetoric than his son seemed to be. The elder Bush might have prioritized the diplomatic relationship with Western Europe as the greatest good of American foreign policy. Since World War II, Western Europe and the United States together constituted the West, and in Western Europe skepticism about the invasion of Iraq ran high. George Bush Sr. might have been less certain that the Western political model—democracy—was applicable outside of Europe. He might have banked on the long-term and limited attractions of this model rather than on the project of exporting Western-style democracy at the barrel of a gun. On the basis of these attractions, he might have been prone to contain the threat of Islamist terrorism rather than to attempt its eradication through war, as his son would try to do in Afghanistan and Iraq: to defend the West rather than to march at the head of it. With the actual Iraq War of 2003, George W. Bush found the most bellicose way possible of not mounting a crusade.

THE ABANDONMENT OF THE WEST answers the question of what changed from the crusades of Wilson, Truman and Eisenhower to the anti-crusade or the un-crusade of George W. Bush. It does so through the examination of foreign policy, culture and ideas. It is a history of the West within American foreign policy, a West that is not exactly a cultural affinity or a strategic posture but some complicated, fluid combination of these two things. Cultural affinities vis-à-vis the West can suggest or negate certain strategic positions. Cultural tendencies can augment internationalism or isolationism. Likewise, strategic or military success could consolidate a cultural affinity for the West, as did World War II, and strategic or military failure could disrupt the cultural attachment to the West, as did the Vietnam War. To gain a clear understanding of the West in American foreign policy, its rise and fall must be charted across multiple worlds. One is the world of those who make foreign policy, the world of presidents, legislators and senior diplomats. Another is that of the university, of the figures who set curricula, who instruct students in the books they should love and the books they should deplore and who teach those who will one day make and explain foreign policy. The biggest world related to the West is that of the general public, the polity that contends daily with the vexed questions of American identity and the polity that through elections sets the course of American foreign policy. Identity and policy constitute two open questions that are deeply and permanently intermingled.

The Abandonment of the West begins well before Eisenhower's crusade in Europe. Though it can be traced back to the American Revolution, the concept of *the West* became key to foreign policy around the time of World War I. Confusingly, the West is a place, an idea, a value—or places, ideas and values. In addition to the geopolitical definitions already provided, *the West* can indicate a range of cultural and philosophical constellations. Many of them are mutually contradictory. An incomplete list would include the classical antiquity of Greece and Rome, Christendom, the culture of the Renaissance, the Reformation, the separation of church and state, the scientific revolutions of the seventeenth century, the Enlightenment, the democratic revolutions of the eighteenth and nineteenth centuries, a coded term for white supremacy, European and American imperialism, the spirit of democracy, the rule of law, the practice of social democracy, the practice of capitalism, the preoccupation with rights and eventually with human rights, and the transatlantic merger of ideas and culture since 1945. Even in the hands of a single author or politician, *the West* can be a comically imprecise term of art. Perhaps the label is so ubiquitous in the discussion of history, politics, culture, art, literature, philosophy and international affairs because it is so obligingly imprecise.

Any history of the United States and the West must take these ambiguities into account. They dominate the debates and disagreements over the West: the precious West of Eisenhower versus the disturbing West of his contemporary W. E. B. Du Bois, the luminous West of John F. Kennedy versus the menacing West of his critic Noam Chomsky, the liberating West of Ronald Reagan versus the colonizing West of his critic Edward Said. The West lives most fully in the never-ending battles over what it is, what it means, what it has been. In this book, the West is many things: Winston Churchill's civilization-saving Anglo-American alliance, Truman's wall against communist tyranny, the object of antiwar fury at the time of the Vietnam War, the object of desire in street protests in communist East Berlin and Warsaw and Prague in 1989, the arduous day-to-day work of self-government, the diplomatic efforts to institutionalize peace and cooperation, and the application of military force and covert action in the name of liberty. The West can be all of these things, and more. Even a pared-down definition of the West contains multitudes. Yet in the telling of its story, *The Abandonment of the West* follows one particular definition of the West in American foreign policy. This is the West embedded in a Euro-American narrative of self-government and liberty, a history of liberty, a project of building liberty, a future-oriented heritage of liberty. *The Abandonment of the West* documents this narrative as well as the conflicts and disagreements over Western liberty, over narratives that equate the West with liberty and narratives that equate the West with racism and imperialism.

Accenting liberty and self-government as it does, *The Abandonment of the West* grounds the West of American foreign policy in the Enlightenment. The Enlightenment had its centers in England, Scotland, France, the German lands and the American colonies, from Königsberg in Europe's East to Philadelphia in the American colonies. The United States is a country carved from the stone of Enlightenment thought. Enlightenment ideals of liberty, self-government and reason were incorporated into the US Constitution. More than anyone, Thomas Jefferson forged the bond between the Enlightenment and the main lines of American foreign policy. In much of what he did, he anticipated what would come to be known over time as the West. Jefferson did this best in the Declaration of Independence. "We hold these Truths to be self-evident," runs his incantation, "that all men are created equal, that they are endowed by their Creator with certain inalienable Rights, that among these are Life, Liberty, and the Pursuit of Happiness." Equality is a given, a gift of the Creator. Rights are native and therefore inalienable, and they cannot be made alien. The word *life* pushes Jefferson's sentence open, while *liberty* is its three-syllable keystone, holding up the philosophical architecture. The *pursuit of happiness* comes as its unexpected climax, a happiness to be pursued as one might pursue the truth in a scientific experiment, and happiness as a right endowed by the benevolent Creator. For Jefferson, the opposite of independence was the hierarchy, the disempowerment, the falsehoods, the blasphemy and the terrors of despotism, or Oriental despotism, as he might have put it.

In the no-longer-dependent country, the Declaration's author went on to become the second secretary of state and then president. Sketching his Enlightenment faith in progress in a 1795 letter, Jefferson wrote "that this ball of liberty, I believe most piously, is now so well in motion that it will roll round the globe, at least the enlightened part of it, for light & liberty go together." The American Revolution had been made for export, for politics around the globe, despite the early republic's many weaknesses, its stubborn provincialism and its place on the distant periphery of international power politics.[13]

Thomas Jefferson offers one further clue to the history of the West in American foreign policy. The epitaph on his tombstone lists three distinct accomplishments. By Jefferson's decree, it reads: "Author of the Declaration of Independence and of the Statute of Virginia for religious freedom & Father of the University of Virginia." The Declaration of Independence was penned by a compiler of statutes, which had been woven into Virginia and US law. Philosophical and statutory liberty demanded an institutional vehicle which (according to Jefferson's tombstone) was not the State Department, not the Supreme Court and not the presidency. Political office was glaringly omitted from his stylized self-remembrance. Liberty's vehicle was the new country's first secular university, the University of Virginia, designed with Palladian flair by Jefferson himself. To found a great university, to guide it, to send out from its gates generations of able students may well be a power more extensive and more consequential than the bounded powers of the American presidency. In this linkage between learning and liberty and between politics and ideas, Jefferson was prescient. His contribution to the West in American foreign policy would prove crucial, a virtuous circle of Enlightenment thought and action, and universities (of many kinds) would never cease to have a decisive impact on American foreign policy.

The Abandonment of the West, having defined the West as a transatlantic idea of liberty, traces this Enlightenment idea through two forms and through a drama in four acts. The forms are messianic and military, on the one hand, and legalistic and multilateral, on the other. With Jefferson, liberty could adopt both forms. The Declaration of Independence, in which the "we" is humanity itself and the cause is revolution, is a joyfully messianic document. It boldly decrees that the future United States would be an extraordinary nation destined to play a world-changing role in international affairs. This was not a military proposition for Jefferson. Nor could it have been, given the early republic's precarious strategic situation. Nevertheless, the United States would actively roll the ball of liberty around the world. In this reading, the United States would lead the West because American democracy was the very soul of Western liberty, not the form of government of a nation among nations. Almost every president since Jefferson has been touched in one way or another by the messianic fires of American liberty, and in the twentieth century by the fires of Western liberty.

Idealistic as its wording is, the Declaration of Independence would have been a Jeffersonian fantasy without the US Constitution and related statutes in which liberty was put into practice. The Constitution's legalistic, compromise-centered idea of liberty is the foundation for American self-government and for a distinctively American notion of international order. Through diplomacy, the United States would try to instill greater deliberation, conciliation and cooperation in international relations. This strain of Western liberty follows an argument of John Stuart Mill that "there is not a more accurate test of the progress of civilization than the progress of the power of co-operation." Walter Bagehot, another great nineteenth-century British liberal thinker—much admired by Woodrow Wilson—stated that "progress of *man* requires the co-operation of *men* for its development." An ideal-typical expression of this vision came from the Enlightenment philosopher Immanuel Kant in his *Idea for a Universal History from a Cosmopolitan Point of View:*

> If one follows the influence of Greek history on the construction of and misconstruction of the Roman state which swallowed up the Greek, then the Roman influence on the barbarians who in turn destroyed it, and so on down to our own times; if one adds episodes from the national histories of other peoples insofar as they are known from the history of the enlightened nations, one will discover a regular progress in the constitution of states on our continent [Europe] (which will probably give law, eventually, to all others).

What separates Kant's barbarians from the enlightened is law, the state and an advanced government. In Kant's view, the Romans had construed their state from Greek history at the beginning of the Western narrative. True to his philosophy, Kant does not propose war, spheres of influence, the balance of power or *Realpolitik* as the rhythm of international politics but rather the spread of the Enlightenment itself. This equation of Greco-Roman or Western civilization with legalized cooperation, an increase in the number of enlightened nations and the spread of international law has been among the most durable impulses in American foreign policy. Many American presidents saw in the twentieth-century United States the Kantian superstate of the modern era, the law-giving guarantor of a *pax americana*.[14]

Since the 1890s, the messianic and the legalistic strains of Western liberty have combined and collided in American foreign policy. The most eagerly messianic presidents were John F. Kennedy, Lyndon Johnson, Ronald Reagan and George W. Bush, though Ronald Reagan started no major war during his presidency and found a way to conduct arms control and other negotiations with the despised Soviets. JFK, LBJ and George W. Bush all indulged in high-level military adventures, wars of choice or wars dictated by a love of liberty. Teddy Roosevelt, Woodrow Wilson, Franklin Roosevelt and Harry Truman were messianic-legalistic, balancing military ventures with the furtherance of international order and the construction of multilateral arrangements and institutions. They saw the United States as democratic juggernaut and peace-oriented mediator alike. Calvin Coolidge, Herbert Hoover, Richard Nixon, Gerald Ford, Jimmy Carter, George Bush Sr. and Barack Obama toned down the messianism of the other presidents, pulling back at times from international activism, seeking order in tandem with liberty and usually with one or several inherited wars raging in the background. George W. Bush campaigned in 2000 on a platform of greater foreign-policy humility, on the avoidance of nation building, on a seeming realism, only to take up the program of democratizing the Middle East in 2003 and of "ending tyranny in our world," as he put it in his expansive Second Inaugural Address of 2005. He campaigned as one kind of president and governed as another.

The non-crusade of the Iraq War underscores a final definition of the West in American foreign policy. To exist as a foreign-policy principle, the West needs to be invoked. It must be part of the conversation and part of the story, either as hero or as villain. Though Jefferson did not write or speak about the West as such, he inhabited an intellectual and political culture that was so European that there was no real need to identify a West. This was no longer the case for "the Western Powers" in World War I: they shared the stage with other powers and with other civilizations, of which there was greater and greater knowledge in Europe and the United States. From that point forward, invocations of the West were consequential. The presidents who spoke most often and most glowingly about the West were the Cold War presidents, from Truman to Reagan. After Bush Sr., the transatlantic West was immensely powerful, but the West as a concept, a term and a phrase was fading away. En route to becoming an intellectual artifact of an earlier era, it was losing its coherence, which (putting it mildly) had never been absolute. With the Cold War over and economic interdependence increasing, *the global* started to take precedence over *the Western*. On the Left, the West had mostly negative overtones in the 1990s. It was the shield and crest of empire and white supremacy, while the Right was divided in its commitment to the West. Some, like George W. Bush, wished to make all the world democratic—North, South, East and West. Other conservatives affirmed an American nationalism; a republic, not an empire; a faltering American republic that need to be sheltered from the cold winds of globalization. This republic would be shaped by the racial and religious exclusions that the nationalist Right associated with the West, and its standard-bearer in the 2016 election altogether abandoned the Jeffersonian West of liberty, multilateralism and law in favor of an ethno-religious-nationalist West. From the 1990s onward, *the West* went from a unifying idea to an idea that was either divisive or disappearing.

THE STORY OF the West in American foreign policy is a four-act drama. At every stage, the drama reflects the connection Jefferson established between the Declaration of Independence and the University of Virginia, between idea and foreign policy, foreign policy and idea. A precis of this four-act drama goes as follows. From 1893 to 1963, the West was an ascendant cause in American intellectual life and in American foreign policy, and a frequently invoked cause. Elements of this cause were assembled in the 1890s, by which time American membership in the West had been achieved. Asserting American leadership of the West—not just membership—was difficult and, in a sense, accidental. It took two world wars for American leadership of the West to make sense. Such is the lesson of Act One: Woodrow Wilson failed to bring his vision of liberty to Europe. Likewise, he failed to convince his fellow Americans that American leadership of the West was in their own national interest. After Wilson, the interwar presidents observed the encroachment of fascism and communism in Europe until Franklin Roosevelt could stand by no longer. Never did the fortunes of European or Euro-American or Western liberty seem darker than in the 1930s. Never were Europe and the United States more violently at odds than during the Second World War.

Act Two covers the 1920s and 1930s. At its heart, the West was a development outside of Washington, DC, outside the White House and outside the State Department. The First World War prompted the creation of Western Civilization programs, starting at Columbia University. These programs permeated academic culture, training students' eyes on the great books of Europe and instilling in many of them a sense of cultural kinship with Europe. This secondary story of the 1920s and 1930s, the proverbial high-water mark of American isolationism, contributed to the rise of an American-led West in the 1940s and 1950s. For the United States, this ascent meant a massive commitment to European security, substantial financial assistance and an involvement in the building up of transnational institutions for and within Europe, a thoroughly messianic-legalistic mix. (One of these American-supported innovations in Europe, the European Coal and Steel Community of 1951, would grow into the European Union.) Truman, Eisenhower and Kennedy waxed lyrical about the West. JFK had been educated in Western culture at Choate and at Harvard, class of 1940. JFK gave his effective, effervescent speech about transatlantic liberty in West Berlin in 1963, the same year the University of Chicago historian William McNeill published his academic blockbuster *The Rise of the West: A History of the Human Community*. For decades,

McNeill's was the standard volume on international history at American universities, its title indicative of a certain mood in American academia and in American foreign policy.

In *The Abandonment of the West*, 1963 is the turning point. The 1960s—Act Three—witnessed transformative changes across American political culture. A shift that long predated the decade was the realization that the European settlement of the Americas was not merely an extension of European history but an interaction. So too was all of American history an interaction between the European and the non-European. From 1619 onward, this interaction entailed the enslavement of Africans and their forced migration to the American colonies and later to the United States. Similarly, the Native Americans Columbus encountered in 1492 did not trace their ancestry back to Greece and Rome, or their religion back to Jerusalem. As the historian Thomas Borstelmann writes, "Natives of three continents—Europe, Africa and North America—gathered in the land that became the United States, later to be joined by immigrants from Asia . . . slavery and westward expansion wove together issues of race relations and foreign relations from the very beginning of American history." These are not twentieth-century facts, and they were not discovered in the 1960s. Their revelation had been the life work of the historian and intellectual W. E. B. Du Bois (born in 1868), among many others. Yet the recognition of a wider America in the midst of the civil rights movement, the Vietnam War and the decolonization of Asia, Africa and the Middle East redrew American culture and American intellectual culture—not to mention American foreign policy. Starting in the 1970s, universities fostered a reconceptualization of American history and politics. Ties between the West and white supremacy, and between the West and empire, often invisible to those enamored of Western liberty, became the subject of essays, books and college courses. In academia, the summa of these inquiries into the misdeeds of the West was a 1978 book, *Orientalism*, written by the Columbia professor Edward Said.

Simultaneously, in the 1960s and 1970s, a new kind of American conservatism was being born. It was not critical of the West, but its adherents were almost as worried by the peril of American liberalism as they were by the peril of Soviet communism. The initial rise of the West had been a bipartisan project, culturally traditionalist in part (implicitly Judeo-Christian) and politically progressive in part (broadly supportive of the welfare state). Western liberty and Euro-American cooperation were Eisenhower's bequest to the Republican Party, an internationalist approach steeped in the rhetoric of the West. The hero of D-Day, Eisenhower had gone from leading the North Atlantic Treaty Organization (NATO) to the White House, where he continued the foreign-policy work of his Democratic predecessors, FDR and Truman. This was too conciliatory an approach for the conservative movement of the 1960s. In a despairing book, the conservative intellectual James Burnham decried the enemies within, the liberals who could not see beyond their imprudent optimism (in Burnham's view), who disdained the heritage of the West and who had more appreciation for decolonizing countries and for nonwhite minorities than for those who stood at the center of the West. Burnham's book had a striking title when it came out in 1964: at that moment of enormous American power and Western European recovery, Burnham released *The Suicide of the West*. He had written the prototype for scores of later conservative polemics.

Act Four is an exercise in irony. It could be pegged as the ultimate triumph of the West, as the Cold War concluded on such Western terms. On the American side, the West had a vigorous champion in Ronald Reagan. Even among Democrats, "Reaganesque" would remain a term of foreign-policy praise for decades, seemingly the foundation for an assertive post–Cold War American strategy. This was on the surface. Beneath the surface was ever greater polarization, a split between internationalist and nationalist visions within the Republican Party coupled with a Left-Right divide known as the culture wars. There were endless disputes about the kind of nation the United States should be, disputes about what should be taught in schools and universities and disputes about the legacy of the West in American life. James Burnham's conservative distrust of liberals continued apace, as did the American Left's distrust of antiquated notions like the West. The universities, ground zero for the culture wars, hastily discarded such affirmative narratives as the rise of the West. The scholar's and the patriot's flame kindled by the thought of a democratic Greece—"reviving Greece!"—had been one and the same for Edward Everett in the nineteenth century. Scholarship and patriotism coalesced far less seamlessly in the contentious political landscape of the late twentieth and early twenty-first centuries.

As it had in the 1940s and 1950s, American foreign policy moved with the universities. It moved away from invocations of the West. Bill Clinton consolidated the Western gains of 1989 and 1991 and expanded NATO across Europe without really having to argue for the West. Clinton grounded the Kosovo War of 1998 in legalistic claims, the humanitarian protection of the Kosovar Albanians, and in the responsibility of the United States to guarantee European order. Clinton's actions in Europe upheld his aspiration to global order, and in the 1990s this aspiration was increasingly economic. George W. Bush retained this economic notion of global order but added the Iraq War to it, the pursuit of liberty drowned in undisciplined messianism. The liberal international order, the organizing agenda of the Obama administration, hearkened back to the happy 1990s: humanitarian intervention here and there, the promotion of global free trade and an expectation of liberty advancing in emulation of the American model. A technocrat's idea of the West, the liberal international order was a recognizably Wilsonian concept. It led to much diplomatic excellence, but it had no cultural resonance. It spoke to no recognizable American identity and no historical pattern. Nor did the word *liberal* in the liberal international order endear it to those on the conservative side of the aisle.

At the end of Act Four the West exits stage right. A construct of academics and foreign-policy experts, the liberal international order was not something Americans were necessarily ready to sacrifice for. It is hard to say how many American voters knew what the term meant or whether they were even familiar with it. During the Obama administration, the liberal international order also endured the slings and arrows of outrageously partisan politics. Division and partisanship exerted themselves when Obama's secretary of state from 2009 to 2013, Hillary Clinton, counterposed the liberal international order to the slogan of her opponent in the 2016 election, "America First." In this matchup, the liberal international order did not fare well. By 2016, it had also fallen victim to the vicissitudes of international disorder: the financial crisis of 2008 and its aftershocks, chaos and continuing authoritarianism in the Middle East, the anti-Western agitation of Russia and China, a populist nationalism brewing across the globe. First, the West receded from view in the 1990s: that was one reason why in 2001 George W. Bush did not want to affiliate himself with a crusading West. Then, in 2016, the West fell from grace. The demise of a West defined as liberty, law and self-government was a cheerful prospect to the winner of the 2016 election.

And so, as Bishop Berkeley wrote in another era and with another historical cycle in mind, the first four acts are already past. Importantly, for Berkeley the westward course of empire was a drama in *five* acts. Prioritizing evolution over finality, Berkeley avoided the built-in association of the West with sunset in his poem. He had dawn close with the day rather than evening with the night, and his were verses about the planting of arts and learning, about growth and generation. They were verses about the rising of the civilizational sun and the loveliness of its most recent rotations: *Time's noblest offspring is the last.* The Americans who most energetically willed themselves into Berkeley's fifth act were the arbiters of policy and culture in the 1890s, those who ran the government and those who ran the universities. These Americans believed they were the inheritors of a European tradition and the inhabitants of a rising power—a rising global power, not just a rising hemispheric power. (They were right about inhabiting a rising global power.) They labored to encase this power in forms that would reflect the international stature of the United States. In their political and cultural ventures and in the architecture they sponsored, the educated American elites of the 1890s wanted to show the world that civilization's westward course was at its most interesting, most optimistic and most meaningful in California, in New York, in Washington, DC—and in the recently rebuilt city of Chicago, which had been devastated by fire in 1871. It is with the Chicago World's Fair, the World's Columbian Exposition of 1893, that the story of the West in American foreign policy truly begins.

PART I

The Rise of the West

1

The Columbian Republic,
1893–1919

> So, on beyond Zebra!
> Explore!
> Like Columbus!
>
> DR. SEUSS, *ON BEYOND ZEBRA!* (1955)

CHRISTOPHER COLUMBUS HAD been worshipped in America since at least the eighteenth century. A historical reference point, his name was transformed into the goddess Columbia, and so divinized Columbia came to represent the civilizational pedigree and novelty of the United States. Columbus was perceived as the exemplary Christian explorer, the man of science, the conqueror who planted Europe's flag in the Americas. Too restless to stay within the known confines of the Old World, he was both brave and curious enough to go out in search of the new. Such were the trappings of the Columbus legend. He had set out to explore on his own, the immigrant navigator and traveler, and he was certainly different from those he met in the India of his imagination. He was so different that he stood on their land with the expectation of converting them and changing their ways to the religion, language and customs that were unapologetically his.

Luckily for Americans on the lookout for a national hero, Columbus was not British. He was thus entitled to serve as the patron saint of the new republic, an American before the fact. Destiny made him the one to join America and Europe into a shared civilization and to advance a distinctively American impetus within this civilization. Americans adored him for his twinned European and American roles. "Fixed are the eyes of nations on the scales / For in their hopes Columbia's arm prevails," the poet Phyllis Wheatley wrote in a 1776 ode to George Washington. The Columbia of Wheatley's poem did not just represent an incipient American nation in the watching eyes of the other nations. Columbia was the American nation itself, the republic George Washington had pried loose from the British Crown. The Latinate word, *Columbia,* depicting a goddess rather than a saint, was coined in 1697. Almost a century later, Wheatley was writing in the established genre of the "Columbian ode."[1]

Christopher Columbus the American prefigured George Washington, and Washington fulfilled the Columbian mission. In the national legend, the two of them brought the gift of freedom. A few years after Phyllis Wheatley penned her ode, the minister-scholar Timothy Dwight contrasted Columbia's Western liberties with the bloodletting of a despotic East: "Let the following crimes of the East ne'er encrimson thy [Columbia's] name / Be freedom, and science, and virtue, thy fame." Americans found countless ways to honor their homespun and de facto saint. The *Columbian Magazine* was launched in 1786, and one of Washington, DC's first major intellectual societies, the Columbian Institute, was founded in 1820. In 1791, shortly before the three-hundredth anniversary of Columbus's arrival, the still unbuilt national capital on the Potomac was declared the "Territory of Columbia," which would evolve into the District of Columbia. Today's Washington, DC, continues Wheatley's association of George Washington with Christopher Columbus, and vice versa: the American and the Columbian Republic were the same. In the beginning, "Columbian" had more cultural meaning than the inscrutable adjective "American," homage to

Amerigo Vespucci, the lesser known explorer in 1776, and at that point a word without a history.[2]

Having been absorbed into the American Revolution, Columbia and the Columbian motif continued to spread across the early republic after the War of 1812. "Hail, Columbia," the unofficial national anthem since 1798, gave way with the War of 1812 to the "Star-Spangled Banner," but everywhere else Columbia was gaining ground. George Washington proposed the idea of a national university in Washington, which would carry the name Columbian College. King's College in New York was renamed Columbia in 1794. The Columbian College in Washington was duly founded in 1821, and in a typical switch it later became the George Washington University. A popular Columbus biography, authored by Washington Irving and emphasizing Columbus the pious Christian, was published in 1828. The first permanent monument to Columbus, the Columbus Obelisk, went up in Baltimore in 1792. Other place names traced a story of their own: Columbia, South Carolina (1786); the Columbia River (1792); Columbus, Ohio (1812); Columbia, Missouri (1821) and Columbus, Georgia (1828).

If anything, the intoxication with Columbus intensified over the course of the nineteenth century. Columbus's close proximity to American nationhood was sculpted onto the Columbus doors of the US Capitol. Cast in Munich and installed in the Capitol in 1863, the bronze doors were modeled on the Ghiberti doors of the Florence Baptistery, with scenes from Columbus's life engraved on them—*The Departure of Columbus from Palos (1492)*, for example, and *Landing of Columbus in the New World (1492)*. The doors were moved inside to the Pantheon-like Rotunda's entrance in 1871, where one could also take in John Trumbell's painting *The Landing of Columbus* (installed in the Capitol in 1847). At the portal to the American republic was the story of Columbus, the archetypal American in this historical scheme. Columbus was the benefactor who had discovered, among other things, the landscape of American freedom. In 1876, on the hundredth anniversary of the republic, a Columbus statue was placed near Philadelphia's Memorial Hall, and on October 13, 1892, New York

City commemorated the four-hundredth anniversary of Columbus's voyage with the unveiling of Columbus Circle. Manhattan mounted its Columbus on a pedestal amid five full days of Columbian celebration. A Columbian ode was composed to celebrate this particular anniversary: it would become the Pledge of Allegiance. When Woodrow Wilson launched his national tour to promote the League of Nations in September 1919, he did so in Columbus, Ohio, as if to bookend this entire chapter in the life of the Columbian Republic.[3]

Between the dedication of Columbus Circle in 1892 and Woodrow Wilson's efforts to create a League of Nations in 1919, what had long ago been defined as the Columbian Republic consolidated itself economically and militarily. The pieces were in place for American leadership of the West, but they were not yet assembled into a workable arrangement in 1892 or in 1919. According to the historian Adam Tooze, "When an American sense of providential purpose was married to massive powers, as it was to be after 1945, it became a truly transformative force. In 1918 the basic elements of that power were already there, but they were not articulated by the Wilson administration or its successors." The articulation took time, and one of its main elements was cultural. An allegiance to the cosmopolitan West and to a larger Europe was forming, though more locally Protestant and Anglo-Saxon ties were also strengthening in this period. They would culminate in the Anglo-Saxonism of the 1920s, in a reassertion of Protestantism and Anglo-Americanism against the many cultures of immigration. In the 1890s, American universities and American cities were already exceeding the borders of the Protestant small town around which the early republic had taken shape. By dressing themselves in the garb of Western civilization, these cities and universities could write themselves into a less parochial story. Appropriation of a classical past and of contemporary European idioms in the great train stations and civic architecture of the turn-of-the-century United States alluded to participation in a broadly European future.[4]

The acquisition of haphazard power circa 1893 instilled a taste for concerted power. The early republic took comfort in being outside international relations as Europe practiced these cunning arts. It was proudly anti-imperial, self-consciously virtuous and indigenously republican. Its presidents might worry about entangling alliances and going off in search of monsters to destroy: the monsters were far away; at home there was safety in the distance from the monstrous outside world. In the 1890s, the ascendant Columbian Republic won a war against Spain and became an empire. For the president and vice president overseeing this war, William McKinley and Teddy Roosevelt, respectively, imperialism was the next logical step in American foreign policy. If it was not the United States, it would be some other power colonizing the Philippines and asserting itself in the Caribbean, they feared. With international affairs a going European concern, the United States would have to play by European rules. Europe's rules were the only rules, McKinley and Roosevelt seemed to be saying: they granted no American exception. This concession raised questions about liberty and self-government as aspects of American foreign policy. By adopting colonies, the United States was reversing the calculus of the American Revolution. Somehow it found itself on the side of the Red Coats facing an array of latter-day Minutemen. Membership in the club of Western powers, however gratifying to some, tarnished the ideals of the American Revolution.

Woodrow Wilson's self-styled mission was to realign American foreign policy with liberty and self-government, and so to contemplate American-style leadership of the West. He built upon the work of his predecessors, continuing treaty-making projects that were important to the budding foreign-policy establishment of the early twentieth century. Liberty and self-government hammered out through deliberation and multilateral treaties were ideals Wilson inherited from Roosevelt and his energetic secretary of state, Elihu Root. Wilson also profited policy-wise from the military investments Roosevelt and others had made, but the international scene around him was startlingly new. France and Britain were the only empires to emerge from the Great War unscathed. The German *Kaiserreich* Empire, the Russian Romanov Empire, the Austro-Hungarian Habsburg Empire and the Ottoman

Empire all collapsed as a result of the war and with them the European stranglehold on international affairs. It was an extraordinary opening for the United States, and Wilson tried to make the most of it. Yet Wilson's bid for an American-led West and his gesture toward liberty and self-government were as premature as they were consequential. They died in the US Congress. The road not taken before World War II, the American-led West of the 1940s would not have come together into a transformative force had the preconditions—the power and the cultural and political missions—not been approached long before. They were first approached by the Columbian Republic of the 1890s.

THE APOGEE OF Columbian fervor was reached four centuries and a year after the Italian explorer crossed the Atlantic. It occurred not in New York or in the District of Columbia but in the landlocked Midwest. In 1890, the House of Representatives passed an act "to Provide for the celebration of the four-hundredth Anniversary of the Discovery of America by Christopher Columbus by holding an International Exhibition of Arts, Industries, Manufactures and the Products of the Soil, Mine, and Sea, in the City of Chicago, in the State of Illinois." The World's Columbian Exposition exceeded its congressional mandate, demonstrating the stunning modernity of the United States to a global audience, the vitality and the might of the maturing Columbian venture. A child of European civilization, the United States was asking Europeans to travel to America in 1893 and to gaze in wonder at the Chicago World's Fair. Many Europeans—from the Duke of Veragua, said to be a descendant of Columbus, to Archduke Franz Ferdinand, whose assassination would launch the First World War—were happy to oblige.[5]

The Chicago World's Fair was a laboratory sample of the Columbian Republic. Columbus was its more-than-allegorical hero. Spain sailed replicas of the *Niña, Pinta* and *Santa Maria* into Chicago. At the fair itself, a copy of the monastery where Columbus decided to make his voyage—La Rabida in Palos, Spain—was among the attractions. A separate Columbus statue, fashioned by the sculptor Mary Lawrence, depicted Columbus with waving flag, cross and sword—Columbus the onward-rushing Christian soldier. On the fair's enormous columned peristyle was the quadriga, a statute of Columbus in a chariot and in Roman garb, staring over at the Statue of the Republic and across to the Columbian Fountain. The fountain was elaborate, a huge boat flanked by statues of Fame and Time. Famous over time, the remembered Columbus was transformed into a symbol of America, a center of industrial power, art and democracy. At the World's Fair, Columbus and Columbia were also inchoate symbols of American foreign policy. The historian Frederick Jackson Turner indicated this obliquely in the lecture he gave in Chicago during the fair. He noted the closing of the frontier: "And now, four centuries from the discovery of America, the frontier was gone, and with its going has closed the first period of American history." (In this same lecture, Turner dissociated the United States from Europe, contending that "the growth of nationalism and the evolution of American political institutions were dependent upon the advance of the frontier.") The fair suggested that the next frontier would be the outward expansion of the United States in the Pacific and the Atlantic. Hoping to unite Europe with Asia, Columbus had not stood still. Neither would the country that defined itself as the living embodiment of his legacy.[6]

The Columbian Republic's grandiose foreign-policy ambitions were intimated in less-than-eternal poetry and prose. At the fair's dedication ceremony, Harriet Monroe's "Columbian Ode" was put to music and sung by a chorus of five thousand:

> *Columbia, my country! dost thou hear?*
> *Ah? dost thou hear the song unheard of time?*
> *Those strange sounds lure thee on, for thou shalt be*
> *Leader of nations through the autumnal gales*
> *That wait to mock the strong and wreck the free*

Monroe placed American leadership of nations somewhere in the future—"thou shalt be"—its current strength necessary against the mocking and illiberal autumnal gales. At the opening ceremony, President Grover Cleveland associated the fair's magnificent buildings, their gargantuan size and scale, with the grandeur of liberty and self-government, which he termed popular government. President Cleveland did not limit his purview to the United States. He spoke in a global vocabulary: "We have built these splendid edifices; but we have also built the magnificent fabric of popular government, whose grand proportions are seen throughout the world." This optimism and this hunger for an audience ("seen throughout the world") were the fair's obvious program. According to Henry Adams—the historian, grandson of John Quincy Adams and the great-grandson of John Adams—"Chicago was the first expression of American thought as a unity." Foreign policy, industry, architecture and art were all aspects of the national unity Adams sensed in Chicago.[7]

The Chicago World's Fair conveyed unintended messages in addition to the pompous official ones. The fair drove home the country's social and racial stratification. Its prestigious center was Euro-American, neoclassical and dedicated to the achievements of industry and high culture. (Antonin Dvorak conducted a concert at the fair.) Outside this neoclassical core, the so-called Midway Plaisance was given over to popular pleasures—the fair's beloved Ferris wheel, a German beer garden, burlesque and variety shows. (In a charming irony of American intellectual history, the Midway Plaisance was eventually absorbed into the campus of the nation's most serious university, the University of Chicago.) The Plaisance also featured Orientalist entertainment and zoo-like displays of non-European peoples, a Dahomey village and a Java village. Frederick Douglass criticized the Dahomey village for featuring "African savages brought here to act the monkey." Others referred to Chicago's fair as "white America's World's Fair," a pun on references to the fair as the White City because so many of its buildings were white. Just outside the fairgrounds, crowds flocked to Buffalo Bill Cody's Wild West Show, a further association of non-European peoples with lowbrow entertainment. Despite Harriet Monroe's accent on freedom and President Cleveland's accent on popular government, the fair was more stylistically in tune with European imperialism than it was with an open-ended democracy, although ethnic and racial division was hardly a foreign import to the United States. These hierarchies and divisions were the melody of post–Civil War American politics. The rallying around Columbus, the progenitor of Spanish dominion in the New World, tipped the scale further toward a celebration of empire.[8]

After the fair, with all its contradictions, was taken down in the fall of 1893, a germinating idea of the West drew on the vast, almost limitless reservoir of neoclassicism and general Europhilia in American life. In the Columbian Republic, the institution that domesticated Western civilization was not the state and not the church. It was the university, which in the 1890s and early twentieth century was manufacturing Western civilization on native ground. Many of the nation's colleges and universities were islands of a dream Europe superimposed onto the American landscape, quasi-European institutions with an American purpose. They were suggestive of an antiquity that had nothing to do with the Western Hemisphere. Columbia University situated an oversized Pantheon in New York City with Low Library (1895), its campus a neoclassical haven as far in spirit as could be from the skyscrapers and frenetic streets of Midtown and Downtown. The University of California at Berkeley erected its lovely Greek Theater (1903) in a Mediterranean setting, with some financial support from William Randolph Hearst of newspaper fame, money from a grubby modern business washed clean by a sparkling bit of academic neoclassicism. Harvard University finished building its massive pillared temple to learning, Widener Library, in 1915.

Turn-of-the-century American universities were eager to make the classical or Western heritage more accessible. This was hardly education for all, but its effects were supposed to ripple beyond the miniscule elite who attended college. The universities tried to reach out by building antiquities museums and by cultivating great-books programs in English. Harvard ceased making the command of classical languages compulsory in 1883. By 1905, most American colleges had dropped Greek and Latin requirements, paving the way for a Western civilization curriculum of translated texts to which any able high school student could be introduced. Even so, between 1890 and 1915 more American high school students studied Latin than all other foreign languages combined. In these years, it could be hard to study either American history or American literature at American schools and universities. It was certainly less prestigious than studying European letters. In a representative example, the young W. Averell Harriman, a future giant of Cold War diplomacy, graduated from Groton in 1909. There he absorbed Latin, Greek, ancient history and the history and culture of England. His teachers encouraged him to look down on the study of American history.[9]

The will to Americanize a classically inflected Western civilization was widespread, and it served more than educational ends. For Chicago's Jane Addams, access to classical culture was a way to combat poverty and to raise the poor to a higher level of respectability. Charles Eliot Norton, a nineteenth-century polymath, "concocted Western civilization" at Harvard, in the words of his biographer James Turned. For Norton, the very origins of Americans' lives are classical: "With the Greeks our life begins," he wrote. Education must connect American students to "the historic evolution of our civilization," he argued, a trust held in common and accessed (for Norton) through study rather than through biological lineage. For Norton, Greek and Roman antiquities gave Americans access to their civilizational self. Classical antiquities also held within them the secrets of power, the wonders of civilization that were case studies in the exercise of power. Through antiquities students could "gain fuller acquaintance with the genius of these commanding races, and a truer appreciation of their works, and thus a better understanding of the origins and nature of their own civilization," Norton wrote. His logic was not at all atypical in 1900. Students gain understanding of their own civilization through the appreciation of ancient works, and by doing so they come to know the genius of the commanding races. This was not an education in speaking truth to power. It was an education in refining power with truth and in learning the truth so as to hold power in the right way. Norton's pedagogic convictions delineated the typical Columbian aptitudes. In the Columbian Republic, as at the Chicago World's Fair, genius and command were cognates.[10]

Building on the fair's eclecticism and global reach, American universities had a fixation on the West that might open students' minds. The West could be simultaneously modern and classical, pagan and pious, Catholic and Protestant. It was a civilization of stimulating, irresolvable contradictions, which suited a country of immigrants that was heading out into the world commercially and in its foreign policy. The historian Lawrence Levine writes of the Western Civilization programs as integrative: "Western Civilization promised to be a unifying and assimilative force which taught the separate groups that they had common and deeply rooted heritage that bound them together." Classical antiquity led to medieval Europe, which led to the Renaissance, which led to the medley of modern times. Such was history's three-part rhythm, and to know it as an American was to know (however improbably) our own civilization—that was the overarching idea. This capacious West overflowed the boundaries of Anglo-American or Anglo-Saxon Protestantism, which otherwise continued to drive elite American culture. A popular 1916 textbook, *Ancient Times: A History of the Ancient World*, by James Breasted, gave students a narrative of civilization to which Christianity was peripheral. In 1816, despite the overweening obsession with classical antiquity, Breasted's dislodgement of the Christian faith would have been less popular. It might even have been scandalous. In 1916, it was within the academic mainstream.[11]

The ethos and architecture of the Chicago World's Fair redefined the American city as well as the American university. It launched the City Beautiful movement, which consisted of large-scale planning, grand buildings, open spaces and neoclassicism run amok. Nowhere was the effect more meaningful than in the nation's capital. The only planned city in the United States, Washington once had a Tiber Creek. The city had been envisioned from the start as the Rome of the Western Hemisphere. The Capitol Building, a work in progress from 1793 to 1863, was no Athenaeum. Its enormous dome signaled the power of the people or it signified power as such. When finally completed, the Capitol was a building that sacrificed graceful proportion to gargantuan size. The Capitol was a republican structure that could fit the continental empire manifestly destined to be American: the *o* in its name was there to remind Americans of their ancestral ties to Rome, to the Roman Senate and to the Capitoline hill that had once been the locus of Roman governance. Such ancestry ran through an appropriated political philosophy more than through any one recognizable genetic line (British or American).

Yet the city that had grown up around the Capitol was anything but Roman. It had all the hallmarks of a backwater: a modest White House and a few administrative buildings surrounded by muddy roads, taverns and inns. A mess of railroad tracks wound its way through the city center. In the satiric cadences of Charles Dickens, who visited Washington in 1842, this was the "City of Magnificent Intentions . . . [of] Spacious avenues, that begin in nothing, and lead nowhere; streets, mile-long, that only want houses, roads and inhabitants; public buildings that need but a public to be complete; and ornaments of great thoroughfares, which only lack great thoroughfares to ornament." Washington was a place to conduct business, to pass through or to get through. Its very lack of grandeur could be deemed democratic. Washington had the republican virtue of not being Paris or London or Saint Petersburg, leaving the American will to power—for a while—to Chicago and New York City, which had always had a taste for megalomaniac architecture. But neither Chicago nor New York was the capital. Whatever it could do, New York could not set the cultural tone for American politics. Still less was it the site of American diplomacy.[12]

For the late-nineteenth-century capital city, the Chicago World's Fair pointed the way forward. The fair had been the product of elaborate top-down design, and its design merged the modern with the neoclassical. Steel frames held up ancient decorative motifs, with ample space devoted to the planned integration of nature. The fair buildings were required to be white, their geometry carefully predetermined.

They re-created an American idea of Rome and of Venice on Lake Michigan, yet their construction involved the most advanced technology. That was the American twist—blueprints from antiquity plus the latest in engineering and convenience. The Chicago World's Fair was first the architectural fantasy and then the designed reality of Daniel Burnham, Charles McKim and Frederick Law Olmsted, two superstar architects and one superstar landscape architect. (Olmsted had designed Central Park long before he worked on the Chicago World's Fair.) After their spectacular triumph in Chicago, these designing celebrities turned their gaze to Washington, DC.

Burnham and Olmsted would leave their mark on Washington, but the architect who did more than any other to enshrine the Columbian Republic in stone was Charles McKim. Educated at Harvard and at the École des Beaux-Arts in Paris, McKim had been trained to imagine new buildings from ancient ruins. With his classicizing eye, he conjured the library, the university, the city and the polity from one architectural aesthetic. (Columbia's Low Library is his design.) Drawing on Parisian and Italian models, he designed the Boston Public Library (1895). That same year, he Romanized New York by providing it with a triumphal arch, Washington Square Arch, which commemorated Washington's inauguration in New York in 1789, not an event most New Yorkers would remember, but a good excuse to give New York the arch that would elevate it to the first rank of cities. In the absence of a Constantine or a Napoleon, George Washington would have to do. In 1894, McKim founded the American Academy in Rome. Coming from McKim, Burnham and others, the impetus for this institution was the Chicago World's Fair. McKim's studio designed the academy's gorgeous main building (1914) on the Gianicolo Hill. McKim was invited to redesign the White House interior in 1903, and in 1910 he completed a masterpiece inspired by the Baths of Caracalla ruins in Rome, New York's Pennsylvania Station.

Having met up with Burnham and Olmsted at a fateful American Institute of Architects meeting in Washington, DC, in 1900, McKim and his colleagues conceived of a new capital city that was also a revival of Pierre L'Enfant's 1792 vision for Washington. Miraculously, Congress endorsed and funded their plans. Their recent success in Chicago and the immediate popularity of the fair's style must 'have convinced Congress that these were the men to lift Washington from its dingy nineteenth-century mediocrity into twentieth-century dignity and elegance. The Senate Park Commission, formed in 1901 with a push from Michigan senator James McMillan, released a plan in 1902 (since known as the McMillan Plan) for a core monumental city that would feel timeless, neither of the eighteenth or the twentieth century. The McMillan Plan realized the Founders' ambition to derive the best from antiquity and to make it American. At the beginning of the twentieth century, the city of Washington made itself modern, not by conceding to the skyscraper, an obvious symbol of Americanness and of industrial engineering, but by forming neoclassical structures into the civic representation of democracy—the legislature, the library, the museum, the memorial—aerated by the open green spaces of the National Mall.

To build this new city, some existing parts had to be destroyed, some parts had to be developed and some added. An anarchy of train tracks was removed to make way for the National Mall. The tracks found their new terminus in Union Station, a station modeled on the Baths of Caracalla and Rome's Arch of Constantine. No backwater could be entered or left through Union Station in Washington, DC. Harvard's president Charles Elliot was asked to choose the allegorical statuary for the building's Main Hall. He picked out Greek gods representative of creativity and technology—the great Columbian themes. Opened in 1907, Union Station was a version of the enormous structures Burnham had designed for the Chicago World's Fair. In Washington rather than in Chicago, this neoclassical behemoth belongs spatially and thematically to the National Mall and is in effortless dialogue with the neoclassical US Capitol Building. From it, one could of course travel up the East Coast to McKim's similarly styled Penn Station.

Though the Thomas Jefferson Building of the Library of Congress predated the McMillan Plan, it fit comfortably within it. Completed in 1897, its Italian Renaissance style was of a piece with the US

Capitol. A soaring interior clarified America's place in the tapestry of civilization in general and in Western civilization in particular. Nine names are etched over the main entrance honoring science, history and literature. They too had been selected by Charles Elliot: Demosthenes, Emerson, Irving, Goethe, Macaulay, Hawthorne, Scott, Dante, Franklin. The reading room dome provides the following road map of civilization: Egypt (written records), Judea (religion), Greece (philosophy), Rome (administration), Islam (physics), Middle Ages (modern languages), Italy (fine arts), Germany (painting), Spain (discovery), England (literature), France (emancipation) and the United States (science). The reading room contains sixteen bronze statues grouped into pairs: Moses and Saint Paul (religion), Christopher Columbus and Robert Fulton (commerce), Herodotus and Edward Gibbon (history), Michelangelo and Beethoven (art), Plato and Francis Bacon (philosophy), Homer and Shakespeare (poetry), Isaac Newton and Joseph Henry (science). Edwin Blashfield's mural on the top of the dome was titled—naturally—*The Evolution of Civilization*. In its design, statues, murals and lists of honorific names, the Boston Public Library (constructed during 1888–1895), outlined a cultural program similar to that of the Library of Congress.

The lamp of learning, lit in European antiquity, was burning brightly in the modern United States. In fact, a twelve-foot torch of learning stands atop the Library of Congress dome. Given its proximity to the Capitol, the Library of Congress repeated a thesis statement that informs the entire ensemble of buildings around the National Mall: *translatio studii,* the geographic movement of learning, mirrors *translatio imperii,* the geographic movement of power. These were twinned processes. They can be fulfilled only if pursued in tandem. Large and somewhat bland neoclassical office buildings, for the House and the Senate, were put up in 1908 and 1909, filling out the Capitol into a legislative complex. This complex occupies the eastern side of the Mall, furnishing the place where presidents take the oath of office. A 1922 statue of Ulysses S. Grant looks westward across the Mall, the largest equestrian statue in the United States. His gaze takes in the US

Botanic Gardens to his left, a 1933 building designed in the style of a seventeenth-century French greenhouse. To his right stand two assertively neoclassical museums, the National Museum of Natural History (1881) and the National Gallery of Art (1941).

On the western side of the Mall, a centerpiece of the McMillan Plan was constructed between 1914 and 1922. Congress had established a Lincoln Monument Association in 1867. The McMillan Plan determined the spot for the memorial. Henry Bacon's design for the structure, which unites Greek and Roman motifs, was approved in 1913. Daniel Webster French's statue of Lincoln is more meditative and more melancholic than the typical neoclassical monument to a great leader. Lincoln seems to be reflecting on the losses of the Civil War. The Great Emancipator is seated on a chair rather than a horse. He has no weapon, no cross, no hand raised in victory, but in his scale and serenity he is clearly a god. He is entitled to the temple that honors him and to the worshippers who ascend its steps to pay their respects to his memory. Despite the relatively late date of the Lincoln Memorial's construction, the National Mall and the city of Washington would be unthinkable without this twentieth-century Pantheon made of Colorado marble and Indiana limestone.

The McMillan Plan set the tone for public architecture in Washington well into the 1930s. Three structures designed by John Russell Pope, an alumnus of the American Academy in Rome and Franklin Roosevelt's architect of choice, extended the National Mall: the National Archives (1935), with its attic friezes and seventy-two Corinthian pillars; the Jefferson Memorial (1943), another remake of the Pantheon and a tribute to the rotundas Jefferson had himself designed for Monticello and the University of Virginia; and the National Gallery of Art on the site where the Baltimore and Potomac Railroad Station had once stood. In addition, Cass Gilbert's 1935 white marble Supreme Court Building has a profusion of statues and mural cycles that honor the long civilizational legacy of law in America, Western civilization ad infinitum. The McMillan Plan left Washington an indelibly neoclassical city. Throughout the twentieth century, statehouses and city halls (and banks) around the country copied Washington's governing aesthetic, especially its fondness for domes and neoclassical columns. The progress of civilization painted in the Library of Congress dome captured an enthusiasm for progress and civilization that was a leitmotif of the 1890s. Once the buildings were built, expressing civilization's progress in America, expressing the happy marriage of learning and liberty, they could not be unbuilt. They stood there with a message to be accepted or rejected or ignored by future generations.

As THE INSPIRATION for a new capital city, the Chicago World's Fair prompted an awkward foreign-policy question. Was the United States becoming an empire? Was that what these refurbished Baths of Caracalla were about? Was the new Rome awaiting its emperor? Or was the democratic United States going to take on European imperialism and fight for an international order for which there was no historical precedent? Until 1914, the makers of American foreign policy could not figure these questions out, and in a world that belonged to European empires, they were in no hurry to figure them out. It was challenge enough to rise up in an international system that, before 1914, seemed destined to last forever.

In foreign policy, the Columbian Republic drew upon Western civilization with lingering uncertainty and increasing self-assurance. Europe was the beau ideal, and it was an obstacle to overcome. In the abstract, a West of liberty and self-government was not less appealing than it had been in Jefferson's day, but imperialism was an alternate and tangible American attraction. Even Jefferson's cherished empire of liberty had included the Louisiana Purchase and the mission of Lewis and Clark, practical stages in the early republic's growth beyond its original territorial limits. They were long-term incitements to imperialism in the Pacific, in the Caribbean and along either the Spanish or the Mexican border. The hierarchical civilization on display at the Chicago World's Fair led to the foreign-policy adventure of the Spanish-American War and to formal American imperialism after that. At the same time, an emerging American ambition of the 1890s was diplomatic mediation, the desire to play the role of peacemaker and thus to polish the lamp of civilization. Empire, a problem-solving civilization and cosmopolitanism pleased the East Coast foreign-policy establishment of the early twentieth century. Less and less the gentlemen amateurs of nineteenth-century American diplomacy, members of this gathering establishment were professionals in law, banking, academia and diplomacy. Woodrow Wilson was one such educated cosmopolitan fascinated by the world-historical responsibilities accruing to the United States.

Civilization was the word of the day, and it resonated throughout American foreign policy. In a *New York Tribune* article, none other than Karl Marx labeled the United States "the youngest and most vigorous exponent of Western Civilization." Marx had the accumulation of capital and industrial expertise in mind, but the United States as an exponent of Western civilization entailed more than economics and raw power. An American foreign policy of Western civilization jumbled together empire and democracy, military affairs and culture, bowing to the international relations status quo, while also aspiring to greater democracy in international affairs. The contradictions were hardly new. They had been remarked upon by the Mexican intellectual Lucas Alamán during the Mexican-American War (1846–1848). In Alamán's opinion, it was the "most unjust war in history . . . provoked by the ambition not of an absolute monarchy but of a republic that claims to be at the forefront of nineteenth-century civilization." An absolute monarchy can conduct imperial wars more convincingly than a self-proclaimed republic can. For Alamán, the American hypocrisy was to position the United States at the avant-garde of history, at the highest stage of development, at the highest pitch of democracy and at the forefront of nineteenth-century civilization, while waging unjust imperialist wars.[13]

As Alamán must have sensed, civilization was never a racially neutral concept in the United States. After the Civil War, the culture of Europe and the United States was permeated with pseudoscientific theories of race. Darwin provided some of the intellectual substance, and the international system as constituted in the 1870s and 1880s provided a kind of empirical proof. The imperial sway of Britain and other European powers emanated from their alleged racial superiority. Colonizing Europeans were the fittest at surviving, and the United States, which had previously regarded European diplomacy and great-power politics with genuine suspicion and disgust, was falling under Europe's diplomatic spell at this very moment. The United States participated in the Berlin Congress of 1884, when Africa was ruthlessly divvied up. The racial prejudices at work in European diplomacy were the domestic and original prejudices of the United States, and through segregation, they were being made into law in the 1880s and 1890s. The international system, in which disparities of military and economic power were being resolved into Western hegemony, made cultural sense on both sides of the Atlantic.

Civilization's cultural-biological hierarchy was reflected in US immigration policy. Not the same as foreign policy, US immigration policy mediated the nation's relationship to the outside world as much as its formal foreign policy did. Late-nineteenth-century policy and the kind of immigration it fostered were paradoxical. Unprecedented numbers of Catholics and Jews were passing beneath the Statue of Liberty, running the gauntlet at Ellis Island and becoming American citizens. "America is God's Crucible, the great Melting-Pot where all the races of Europe are melting and reforming" was a telling line from Israel Zangwill's 1908 play, *The Melting Pot*. Twentieth-century America would belong as much to the melting immigrants as it would to the Anglo-Saxons who let them into the pot. Their arrival sounded the death knell of the eighteenth-century Anglo-Protestant republic: in 1910, immigrants composed almost one-third of the American population. Radical as this shift was, it still reflected an immigration policy with a bias toward the races of Europe, as Zangwill had directly stated. In keeping with this bias, the Chinese Exclusion Act was passed in 1882 amid a wave of anti-Chinese sentiment. Greeks, Italians, Jews and Irish were less than white on the racial hierarchy; the Irish and the Jews were other than the Germans and the Scandinavians; but all of these immigrant groups had assimilative options that were not available to those of Asian, African and Hispanic descent. Not by design, US immigration policy was creating a Western rather than an Anglo-American society.[14]

Where race and civilization intersected in the 1890s, the ideal of Western civilization encouraged narratives of decline as well as ascendancy. The exclusion of Chinese immigrants betrayed a fear of Chinese immigrants. No sooner had Americans introduced themselves to Western civilization as a phrase (in the late nineteenth century) than they were being asked to contemplate its decline and demise. Civilizational affirmation and civilizational anxiety tend to walk hand in hand. This would prove a common counterpoint throughout the twentieth and into the twenty-first century in both Europe and the United States, with decline and fall the feared fellow travelers of an ascendant civilization. Western hegemony was a wave always about to crest, though the West was at its most beguiling when it was near death or, better yet, being sped toward decline by the Asiatic hordes or by its enemies from within. The art, philosophy, literature and music of fin de siècle Europe often evoked the theme of inner rot—the decadence of the domineering West. The Zionist intellectual Max Nordau sketched this theme in Darwinian terms, as racial decadence, in an 1892 book, *Degeneration*. Unencumbered by racial anxiety, Thomas Mann's exquisite 1912 novella *Death in Venice* depicted the sickening of Western culture, its exhausted spirit, through the tale of a once disciplined German writer lured to his death by a homoerotic vision of beauty. Decayed, moldering Venice was Mann's effortless metaphor. A healthy culture had lost its mooring and ripened into decadence. The sun is always setting in the West.[15]

Very often, the alleged unraveling of the West had a racial subtext. The British sociologist James Stanley Little published *The Doom of Western Civilization* in 1907. The American journalist and historian Lothrop Stoddard turned out his sensationalist treatise, *The Rising Tide of Color against White World Supremacy,* in 1920 followed by *The Revolt against Civilization: The Menace of the Under Man* in 1922. A Ku Klux

Klan member, he divided the world into white, yellow, black, brown and Amerindian races in order to evaluate his worries about the white future. This was the book F. Scott Fitzgerald parodied in *The Great Gatsby* (1925). "Civilization's going to pieces," the character Tom Buchanan laments in *Gatsby*. "I've gotten to be a terrible pessimist about things. Have you read 'The Rise of the Colored Empires' by this man Goddard? . . . The idea is if we don't look out the white race will be— will be utterly submerged. It's all scientific stuff; it's been proven." Tom Buchanan is the novel's least civilized character, though taken as a whole *The Great Gatsby* does little to disprove his intuition that civilization is going to pieces. The shrill self-celebration of the World's Columbian Exposition, viewed some thirty years later through Fitzgerald's discerning lens, was an early protest against the prospect of a West in chronic decline. With Victorian work ethic, the organizers of the fair had struggled to disprove their underlying fear of decadence.[16]

Race and civilization were scrutinized from a different angle by W. E. B. Du Bois, one of the era's most original scholars and public intellectuals. The status quo was desperate enough for Du Bois, who wanted progress more than he feared decadence. Du Bois grew up in Great Barrington, Massachusetts, attended Fisk University, Harvard University and the Kaiser-Wilhelm University in Berlin. He completed his PhD at Harvard in 1895 (at age twenty-seven). An African American in New England and in Germany, Du Bois experienced his education as a contradiction: "In the folds of this [late nineteenth-century] European civilization I was born and shall die, imprisoned, conditioned, depressed, exalted and inspired," he wrote in his 1940 memoir *Dusk of Dawn*. In a stroke of good fortune, his high school principal had insisted that he learn Latin and Greek, then the ticket to higher education and to the liberal arts of which Du Bois was a lifelong champion. Du Bois was among other things a Europhile. "Europe modified profoundly my outlook on life and my thought and feeling toward it," he wrote in his memoir. "Something of the possible beauty and elegance of life permeated my soul." Equally decisive to his education was a Hampton Quartet performance of "Negro folk song [at which] I was thrilled and moved to tears and seemed to recognize something inherently and deeply my own," he recalled. Du Bois's first academic position was as "chair of 'classics'" at Wilberforce University in Ohio, a historically black school. Du Bois the student and professor was imprisoned and inspired, depressed and exalted in multiple traditions. Segregation and the racism behind it demonstrated the incompatibility of these traditions.[17]

In his books and articles, Du Bois presaged a new American relationship to the West. He was a critic of American foreign policy before the Chicago World's Fair. In an 1890 commencement address given at Harvard, he discussed Jefferson Davis, a noble specimen of "Teutonic civilization," in Du Bois's mocking characterization. Warlike Teutonic civilization suited American foreign policy in 1890. It had cultural meaning in a country that was piling up wealth, military power and dominion overseas. As Du Bois would not allow his New England audience to forget, the advance of civilization had a price: the South may have lost the Civil War, but Jefferson Davis was a representative American in 1890. The country, North and South, was going backward. In Du Bois's words, "Advance in civilization has always been handicapped by shortsighted national selfishness" in the United States. Power and civilization are selective. "The Teutonic met civilization and crushed it—the Negro met civilization and was crushed by it," Du Bois declared. Du Bois concluded his address with a request. Americans "whose nation was founded on the loftiest ideals" have a duty and "a debt for this Ethiopia of the Out-stretched Arm." Over the decades, Du Bois became less and less convinced that the duty would be honored and the debt repaid.[18]

In 1903, Du Bois found a way to synthesis, in his book, *The Souls of Black Folk*. Rather than compounding America's own racial pathologies with the perversity of European imperialism, the United States had the potential to reverse the standard equation between race and empire, Du Bois thought. If the United States could address its own racial pathologies, it could devise a postimperial and democratic approach to foreign policy. European and African heritage, cruelly contrasted by segregation, were both burden and gift: "After the Egyptian and Indian, the Greek and Roman, the Teuton and Mongolian, the Negro is a sort of seventh son, born with a veil, and gifted with second sight in this American world." It is white Americans who see less and who think more monolithically—to the detriment of American foreign policy. Accustomed to two-ness, gifted with second sight, African Americans have a history of developing self-consciousness. Lucky to have such a history, the African American "would not Africanize America, for America has too much to teach the world and Africa." Instead, within the United States the African American should achieve parity and respect and equal opportunity, which is not equivalent to sameness. Just as America would not be Africanized, the African American "would not bleach his Negro soul in a flood of white Americanism, for he knows that Negro blood has a message for the world." Large parts of the world for which Negro blood has a message are nonwhite.[19]

Du Bois envisioned an inclusivity larger and better than white Americanism and the imperial sway of contemporary international affairs. If American foreign policy could incorporate this multivalent democracy and this flexibility, it would realize the Negro blood's message to the world. One foundation for this vision, naturally enough for an 1890 graduate of Harvard College and a professor of the classics, was the great-books ethos that Columbia University would spin into a Western civilization curriculum roughly a decade after *The Souls of Black Folk* came out. In a chapter titled "Of the Training of Black Men," Du Bois weaved together a series of rhetorical questions, writing himself into Western civilization and claiming Western civilization's treasures for someone with his second sight:

> I sit with Shakespeare and he winces not. Across the color line I move arm and arm with Balzac and Dumas. . . . I summon Aristotle and Aurelius and what soul I will, and they come all graciously with no scorn or condescension. So, wed with Truth, I dwell above the veil. Is this the life you grudge us, O knightly America? Is this the life you long to change into the dull red hideousness of Georgia? Are you afraid lest

peering from this high Pisgah, between Philistine and Amalekite, we
sight the Promised Land?

WHAT IF WESTERN civilization could be turned into the tool of his
liberation and of his people's liberation, Du Bois was asking. Well before 1903, his questions were rhetorical because such liberation had
already taken place in Du Bois's mind. Shakespeare and Aristotle
had lifted him above the veil segregation imposed on white and black
Americans alike, and Shakespeare did not wince when he was read in
this way. (In his 1931 satirical novel *Black No More,* George Schuyler
poked fun at the high-culture aura of Du Bois's writing through the
absurdly named character "Dr. Shakespeare Agamemnon Beard . . . a
graduate of Harvard, Yale and Copenhagen.") Du Bois wanted white
America—knightly, Anglo-Saxon America—to acknowledge his liberation and thereby to encourage the liberation of other African American readers and citizens.[20]

In *The Souls of Black Folk,* Du Bois contended that the problem of
the twentieth century would be the problem of the color line. He had
in mind the global disease of white supremacy, the dislocation of peoples, the racism, the plight of empire and the colonization that went all
the way back to the days of Columbus. Du Bois laid out these themes
in "Address to the Nations of the World" for the first Pan-African Conference held in London in 1900. Du Bois presumed that the formerly
enslaved and the currently colonized would not be passive. They would
assert themselves by rethinking the color line, revising it from the line
between empire and the servants of empire to something less unjust. In
the best-case scenario, the line would cease to exist and decolonization
would be accomplished. Within the United States, Du Bois's words
had a unique complexity. The organizers of the Chicago fair had gotten
the United States wrong. They had whitened it. The color line ran right
through the United States, not around it: the country was white and
black, its history white and black, its culture white and black; its people
were white and black as well. The white-and-black Chicago outside the
fair was the real American city, and so too was Washington, DC, a city

white and black. The authors of the McMillan Plan had also gotten things wrong. To them, as to so many educated whites of the period, the color line was invisible, or if it was visible at times the color line did not register deeply.

THE PRACTITIONERS OF American foreign policy were not reading Du Bois in the 1890s. They scrupulously upheld the civilizational boundaries of the World's Fair and the McMillan Plan. Presidents McKinley, Roosevelt and Wilson were the first presidents to enact a truly global foreign policy for the United States, scoring notable victories on the battlefields of Europe, Asia and the Caribbean, and on the battlefield of ideas. Their foreign policy was imitative but not derivative of Europe's. It was true to the Columbian Republic in which they had come of age. They were too self-confident to defer to the European empires and the international system as it was. They could imagine and advocate for a republican or democratic future that would one day supplant the aristocratic age of empire, ridding the world of spheres of influence and transforming the balance of power into an international community. More than any other figure, Woodrow Wilson brilliantly and lastingly drove democracy to the heart of international affairs, and not just in the United States. When it came to foreign policy, McKinley, Roosevelt and Wilson were all Columbian in their experimental boldness, Columbian in their passion for reinvention. They were no less Columbian in their blindness in the lines they were unwilling to see and in the lines they sought to impose upon the outside world.

The turning point was the war with Spain. "No war ever transformed us quite as the war with Spain transformed us," Woodrow Wilson noted in 1902. "The nation stepped forth into the open arena of the world." Already in 1901 Wilson had proclaimed America's "full self-consciousness as a nation." Before 1898, the United States had tended to define itself against the European powers. The early republic had brushed the Spanish, French and Russian empires back from territory it coveted, using guile, force and money. Against the odds, the United States had survived and grown. The North muddled through the zig-zag intricacies of Civil War diplomacy, after which the supreme achievement of American diplomacy was the avoidance of great-power conflict in the Western Hemisphere. Impossible in theory, the Monroe Doctrine worked in practice, but it may have worked because the United States was on the margins of the international system, too peripheral to be worth disturbing. At any rate, to work the Monroe Doctrine relied on the British navy, while American strategy and interests did not factor much in nineteenth-century European calculations. Until 1892, European countries did not even have ambassadors in Washington. There was not enough to discuss in this rich, rising but still remote country. Even after 1892, mosquito-ridden Washington was not the place for ambitious international diplomats to be. The City of Magnificent Intentions continued to attach an aspirational foreign policy to a provincial government long after Dickens's visit to the United States.[21]

The Spanish-American War altered the City of Magnificent Intentions, marking the more proactive presence of the United States within the international system. The more territory a country has and the more it acts on the open arena of the world, the more it is compelled to act and to acquire territory. Assets in the Pacific demanded more overseas involvement in order to defend the territories the United States had won from Spain, a vicious circle. As had been the case with the Mexican-American War and as was definitely the case with the European empires of this period, civilization was made to justify the projection of power. Major civilizations had and were measured by territorial power. The winning of territory was proof of civilizational excellence: Rome's civilization was superb because so much of the world had fallen within its scope. Observing an ascendant United States, an American foreign-policy elite arose, comfortable with the projection of power but also eager to put an American stamp on the international system, to ensure that the progression of civilization and the rise of the West would be synonymous with treaty making and the promotion of law. Not just territory was the sign of civilization at the turn of the century. Order was the sign of civilization, and in the international affairs of the 1890s the United States was starting to seek a civilized order of its own.

The claim that American power might augment "civilization" abroad had been audible decades before the Spanish-American War. An American diplomat, Townsend Harris, who worked on opening up Japan to outside influence, speculated about raising Japan to "our standards of civilization." James Blaine, who served as secretary of state under Presidents Garfield and Harrison, sketched an American will to raise "the standard . . . of civilization" in Latin America. By not placing the adjective *Western* or *European* or *American* before the noun *civilization,* Harris and Blaine could argue that Japan and Latin America might be culturally or historically different from the United States and from the West, but with sufficient tutelage or sufficient force they would achieve the American standard of wealth, education and comfort. Properly raised up, they could enter into the global supply chains and industrial productivity that described modern civilization. This was civilization as process, as technique, civilization as a matter of economic stages. The twentieth-century language of economic modernization and development has its precursors in the nineteenth-century language of civilization. By contrast, Western civilization was more than a technical process, and it was closer to home, intersecting with the particulars of culture, religion, politics and race. In the judgment of an 1897 editorial in the *Hawaiian Star,* if "the Japanese ever got the franchise here [in Hawaii], good bye to Western civilization." Western civilization was what some had, and others did not.[22]

Talk of civilization and of Western civilization easily countenance the waging of war on civilization's behalf. In 1898, at a time of war, Secretary of State Richard Olney promised not to forgo any "fitting opportunity to further the progress of civilization." The American war against Spain was not a war for civilization, per se. Nor was it a war for the West, because Spain was a European power. Yet the consequences of the Spanish-American War dangled a civilizing mission before American politicians and diplomats. Kipling versified about the "white man's burden" a year after the Spanish-American War, a burden President

William McKinley was glad to adopt as his own in the Philippines and a handful of other places. McKinley combined the messianic and the legalistic elements of American foreign policy into a mix of his own making. Born in 1843 and trained as a lawyer, McKinley went from a seat in the House of Representatives to the White House in 1896. He was keen on negotiations and treaties, working out an arrangement with Britain for North American borders and fisheries, and having his secretary of state, John Hay, finalize the Hay-Pauncefote Treaty in 1901, a precondition for the construction of the Panama Canal. The 1898 Treaty of Paris codified American support for a Cuban uprising against Spain, a support that could be sold as the advancement of liberty. In fact, this war over Cuba ushered the United States into the club of imperial powers with the annexation of Hawaii and the absorption of the Philippines, Guam and Puerto Rico into the American orbit. McKinley even sent American troops as far as Beijing in 1900.[23]

In its foreign policy and its norms of civilization, the McKinley administration was joining the European foreign-policy rat race. Speaking before an audience in Boston in 1899, McKinley characterized US control of the Philippines, Cuba and Puerto Rico as a "great trust . . . under the providence of God and in the name of human progress and civilization." To a group of visiting churchmen McKinley is supposed to have described the need to "educate the Filipinos, and uplift them and civilize them and Christianize them, and by God's grace to do the very best we could by them." Teddy Roosevelt, a proud veteran of the Spanish-American War and the archetypal American expansionist, personified this civilizing mission. He characterized the pacification of the Philippines as civilization's struggle against the "black chaos of savagery and barbarism." The historian Thomas Borstelmann writes that "U.S. policy toward its new colonies after 1899 derived from its prior policies toward Native Americans." So did the rhetoric of civilization and barbarism. Some Americans were horrified by the advent of an outright American empire, around which talk of civilization was so thick and so self-righteous that it could be distilled into satire. The journalist E. L. Godkin quipped, with the Philippines in mind, that "we do not want any more states until we can civilize Kansas." At the time of the Mexican-American War, the newspaper editor Horace Greeley had counseled Americans to read "the histories of the ruin of Greek and Roman liberty consequent on such extensions of empire by the sword." An Anti-Imperialist League was founded in the United States in 1898.[24]

When McKinley was assassinated in 1901, his vice president became president overnight. Teddy Roosevelt altered the culture of American foreign policy in a way that the less charismatic though possibly more transformative McKinley did not. An 1880 graduate of Harvard College and scion of an affluent New York family, Roosevelt was a Republican from the Northeast who heeded the call of public service. In his writing and in his person, he linked the American conquest of the West—as in the western portion of the North American continent—with the great-power contest for prestige and empire that pervaded the first decade of the twentieth century. Between 1889 and 1896, Roosevelt completed several volumes in *The Winning of the West*. From Roosevelt to Lyndon Johnson to George W. Bush, the image of the American cowboy would be associated with the main lines of American foreign policy: John F. Kennedy's mantra was the "new frontier," a westward extension into modernity and outer space. The romance of the American West signaled the application of European power, technology and law outside of Europe. It was civilization on the frontier, the opposite of civilization as decadence or overrefinement, civilization honored in the breach, mythically vigorous and thrilling. (Francis Fukuyama would conclude the *End of History* [1992] with a long comparison of the Western triumph after 1989 and the winning of the American West in the nineteenth century.) The historical reality was distressingly at odds with Teddy Roosevelt's Western romance: the suppression of Native peoples and the theft of their land, the crimes of civilizational entitlement and of empire. The TR-style fantasy of the West and the reality that shadowed it mixed together in Roosevelt's larger-than-life cultural legacy.

Under both McKinley and Roosevelt, furthering civilization had its militant and its pacifist dimensions. A civilized war was one fought for the sake of peace: at some point the cowboys were supposed to give way to the sheriffs. For Roosevelt, the civilized actors in international affairs were charged with keeping the peace, with beating back the black chaos of savagery and barbarism and eventually with translating barbarism into civilization. To this degree, imperialism was a civilizational good in Roosevelt's view. The outlines of a civilized peace had been drawn in the Peace of Westphalia (1648) and after the Napoleonic Wars at the Congress of Vienna. Diplomacy existed to perpetuate the peace, and a balance of power in Europe was gradually to be applied to the entire world—by enticement and commerce if possible, and by force and imposition if necessary. When Teddy Roosevelt was president, the preponderance of Western power was near absolute, with Japan the one rising Asian power. Within this Western preponderance, the United States was making its great-power debut, prompting Roosevelt to speak grandly of "we, the great civilized nations." In a 1902 message to Congress, Roosevelt noted that "more and more, the increasing interdependence and complexity of international political and economic relations render it incumbent on all civilized and orderly powers to insist upon a proper policing of the world." This was not a unique mission for the United States, in Roosevelt's eyes. It was the identical mission of all the orderly and civilized powers.[25]

Like the European empires it was copying, the United States could be an arsenal of civilization and a guarantor of order, roles that appealed to the budding American foreign-policy establishment. To act in this capacity, it would need powers that even President McKinley had been unable to summon. Roosevelt devoted great energy to military modernization. Power equaled civilization, which equaled the exercise of power for a president who relished the bracing effects of war. Without the experience or feel of war, Roosevelt believed, "we shall indeed reach a condition worse than that of the ancient civilizations in the years of their decay." Roosevelt's secretary of state from 1905 to 1909, Elihu Root, synthesized his president's vision of civilization, international order and an assertive American foreign policy. A lawyer before entering government, Root had been secretary of war under

McKinley, a position he used to expand and improve the American army. Root's improvements merged with Roosevelt's enhancement of the American navy. As assistant secretary of the navy from 1897 to 1898, Roosevelt had sent the Great White Fleet, sixteen battleships and fourteen thousand sailors, around the world from 1907 to 1909 in the Western Hemisphere, the United States was Rome, a territorial empire; in its newfound naval power it could be Athens as well, a maritime empire. Secretary Root reformed the State Department, which in 1898 had had a Washington, DC, staff of some sixty people. He brought it closer to the European standard, with geographical divisions and a more pronounced work ethic. In 1906, Congress created a more professional consular service. After leaving the State Department, Root helped to forge the East Coast foreign-policy establishment just then coming into its own—educated, self-confident, civic-minded, bipartisan, Europhilic and accustomed to moving among the worlds of finance, law, academia, diplomacy and military affairs. Root was president of the Carnegie Endowment for International Peace from its establishment in 1910 until 1925 and president of the American Society of International Law. In 1912, he was the second American to receive a Nobel Peace Prize. Teddy Roosevelt had been the first—in 1906. Root was also the founding chairman of the Council on Foreign Relations, an institution he was instrumental in creating in 1918.[26]

President Roosevelt wanted diplomacy, finance, engineering and an advanced military to imbue American foreign policy with the full force of civilization. In 1905, Roosevelt brokered peace negotiations between imperial Russia and Japan. The result of his labors, the Treaty of Portsmouth, reflected Roosevelt's notion of civilization. This was a state of peace enabled by negotiation and the Anglo-Saxon genius for compromise (in his eyes). Diplomatic accomplishments like the Treaty of Portsmouth would ideally have the status of law, a microcosm of what would later come to be known as the rules-based international order. Portsmouth was followed by the Central American Peace Conference of 1907, the Second Hague Conference of 1907 on international peace and disarmament, creation of the Central American Court of Justice (1907) and the Canada Fisheries Arbitration of 1909. In his Nobel Prize acceptance speech, Teddy Roosevelt had sketched out a World League, a prototype of the League of Nations or the United Nations. As Woodrow Wilson would after him, Roosevelt believed international affairs should be fit to the shape of domestic American politics. American politics begins in conflict, and over time conflict gets enmeshed and moderated in legal precedent. Conflict gets resolved (or postponed) through the separation of powers. All is regulated by the Constitution, the rule of rules and the law of laws. Once the system arrives at a judgment—a Supreme Court ruling, for example—it must be accepted by the parties to the conflict and accepted peacefully. A tool of civilization as attested by the murals and friezes of the Supreme Court Building in Washington, the Constitution anchors civility and liberty in the United States. Teddy Roosevelt considered the Constitution an example and a bequest of Western civilization that the United States could advance abroad—even in Western Europe where constitutional republics were not the norm in 1906.

For Roosevelt, civilization's more pragmatic side was revealed in modern engineering. His signature project was the construction of the Panama Canal. The aggressive diplomacy behind it exposed the strong sense of civilizational self-righteousness Roosevelt and many of his countrymen harbored. The United States merged rhetoric and military pressure to present Colombia and the newly created country of Panama with an offer they could not refuse: the civilized and the less civilized did not play by the same rules. The canal was also a tool of civilization that would redirect the American future. En route to India, Columbus had made it to the New World because of Europe's naval superiority, civilization and sea power combined. The civilized United States had the technical capacity to build the East-West canal and thereby to link the Atlantic and Pacific Oceans. Commerce would flow faster as a result. The American navy and commercial vessels could start to move in broadly hemispheric and global arcs, placing the Columbian Republic at the center of the global crossroads. Roosevelt would not have been wrong to say that the Panama Canal, ready for use in 1914, redrew the map of civilization—at least as Roosevelt and his contemporaries understood the word. It was *translatio imperii* by dint of shovel and crane.

By the time the Panama Canal was completed, Woodrow Wilson had been president for two years. It fell to him to convert the geopolitical advances of the United States into a modern American foreign policy, and a foreign policy that was not a rehashed version of European great-power politics, more imperial than republican in orientation. Born in Virginia in 1856, Wilson graduated from Princeton in 1879 and went on to law school at the University of Virginia, Thomas Jefferson's university, as Wilson was well aware. Wilson then finished a PhD at Johns Hopkins University and devoted his early career to the study of American politics. In 1885, he published *Congressional Government*, and in 1889, *The State*. In 1908, he added *Constitutional Government in the United States*. Wilson the political scientist made the leap from academic administration to politics, from Princeton to the governorship of New Jersey and then on to the White House. He was confident in the excellence of the American experiment going back to Jefferson. The first self-consciously Southern president since the Civil War, he was an avid segregationist. He also believed that the American experiment had international application, going beyond McKinley and Roosevelt on this point. The goal was not just to act on par with the European powers. Joining the West was not enough. It was incumbent on the United States to lead the West, and in doing so to imbue the West with Jeffersonian liberty.[27]

Original in so many ways, Woodrow Wilson's foreign policy was a variation upon the themes set by Roosevelt, Elihu Root and McKinley. The Panama Canal was a set-piece example of an integrating global economy. When Wilson became president in 1913, after the humdrum "dollar diplomacy" of his immediate predecessor William Taft and Taft's secretary of state, Philander Knox, Wilson could not ignore global economic interdependence of startling complexity and scope. The United States could no longer pretend to be the agrarian republic Thomas Jefferson had hoped for, with yeomen farmers harvesting virtue on their detached and independent properties. Nor could George Washington's

and John Quincy Adams's sage advice about avoiding foreign entanglements and not going out in search of monsters to destroy have the same
meaning in 1912 as it did for the early republic. If the entanglements
and monsters were less and less avoidable, technology and economics
were to blame. Finance and commercial exchange, coursing through
Asian and European markets, ran through the United States as well.
Industrial civilization was at its apex in 1912, and with it the United
States was one of its biggest motors. An outside world dependent on the
United States dovetailed with a United States dependent on the outside
world. Woodrow Wilson understood that twentieth-century civilization was associative, synthetic and in rapid motion.

Like Roosevelt, Wilson believed that civilized nations needed to
keep the peace and at times fight for the sake of reaching peace. Wilson sought a "progressive order" in international affairs, and through
this order "the development of constitutional liberty in the world."
McKinley, Roosevelt and Taft had all been imperialists. Like them,
Wilson was confident in the high stage of civilization the United States
had reached, with an arrogant attitude toward the states south of the
border. Although Wilson's secretary of state, William Jennings Bryan,
was an outspoken anti-imperialist, for Wilson the United States had
the purview of the European imperial powers: in the Western Hemisphere it was the teacher, and Latin America, the unwilling pupil. This
attitude prompted several military interventions in Latin America. In
1915, Wilson sent US soldiers to Haiti, and in 1916 to the Dominican
Republic. When Wilson sent American troops to Mexico in 1915, he
promised that "I am going to teach the South American Republics to
elect good men." The Panama Canal expanded American economic
and military interests in Latin America. This combination of widening interests and a patronizing foreign policy did little to endear the
United States to the peoples of Latin America. All the countries of
the Americas could claim Columbus if they wished. Colombia did so
by name. The special claim on Columbus put forward by the United
States before and after the Chicago World's Fair was a thorn in the side
of its hemispheric diplomacy.[28]

As opposed to his predecessors in the White House, Wilson had to contend not only with Europe's imperious great powers but also with the crack-up of multiple great empires. In general, Wilson divided the European powers into two camps. On the one side were the authoritarians—Germany, the Austro-Hungarian Empire, the Ottoman Empire. This was the side that had to be defeated politically and morally as well as militarily, after which the uniform-wearing emperors could be consigned to history. The authoritarians had to be civilizationally defeated. (Imperial Russia was that American inconvenient thing, an authoritarian ally.) On the other side were France and Britain. The decorative imagery of the Library of Congress associated France with emancipation, and if France and Britain were not democracies in the true sense of the word—both were unrepentant empires, Britain was a monarchy—they were internally democratic. They had parliaments; they believed in the separation of powers, in a rough separation between church and state; and they upheld the rule of law. By fighting with them, the United States would be fighting for civilization, but it would be doing so in an American fashion. France, Britain and the United States were to make the world "safe for democracy," Wilson memorably declared. A giver of Western civilization, Columbus had given the Columbian Republic its liberties. Now it was time for the United States to defend the liberties of Western civilization and to hand them back to Europe in its hour of need.

Like Roosevelt, Wilson pictured the United States as a mediator. As early as 1915, Wilson sent his close advisor Edward House to Europe to find a path out of the diplomatic-military labyrinth. House could not bring Britain, Russia, Austria and Germany to terms. Also in 1915, Wilson announced a League to Enforce Peace, a draft proposal for universal collective security, and speaking to the US Senate in that year of incalculable European losses, he broke from the diplomatic norms of the European nineteenth century. The nineteenth-century concert of Europe, the balance of power transcribed into an art form by diplomats like Prince Klemens von Metternich and Otto von Bismarck, had fallen to pieces in the summer of 1914. Wilson was glad to bid it farewell. From the ashes of the old international system a new system could rise up. Wilson imagined its contours in his speech to the Senate: "There must be, not a balance of power, but a community of power; not organized rivalries, but an organized common peace." A community of power would demand deliberation; deliberation would demand institutions and procedures. Through deliberation, individual nations could act on the reasonable premise that a community of nations would organize a common peace. Wilson's idealism was qualified by the experience of the many participants in World War I. Amid so much death and destruction, amid the crumbling of the old political and social orders, even the victors were among the First World War's losers. For Wilson, the organized rivalries of the past proved the madness of war and the moral necessity behind a community of power.

Wilson articulated his goals in a war message to Congress, which he delivered on April 2, 1917. These goals were not economic, and they were only tangentially military. Wilson was outraged by German naval activity in the Atlantic, but the United States was not going to war simply to secure freedom of navigation. The United States would foster peace by eliminating autocratic governments, the real cause of the war in Wilson's view: "Our object . . . " Wilson told Congress, "is to vindicate the principles of peace and justice in the life of the world as against selfish and autocratic power and to set up amongst the really free and self-governed peoples of the world such a concert of purpose and of action as will henceforth ensure the observance of those principles." The principles of peace and justice demanded a "partnership of democratic nations," partnership crucial to winning the war and no less crucial to preserving the postwar peace. It was Wilson's skill as a politician to present this revolution in American foreign policy as a return to first principles:

> We shall fight for the things which we have always carried nearest our
> hearts—for democracy, for the right of those who submit to authority
> to have a voice in their own governments, for the rights and liberties
> of small nations, for a universal dominion of right by such a concert of

free peoples as shall bring peace and safety to all nations and make the world itself at last free.

ONE PHRASE STANDS out in this unspooling of idealistic political rhetoric—the rights and liberties of small nations. Neither the United States nor Wilson had a perfect record of defending the rights and liberties of small nations. Wilson's was a stirring idea, however, especially when linked to a concert of free peoples. This was the League of Nations and the United Nations in embryo.[29]

In January 1918, a few months before the war was over, Wilson released his Fourteen Points. A Jeffersonian hymn to enlightened politics, it combines a list of specific requests with a series of sweeping pronouncements. In the Fourteen Points, Wilson's language was also a prophetic appeal to peace, righteousness and reconciliation—the Book of Woodrow. In this vein, he wrote that "the day of conquest and aggrandizement is gone," in his first paragraph. Justice and fair dealing are supplanting "force and selfish aggression," though Wilson does not explain how this extraordinary transformation is coming about—whether it is some slow process of global enlightenment, or whether the war had so discredited force and selfish aggression that a new page in international affairs would inevitably be turned. Coming into view is a kind of diplomatic Golden Rule when Wilson writes: "we see very clearly that unless justice be done to others it will not be done to us." Wilson concludes with reflections on a "general association," part of the settlement of old colonial claims (point 5) and the best means of giving "political independence and territorial integrity to great and small states alike." The general association would be a new covenant, the floods having lasted for four years and, by January 1918, the dove and the olive branch already in sight. Wilson had managed to put liberty and self-government at the center of that most dispiriting of wars, a feat of the political imagination.

Wilson traveled to Europe in 1919 to attend the peace conference in Paris, a statesman, a diplomat, a mediator. In his top hat and frock coat and with his natural clarity of mind, he played the part beautifully.

Adoringly received in France, he had a major role in the negotiations, pushing for a League of Nations as the postwar covenant among peaceful, democratic nations. Hu Shi, a Chinese intellectual educated at Columbia University, contemplating Woodrow Wilson at Versailles, called him "the supreme product of Western civilization." He was the one with vision, and for it he was awarded the Nobel Peace Prize in 1919. Interestingly, Wilson's own secretary of state, Robert Lansing, preferred "an Atlantic Union of Democracies" to "a League of Nations," a precursor to the NATO alliance arguably, but not a format destined to succeed in 1919. Lansing also recommended that the American delegation in Paris include Republicans such as Elihu Root, but Wilson disagreed, to disastrous effect at home. Wilson's foe on the Senate Foreign Relations Committee was Henry Cabot Lodge, one of the Republicans not invited to Paris. Lodge could agree to security guarantees for France and Britain. Up to a point he was persuadable, but he was also bent on witnessing Wilson's political defeat and was delighted to see the League of Nations fail in Congress. The purest humiliation in Wilson's career took the form of democratic action. The American people and their elected representatives were not sure that the day of conquest and aggrandizement was gone. With the many covenants of their domestic politics long ago signed, they were reluctant to approve a covenant tying them to the destiny of countries not their own.[30]

Wilson's political failures coincided with an age of unforgiving turbulence in international affairs. Between 1914 and 1919, Europe and the United States were adrift, World War I being the war that refused to end. Both France and Britain were in denial as to how much had changed around them. They would expand their overseas empires in the interwar years without the internal European stability that had stretched more or less from the early nineteenth century until the assassination of Archduke Ferdinand. Postwar European order, balanced on a ridge of fledgling nation-states and an intemperate Germany, was a house of cards. Imperial Russia had undergone a revolution in 1917, something so strange to most Americans that they kept expecting the Soviet experiment to come apart in 1918 and 1919. The United States refused to recognize the Soviet Union diplomatically and would persist in this refusal for some fifteen years. Miniature versions of the Bolshevik Revolution flashed across Europe after the war, none of them lasting, all of them omens of the coming chaos. Everywhere there were dazed veterans and paramilitary units forming into a combustible mix, an international system born in the violence of war and understood by nobody. In the most traumatic way possible, Europe was entering the age of mass democracy in 1919. In a sense, Wilson was fortunate not to have succeeded at home and not to have secured a greater share of international leadership for the United States of the 1920s. In the shadow of so many World War I trenches and cemeteries, Europe was not ready to adopt democracy, and in the project of democracy promotion, the United States was not ready to lead.

Yet this same deteriorating international order turned Wilson's political failure into a tragedy. To develop to the point that the United States had reached in 1893 or in 1914, to gather that degree of economic might and that degree of optimistic ambition, the Columbian Republic had depended on others. The European powers, and Britain especially, had devised a nineteenth-century international order that was more than kind to the United States, with the British navy wedged between the United State and any potential European aggressor. Over the centuries, a system of international trade had arisen among the European powers, and even those Americans who disliked European politics and diplomacy profited from the trading system that Europe had built—the laws, the protected sea lanes, the geopolitical predictability of the long nineteenth century. Europe had made the door the United States wanted kept open in Asia. Not for nothing was the Columbian Republic preoccupied by Columbus the navigator and seaman. His Europe had given the United States stability and wealth. And then, the European predilection for balance of power and spheres of influence, the juggling act that had been perfected after the Napoleonic Wars, vanished overnight. Rivalries of power and colliding spheres of influence resulted in war, first in the Balkans in 1914 and then everywhere. Woodrow Wilson clearly grasped the bankruptcy of the old diplomacy.

Perhaps he intuited some of the horrors to come in the 1920s and 1930s and concluded that the international application of liberty and self-government had to replace a balance-of-power and spheres-of-influence approach. American leadership of a West imbued with liberty and self-government—rather than an America seduced by European imperialism—was a solution to the problem. To be led by the United States this democratic West first had to be created. That was Wilson's incompletely realized insight, and in 1919 he was in the unenviable position of possessing a solution in theory without knowing how to implement it in practice. Unreconstructed, the rivalries of power were destined to keep on smoldering and once again to ignite into world war.

2

The Case for the West,
1919–1945

I have one earnest conviction in this war. It is that no other war
in history has so definitely lined up the forces of dictatorship
against those of human rights and individual liberty. My single
passion is to do my full duty to smash the disciples of Hitler.

—Dwight Eisenhower, April 1943

OSWALD SPENGLER, A high school teacher turned best-selling
author, placed his bet on the Russians. He narrated much of
human history in *Decline of the West*, a two-volume book released in
German between 1918 and 1923, and in English in 1926. Spengler
ran through the major world civilizations, ruminating grandly on the
downward movement of the West, *das Untergang des Abendlandes* as his
title reads in German. In Spengler's judgment, the United States was
at the heart of this descending West. America had a "Faustian civilization," in Spengler's terminology. By "Faustian," he meant a civilization
bent on action and conquest and besotted with technology. Columbus
had been a Faustian man. The turbines and massive artillery pieces on
display at the World's Columbian Exposition were Faustian objects,
as were Union Station in Washington and Penn Station in New York.
American mechanical power and American cultural inferiority were

comparably Faustian. Perhaps "the best Germans . . . would represent a new kind of America," Spengler hoped, "[yet] more refined, nobler." More likely, a Russia alight with Christian guilt and fervor would surge forward. Faustian civilization would make way for Magian civilization, another of Spengler's invented terms. Pious and proudly irrational, Magian Moscow might be the one to surpass the counting houses, the factories and the gunboats of the Western world.[1]

For Spengler, Russia's civilizational triumph was a foreseeable future. In his reckoning, Faustian civilization was roughly a thousand years old. Before it and around it other civilizations had risen and fallen, and Spengler took a morphological approach to them. To him, civilizations resembled plants. Variety and the life cycle, seeds dying out and regenerating, growth and decay give direction to *The Decline of the West*. Spengler declared progress an illusion, denigrating the recent triumphs of the West as commercial, predatory and depressingly Anglo-American. This was the cautionary geopolitical tale of "England, the Anglo-Saxon element, whose maritime bases today are spread over the whole world, and which could have its center of gravity one day in North America instead of London." England's power worried Spengler: "It is the only opponent that necessarily stands in the way of the Pan-German future because only undivided rule is possible. Russia in comparison with it is only a local North-Asiatic power." The rise of Christian Russia was simply an interesting hypothetical.[2]

Spengler's extravagant combination of history, civilizational speculation and prophesy washes over the reader in waves of never exactly coherent prose. Spengler does not persuade when he can overwhelm. Coupled with the cultural allure of decline, however, the bombastic vagaries were the stuff of his intellectual celebrity. Spenglerian pessimism was en vogue as soon as *The Decline of the West* started appearing in 1918. In Germany, Spengler was a native son whose aspirations for a pan-German future softened the horrors of the war. As for Russia, Spengler was an antidote to Marx and to the Soviet invention of Marxism-Leninism, a doctrine of linear progress if ever there was one. In 1926, Spengler was invited to the United States to debate the novelist H. G. Wells at a "Philosophy of History" conference in Cambridge, Massachusetts. Author of the popular *Outline of History,* Wells was to defend progress and Spengler to scoff at it, but regrettably Spengler never made it to Cambridge or to America. *The Decline of the West* still enjoyed decades of popularity in the United States. Once encountered, the title (at least) was unforgettable.

Many of Spengler's predictions overshot reality. In Russia, the twentieth century belonged to the Bolsheviks and not to some Dostoevskian fabrication of Spengler's active imagination. On the other hand, Spengler's claim that Europe could countenance only undivided rule was an astute expectation for the interwar years. In the 1920s and 1930s, Europe was fought over not only on battlefields, as it had been during the Great War. It was fought for on the terrain of civilization, which is to say of ideas and culture. The main contenders for leadership of the West were fascist Germany and Italy; democratic Britain, France, the United States and their assorted allies; and the Soviet Union. These contenders were fighting for rival civilizational visions, guaranteeing division. Rather than ultimate victory for any single version of the West, the defenders of fascism, communism and democracy reached a nervous, exhausted stalemate in 1945. A type of fascism was consigned to the Iberian peninsula and to the margins of European politics, while an East-West line ran right through the city of Berlin and through the center of Spengler's Germany. The Soviets lay claim to much of Central and Eastern Europe. Rather than a pan-Germanic future for Europe, Germany and Europe were broken into ill-defined communist and noncommunist halves.

Without a developed strategy, the United States moved closer to leadership of the West in the 1920s and 1930s. Despite the Great Depression, the American economy grew miraculously in the interwar years. It would be among the most decisive factors in the outcome of World War II. Geographic remove from most of the wartime fighting left the United States an inarguable superpower in 1945, when so much of the industrialized world had been bombed into rubble. American diplomacy kept its instinct for mediation and peacemaking after World

War I, an attitude that was out of sync with the 1930s but hardly irrelevant to the international scene in 1945, when the avoidance of war was the cardinal geopolitical challenge. Woodrow Wilson's posthumous influence expanded over time. The president who led the United States through World War II, Franklin Roosevelt had been Wilson's assistant secretary of the navy, a dedicated Wilsonian who kept getting re-elected until he won the war. American leadership of the West (defined as liberty and self-government) also had real academic and intellectual stature in the 1930s and 1940s. While Europe slipped into political insanity in the 1930s, American universities devoted to Western civilization were solidifying a connection to European culture and history. For educated Americans, a cosmopolitan West was an alternative to the anti-immigrant sentiment and rampant Anglo-Saxonism of the 1920s, encouraging postwar American policy toward Europe to be larger than the special relationship with Britain. The military, economic and cultural pieces that did not yet fit together in 1919 fostered a counter-Spenglerian rise of the West in 1945. At its helm was the United States.

FASCISM AND COMMUNISM were twentieth-century newcomers to Western political culture. They were the Great War's offspring, whereas Britain, the United States and France were states with an established relationship to political economy, diplomacy and culture. Each had a history of colonialism—of imposing Western influence economically and militarily—and each of these three stereotypically modern countries had a claim on classical antiquity. They had an affinity still for Latin and Greek and a strong bond with the Enlightenment. They saw themselves as Western because they had inherited a practical understanding and a traditional love of liberty. The Anglo-Franco-American ideal of liberty entailed limitations on executive power; it entailed the sanctity of private property and some degree of separation between church and state: absolute in France, negotiable in Britain and always ambiguous in the United States. Perhaps liberty in interwar France, Britain and the United States also entailed the providential support of the Christian God or the foundation stones of a Judeo-Christian ethical sensibility. In the 1920s, Western liberty and democracy drew closer together as words and as concepts, even if Britain retained its king and queen; France, its far-flung empires; and even if the United States had codified an antidemocratic racial segregation in its laws and civic life (never more zealously than in the 1920s). The rise of fascism heightened the appeal of democracy for the antifascist powers to the west of Nazi Germany.

After World War II, fascism would be anathematized across Europe and the United States as a deviation from Western norms. This made moral sense at the war's end, but in the interwar years fascists fancied themselves the saviors of an ailing West. Fascism's very name—from the Latin word *fasces*—was a reference to classical antiquity. Its geographical basis was at the heart of Europe and of the erstwhile Roman Empire, its governing ideology a hodgepodge of European ideas from Nietzsche's will to power to social Darwinism to the celebration of the nation-state and the people (*il popolo, das Volk*). Fascism was also a fantasy of European purity and Western dominance exerted through the nation-state. Its enemies were the internationalist Bolsheviks to the East and the Anglo-Saxon capitalists to the West. Fascism promised to save the West from its most debilitating impurity, the Jews, who were present and active everywhere. Somehow, while running the Soviet Union the Jews were the puppeteers behind the world's banks as well. Until Nazi Germany and Fascist Italy were forced into unconditional surrender and their crimes were exposed, a Europhilic, anti-Semitic, fascistic nationalism—the aspiration of a uniformly fascist West— resonated throughout Europe.

Once there was a Cold War, the Soviet Union would likewise be anathematized in the West as the implacable East. This was a defensible claim, and it was geographically impeccable. The Soviet Union was in the East, but categorizing the Soviet Union as the political Orient could be simplistic and misleading. It could erase the plans the Soviet Union drew up for itself after 1917, obscuring the origins of Bolshevism and the appeal of Soviet communism across Europe and the United States in the 1920s and 1930s. One day all the world would be communist, the Bolsheviks believed. It had been decreed in books and essays with the finality of scientific law. The communist holy land was supposed to have been Germany, the birthplace of Karl Marx and the home of the world's most advanced economy and culture, most communists believed in 1917. But oddly revolution had come to Russia first. Like fascism, Soviet communism had a civilizational thrust, and the civilization in question was the civilization of the West. Before history came to its soothing end, as Marxism promised, Europe would follow in the Soviet Union's footsteps. Its preordained revolutions would progress with Soviet planning and assistance. Alive with world-changing fervor after 1917, the Soviet Union applied its revolutionary tactics and example wherever it could. Lenin and his generation of Bolsheviks lived in the political West.

From 1917 to 1945, the geometry of the contest among fascism, communism and democracy was kaleidoscopic. After 1917, the fascist–Soviet, Right-Left confrontation was immediate and intense. Fascism was in part a response to the Russian Revolution and to the fears it provoked. Simultaneously, the fascist leaders imitated Soviet governance with a single-party state, a leader cult, a permanently mobilized population and a reliance on secret police. Lenin, Mussolini, Hitler and Stalin were assembling the interlocking geopolitical puzzle of the 1920s and 1930s. Fascist Italy, Nazi Germany and the Soviet Union were sworn enemies who needed one another as enemies and who resembled one another as enemies. An under-the-surface commonality was made apparent in the word *totalitarian,* which surfaced (first in Italian) in the early 1920s. Whether fascist or Soviet, the totalitarian states pioneered the practice of total war, which brought fascist and communist governance to all spheres of life after 1939. The ensuing clash of totalitarianisms was felt across the world. Fittingly, the Second World War was decided in the winter of 1942–1943 by the defeat of Hitler's armies at Stalingrad.

Meanwhile, Britain and France were the beleaguered status quo powers of the interwar period. They tended to their empires and did what they could to manage the failing order in Europe. A quixotic

Anglo-American and European effort was made to support the coun-
terrevolutionary Whites in the Russian civil war, made and quickly
abandoned. Britain and France mostly reacted to the novelty of fascism in Germany, Italy, Spain and elsewhere. Their struggle was to
hold on and to defend their idea of the West from the rabble-rousing
totalitarian imposters. By the summer of 1940, Britain was barely
holding on. Democratic France had been banished to a government-
in-exile not long after British soldiers had endured a panicked retreat
from Dunkirk back to the British Isles. After the fall of France, Britain's resolve was not merely national. In the spirit of the times, it was
avowedly civilizational. Winston Churchill emerged as the war's greatest orator and the statesman most enamored of Western civilization.
For Britain's American and European Allies, Churchill's words were
a crusader's banner. So bracing and clear-cut was the experience that
they would find themselves marching beneath the same banner in the
Cold War.

In the 1920s, the United States was not in the mood to march
under anyone's banner, not even one of its own making. Memories
of the most recent crusade were still too painful. The United States
was a rising power nevertheless. Its economic ties to the outside world
were radically expanding after World War I. "No other power had
ever wielded such global economic dominance," the historian Adam
Tooze writes of the United States in the 1920s. The earlier attempts of
McKinley, Roosevelt and Wilson to mediate and instill managed deliberation into international politics had not been abandoned, despite
the isolationist label that sticks to this period. One of the few presidents with a background in journalism, Warren Harding employed
what he called an "America first" approach to foreign policy. He did
not wish to join the League of Nations and was intent on not repeating
Wilson's mistakes. Yet Harding was interested in the World Court that
was emerging in the 1920s, very much an international institution.
(After Harding's death in office, in 1923, Calvin Coolidge was president when the Dawes Plan was instituted in 1924, restructuring German war debt.) With the Washington Conference and the Four-Power

Treaty of 1921, Harding tried to broker the Anglo-Japanese naval arms race in the Pacific. Harding's secretary of state, Charles Evans Hughes, the chief American negotiator at the Washington Conference, was a legally minded internationalist not unlike Woodrow Wilson in out-look. He was also president of the American Bar Association. Teddy Roosevelt once called him "a whiskered Wilson."[3]

Calvin Coolidge, the tight-lipped Vermonter, was not anti-internationalist. In 1926, he succeeded in getting the United States to join the World Court. If not leadership of the West, it was still interna-tional leadership. In addition, President Coolidge selected the Republi-can internationalist Frank Kellogg as his secretary of state. Kellogg had been a friend of Teddy Roosevelt's and part of the moderate resistance to the Treaty of Versailles—the Republicans whom a less doctrinaire Wilson might have been able to bring on board. Kellogg became secre-tary of state in 1925, in which position he consulted often with Elihu Root. Kellogg helped negotiate the remarkable Kellogg-Briand Pact, which was signed in Paris in August 1928. Its fifteen signatories agreed to relegate war-making to history. For his efforts, Kellogg was awarded the Nobel Peace Prize in 1929, the first American to win this prize in nineteen years. (Charles Dawes, the businessman and diplomat, and Coolidge's vice president from 1925 to 1929, had won a Nobel Peace Prize in 1925 for his work on restructuring German war debt.) From 1930 to 1935, Kellogg would serve on the Permanent Court of In-ternational Justice, a multilateral institution at odds with an increas-ingly fascist Europe. Kellogg's star-crossed diplomatic commitment to world peace was either a less astute version of what Wilson had been trying to do, or it was yet another iteration of Wilsonian naivete, but Kellogg's tilting at windmills was not an experiment in American iso-lationism. It was bona fide internationalism, and it lived on even after World War II. The Kellogg-Briand Pact was, according to the historian Richard Current, "cited as the basis for the Nuremberg trials of 1946, involving Nazi leaders accused of war crimes."[4]

To be sure, the Kellogg-Briand Pact was a toothless answer to Europe's dual challenges in the interwar period, both dimly on the horizon in 1928. These were the disruptions of fascism, on the one hand, and of communism, on the other. Before he became president in 1929, Herbert Hoover had fine preparation for handling European affairs. An 1895 graduate of Stanford University and a brilliant engineer, Hoover was nominated for high office by Woodrow Wilson. He led the US Food Administration from 1917, and the American Relief Administration in Europe from 1919 to 1920. His performance made him internationally famous. From 1921 to 1928, he served as secretary of commerce, a virtuoso of modern administration. As president, Hoover pioneered a "good neighbor" policy toward Latin America, one which Franklin Roosevelt adopted, and signed the Pan-American Treaty of Arbitration. Hoover's secretary of state, the hawkish Henry Stimson, promulgated the "Stimson doctrine," whereby the United States would not recognize the fruits of aggression. The United States could not prevent Japan from taking Manchuria between 1931 and 1933. The Stimson doctrine prevented Hoover and Stimson from normalizing Japanese aggression, although their nonrecognition of aggression was not a step toward war. (After World War II, Hoover condemned both American Cold War policy in general and the NATO alliance in particular as military overreach, falling out of line with the foreign-policy consensus of the times.) World War I had left its mark well into the 1930s, and the business of the United States was business, the Republican presidents from Harding to Hoover were sure. They also inhabited a world in which Adolf Hitler was an improbable German leader and Joseph Stalin was still securing his grip on the Kremlin.

But by 1933, Hitler and Stalin were empowered, ambitious statesmen. From its inception, fascism was an immediate, acute and Europe-wide threat to liberty, and in the 1920s fascism was percolating throughout Europe. Belligerently European in orientation, fascism rested on hierarchies of race and nation that were sharply exclusionary and that would lead from World War I to the next conflagration, a battle to the death of *Übermensch* against *Untermensch*. Fascists embraced some Europeans and not others, and they tended to despise Americans as icons of capitalist and interracial decadence. The fascists' rejection of Asiatic

Bolshevism and of global finance, epitomized by the New York Jew or the Frankfurt Jew—Judeo-Bolshevism was their preferred phrase, as hazy as it was deadly—gave them a European idea to which each fascist nation could contribute in its own way. Fascists longed for a West of blood and soil, *Blut und Boden,* one part revival of antiquity, one part militant program to colonize the European and global future. The best of an imagined past would be reclaimed by Europe's awakened, restored and racially cleansed nations.

Hitler and Mussolini partnered on the construction of a fascist Europe. In Italy, in addition to the militarism of his movement, which flowed from the recently concluded war, and the fascist principles of governance, which were monarchy superimposed onto the modern bureaucratic state, Mussolini sought a fascist aesthetic that was at once industrial and neoclassical—much as the Chicago World's Fair had been—an architecture for the masses and an architecture that acknowledged Italy's unsurpassed civilizational heritage. With this architecture in mind, Mussolini stated in 1931 that "Rome must appear marvelous to all the people of the world—vast, orderly, powerful, as in the time of the empire of Augustus." Mussolini's was the generic wishful thinking of fascist statesmen, all of whom were latter-day Caesars. Hitler and his architect Albert Speer poured their empire-building enthusiasm into a fictional fascist metropolis, Germania, a Germanic Rome of cupolas and monumental neoclassical buildings. Hitler and Mussolini had architectural, political and foreign-policy affinities. Their foreign policy encompassed the promotion of fascism throughout Europe and territorial acquisition where possible. Its initial goal was a European order with allowance made for a condominium with Japan. Hitler intended the Second World War to defeat the Soviet Union, subdue Britain and isolate the United States, leaving Germany and Italy and their Europe at the political and commercial center of the world. Once the war was won, there would be no dispute as to whom the twentieth-century Romans truly were. Japan and the United States would be too far away to contest the fascist states for Europe. Then the world could revolve around its fascist axis.[5]

In Europe, fascist foreign policy found its analogue in fascist cultural diplomacy. The fascist Union of National Writers released a 1934 statement, coauthored by two German writers, Hanns Johst and Gottfried Benn, outlining their ideal of the West. The statement had the standard fascist jumble of feared disarray and anticipated unity, of predicting and trying to forestall the decline of the West. "In the threatened condition in which Occidental culture finds itself, no intellectual reordering of Europe can take place, no style can be formed, no literature can rise up from such dissolved elements, indeed no history can come from this continent at all," Johst and Benn wrote, "unless the high concept of moral Fatherland—as genealogical fact, legacy, and linguistic *Mysterium*—forms the highest, most guiding concept of the future." The rooted Fatherland was made up of language and history and blood. The rooted moral Fatherland and the land freshly conquered from the nonfascists and the weak would shore up Europe's heritage, as was the intent of the Permanent Council for International Cooperation among Composers (1934), the International Film Chamber (1935) and the European Writers' Union (1941). These fascist cultural foundations harmonized with the Anti-Comintern Pact signed by Germany, Japan and Italy in 1937, which was charged with dispelling Soviet cultural influence. Another mission was to repel American culture. The European film market, in Nazi propaganda minister Joseph Goebbels's 1942 wish, would be so robust that "when the decisive hour comes after the war we can confidently take up the struggle with America." (Goebbels must have expected the United States to surrender or to sue for peace but to keep on selling its films in Europe after the war.) Fascist Europe would also be free of Jews, not just of Judeo-Bolshevism. This ideology of purity had murderous overtones. The *Frankfurter Zeitung*, marking the German-Italian cultural accord of 1938, predicted "a gradual cultural union among all European nations that will have purified themselves of the Jewish element."[6]

Comparably megalomaniac, though very different in orientation, Soviet foreign policy originated in the miracle of the revolution. Having traveled in 1917 to Saint Petersburg from the alpine obscurity of

Zurich, from West to East, Vladimir Lenin knew firsthand the potential for transformation. He wanted the star of revolution to travel from East to West: westward the course of communism would take its way. In Western Europe and the United States, capitalism was at its worst, and through empire its evils were being globalized. Lenin had written the book on this subject, *Imperialism: The Highest Stage of Capitalism,* published in the year of the Bolshevik Revolution. Yet having taken Russia, the Bolsheviks found they could not take Europe. Lenin could not even take Poland, which the Soviets unsuccessfully invaded in 1921. A revolutionary war would have to be waged by other means. Founded in 1919, the Comintern (Communist International) blended subversion and espionage, propaganda and cultural diplomacy, politics and geopolitics, drawing upon communist enthusiasm within Europe's intelligentsia and working classes. Communism's fortunes were buoyed by the stock market crash of 1929, by the rise of fascism and by the appeal Stalin's manically industrializing Soviet Union had for many Europeans.

Apart from communism's promise of a classless society and of eventual peace and good will among men, the Bolsheviks' passion for Western civilization made them familiar and accessible to Europe's Left. The Bolsheviks had inherited their appreciation for Western literature, philosophy, music and architecture from Marx himself. A 1940 Soviet manual on urban planning characterized socialist-realist art as "Rembrandt, Rubens and Repin in the service of the working class and socialism." (Rembrandt happened to be among Hitler's favorite painters.) The culture hero of the communist West was Leon Trotsky, a fluently European intellectual and a real-life radical. Trotsky had a sparkling prose style and literary eye that neither Lenin nor Stalin could match. He was the most civilized of the early Bolsheviks and his was self-evidently the civilization of the West. In his 1924 book *Literature and Revolution,* the man who forged the Red Army rhapsodized about the coming of communism. Trotsky imagined a communism in which "social construction and psycho-physical self-education will become aspects of one and the same process." Previous ages had limited self-creation to a handful of privileged talents, whereas "the shell in which the cultural construction and self-education of Communist man will be enclosed, will develop all the vital elements of contemporary art to the highest point. Man will become immeasurably stronger, wiser and subtler." Communism will produce a new Adam: "his body will become more harmonized, his movements more rhythmic, his voice more musical. The forms of life will become dynamically dramatic. The average human type will rise to the heights of an Aristotle, a Goethe, or a Marx. And above this ridge new peaks will rise." Civilization did not serve communism. Communism served the civilization of Aristotle, Goethe and Marx.[7]

The Moscow of the 1930s would be the capital of this communist West, yet another modern Rome. Boris Iofan was the architect selected to design the Palace of Soviets, Moscow's government showcase that was never built. Iofan took some of his cues from the Rome of Mussolini and Augustus. He would have had notes to compare with Albert Speer, but he was also interested in Washington, DC, which had asserted its belonging to the West well before the twentieth century. In a 1936 article, Iofan expressed admiration for the Lincoln Memorial and the Folger Shakespeare Library (1932). Otherwise, he thought Washington a capitalist wreck of a city, a derivative collection of "soulless copies [that] fail to evoke the solemnity and monumentality to which they aspire." On balance, he concluded, "the architecture of U.S. government buildings is monumental decoration aimed at persuading ordinary Americans of the permanence of the existing political order." Iofan was comparing communist Moscow with capitalist Washington. What similarity there was between the Soviet Union and the United States would prove helpful between 1935 and 1939, when a truce in their recurring enmities was declared. From 1928 to 1934, the Comintern was in its "Third Period," a war of attrition against the moderate Left, against capitalism, against fascism and against Trotsky, whom Stalin would have murdered in 1940. Hitler's coming to power and subsequent liquidation of the German Communist Party ended the Third Period. A loose conglomerate of left-wing antifascist conviction, from Soviet communism to European social democracy to American progressivism, the Popular Front took its place. The Popular Front was en vogue in the late 1930s, chalking up such artists as Pablo Picasso and Ernest Hemingway as its celebrity affiliates. Moscow and Washington had harshly irreconcilable visions of the West, but they could at least agree on fascism as civilization's mortal enemy. Hitler had unwittingly brokered both the Popular Front and a certain commonality of national interest between the Soviet Union and the United States.[8]

AFTER WORLD WAR I, the United States was more reluctant than the Soviet Union and Nazi Germany to seek leadership of the West. A Western frame for the American relationship to Europe would prevail by the war's end, but initially a more limited Anglo-Saxon frame was stronger. Anglo-Saxonism had a long history in the United States. Thomas Jefferson referred to "our Saxon ancestors," and Ralph Waldo Emerson believed, in historian Nell Painter's words, in "the chain of association linking Saxons and Protestants, Protestantism to the English church, the English church to the Magna Carta, and the Magna Carta to 'liberty.'" Anglo-Saxonism was also in tune with the spirit of racial segregation that was intensifying in the 1920s, comfortably aligned with the Anglophilia and Protestant tenor of the American political elite. Though Anglo-Saxonism might tie American heritage to Germany, where Saxony was to be found after all, it became the glue of the Anglo-American relationship in the early twentieth century. The First World War was one pillar of Anglo-American comradeship. Defeating fascism would be another and related pillar, leading not to a marriage of convenience but to something like an actual marriage based on language, religion and all the other connective tissue between the United States and Great Britain. Intertwined as they were historically, capable as they were of alliance building, France and the United States were sister republics with less in common. The term *Anglo-Saxon* is a foreign and unflattering adjective in the Francophone world, as it is in the German-speaking world, an adjective that distances, while

Anglo-Saxonism in the United States could be a synonym for *American-ism*. This was especially the case in the 1920s.[9]

Potent throughout the nineteenth century, Anglo-Saxonism was advancing in the United States of the early twentieth century. The 1920s were the high-water mark of the Ku Klux Klan, a racist, anti-Semitic and anti-Catholic group that was reconstituted on Stone Mountain, Georgia, in 1915, with civilizational despair as one of its inspirations. The KKK's membership rose to five million in the 1920s, the decade in which immigration was dramatically curtailed along lines amenable to the KKK. The 1924 Immigration Act cut off new arrivals from Southern and Eastern Europe, and the immigration quotas imposed in 1924 would remain in effect for some forty years. The prior immigration that had made the United States more Catholic and more Jewish—and much less homogeneously Anglo-Saxon—was being reconsidered. Perhaps it had been a cultural mistake. For the authors of the Immigration Act, the Northern European was the model American. Championing this same Northern European model, the Rhodes Scholarship acted on the hope of joining the United States and the British Commonwealth to the United Kingdom. It had been established in 1902, and its founder Cecil Rhodes was a prominent symbol and progenitor of the Anglo-Saxon myth. He lent his name to the African country of Rhodesia, which was renamed Zimbabwe in 1979, and his adventures in Africa had all the lurid cultural hallmarks of late-nineteenth-century Anglo-American imperialism. What Rhodes correctly recognized was that cultural affinities cultivated and secured in a great university might evolve over time into strategic affinities between the United States and the British Commonwealth. The University of Oxford was the logical home for the Rhodes Scholarship and for its Anglo-Saxon political ethos.

In the early decades of the twentieth century, the Anglo-Saxon underpinnings of the Rhodes Scholarship were evident across American academia as well. On American campuses, the collegiate gothic was a tribute to Oxbridge and an alternative to the neoclassical style Charles McKim and many others had popularized in the late nineteenth century.

It was a Northern European rather than a Mediterranean style. American collegiate gothic architecture dates back to 1827 and to a building on the Kenyon College campus in Ohio. Harvard put up the gothic Gore Hall in 1838, and Yale a gothic library in 1840. In 1891, the University of Chicago adopted a gothic plan for its campus, as did Duke University in the 1920s: a massive gothic chapel became the center of the Duke campus in 1928. A virtuoso of the collegiate gothic, Ralph Adams Cram was an American architect who had lived in Rome. He left a formidable gothic imprint on the East Coast. Cram got the commission to design the West Point Cadet Chapel (1910) in 1902 and New York's enormous Cathedral of Saint John the Divine (2008) in 1911. From 1907 to 1929, he was the supervising architect at Princeton University, the spirit behind its twenty-five mostly gothic buildings. Cram designed the Princeton University Chapel, a bit of simulated Oxbridge in America, which was completed in 1928. Yale received its ornately gothic Sterling Library and Sterling Law Building in 1931, both from the architect James Gamble Rogers, who bestowed a gothic library on Northwestern University in 1933. Setting foot on the University of Chicago campus in 1945, one fifteen-year-old student "saw the University of Chicago campus for the first time and somehow sensed that I had discovered my life," Allan Bloom (who would go on to teach at the University of Chicago) recalled as a wise-cracking adult, "longing for I know not what suddenly found a response in the world outside. It was, surely, the fake Gothic buildings." The 1987 gothic scheme for a part of Boston College is among the last examples of the collegiate gothic in the United States.[10]

Another conspicuous early-twentieth-century Anglo-Saxonist project was Washington's National Cathedral. The world's sixth-largest cathedral was a bizarre addition to a country constitutionally required to separate church from state and state from church. It was built from 1906 to 1990, though its origins date back to 1893 and to an act of Congress that chartered the Protestant Episcopal Cathedral Foundation. The cathedral was built by an English architect, George Bodley, and an English-born architect, Henry Vaughn. It is the most English of structures, a forceful answer to Henry James's famous list of vacancies in American life: "no cathedrals, nor abbeys, nor little Norman churches; no great Universities nor public schools—no Oxford, no Eton, nor Harrow; no literature, no novels, no museums, no pictures." The National Cathedral's Canterbury Pulpit is constructed with stone from the Church of England's Canterbury Cathedral. It boasts a Churchill Porch and a Pilgrim Observation Gallery, and it made cultural, religious and perhaps even political sense that Woodrow Wilson was buried in 1924 in the National Cathedral, also known as the Cathedral Church of Saint Peter and Saint Paul. His body would later be moved to the church's Woodrow Wilson Bay, which was completed in 1956. Beneath a stained-glass window depicting war and peace stands Wilson's tomb, a Crusader's sword carved on its top. From 1951 to 1978, Wilson's grandson, Francis Bones Sayre, was the dean of this cathedral. State funerals and memorial services have been given in this building for Taft, Harding, Coolidge, Eleanor Roosevelt, Truman, Eisenhower, Ford, Reagan, George Bush Sr. and many other major American political figures. America's de facto Westminster Abby reinforces what appears to be a formal connection among English beginnings, Protestant gravitas and the American presidency—Emerson's genealogy of Anglo-Saxon liberty. In 1924, the year of Wilson's burial, this connection was quasi-official.[11]

These twentieth-century American gothic buildings were put up without embarrassment in a country that has no medieval past, grafting the history of Britain and Northern Europe onto that of the United States. As such, the collegiate gothic was the perfect style for producing an American elite trained to be at home in an Anglo-Saxon landscape and cityscape. Walter Isaacson and Evan Thomas write of "the Anglo-Saxon code" shared by the foreign-policy elites of Britain and the United States in the early twentieth century. When not learned in church, the code could be assimilated in American prep schools and universities. The First World War, which the United States entered in its third year, did not activate the Anglo-Saxon code as emotionally as the crises of the late 1930s did. The Soviet Union was off the

Anglo-Saxon map, a menace from afar. Germany was on the map, but under Hitler it was a horrific repudiation of Anglo-Saxon liberty and fair play. Once Winston Churchill replaced Neville Chamberlain as Britain's prime minister in 1940, Americans had an Anglo-Saxon object of adoration across the Atlantic, an English aristocrat who had to interrupt writing *The History of the English-Speaking Peoples* to guide Britain through the Second World War. (Conceived between 1937 and 1939, Churchill's language-driven history was published between 1956 and 1958; he had received the Nobel Prize for Literature in 1953.) "The whole English-speaking world will be in line together," Churchill promised the House of Commons on June 20, 1940, with the United States very much in mind. Churchill even had an American mother.[12]

To complete the Anglo-American symmetry, Churchill's comrade in arms in World War II was Franklin Roosevelt, quite possibly the most Anglophilic president in American history. Roosevelt's family history, his style and his mannerisms tied him visibly and audibly to Britain. Born in 1882 and educated by Swiss tutors, FDR attended Groton from 1896 to 1900 and Harvard after that. In 1913, he was appointed assistant secretary of the navy. Like Herbert Hoover, he had served in the Wilson administration, and FDR's beloved uncle Teddy had also occupied the assistant secretary of the navy position. (First Lord of the Admiralty from 1911 to 1915, Churchill liked to sign his correspondence with FDR "Former Naval Person," from one former naval person to another.) In addition, FDR's fervent Protestant piety did for him what the gothic chapels at West Point, Princeton, Duke and Northwestern were meant to do for the students who studied in their ambiance. FDR's Protestant piety retraced a religious impulse that began in sixteenth-century England, continued on in the British colonies and was common enough in the modern United States. No line had to be crossed in the back-and-forth between the British past and the American present, no theological barrier and no linguistic barrier, especially for the Episcopalian FDR whose diction had a non-American crispness and lilt. Despite his Dutch surname, Roosevelt brought a touch of the British royal family to the White House. In June 1939,

FDR literally hosted the royal family at his home in Hyde Park, New York, where he served them hot dogs (to their delight).

Not quite the man of ideas that Wilson had been, FDR had internalized Wilson's foreign-policy thinking. FDR ended up applying it to crises even greater than those Wilson had lived through. The sway of Wilsonianism in the Roosevelt administration was substantial. In October 1943, a few months after the battle of Stalingrad, FDR's secretary of state from 1933 to 1944, Cordell Hull, went to Moscow. A lawyer by training, Hull had served in the Spanish-American War, in the Senate and as chairman of the Democratic National Committee. According to the historian Donald Drummond, Hull's "sense of identification with Wilson's proposals [for a League of Nations] embodied a ready acceptance of their idealistic content." When Secretary Hull returned to Washington from his 1943 visit to Moscow, he spoke before Congress, explaining that once the war was over "there will no longer be need for spheres of influence, for alliances, for balance of power, or any other of the special arrangements though which, in the unhappy past, the nations strove to safeguard their security and promote their interests." Given the historical moment, this was an astonishing repudiation of a balance-of-power and sphere-of-influence approach. Hull's was an astonishing affirmation of a new world order, with the Soviet Union of all places as its backdrop. Another world war had reactivated Wilson's hope for a community of powers and for an end to a rivalry of powers. Joseph Stalin was no Wilsonian, as Hull may or may not have realized, but that was a problem for another time. For the Wilsonian sweep of his foreign-policy thinking, for his aspiration to build a new world order, Secretary Hull was awarded a Nobel Peace Prize in 1945, the second US secretary of state to receive the honor (after Frank Kellogg).[13]

Before the peace prizes could be handed out and the unhappy past forgotten, the war itself had to be brought to a close. FDR had two choices when German soldiers invaded Poland in September 1939. President of a United States not ready for war in 1939, he could have cemented a policy of neutrality. The United States was a noncombatant, not an aggressor, and for a while the overseas conflict was a phony war anyway. It was gathering steam but reassuringly far away. Nobody in the United States, including FDR, wanted war, and in the abstract, neutrality was an attractive option, the only way to avoid entangling alliances. As a second choice, FDR could forgo neutrality and align the United States with an embattled France and Britain, risking the wrath of Nazi Germany and its partners. FDR did not arrive at his conclusion for sentimental reasons. He had taken the measure of Hitler and did not believe the United States could manage the German threat through neutrality; but a love of England confirmed his policy prescriptions. It made these prescriptions seem not just right but righteous. President Roosevelt would test the patience of his electorate and stretch the letter of the law to do whatever he could for Britain. He was helped along by institutions like the Committee to Defend America by Aiding the Allies, which was formed in May 1940 with Roosevelt's support.

Another side to FDR's internationalist sensibility proceeded from his domestic political vision. FDR had witnessed the upheavals of the First World War. He had seen imperial Russia slide into the Soviet Union, and Italy pass over to fascism not long after the war's end. Reeling from the Great Depression, Germany succumbed to Hitler at almost the same moment FDR came to power in the United States. Not only were the economic woes of the post-1929 period contagious. The interwar years were proof that democracy and stability were anything but guaranteed. The British historian and philosopher Isaiah Berlin associated democracy's strength and its fragility with FDR in a retrospective essay he wrote in 1955:

> The only light in the darkness [of the 1930s] was the administration of Mr. Roosevelt and the New Deal in the United States. At a time of weakness and mounting despair in the democratic world, Mr. Roosevelt radiated confidence and strength. He was the leader of the democratic world, and even today upon him alone, of all the statesmen of the thirties, no cloud has rested—neither on him nor on the New Deal, which to European eyes still looks a bright chapter in the history of mankind.

For FDR, democracy and stability had to be secured at home, and they had to be secure at home if democracy was to be advocated for abroad. Teddy Roosevelt and Woodrow Wilson had married progressive domestic initiatives to an internationalist vision. FDR did this more comprehensively, starting in the 1930s. With Europe in such bad shape politically, the stakes of FDR's New Deal were especially high. Democracy rested on institutions and leadership and some degree of economic normalcy. For FDR, these were geopolitical and domestic political concerns, civilizational and socioeconomic. His New Deal would be folded into his four freedoms at home and abroad. Setting them before the public in his 1941 State of the Union speech, FDR espoused freedom of speech and expression, freedom from want, freedom of worship and freedom from fear. As the historian William Leuchtenburg put it in a 1995 book, *The FDR Years,* "Roosevelt came to office at a desperate time, in the fourth year of a worldwide depression that raised the gravest doubts about the future of Western civilization." Only with an economically viable United States, FDR reasoned, could Western civilization be successfully defended abroad.[14]

The 1940 election made it easier for FDR to accent to his favored internationalism. Harding, Coolidge and Hoover had been modestly internationalist, but they had been cautious, and they had had to manage a Republican Party that was divided between Midwestern isolationists and Northeastern internationalists. Wilsonianism had already been punctured once by Republican senators. In 1940, however, Wendell Willkie, a stunningly dark-horse candidate, appeared. His internationalism presaged that of the postwar Republican Party. Willkie, a young lawyer and tempered critic of the New Deal, was so unconventional in his foreign-policy thinking that the Republican Party dropped him in 1944, but Willkie got 45 percent of the popular vote against the godlike FDR in 1940. After losing, Willkie traveled the world in 1942, meeting with leaders in Africa, the Middle East, the Soviet Union and China. In his 1943 best-seller, *One World,* Willkie argued for Western responsibility, for the replacement of imperialism and colonialism with the political independence of the formally colonized countries.

To flourish under this new multiracial international order, the United States would have to address its problems with racism at home, Willkie contended. It was an argument that most Republican and Democratic politicians did not want to hear in 1943.

The 1940 election behind him, FDR pushed the United States a step closer to Great Britain. In August 1941, he met with Churchill on the Atlantic Ocean. Had theirs been a treaty alliance, the United States would have been in the war already. Four months before Pearl Harbor, FDR could not go that far, but he could show Hitler and Mussolini that he and Churchill stood by one another, and not for purely pragmatic reasons. Churchill and Roosevelt bowed their heads together in prayer. They sang "Onward Christian Soldiers" and affirmed a common Anglo-American view of international affairs, a vision of peace and unimpeded commerce that was to be guaranteed by the American and British Navies. At the heart of the Atlantic Charter was a hoped-for international order of liberty and self-government. The signatories rejected "territorial changes that do not accord with the free expressed wishes of the people concerned" and affirmed "the right of all peoples to choose the form of government under which they will live," expressing their wish "to see sovereign rights and self government restored to those who have been forcibly deprived of them." Just two months before, in June, Hitler had cast aside the Nazi-Soviet pact, launching Operation Barbarossa. Day by day, Hitler's armies were plunging toward Moscow. Europe's situation was in every way desperate, and by meeting with Churchill, FDR was qualifying American neutrality: lend-lease, an American method of providing aid to Britain and other countries, including the Soviet Union, had been in place since March 1941. The United States was on one side and not on the other. After December 7, 1941, the FDR-Churchill friendship and the special relationship were the soul of the American war effort.[15]

Close as it was, the alliance with Britain was not the totality of the American war. The American war in the Pacific pitted the United States against an Asian power that would be demonized throughout the war as a racial and civilizational other. Though Churchill and Stalin supported the war against Japan, it was largely an American endeavor. Its dynamic was different—strategically and culturally—from the British and American campaigns in North Africa and Europe. Nor were the Allies just the British Commonwealth and the United States. The Free French under Charles de Gaulle's command were American allies. Likewise, Poles and Czechs and soldiers from other occupied European countries were part of the Allied war effort, numerically small but morally and emotionally important. The pre-1933 mayor of Cologne, Konrad Adenauer, was in exile during the war. So too was another future West German chancellor, Willy Brandt. Those Italians liberated from fascism could turn into allies. When General Mark Clark led American troops into Rome in the summer of 1944, the event was excitedly celebrated on the American home front and not just for its military significance. The pivotal wartime partner was the Soviet Union, the nemesis of Nazi Germany that was difficult (for Americans) to fit on any civilizational map. During the war, American propaganda did not shy away from praising Uncle Joe Stalin and affirming the bravery of the Russian people. At Stalingrad, in the winter of 1942–1943, the Soviet Union reversed the direction of the war, and out of deference to this fact General Eisenhower believed that Soviet soldiers should take Berlin in the spring of 1945. The Allies owed them that honor.

In addition to having allies across the Eurasian continent, the American government and society at war were not composed only of Anglo-Saxons. Anglo-Saxonism was an incomplete cultural foundation for the war, because American soldiers and officers came from all backgrounds. They were black and white and of every Christian denomination. They were Jews and Native Americans. Awkwardly, some were of German, Italian and Japanese descent. The variety was a function of immigration and migration patterns going back centuries. Not every barrier fell during the war. America's World War II military was as segregated as the society that peopled it. Those of Japanese background endured considerable persecution—those of German and Italian background considerably less. At FDR's order, internment camps for people of Japanese descent, many of them American citizens, were set up shortly after Pearl Harbor. Japanese Americans were the only group to be targeted in this brutal way, whereas for the immigrants and the children of immigrants recently arrived from Eastern and Southern Europe, the nativism of the 1920s did not survive the war intact. The war may have begun with the Anglo-Saxon ideal, with the cultural lineage that FDR and Churchill so proudly upheld on the *Prince of Wales* in Placentia Bay on August 9, 1941, when they signed the Atlantic Charter. As the war progressed, a category broader than Anglo-Saxonism was necessary.

That category was the West. It was a Euro-American and not a universal category. In the Pacific it might be a war of East against West, the very trauma of the war the fact that an Asian power had been so bold as to attack the West at Pearl Harbor. In Europe, it might be— and was—a war for the West. Within Anglo-American discussions, the West was a key category, in the parlance of the times. In 1942, according to a reporter, FDR's emissary Harry Hopkins met with Churchill to "discuss the grave predicament of Western Civilization." For Eisenhower, this was a war to reconstitute Europe, a crusade in Europe that helped gather the full American population behind the war. FDR had already invited urban "ethnics"—the working-class Jews and Italians and Irish—into his electoral coalition. A general with a German name could lead them into a war in and for Europe. A war for the West and not just for the English-speaking peoples clarified American strategy. It was a war to allow the West to remain what it was, to excise the cancer of fascism and to restore liberty in its ancient European homeland. Wartime places and dates arrayed themselves into a stirring Euro-American narrative: Rome (liberated June 4, 1944); Paris (liberated August 25, 1944); Athens (liberated October 14, 1944). The destiny of these cities and the prominent American role in saving them from the fascists was the cradle of postwar Euro-American or Western liberty.[16]

American leadership of the West in 1945 changed the nineteenth-century relationship between race and civilization. The US military fought the war with a segregated military. As in World War I, the democratic rhetoric of an American president was contradicted by the racial barriers to democracy at home and to the conduct of the war itself. Yet World War II was unequivocally a war against Hitler. Hitler had derived *Lebensraum* in part from the US government's treatment of Native Americans: he had a lifelong addiction to the Westerns written by the German writer Karl May. Hitler analogized Europe's East to America's West, analogizing Jews to Native Americans. Segregation in the United States bore some resemblance to the racial laws established in Germany in 1935 and thereafter, but Hitler's racism was so extreme that its eradication became an American war aim, of sorts. When the liberation of Europe turned to the liberation of Germany from Nazism—when the war reached German territory, that is— Americans soldiers were confronted with evidence of the Holocaust. News of the death camps in Poland and elsewhere outlined the unbelievable story of German anti-Semitism. As the historian Thomas Borstelmann writes: "Hitler forced the world to see where racist thinking ultimately could lead, thereby sharply reducing its legitimacy for the postwar era. This encouraged popular opinion in the Western nations like the United States to begin to support the antiracist consensus that had been building in the scientific community since the 1920s." (This was the consensus that race is not a scientific or biological fact but a pseudoscientific fiction.) The battle against Hitler was one of many tributaries into the civil rights movement, as in its way World War I had been in the 1920s. Hitler discredited without destroying the seductions of a white West.[17]

THE CRUSADE IN Europe, the joy of liberating the West, was an essential wartime commodity. It could be appreciated because it had been disseminated in elite circles long before the war. The universities started putting their energy behind the West at the time of the First World War. They spent the interwar years ignoring cultural isolationism, ignoring the fashion for Spenglerian pessimism and not succumbing to nationalism. They spent the interwar years educating American students in the achievements of the West and aligning the notion of the educated American with a command of Western civilization.

Columbia University was the pioneer of the Western civilization curriculum. It merged commitments to Western civilization and to great books into its General Honors program. Columbia substituted Western civilization for a requirement that had once been self-evident—that educated Americans know Greek and Latin. Latin had been the language of learning for millennia, and Greek was the bridge to many of the greatest of the great books. In the eighteenth and nineteenth centuries, to have labeled higher education at American universities Western would have been beside the point. There was no education other than the one that had descended through the ages from Greco-Roman antiquity. Columbia's recognition of Western civilization as a distinct subject demonstrated an educational outlook of widening breadth and cosmopolitanism. With Latin and Greek no longer required, however, students might attend college and bypass a real education altogether, Columbia and its alumni feared. The university's motto—*in lumine Tuo videbimus lumen,* "in thy light we shall see light"—might be illegible in more ways than one. So, for the first time, Western civilization as such was something that had to be taught.

In Columbia's General Honors course, to learn about Western civilization was not to look backward. The great-books element, mostly books read in translation without much scholarly or historical context, dropped undergraduates into the world of Plato or Dante as if it were already their world. The ideas were close at hand. They belonged to the students. First a student and then an instructor in the program, the Columbia professor Lionel Trilling recalled "that enchanting General Honors course that [John] Erskine had devised" and had constructed around the premise that "the best citizen is the person who had learned from the great minds and souls of the past how beautiful reason and virtue are and how difficult to attain." Reason and virtue as the soul's educators: Thomas Jefferson might have used the same Enlightenment language to explain the purpose of the University of Virginia. John Erskine was an English professor, and he detailed his agenda for General Honors in a 1928 volume, *The Delight of Great Books.* "The approach to literature is always through life," Erskine explained, "and if a book no longer reflects our life, it will cease to be generally read, no matter what its importance for antiquarian purposes." He meant *our* life as Columbia students and professors and by extension our American life in great books. The books, too, were ours, wherever they had been written and in whichever language, for "until we have discovered that certain books grow with our maturing experience and others do not, we have not learned how to distinguish a great book from a book."[18]

Over time, General Honors modulated into a colloquium, "The Classics of the Western World." This colloquium was put together by Jacques Barzun, a Columbia professor who would direct his attention to the Western world decades later in a despairing and polemical book, *From Dawn to Decadence: 1500 to the Present; 500 Years of Western Cultural Life.* Assigned readings for the 1930s colloquium included Homer, Aeschylus, Sophocles, Euripides, Plato, Vergil, Dante, Rabelais, Cervantes, Hobbes, Milton, Moliere, Goethe, Adam Smith, Gibbon, Balzac, Stendhal, Dickens, Dostoevsky and Tolstoy. This row of authors formed a chronological and civilizational line, European culture sprung from the godhead of the Homeric epic. Two Russians made the cut. No Americans did. Gibbon was the only historian, and Smith the only economic thinker. Balzac, Stendhal and Dickens were the less-than-avant-garde exemplars of modern literature. The British strain was prominent, but not overpowering. Protestant Milton was obliged to share the stage with Catholics, Orthodox Christians and pagans. The Bible was handled as another great book at Columbia, and it was not approached as scripture. The onus was on it to reflect our life.[19]

The point of departure for the Columbia program, with its literary and Greek bias, was Greco-Roman antiquity. As Herbert Edwin Hawkes put it in a 1937 essay, "The Evolution of the Arts College: Recent Changes at Columbia": "the first year will be devoted to the literature of Greece and Rome . . . literature which has through the ages meant the most to mankind," a forthright pedagogic claim. A university in a city of immigrants, Columbia was the elite American university of the 1920s and 1930s most open to non-Protestant public high school graduates. The curriculum of Western classics was a letter of welcome to them. In no way was Columbia catering to Jewish students like Lionel Trilling, an early alumnus of the program. Apart from the Bible, religious Judaism and modern Jewish authors were a blank space. Jewish students were accepted into Columbia in order to acquire a non-Jewish intellectual patrimony, but neither was the Columbia curriculum being denied to Jewish students like Trilling. For Columbia's Catholic students, the classics—and Dante especially—could be studied as the legacy of their world. For all that the Anglo-Saxon Protestant remained the model American in the 1920s and 1930s, and the model university student, the academy under the firmament of Western civilization was becoming an increasingly hospitable place for Catholic and Jewish students alike.[20]

Between 1931 and 1934, as a visual compliment to the classics of the Western world, a new library was erected on the Columbia campus. Its architect was the same as Sterling Library's at Yale, James Gamble Rogers. The Columbia library would become known as Butler Library after Nicholas Murray Butler, Columbia's president from 1902 to 1945, and Rogers's library was neoclassical rather than gothic. It faces Charles McKim's Low Library, the alpha and the omega of the Columbia campus. The entryway of Butler Library has a mural, *Videbimus Lumen,* that is a graphic depiction of the university's motto. It portrays Athena beating down malevolent influence and disorder, a metaphor for education and scholarship. The library's exterior reinforces the civilizational line of the assigned reading. As was typical of so many American buildings associated with learning, it presents a long list of honorific and non-American names: Homer, Herodotus, Sophocles, Plato, Aristotle, Demosthenes, Cicero, Vergil, Cervantes, Shakespeare, Milton, Voltaire, Goethe, Horace, Tacitus, Saint Augustine, Saint Thomas Aquinas, Dante. From Homer to Dante: epic poetry reigns supreme far above theology. On the Butler Library façade, the English-language luminaries number only two, Shakespeare and Milton, the same as the number of Catholic saints. Seemingly against his will, Voltaire, the satirist of Christianity, is up there as well (keeping company surely with Cervantes). Relative to the nineteenth-century

American university, resolutely Protestant and inward looking, the Western culture etched onto Butler Library reflected the opening of the American mind. Butler Library was no Anglo-Saxon haven. Nor was the city that surrounded it.

An alumnus of Columbia's General Honors program, Mortimer Adler, transplanted the great-books model to the University of Chicago. Adler worked in tandem with Robert Hutchins, since 1929 the youthful president of the University of Chicago, to have Chicago surpass Columbia as a beacon of Western civilization. Chicago's program was the common core, and within and beyond the university gates Adler was its vigorous promoter. He published *The Great Ideas: A Syntopicon of Great Books of the Western World* in 1952, a summation of his career. Stanford University set up its Western Civilization program in 1935. Drawing inspiration from Chicago, St. John's College in Annapolis adopted a strenuous great-books program in 1937, its undergraduate education an education in great books alone. Assigning the great books of the Western world was a national trend. International background to this trend was the public burning of books in Germany, the country where not a few great books had been written. Noting the link between fascism and willed ignorance, the journalist and foreign-affairs pundit Walter Lippmann identified St. John's as a center of antifascist resistance and simultaneously of American political and intellectual rebirth. The classics well studied were the antithesis of fascism, which rested on propaganda and the perversion of ideas, the tyranny of ignorance and force rather than the difficult-to-attain harmonies of reason, virtue and self-government. "In the future," Lippmann wrote, "men will point to St. John's College and say that here was the seed-bed of the American renaissance."[21]

EXTRAVAGANT AS HIS wording was, Lippmann was right to see geopolitics in a university's choice of which books to assign, which courses to teach and which curricula to require. Only a small number of American men and a smaller number of women were getting university educations in the 1930s. Homer and Aeschylus were of no use in determining the fine points of tank warfare, in protecting against aerial bombardment and in managing the economics of modern war. They could not help to assess the balance of power in 1930s Europe or 1930s Asia. Nevertheless, even defensive wars must be fought for reasons, and all alliances are grounded in more than a common threat perception. This much the US-Soviet partnership would prove when it collapsed immediately after World War II. Alliances rely on culture, religion, kinship and language as well as strategic affinity, all of which has to be comprehensible to the people within the alliances. The curricular West anticipated and amplified an antifascist Western alliance to the citizens who composed it. The Western civilization curricula made plausible the idea that by not appeasing and surrendering to the fascists, the United States and Britain were meeting their responsibility to uphold Western civilization, to fight for it and ultimately to bring it back to the European continent. The war's leaders and planners and a portion of its soldiers had been educated to conduct a crusade in Europe.

Harry Truman and Dwight Eisenhower, two Midwesterners, left an oversized mark on this great crusade. They would move from major roles in World War II to the position of first and second Cold War president, further linking these interlinked wars. Truman and Eisenhower were both regular American guys in a way that Franklin Roosevelt was not, and neither had noticeable English or even Anglo-American pedigrees. As with the vast majority of people they governed, Truman and Eisenhower happened not to be English gentlemen. Despite serving in two world wars against Germany, Eisenhower was proud of his German heritage. Truman had grown up on a farm and did not attend college. Although Roosevelt's Harvard diploma and aristocratic lineage were not political liabilities for him when he stood arm in arm with Churchill, the unabashed elitism of their Anglo-American leadership was a limitation. (Remarkably, Churchill was voted out of office in July 1945.) One could look up to the Churchill-Roosevelt partnership, one could admire its dignity, but for many Americans it was hard to feel an equal part of it. An excess of Anglophile elitism in the Roosevelt administration was balanced out by Truman, Eisenhower and others like chief of staff of the US Army George Marshall, who were Euro-peanists first and Anglophiles second. These members of the Roosevelt administration helped to popularize the West as an element of American foreign policy.

Not one to quote from Aeschylus and Sophocles in his speeches, Eisenhower was an army man, unpretentious and unassuming, but he was a reader as well. He was a rural Midwestern intellectual rather than an urban East Coast intellectual. (Born in Texas, Eisenhower grew up in Kansas.) According to Stephen Ambrose, Eisenhower's biographer, Eisenhower's father was "excellent in Greek" and an avid student of the Greek Bible. Eisenhower himself studied Latin in school and had a childhood fascination with Hannibal, whose invasion of Europe Eisenhower would replicate, with amphibious landing craft instead of elephants. In his Abilene High School yearbook, Eisenhower predicted that he would become a professor of history at Yale. A graduate of West Point, Eisenhower read Clausewitz's classic study of war three times. He spent quite a bit of time in Europe after the First World War. From 1928 to 1929, he lived in Paris, where he helped to compile a guidebook on World War I monuments. This background led to a particular interpretation of the Second World War. Fascism was a betrayal of European civilization and European liberty in Eisenhower's view—a take on European civilization with an American tinge. He did not see empire or stale monarchy or entrenched malice in continental Europe. He did not at all equate Hitler with Europe. He equated Europe with the time before and after Hitler. As Eisenhower wrote to his son at the time of the D-Day invasion, "No other war in history has so definitively lined up the forces of arbitrary oppression and dictatorship against those of human rights and individual liberty." No historical or geographical rule separated human rights and individual liberty in the United States from human rights and individual liberty in Europe, according to Eisenhower. When he looked at Europe, Eisenhower saw the potential for liberty because he saw the precedent of liberty.[22]

When D-Day was over and the Allied soldiers were marching toward Berlin, General Eisenhower insisted that his soldiers fight a war for civilization. Having trampled on human rights and individual liberty, having shamed Western civilization with arbitrary oppression and dictatorship, Hitler could not be defeated by trampling on human rights and sullying individual liberty. To defeat Hitler would be to uphold Eisenhower's jewel of Western civilization. For this reason, as Stephen Ambrose writes, Eisenhower "issued stern general orders that no fighting should take place in areas containing important historical or religious monuments, explaining that they represented, in large part, what the Allies were fighting for." This was a remarkable war aim, especially for the American soldiers involved. They were being asked to incur greater practical difficulty and perhaps greater casualties for the sake of historical and religious monuments in countries most of them were seeing for the first time. Needless to say, no such provision was contemplated or enforced in the Pacific war, in which a civilizational affinity for Japan on the part of most American troops and officers was nonexistent. The firebombing of Tokyo and the bombing of other Japanese cities generated little remorse for the countless historical and religious monuments that were destroyed.[23]

Eisenhower's reverence for the civilization of the Allies and even for the countries he was fighting against set the tone for his wartime diplomacy. Alliance building was a necessity for the United States, though that which is necessary is not always easy. Eisenhower's character, his lack of theatrical egotism and his reading of the war smoothed a network of fraught relationships—with General Bernard Montgomery, leader of Free France Charles de Gaulle, Churchill and others. Eisenhower's belief in a Euro-American affinity gave him the patience to maintain the transatlantic alliance. So too did his capacity to observe Europe through European eyes. The Falaise battlefield "could be described only by Dante," Eisenhower wrote. Dante's inferno was a cliché here, but a tellingly European cliché. Eisenhower anticipated JFK's far more famous identification with Berlin—"*ich bin ein Berliner*"—by eighteen years when he gave his victory speech in London on June 12, 1945. Among his British friends he confessed that "I am now a Londoner myself." The phrase is not startling, not controversial, not memorable, but it is more evidence of Eisenhower's personal identification with his European partners in the Second World War. Not every American general felt this kind of identification, and not every World War II general would go on after the war to become the Supreme Allied Commander of Europe and a two-term president after that.[24]

Harry Truman's attitude toward Europe was more or less the same as the general's. A Democrat and a politician, rather than a dyed-in-the-wool military man, and six years older than Eisenhower, Truman was an autodidactic scholar of the West. When he was a child, he, an excellent pianist, had met the legendary Polish virtuoso Ignacy Paderewski (who had performed at the Chicago World's Fair). From a young age, Truman spent considerable time reading European books. Like Eisenhower, Truman studied Latin in school and was captivated by ancient history. He especially loved Plutarch's *Lives,* a meditation through biography on politics and statesmanship, which his father had given him. He read Caesar's *Commentaries,* translated Cicero and was enamored of Marcus Aurelius, as Bill Clinton, another autodidact from rural America, would be later. A more-than-amateur farmer, Truman consulted Cato's *de Agricultura* for insight into how best to plant beans. "I was reading Plato's Republic this morning and Socrates was discoursing on the ideal Republic," Truman wrote in a not atypical note to his wife. Dean Acheson, Truman's aristocratic and learned secretary of state, would later describe himself as "awed" by Truman's command of history. Truman's identification with Europe also accorded with the Southern folkways of his childhood and with a Southern penchant for the classics, reinforcing his status as a white American. He grew up not long after the Civil War in the former slave state of Missouri, the grandson of slave owners. As a young man, Truman considered joining the KKK.[25]

Truman's love of the European past sharpened his image of himself as an American politician. More than agricultural advice, Truman adopted a norm of liberty and self-government from his reading in ancient Greek and Latin letters. He had an eighteenth-century American's reverence for Cincinnatus, dear to Truman's heart as a fellow tiller of the soil and dear to Truman's commander-in-chief heart as someone who did not give in to the temptations of power. As president, Truman kept a miniature plow on his desk, symbolic of the restraint Cincinnatus had once embodied. Truman connected republican excellence and ascendance with the limits on executive power. He connected executive overreach with imperial decline, writing when he decided not to run for reelection in 1952 that "this is a republic . . . Cincinnatus and Washington pointed the way. When Rome forgot Cincinnatus its downfall began." More to the point, when he was a senator from 1935 to 1945, Truman was an internationalist Democrat in the Wilsonian vein. The First World War had been his ticket to Europe. Before the Second World War, Truman focused on military preparedness, employing his skills as a legislator to expose and condemn the misuse of military appropriations. Truman also shared FDR's and Eisenhower's appreciation of alliances. The Midwest in which Truman grew up may have been an isolationist stronghold, the America not on the coast and the America not preoccupied by European politics, but such regions were politically crucial to the running of American foreign policy. Whatever its outlook was, the Midwest would supply many of the soldiers and much of the funding for America's wars. Other senators may have known more about international affairs. They may have had the academic degrees and diplomatic experience that Truman did not have. Few American politicians have ever matched Truman's ease with domestic politics *and* foreign policy, with the way in which foreign policy is dependent on domestic politics. As president, he would prove a Wilsonian far more skilled at implementing his foreign policy than Woodrow Wilson.[26]

THE CONTEST FOR the West was coming to a head in 1944, the year Truman became the vice president elect. Germany was fighting and losing on two fronts in 1944. Mussolini, who had been living in exile in northern Italy since 1943 while Italian fascism was collapsing, was hung in April 1945. Contrary to its military mystique from 1939 to 1941, fascism was not invincible, and as information about the

Holocaust trickled out fascism's abominations inflicted a second defeat on Hitler and on Nazi appeals to the high concept of a moral Fatherland. Purifying Europe of Jewish influence meant murdering Europe's Jews. Awareness of the Holocaust, slow and incomplete as it was, altered the war. The Western civilization to which Churchill and Eisenhower regularly appealed had to exceed the preservation of religious and historical monuments. The West could not simply stand for liberty and representative government versus dictatorship. For the war to have moral meaning, Western civilization had to be the inverse of the Holocaust: this was a twentieth-century as opposed to a nineteenth-century reading of Western civilization. In addition to protecting the rights of small nations, the Czechoslovakians who had been betrayed by the West in the 1930s, Western civilization would need to show greater tolerance of minority rights and to provide more safeguards for them. Given Germany's recent descent from civilization to barbarism, Europe would once again need to civilize this big nation, which was a scarcely credible prospect in 1944.

With fascism on the defensive in 1944, Soviet communism was triumphing. Stalingrad was in the past. After the grievous setbacks of 1941 and 1942, the Red Army was not just nearing Germany but also liberating Europe along the way. The liberation cut two ways, of course. The Nazis had enslaved the peoples they ruled in Eastern and Central Europe, murdering Jews and non-Jews at will. Only the most craven of the Nazi collaborators could regret the Soviets' expulsion of the Germans from the territory they occupied. In this light, the Soviet soldiers were heroes, though Stalin had been an architect and a beneficiary of the Nazi-Soviet pact from 1939 to 1941. Yet Stalin also knew what it was to enslave, which did not bode well for the countries falling under his control in 1944 and 1945. The Soviet Union's relative foreign-policy calm from 1921 to 1939 had been a hiatus, a long exception to the rule. The spread of Soviet communism had stalled under Stalin, the Soviet Union getting outperformed by the capitalist economies even during the Depression. In the late 1930s, Soviet culture was middling, forcibly isolated from the Western avant-garde and decimated by the

Great Terror. In the Soviet Union, Trotsky's civilized brilliance had long since been extinguished, and by 1944 the intellectuals of Europe and the United States were losing interest in the Soviet experiment. Stalin had too much blood on his hands. Nevertheless, at this very moment, Stalin was organizing the Soviet Union into a military juggernaut and a European power by default. Not since 1814 had Russian soldiers found themselves traveling so far to the West as they were in 1944. Among the war's biggest victors, Stalin would have the spoils.

Roosevelt, Marshall and Eisenhower were similarly making the United States into a European power in the early 1940s. The Columbian Republic would see itself no other way. Of the West, it was destined to be in the West or simply to be the West. By 1944, American leadership of the West was for the first time a plausible scenario. In uniform for the second time to save the West, Americans had to head East to reach Berlin, but the portion of Europe they would occupy, by geographic accident, was Western rather than Eastern. This reinforced the cultural template many brought with them to the war. The restoration of France, the rescue of Italy, the resurgence of Britain after facing Hitler alone for two endless years prevented the events of 1944 from being an American venture, and to speak of "the Allies" was of course to speak of an alliance with the Soviet Union. As Stalin rightly sensed and acutely resented, however, there were alliances within alliances and partnerships within partnerships. The West was the United States plus Britain and France. Other properly Western European nations—even the one that had started the war and its closest ally, Italy—could be incorporated into the West later. In aggregate, these were the world's wealthiest countries and the most technologically advanced. As the war had shown, if they could work together there was little they could not do. By late 1944, the democratic West was much closer to victory than it was to tragedy or to some Spenglerian downfall.

Leadership of the West fell into Harry Truman's lap. Truman was the vice president from nowhere, Roosevelt's nondescript sidekick suddenly at the helm of the ship. Eight years later, Winston Churchill would join Truman for a sail on the Potomac. On the presidential yacht,

Churchill paid the man from Missouri a lavish compliment. Since the Potsdam Conference, "You [Truman] more than any other man have saved Western civilization." This was Churchill being Churchill, dramatizing through rhetorical excess, but it was also a retrospective statement about FDR's choice of vice president. FDR could have selected someone who would appreciate the Soviet contribution at Stalingrad and elsewhere, detecting in it the foundations of a new international order, Europe a Soviet-American condominium. FDR could have kept on the philo-Soviet Henry Wallace as vice president. FDR could have selected someone with a less internationalist bent, someone for whom the end of the war would have been the end of the United States as a European power and for whom the United States as a hemispheric American power was sufficient. There were domestic problems aplenty for any American president to confront in 1945. Very likely the majority of Americans, who wanted the boys home before Christmas, would have consented to a gradual withdrawal from Europe once the war was over. Yet FDR had put his finger on Truman.[27]

Because of their orientation toward the West, FDR and Truman conducted a more vicious war in Asia than they did in Europe. Hitler may have violated the ideals of the West, but Nazi Germany was closer—racially—to the United States than was imperial Japan. The historian John Dower traces the American racial animus toward Japan back to the nineteenth century, to the wars against the Native Americans and the Spanish-American War, which consolidated the United States as a Pacific power. Dower emphasizes "the fact that anti-oriental sentiment not only had deep roots in American history, but also was embedded in the laws of the land." Dower quotes from an 1866 speech of Teddy Roosevelt as an insight into wartime attitudes toward the Japanese: "I suppose I should be ashamed to say that I take the Western view of the Indian. I don't go so far as to think that the only good Indians are dead Indians, but I believe that nine out of every ten are, and I shouldn't inquire too closely about the tenth." (By "Western" Teddy Roosevelt was referring here to the American West.) A practical consequence of the cultural or racial distinction between

Germans and Japanese was the internment of some 110,000 American citizens of Japanese background. In addition, American bombing of Germany was extensive and resulted in massive civilian casualties, and no doubt atomic weapons would have been used against Germany had it not surrendered before they became available. Still, it was on two Japanese cites that Truman used the atomic bomb. Anti-Japanese prejudices in the American population were in tune with those of FDR and Truman.[28]

Personalities were integral to American strategy, as were cultural affinities and prejudices, but so too was geopolitics. In 1945, these factors favored the evolution of an American-led West. Europe needed American assistance, and the United States needed an end to wars in Europe. The United States was not going to ask anyone's permission to stay in Europe in the 1940s, and fortuitously the United States had much to offer postwar Europe: it could be sincerely welcomed as an occupying power. Having butchered one another for six years since 1939, Europeans were unprepared to present a united front against any potential enemy; Europe was a panorama of rubble. Hunger, poverty and millions of refugees were the immediate political issues, making the Western European dependence on American military power existential in 1945. Only the United States could deflect the Soviet Union's military designs on Europe or on Europe's Western half. Of the Western powers, the United States was the only one with an unspoiled economy. Indeed, it was the booming American economy that had fueled the Allied war effort. After the war, the capitalist United States was a European benefactor and an excellent, if aggressive, trading partner. The United States was the world's sole nuclear power in 1945, a valuable ally and an undesirable enemy.

The United States was also the West's representative democracy in 1945. To Europe's established democracies, the military prowess of the United States proved that democracies could be durable, that not all democratic statesmen were Neville Chamberlains in spirit, that a democracy in concert with other democracies—and one unabashed autocracy, alas—could defeat despotic fascism. In Europe, the American example was even more important to the vanquished fascist countries than it was to the wartime allies. Italy and Germany might well have gone back to authoritarian strongmen in 1945, yet no postwar European country adopted democracy with the same care and the same level of ingenuity as West Germany. West Germany was occupied by the British, the French and the United States, and it quickly occupied itself with the problem of democracy, absorbing the rights and freedoms of the American Constitution and altering them to fit West German circumstances. In 2000, the German historian Heinrich August Winkler published a landmark history of Germany from 1871 to 1989: *Der lange Weg nach Westen* (the long way to the West) describes the journey from authoritarianism to democracy, from Asiatic despotism to the liberty-loving Euro-American West. A Germany within the West made the West much more than the Anglo-American special relationship, and more than Britain or France, it was the United States that sought a democratic and westernized Germany, the keystone to the American strategy for Europe.[29]

Partnering with postwar Europe and forging an American-led West was not an absolute necessity for the United States. It was a choice. In the making of this choice, American leaders, and with them the American electorate, were prepared to accept the costs of an American-led West. The military logic was clearer than the truth, as Dean Acheson was fond of saying. Twice the United States had been dragged into world war by Europe. The domination of Europe by any one power, and especially by a power hostile to the United States, was strategically impermissible. With ongoing global economic integration, it was impossible for Americans to see war in Europe as a pity for Europeans but a matter of irrelevance to the United States. War in Europe spilled over to the United States. The impact might be reduced trade. It might be the sinking of American ships and passengers in the Atlantic. It might be the schemes of European powers to infiltrate Latin American countries and thus to bring their conflicts to the Americas—their military bases, their intelligence services, their subversive intent. Overshadowed by Pearl Harbor, Hitler's unprovoked declaration of war against the

United States in December 1941 demonstrated the folly of sitting on the sidelines once Hitler had invaded his neighbors. One way or another, the United States would be a factor in Europe, a factor in any world war.

The economic angle to German perfidy was apparent to American planners, if somewhat opaque, perhaps, to the American public. Beginning in March 1936, Hitler had occupied the Rhineland, against the spirit and the letter of the Versailles Treaty. The industrial plant Hitler acquired allowed him to modernize the German military, and by 1939 the German military was the strongest in Europe. It had taken only a few years. As of fall 1941, Hitler and his allies had a hold on Europe comparable in reach to Emperor Hadrian's Roman Empire. To the United States, the cost of defeating Hitler was stupendous even with the Soviet contribution and with the role that Britain and the other Allies played. The United States had to launch an invasion of North Africa, drive up Italy's mountainous spine and then launch the greatest amphibious attack in the history of war for the privilege of standing face-to-face with the *Wehrmacht* in France and Germany. To say "never again" to this military scenario was to focus on who in Europe might have access to the key industrial areas such as the Ruhr Valley and the Rhineland. As the historian Melvin Leffler argues, "For U.S. officials, the most decisive and lasting legacy of the wartime experience was that potential adversaries must never again be allowed to gain control of the resources of Eurasia through autarkical economic practices, political subversion, and/or military aggression." According to Harry Truman in January 1951: "If Western Europe were to fall to Soviet Russia it would double the Soviet supply of coal and triple the Soviet supply of steel." Luckily for the United States in 1945, many of Europe's key economic arteries were to be found in the West, in the zones that happened to be controlled by British, French and American soldiers. That was one case for an American-led West.[30]

The other case for the West was political or diplomatic. Once there was an American-led West, Western Europe at least would have to be at peace if World War III was to be avoided; and to be at peace Western Europe would have to be democratic. During the Second World War, Woodrow Wilson had been rehabilitated in the United States. Hollywood released *Wilson* in 1944, a film that polished the reputation of this American transatlanticist *avant la lettre*. Wilson may have been dimly remembered in Europe by 1944, but after the war his (Eurocentric) ideas were due for a second run: if anything, they would be picked up more vigorously at this stage by Europeans than by Americans. Wilson's internationalist vision had been to institutionalize and democratize peace, to create deliberative bodies that would transcend national borders and whose mandate it was to beat swords into plowshares. Perpetual peace was worth the sacrifice of some national sovereignty. It was worth a degree of negotiation and compromise, much as the individual states in the United States had given up some power so that there could be a federal government. Shortly before his death in 1945, FDR captured all that had been learned, politically and morally, in the 1920s and 1930s and during the Second World War:

> We have learned that we cannot live alone, at peace; that our own well-being is dependent on the well-being of other nations far away. We have learned that we must live as men, not as ostriches, nor as dogs in the manger. We have learned that we must live as members of the human community. We have learned to be citizens of the world! We have learned the simple truth, as Emerson said, that the only way to have a friend is to be one.

FDR PAID TRIBUTE to the community of powers, or the human community, by helping to found the United Nations in 1945, the gathering place for a citizenry of the world, and by tipping the human community in Western Europe toward peace. Such cooperation proved the Wilsonian thesis that deliberation grounded in law was preferable to military rivalry and to spheres of influence mapped onto the contours of raw power. For too long the big nations had made decisions and the little nations had made concessions; or in many cases they had simply disappeared from the map. Too many times in European history had the diplomats' artful schemes given way to the brute devastation of war. The West had had enough of the decline it brought upon itself in 1914 and that Spengler had summarized at such great length in *The Decline of the West.* Franklin Roosevelt and his new vice president Harry Truman were sure that the achievement of a democratic, mutually dependent West would guarantee the rise of the West.[31]

3

The Rise of the West,
1945–1963

Give 'em hell, Harricum!
—University of Oxford students to
Harry Truman on June 20, 1956

WILLIAM MCNEILL WAS born in Canada in 1917, and he entered the University of Chicago's gothic quads in 1933, the same year Hitler came to power in Germany. His Presbyterian father had taught church history in the Victorian intellectual milieu of McNeill's studious youth. At Mortimer Adler's and Robert Hutchins's university, William McNeill was directed toward "History of Western Civilization," a humanities course. In this class, his "teachers concentrated attention on ancient Athens and Sparta, then on Rome, Western Europe, and its American offshoot," McNeill wrote in his memoir, *The Pursuit of Truth*. Having been transferred from Columbia University, Chicago's academic introduction to Western civilization was momentous for McNeill. As he later recalled, "Week after week, readings and other experiences incidental to the course had revelatory force for me, since I had been strictly raised within a rather narrow canon of Scottish Presbyterian propriety." The motif of Western civilization resounded throughout McNeill's long career as a teacher and historian, much of it at the University of Chicago. Anglo-Saxon Protestantism, proper or otherwise, could not compete in excitement and status with the West.[1]

McNeill's readings and other experiences at Chicago were part of a much larger tapestry of ideas and politics. Between 1945 and 1963, the Second World War over and the Cold War in full swing, the transatlantic West was in its heyday. A set of policies that institutionalized the transatlantic West, NATO above all, had the bipartisan support of American presidents and policymakers, not to mention the electorate that set the parameters of the possible and the impossible. The headwind this gave American foreign policy encouraged more extensive commitments to Western Europe, and a far-reaching military partnership validated the shared image of Western civilization that Winston Churchill had praised Harry Truman for saving. The president who canonized this partnership was John F. Kennedy in his "*ich bin ein Berliner*" speech given in West Berlin in 1963. Kennedy's was a rapturous affirmation of fellowship with European history, culture and politics, even if he was being cheered by the same Germans who a mere eighteen years earlier had been slaughtering Americans at the Battle of the Bulge. Such was the magic of Western civilization or the magic of the Cold War. A tributary into Kennedy's speech came from American universities, which were busily teaching the courses on the West that the undergraduate McNeill had signed up for in Chicago. After World War II, as many young Americans left the military for academia, their professors were eager to help the government do what it had to do in the Cold War. In the 1940s and 1950s, there were so many ways to articulate, to encourage and to consolidate the rise of the West.

THE RISE OF the West continued to preoccupy William McNeill. Still in thrall to the revelatory force of his undergraduate education, he finished his historical magnum opus in 1962. Published in 1963, it went on to win the National Book Award. McNeill dedicated *The Rise of the West: A History of the Human Community* to the University of Chicago from 1933 to 1963, the period in which the West was the guiding light of the American academy. McNeill's title playfully modified Spengler's

The Decline of the West, that monument to the previous generation's credible pessimism, and McNeill's book mirrored a midcentury fascination with the West that was not limited to universities. On March 17, 1947, the British historian Arnold Toynbee appeared on the cover of *Time* as a well-known intellectual and the author of the massive series A Study of History (1933–1961). In 1949, Toynbee published *The Prospects of Western Civilization*, and in 1952 *The World and the West*, as if to ask and answer the question that seemed to be on everyone's mind: What was to become of the West after 1945? Was its decline as terminal as the Spenglerians would have us believe? Or was the West in decline at all? What if its prospects were on the mend?[2]

With *The Rise of the West*, McNeill distilled Chicago's Western civilization curriculum into a long and surprisingly readable book. His story began before recorded history but took shape with the Greek polis, the citizens of which were "free as men can be from subjection to any alien will; yet this life was rigorously bound by law." Freedom and rule of law, the precursors to self-government, were the seedbed of the West. This evaluation of the Greeks, the progenitors of liberty and law, correlated with the idea of the West in twentieth-century American foreign policy. Similarly, "Greek thought, art, literature, and institutions have always remained a sort of norm for Western civilization," McNeill argued. His canvas and his ambition were as vast as Spengler's. In his book, McNeill followed the "four major civilizations of Eurasia" over thousands of years. An avid student of anthropology, he was especially interested in cultural borrowing and transfer. He believed that "the history of civilization is a history of the expansion of particularly attractive cultural and social patterns through conversion of barbarians to modes of life they found superior to their own." The great civilizations were beguiling, civilization being the story of imitation, adoption and appreciative theft rather than of imposition or coercion alone. The great civilizations were not so much imperial as magnetic, or they were able to be enduringly powerful because they were so magnetic.[3]

Greek norms drew the Romans into a continuous and westward civilizational arc. The Roman legacy was similarly legal, in McNeill's view, "the concept of an objective law applicable to human affairs . . . apart from divine revelation and from human whim and passion." The Roman model spread northward with the four Eurasian civilizations battling it out until around 1500. Then, while Islamic civilization stagnated, Western civilization began its extraordinary ascent. McNeill contrasts the dynamism of the West unfavorably with the Islamic East, an Enlightenment dichotomy between the vigorous West and the static East, writing critically of "the languid and ultimately disastrous immobility that has characterized subsequent Islamic thought until almost our own time." Curiosity and creativity accrued to the West, "a society remarkably open to innovation . . . sure of itself, interested in the wonders of the civilized world, and eager to seize wealth, fame, and learning wherever they could be found." This was the Columbian impulse, Columbus the man of 1492 who brought Europe's innovations to the Americas. His was another forward leap from the "Greco-Roman and Judeo-Christian inheritances . . . [which had] provided the fundamental frame of high medieval and modern European civilization." The result after 1500 was the global rise of the West, "the world-girding civilization of modern times."[4]

McNeill characterized the West as restless, energetic and secular or notably committed to "radical rationality." The modern industrial and democratic revolutions proceeded from the Western civilization that had nurtured them. Interestingly for a book published when it was, McNeill categorized both the Soviet Union and the United States as Western countries. Of the two, it was the Judeo-Christian and antiquity-loving United States, the country that grew directly from Western roots, that was the more organically Western. Yet McNeill closed his book not on a note of Cold War competition and not with an intuition of disaster. His final emphasis fell on all that had been achieved and all that there was to admire in the West's rise. For McNeill, the twentieth-century West had a claim to occupying the best of all possible eras:

Men some centuries from now will surely look back upon our time as a golden age of unparalleled technical, institutional, and perhaps even of artistic creativity. Life in Demosthenes' Athens, in Confucius' China, and in Mohammed's Arabia was violent, risky, and uncertain; hopes struggled with fears; greatness teetered perilously on the brim of disaster. We belong in this high company and should count ourselves fortunate to live in one of the great ages of the world.

TRUE TO ITS dedication to the University of Chicago over three decades of academic life, *The Rise of the West* was very much a product of the 1930s and 1940s. McNeill's title, however, was an artifact of the postwar period. McNeill had himself served for four years in the European war. Had the Germans been victorious, his could not have been the same book. It could not have had the same exuberant and grateful title.[5]

The appearance of *The Rise of the West* in 1963 folded it into yet another war. Against the will of its author perhaps, *The Rise of the West* was indeed a document of the early Cold War. It captured many of the Cold War's key components from an American slant. Western Europe and the United States were smoothly integrated in McNeill's narrative, merging into one another. One sees the same integration in a 1952 statement of Harry Truman on the five-hundredth anniversary of Leonardo da Vinci's birth: "Since the American people have a common interest in the heritage of Western civilization which owes so much to da Vinci, it is fitting that we take note of the anniversary with appropriate observances in our museums and other institutions of art, science, and learning." This synthetic historical frame supported the core project of American foreign policy after 1945, which was the alliance with the states of Western Europe. American readers could encounter themselves in the pages of a book devoted mostly to Western Europe. McNeill was not much interested in the ethnic, racial or religious ties between the United States and Europe, whatever these were. He stressed the cultural and intellectual ties, the borrowing and the imitation, a heritage of aptitudes and attitudes: that for McNeill was the essence of the transatlantic kinship. To European readers, McNeill made clear that the history of New England (for example) was their history, too. It reflected "the most thoroughgoing translation of European-type society to new ground to be found anywhere in the world." *The Rise of the West* was a skeleton key to the NATO alliance, and the NATO alliance a skeleton key to *The Rise of the West*.[6]

Crucial to the fusion of Europe and the United States in *The Rise of the West* was the West's democratic spirit. At the 1893 Chicago World's Fair, President Cleveland had called it "popular government." McNeill labeled this spirit "popular participation in economic, cultural, and political life." For McNeill, the West's democratic or participatory vitality was more consequential than Christianity. In his memoir, McNeill revealed that *The Rise of the West* was "a secular substitute for a Christian worldview." In *The Rise of the West*, McNeill highlighted the "pervasive moral uncertainty" of the West, more the search for truth than the repetition of doctrine, flux over stasis, which made for a West dynamically modern rather than inherently Judeo-Christian. Uncertainty fed into the scientific Cold War, the area in which the contest between the United States and the Soviet Union was at its most equal and most intense. The Cold War battle of the researchers and the technocrats crossed economics, technology and the ideal of a rational society. *The Rise of the West* implied Western excellence at all these things, whereas McNeill paid little attention to the (considerable) communist claim on reason, science and a rational society—in the theories of Marxism-Leninism. For the Soviet Union, these were not just communist attributes. They were the signs of the Soviet Union's European origins, from Galileo to Newton to Marx to Lenin. For McNeill, the United States was implicitly more modern than the Soviet Union because its history and culture were more indelibly Western.[7]

The Rise of the West was a perfect Cold War book and the perfect book for the Cold War university because it was a study of civilization. *Civilization* had been an intellectual buzzword since the eighteenth century. Spengler and Toynbee helped to popularize civilizational paradigms in the twentieth century. Like Spengler, McNeill no longer had the confidence in civilization—or Civilization, as they might have put it—that had inspired Victorian historians and intellectuals and that had very much inspired the organizers of the World's Columbian Exposition of 1893. Like Spengler, McNeill was, as he wrote, "committed to cycles and to the notion of 'civilization' as a historical actor, liable to breakdown." McNeill had lived through one such breakdown between 1914 and 1945. Yet when it was American policy to revive Western civilization in Europe, McNeill was willing to celebrate Western civilization and to associate it with liberty. For American policymakers, Western civilization's revival was West Germany's road to decency and its road back to Europe. Civilization would tame the continent's intractable nationalism, ensure its liberty and save Western Europe from the fraud that was communism. A military without a civilizational alliance would unravel at some point. Only the two together could thrive, which was one secret to the extraordinary role that universities played in America's Cold War. American universities were places of scientific research: the Manhattan Project had begun under a tree on the University of Chicago's Main Quad. American universities were simultaneously the cultural engines of Western civilization, which they had been since at least the turn of the century. After the war, they were emerging as the world's leading universities, and in the Cold War they set the course for American foreign policy, "bastions of our defense," as Michigan State University's president John Hannah daringly put it in 1961.[8]

IN 1963, A Soviet McNeill could conceivably have written a long, optimistic book on the rise of the East or on the rise of the Soviet West. The subject would have been the rise of Soviet civilization or simply the rise of the Soviet Union. As with the United States, World War II was the validating triumph, after which the Soviet Union faced intersecting challenges. One was the construction of a buffer zone in Europe, necessitated by the war, in Moscow's view. The other was to devise something the Soviet Union had never really had—a global foreign policy. Unevenly, the postwar Soviet Union would address itself to both tasks.

Never, not even under the mightiest of the czars, had Saint Petersburg had as much of Europe under its control as Moscow did after

1945. The Soviet Union was one of two dominant European powers from 1945 to 1989, though for the Soviet Union, as for the United States, postwar Europe was a dilemma as well as a trophy. With the possible exception of Berlin, stranded deep in East Germany, there was no place in Europe for the Soviet Union to expand. Because of the American military perimeter, Western Europe was walled off from the Soviet Union. Limitations in one theater sparked activism in another. After 1945, the Soviet Union found real advantages in parts of the world that had a legacy of Western imperialism, large peasant populations and a leadership cadre receptive to communism of one kind or another. The United States may have captured and held Western Europe, the badge of its rise to global power, but the Soviet Union was the communist motherland, where Marx's prophesies were coming into their own. The world's proletariat and especially its peasantry still had nothing to lose but their chains.

Stalin's foreign-policy achievements dramatically outstripped Lenin's. In the 1940s, Stalin built communism in Poland, Bulgaria, Romania, Hungary and Czechoslovakia (and in other places). He brought communism to the homeland of Karl Marx: the resplendent Stalin Allee, a Muscovite boulevard running right through the heart of Berlin, completed in 1951 and now called Karl-Marx-Allee. Across Eastern Europe, the Red Army and the Soviet secret police erected communist governments, blending different degrees of national autonomy with the requisite loyalty to Moscow. Stalin also negotiated Western noninterference, getting Churchill and Truman to live with a Soviet sphere of influence in Eastern Europe. Noninterference in Soviet affairs was not agreement—West was West and East was East, as Stalin had concluded during the war—but the Kremlin could accept being a de facto colonial power in Eastern Europe. The national governments there were the tribute that vice (domination) pays to virtue (autonomy). It was not the first time Europe had been divided along an East-West axis: the historian Nell Painter describes "the notion of the river Rhine as a dividing line between permanently dissimilar peoples," which dates back to antiquity. The Rhine River was not exactly the Cold War line between East and West, but it was close enough. German chancellor Konrad Adenauer described the land east of the Elbe River as the beginning of the "Asiatic steppe," a comment about inner German divisions as much as it was about "Europe" and "Asia" or civilization and barbarism. Whether Asia or Europe, the Europe East of the Elbe was under Stalin's thumb.[9]

Stalin was eager to see communism advance outside Europe after the war. Before World War II, the Soviet Union had been hemmed in in Asia by a noncommunist China, by the French and British empires, by imperial Japan and by the American navy. To improve the Soviet position, Stalin briefly went to war against Japan in August 1945. This whole setup changed completely after the war. Japan was lost to the Americans, but much else was in play—from an independent non-aligned India, which had its grievances against Britain and the West; to Indochina, where the French position had been shattered in the war; to Korea, which had a border with China and could not escape Chinese influence; to Latin America, where revolutionary movements of the Left and the Right were strong; to the Middle East, where antipathy to the West coalesced with Israel's founding in 1948. Surveying the global scene, the Soviet Union had the option of diversifying the Cold War after 1948. Though the Soviet Union had been conditioned to being a European power, not an Asian power, Stalin's Chinese understudy would transform Asia and recast the global balance of power. Outside of Europe, the success of communism would irritate and pin down the United States and the West. If the Soviet Union could inflict defeats on the margins of the Cold War, opportunities might then materialize in the conflict's central theater, which was certainly Europe.

A global Cold War suited Moscow. In Europe, the attractions of the United States were hard to resist and hard to outshine, but many political figures outside of Europe regarded Joseph Stalin as a political maestro. A ragtag revolutionary before World War I, he had taken over a backward Russia and given it factories, electricity and literacy. This furnished the Soviet Union with a top-tier military, which against all odds had prevailed against Hitler's Germany, a Western European great power. Stalin's brutality was secondary given the Soviet Union's recipe for power; such recipes could be learned and then used against the West. In the 1950s, Soviet foreign policy taught itself the grammar and vocabulary of postcolonial revolution, some of which was Marxist-Leninist to begin with. Countries and movements took up the preexisting Soviet formulas in whole or in part, adapting them for opportunistic or idealist reasons. An anti-Western anticolonialism was a platform through which global Soviet aspirations could be projected, and project them Stalin and Nikita Khrushchev did. Having taken the reins after Stalin's death in 1953, Khrushchev gave a blunt speech in January 1961 on the Soviet Union's dedication to "national liberation." Stalin and Khrushchev understood intuitively the global discontents with capitalism and with empire, which their foreign policy and their propaganda pinned on the United States and the American-led West.[10]

FOR AMERICAN POLICYMAKERS, the rise of the West was a best-case scenario in 1945. Though the United States was not directly threatened, postwar Europe suffered from countless crises at the war's end, and in Europe the Red Army enjoyed a disturbing conventional military superiority. US military experts regularly assessed the Soviet Union as having 175 ground-force divisions. It took until 1954 for the Western alliance to muster a hundred divisions in Europe. The Soviet Union did not have an Atlantic between itself and Western Europe. It was adept at using local communist parties across Europe, and not just in the east, to insinuate itself into neighboring countries. How far it would go was anyone's guess. Meanwhile, the German problem was hypothetical but horrific in 1945. Twice Germany had been a cause of world war. Its potential for authoritarian nationalism was beyond dispute. Communism was not the temptation in West Germany that it was in France or Italy, but reversion to fascism was a realistic fear, stemming perhaps from the pooling despair in this defeated and disgraced country. In the late 1940s, American planners had low expectations for the Germany under Western occupation, and many thought that Germany was moving away from democracy in these years. Given Soviet control of the German east, and given Germany's geographic position in Europe, the Soviet and the German challenges could figure as almost one and the same. If Europe was stuck between East and West, divided Berlin was Europe's unhealed wound, ripe for infection.[11]

Facing the Soviet threat, Truman and his advisors improvised their way to a new foreign policy. They used ideas of liberty well established within the American foreign-policy tradition, drawing generously on Wilson and Jefferson. They recognized the potential for a republic of republics that had been dreamt up in the eighteenth century or a community of powers that could be a decent model for postwar Europe. They also saw the United States as ordained to play a special role at midcentury, a messianic country tasked with remaking Europe and articulating the ideas around which historical change would unfold. Americans had to accept "the responsibilities of moral and political leadership that history plainly intended them to bear," the diplomat George Kennan wrote in a 1947 *Foreign Affairs* essay, "The Sources of Soviet Conduct." By disposition and experience the least messianic of American diplomats, Kennan invoked a "history" that might as well have been God, Providence, the *Weltgeist* or some other supernatural power that determines which are the chosen nations. (Woodrow Wilson, whom Kennan generally deplored for such sentiments, had written in an August 1914 letter that "Providence has deeper plans than we could possibly have laid ourselves.") Kennan joined George Marshall, Dean Acheson, John McCloy, Averill Harriman, Lucius Clay and many other Truman administration luminaries who believed in a sustained American commitment to Europe. They did not have to persuade Truman, who had been an internationalist and an Atlanticist well before Pearl Harbor. When the public mood of the 1930s favored caution and reserve, Truman had gone against the grain, which was one reason FDR had selected Truman to be his vice president in 1944.[12]

George Kennan was the first to tackle the Soviet threat for the Truman administration. He was a diplomat's intellectual and an intellectual's diplomat. Born in the Midwest and class of '25 at Princeton, Kennan was an American anomaly, a Russophile enamored of Western civilization. He did not need a great-books program, which Princeton never adopted, to revere European books. He spent some of 1926 in Heidelberg and "took Goethe's *Faust* and Spengler's *Untergang des Abendlandes*" along with him in his backpack. Spengler's pessimism was something Kennan easily shared and never shook off. A hint of Spengler is almost always audible in Kennan's prose and apparent in his strategic thinking. In 1929, Kennan studied Russian in a Berlin institute "for cultures other than Western," as he wrote in his memoirs. Kennan loved Russian literature and the Russian people, and he despised the Russian political tradition, "the result," in his view, "of century-long contact with Asiatic hordes [and] the influence of medieval Byzantium." Hitler, whose rise Kennan observed firsthand as an American diplomat stationed in Europe, was comparably barbaric. Hitler's mission was "uncomplicated by any sense of responsibility to European culture as a whole," Kennan thought, and that in a nutshell was the catastrophe of National Socialism.[13]

In a diplomatic cable from February 1946, the "Long Telegram," and in "The Sources of Soviet Conduct," Kennan sketched a Cold War policy for the United States. He grounded the containment of Soviet communism in the motif of Oriental despotism, a civilizational division between East and West—and never the twain shall meet. Soviet despotism was as Oriental as it was Russian, in Kennan's opinion. (As early as 1894, the translator Nathan Haskell Dole argued for a chair in Russian studies at Harvard in order to study "our nearest Oriental neighbor.") The United States could do nothing about an Oriental Russia, Kennan believed, for it was the product of Russian history and civilization. The Russians would never be democrats, Kennan was sure, but they would not always be Soviets. Therefore, the United States needed to scrutinize the tension between Soviet ideology, based as it was on lies, and the splendors of Russian culture, which militated in favor of an anti-Soviet truth. Eventually, with the assistance of their culture, Russians would transcend the Soviet falsity. Until then, the United States had to keep the Soviet Union out of Western Europe—where it did not belong— and practice Western liberty at home. It had to be the West to lead the

West. Regarding World War II, Kennan believed that "no amount of sacrifice would be too great" to enable "the reestablishment of Europe," and the Cold War was an identically calibrated conflict in his eyes. The rise of the West outside of Europe was too much to hope for in 1947, while containment was not a strategy for defeating the Soviet Union and still less a strategy for democratizing Russia. The reestablishment of Europe was the thing.[14]

Kennan's prescriptions for containing Soviet communism took Washington by storm. They spoke to a host of urgent policy headaches. The Soviet Union had not allowed free elections in Eastern Europe and was taking over country after country. In a Europe deranged by war, the strategic momentum was sliding eastward, something President Truman and his advisors understood in civilizational as well as military terms. Secretary of the Navy James Forrestal noted in a diary entry that Dean Acheson, Truman's undersecretary of state in 1945, "said the greatest crime of Hitler was that his actions had resulted in opening the gates of Eastern Europe to Asia." The Asia in question was of course the Soviet Union. In January 1945, Averill Harriman, then the US ambassador to the Soviet Union, wrote in a note to himself that "unless we wish to accept the twentieth-century barbarian invasion of Europe . . . we must find ways to arrest the Soviet domineering policy." When Harriman wrote these words, the Soviet Union and the United States were still wartime partners. A year later, the partnership wobbling, Soviet domineering policy in Europe got a lot worse. From the East, the barbarians were on the march, exactly Winston Churchill's point when in March 1946—in Fulton, Missouri—he decried an iron curtain falling from "Stettin in the Baltic to Trieste in the Adriatic."[15]

East-West division already manifested itself when Truman and Stalin met at Potsdam in July 1945. Truman's first impression of Stalin was not especially negative: if they could talk with one another, the mutual suspicion might not be insurmountable. Stalin was not Hollywood's Uncle Joe anymore, but Truman found him clever and even charming. Kennan, then an unknown Foreign Service officer, held a view of the Soviet Union that was close to Truman's at this critical moment.

"Never did I consider the Soviet Union a fit ally or associate, actual or potential, for this country," Kennan wrote in his memoir. At Potsdam, Truman decided to inform Stalin of what Stalin already knew—that the United States had a devastating new weapon. But Truman decided to hide the specifics of his atomic secret from Stalin (while Stalin hid from Truman his awareness of the American atomic secret). The Soviet Union not being a fit enough ally or associate, information of such sensitivity could not be passed from Truman's to Stalin's hands. In September 1945, a meeting of US officials was convened in Washington on this very topic. Should the United States give the Soviet Union the keys to the nuclear kingdom, ending the US monopoly on the atomic formula, or should some international mechanism for managing the atomic age be set up? Forrestal spoke for the entire Truman administration when he said no. After all, the Soviets "are essentially Oriental in their thinking," as Forrestal wrote in his diary.[16]

Orient and Occident, Asia and Europe, East and West were at diplomatic loggerheads. These were the inescapable historical referents for the Truman administration. In Truman's view, with the Cold War, the American people "are faced with the most terrible responsibility that any nation ever faced. From Darius I's Persia, Alexander's Greece, Hadrian's Rome, Victoria's Britain, no nation or group of nations has had our responsibilities . . . to save the world from totalitarianism." In 1946, Truman faced a spate of domestic woes—an economic downturn and an uptick in labor unrest. In September 1946, Truman's approval rating stood at a daunting 32 percent, and the Republicans won both houses of Congress in that year. Tied to the political fortunes of President Truman, the liberty-loving Occident was not in the best of shape. The economies of Western Europe were declining fast, and hardship invited communist subversion: Western Europe's economic woes had repercussions beyond Europe. The loss of Britain and France as companion anticommunist powers to the United States was not far-fetched, risking the destruction of the vast overseas empires that had determined the prewar regional order in Asia, Africa and the Middle East. The incapacitation or collapse of Britain and France would have unknowable consequences for American policy, from South Africa to Hong Kong to Vietnam. Western Europe was truly the lynchpin of any serious American Cold War strategy.[17]

Before there was an acknowledged Cold War, crises in Turkey and Greece prompted Truman to act in defense of the West. In Greece, where Britain had fought against Nazi Germany, London was no longer financially able to provide security in 1947. A Soviet presence in Iran and in what would become Yugoslavia endangered Turkey and Greece, which in turn threatened the West's position in the Eastern Mediterranean. On March 12, 1947, Truman went before Congress to speak on Greece's behalf. Truman succeeded in getting $250 million in aid to Greece and $150 million to Turkey, and from this crisis he elaborated the Truman Doctrine, the open-ended policy of supporting "free peoples who are resisting attempted subjugation by armed minorities or by outside pressures." The Truman Doctrine was reminiscent of the American excitement about Greece in the 1820s, with the lurking Soviet Union in the role of the Asiatic Ottoman Empire, except that in 1947 the United States was a global superpower and militarily omnipresent in Europe. In 1947, Americans could do something for Greece other than writing florid poetry.

For Washington, Greece and Turkey were only a part of the problem in 1947. The architect of containment, Kennan assisted in drafting a plan to aid Europe financially. Secretary of State George Marshall had appointed Kennan the director of the State Department's Office of Policy Planning, a Cold War intellectual hub and an office Marshall established in 1947, when he became secretary of state. Among the office's first proposals was the Marshall Plan, policy planning par excellence. The plan spurred European economic growth and halted Western European communism, restoring Britain and France not to the powers they had been before the war—no amount of American aid could have done that—but to the point where they were Cold War assets rather than Cold War liabilities. The Marshall Plan was offered to the occupied Eastern European countries as well on the correct assumption that Moscow would reject the offer. A jealous Stalin forced his Eastern European proxies to turn this American money down. The Eastern European refusal had strategic value for Washington: to Europeans East and West the Marshall Plan underscored the lack of sovereignty in Europe's Soviet precincts. It was also a gesture of good will toward those countries that were able to accept Marshall aid, yet another way to invert the punitive, reparations-fueled diplomacy of the interwar years and to replace a self-defeating rivalry of powers in Europe with a self-governing community of powers.

Where the community of powers ended in the late 1940s and the rivalry of powers began, the NATO alliance was to be the shield of the West. Much more than the Marshall Plan, NATO was a radical departure from earlier American foreign policy. Previously, the United States had consciously done what it could to avoid Europe's tangle of alliances. The United States allocated to itself the right to intervene in Latin America, but not because it had guaranteed the security of Latin America through formal alliances: its interventions were conducted in the name of American security or American economic interests. NATO was different. For the first time, the United States was giving Europe a security guarantee, and doing so before a war was under way. Truman's commitment to Europe was much more than Franklin Roosevelt was able to give Winston Churchill between 1939 and 1941. "Political and indeed spiritual forces must be mobilized in our defense," Britain's foreign secretary Ernest Bevin had admitted in December 1947 with NATO in mind, and these powers must be mobilized within the United States. The British foreign minister's request for help was sensible in the postwar period. What was remarkable was how many Americans appeared to agree with Bevin and were willing to honor his request.[18]

The Marshall Plan and the NATO alliance met Truman's strategic objectives for Europe. As Bevin implied, they met civilizational and strategic objectives—Bevin's political and spiritual forces—which was crucial to their adoption by the US Congress and indirectly by the American taxpayer. The United States was offering Europe something of value, money and a security guarantee, without receiving anything tangible in return. As such, NATO was a hard sell to Congress. Perhaps a stern Congress would do to these policies what it had done to Wilson's League of Nations after World War I: refuse its support, demand that Europe take care of Europe and pull back to fortress America. Truman had the good sense to name the Marshall Plan after George Marshall, the unsurpassed military hero, and not after himself, a less-than-popular president in 1947 and 1948. Marshall, in turn, invoked civilizational duty to justify these policies and to ally the United States permanently with Western Europe. Going before the House Foreign Affairs Committee in January 1948, Marshall expressed himself plainly:

> Left to their own resources there will be . . . no escape [by Europeans] from economic distress so intense, social discontents so violent, political confusion so widespread, and hope of the future so shattered that the historical base of Western civilization . . . will take a new form in the image of the tyranny we fought to destroy in Germany.

MARSHALL CONTRASTED WESTERN liberty with the adjacent tyrannies of National Socialism and Soviet communism. In his statement, Western civilization was the pivot between World War II and the Cold War. Addressing a congressional committee, George Marshall rested the Marshall Plan on the historical base of Western civilization, American history as McNeill conceived of it in *The Rise of the West,* the American extension of the European pattern. According to Marshall, the United States was saving itself from tyranny by saving Europe. A product of Western civilization and a party to the rise of the West, America's geopolitical destiny was forever intertwined with Europe's.[19]

One prominent recipient of Marshall Plan aid was West Germany. On the surface, it was remarkable that Germany should be the beneficiary of American largess at all. Hitler had maliciously declared war on the United States, and his refusal to surrender cost many, many American lives once Germany had lost the war (well before 1945). During the war, the United States government floated a plan for the deindustrialization of postwar Germany, the so-called Morgenthau Plan, after the secretary of the treasury Henry Morgenthau. A Germany put to pasture would have been a Germany removed from the list of potential military problems and a Germany punished, but it would also have been a Germany removed from the global economy, leaving a pastoral no-man's land at Europe's center. With Soviet soldiers parading in East Berlin and Germany the accidental centerpiece of American-Soviet intrigue, there was only one viable US policy, and that was to strengthen West Germany's military and economic position. On the Cold War chessboard, Germany was the most significant square, the place where the East-West border was at its most artificial and insecure. The United States was willing to risk military escalation to keep West Berlin in the West and to contain the Soviets in the East. The airlifting of goods into Berlin starting in June 1948—the Germans dubbed the American planes *Rosinenbombers,* raisin bombers—was a public relations coup. When Stalin backed down in the spring of 1949, it was a substantial victory for the United States.

Secretary Marshall's words to the House Foreign Affairs Committee highlighted the nonmilitary dimension to American policy. World War II had been a battle to destroy tyranny in Germany, Marshall and Eisenhower both believed, and the tyrant was now dead. Since then, according to Marshall, Europe was in a state of economic distress, social discontent and political confusion. The Marshall Plan and the military activity taking shape behind it were addressed to the historic base of Western civilization. Some of Marshall's vocabulary was boilerplate, the obligatory reference to rescuing civilization in desperate times, but the issues Secretary Marshall and the Foreign Affairs Committee had before them were hardly rhetorical. They were facing the literal reestablishment of Europe, which entailed civilizing Germany or recivilizing Germany. Whatever it had become under Hitler, Germany had always been integral to the West: the historical base of Western civilization was no less German than it was French, British or Italian. Germany was the site of the Protestant Reformation, birthplace of Martin Luther. It had produced some of the Enlightenment's greatest thinkers. Literary romanticism arose in Germany, as had much of modern philosophy, including Kant whose thinking had inspired Woodrow Wilson's faith in a cooperative international order. German music suffused any idea of the cultural West. The names of German universities—Heidelberg, Göttingen, Tübingen—were embedded in American intellectual history. Educated Americans did things like travel to Heidelberg with Goethe and Spengler in their backpacks.

Marshall's policies and language made political, cultural and diplomatic sense. Whether they made historical sense was another question. If accurately rendered in Forrestal's diary, Dean Acheson's claim that Hitler's greatest crime had been to open Eastern Europe to Asia was wrong. Hitler's greatest crime was the Holocaust, a crime in which the entire West was complicit to varying degrees. Britain and the United States had taken in distressingly few Jewish refugees. France and Italy had sent off scores of Jews to Auschwitz and other death camps. In Eastern Europe, German policy had left the local population little alternative to collaboration in the mass killings. The Soviet Union and the United States resembled one another in their willingness to move on in 1945, to pretend that the majority of Europeans had resisted the Holocaust—as proto-communists or proto-democrats—and that allegiance with the antifascist Soviet Union or the antifascist United States was sufficient penance for past crimes. There was a Cold War on. To go much beyond the Nuremberg trials and some denazification might be exploited by the other side as a show of weakness. Phrases like "the historical base of Western civilization" or "the reestablishment of Europe" could be a mask that Europeans were only too glad to wear, but this was a moral problem and not necessarily a policy problem. After 1945, a targeted amnesia had political utility.

The transatlantic West needed Germany, though the restoration of Germany attracted some resistance in Europe. One of the architects of Franco-German rapprochement and the future European Union, Robert Schuman, was vigorously opposed to German rearmament. In July 1949, he argued before the French National Assembly that "Germany has no army and should not have one . . . [it is unthinkable] that

Germany could be allowed to adhere to the Atlantic Pact as a nation capable of defending itself or of aiding in the defense of other nations." By contrast, Dean Acheson, Truman's secretary of state by 1949, put a rearmed West Germany in the foreground of American policy. An archetypal member of the East Coast elite, Acheson had come to the State Department from Groton, Yale and corporate law. This Anglo-American gentleman had in Walter Isaacson's and Evan Thomas's words "a lifelong devotion to protecting Germany." The Truman administration's anti-Morgenthau, Acheson lent his influence to the cause of supporting West Germany and of stewarding it into NATO. Acheson and Truman pushed the Europeans to accept the eventual re-armament of West Germany, conditioning American military aid upon it, and in May 1955 the Federal Republic of Germany joined NATO. Two months later, West Germany formed an army of six thousand volunteer troops. Acheson also structured a global American foreign policy around Germany and Europe. He likened the Soviet Union, as a threat to the West, to "that which Islam had posed centuries before," an East outside of Asia. The Korean War began in June 1950, not long after Acheson became secretary of state. He tied it to Europe—as he would the Vietnam War in later years. To hold the line in Asia was to prevent the Soviets from testing the line in Berlin or anywhere else in Europe. Credibility was determined on a global grid of actions and events, but the need for American credibility originated in the question of European security. As Acheson said not just of himself but of his whole coterie at the State Department and the Truman White House, "Europe, we had always believed, *was* the world." If Europe was the world, at the heart of the world was Germany.[20]

THE UNITED NATIONS was the loftiest achievement of postwar American foreign policy. It was the aspiration to mediation and peacemaking made flesh, a republic of republics not just in Europe but of global dimensions. It was a collective achievement, of course, rising from the insanity of the war, from the utter bankruptcy of European great-power politics circa 1945 and from a world order ever less European in texture and tone. The UN's creation anticipated an era of decolonization that, in 1945, was well under way. Yet the American stamp on the UN was distinctive. The United Nations was launched at a conference in San Francisco, which ran from April to June 1945, and the UN's center would be in New York City, much more of a world city than Washington, DC. The United Nations had a precedent in Woodrow Wilson's League of Nations, but where Wilson had failed—domestically, internationally—the United Nations was meant to flourish. The UN reflected the evolving multilateralism of American foreign policy. Also in 1945, the International Monetary Fund was set up in Washington, DC, and so was the World Bank, institutions that were at the outset American-led and Anglo-American in orientation, though set up in theory for international cooperation and decision making. The NATO alliance that came a few years later was military and proudly Eurocentric, a *North* Atlantic rather than an Atlantic alliance, but it belonged to this same story. The UN, the IMF, the World Bank and NATO would be vehicles of democracy, of free trade, of a new international order more open and creative and constructive than the previous international order had ever aspired to be. That was the American hope in 1945.

A fresh American commitment to multilateralism made one appeal to the newly formed UN particularly striking. Delivered in 1947, it did not come from a colonized country or a stateless people. It came from within the United States, a "Statement on the Denial of Human Rights to Minorities in the Case of Citizens of Negro Descent in the United States of America and an Appeal to the United Nations for Redress Prepared for the National Association for the Advancement of Colored People." Among its authors was W. E. B. Du Bois, who wrote the statement's introduction. Du Bois began with an outline of African American history and the internal dilemma of an African American polity within a white-supremacist American polity: slavery had led to segregation, and in 1947 segregation was the law of the land. Any assessment of American foreign policy had to begin with these facts, Du Bois affirmed. Should an African American polity denied its human rights be "strengthening its inner cultural and group bonds" or escaping "into the surrounding American culture," Du Bois asked. The catalyst of this dilemma was segregation, the daily discrimination and the curtailed opportunities of the African American population. Racism, Du Bois argued in the statement's introduction, "has repeatedly led the greatest modern attempt at democratic government to deny its political ideals."[21]

The appeal to the United Nations was a cry for help projected beyond an unreceptive US government. Its goal was to pressure the United States into greater democracy and equality, to question and to shame American foreign policy at a moment of seeming triumph. The internationalist newness of American foreign policy in 1947 shed a revealing light on racial problems within the United States, as Du Bois was well aware. These problems were age-old, and so too were the political contradictions they described—the contradictions of idealist presidents like Thomas Jefferson and Woodrow Wilson, who were thoroughly implicated in either slavery or segregation. Jefferson owned slaves, and the federal government was segregated at Wilson's direct request in 1913. Since the eighteenth century, a philosophical and political internationalism had intensified the internal American contradictions, making them not just repugnant but also repugnantly hypocritical. As Du Bois pointed out, "in its international relations, the United States owes something to the world; to the United Nations of which it is a part, and to the ideals which it professes to advocate. Especially is this true since the United Nations has made its headquarters in New York." The segregated United States was a regressive example to the UN, and the New York–based UN a provocative example to the United States. The country that played host to the United Nations was out of step with the countries and peoples beyond Europe, a foreign-policy conundrum because most of the world's inhabitants were "more or less colored in skin," in Du Bois's words. The Cold War was putting these non-European countries into play at precisely this moment.[22]

The 1947 appeal to the UN did little to alter American foreign policy. For the makers of American foreign policy, from Harry Truman to Dean Acheson to George Kennan, what the United States owed to the world in 1947 was not an apology. (Kennan's racism and anti-Semitism were exposed, though not impossible to discern in his published writings, when his diaries came out in 2014.) The dominant foreign-policy affiliation of the 1950s was with the West, and the dominant sentiment one of hoped-for Western ascendancy. The dominant intellectual concordance was between the Cold War university and the White House under Eisenhower and Kennedy, a concordance that rested on a celebratory, nurturing image of the West, the glittering home of American and European liberties. It was a small intellectual step from William McNeill's *Rise of the West* to Truman's affection for the West to Eisenhower's defense of the West. Or perhaps the lineage ran in the opposite direction, from Eisenhower's defense of the West to Truman's affection for the West to McNeill's eight-hundred-age masterpiece and to similar books. McNeill's history was no doubt representative of American foreign policy and educated opinion, but it was not fully representative. Decades later, McNeill himself had second thoughts about *Rise of the West*. More and more, to him, the book "began to seem archaic and inadequately conceived." McNeill came to feel that "my book retained more than a whiff of Eurocentrism," a lament voiced in the terminology of the 1990s. The lament itself predated the 1990s. It was the substance of Du Bois's unheeded 1947 appeal.[23]

WHETHER OR NOT Europe was the world, as Dean Acheson believed, European security was a bipartisan American enthusiasm in the late 1940s. Acheson and Truman were Atlanticist students of FDR, to whom they owed their positions in government. The Democrats had owned American foreign policy since 1933, but the war had held in check some of the country's natural partisanship, enabling uncommonly high levels of cooperation between the White House and Congress and between Democrats and Republicans. The war had also fostered a new internationalism in American politics. In the parlance of a Midwestern senator circa 1945, "I'm the biggest isolationist that ever lived, but I'm sure as hell not going to vote against the [UN] charter."

Indeed, the policies championed by the Truman administration could not have gone forward without Republican support. George Marshall was neither Republican nor Democrat, which helped him to convince Republicans to vote for the Marshall Plan. The same was true for the NATO alliance, evolving as it did out of the Franco-British mutual self-defense Dunkirk Treaty signed in March 1947. France and Britain remained worried about Germany—why else would they have signed their treaty in Dunkirk?—and everyone was worried about the Soviet Union. The NATO treaty was signed on April 4, 1949, by twelve nations: France, Britain, the Netherlands, Belgium, Luxembourg, Italy, Norway, Denmark, Iceland, Canada, the United States and Portugal. (Strategically vital Portugal was the odd dictatorship in NATO, a contradiction within an alliance formally devoted to democratic values.) When the US Senate ratified the treaty three months later, the vote was eighty-two to thirteen. Acheson spent much of his first few months as secretary of state on Capitol Hill prodding Republicans to vote for an American foreign policy transformed.[24]

Dwight Eisenhower's emotive support added to NATO's Republican pedigree. Like Marshall, Eisenhower was up in the ether above political party. Even if he had not been, he shared the civilizational and strategic outlook of Acheson and Truman, Kennan and Forrestal. As if paraphrasing Secretary Marshall, Eisenhower said of NATO that "I rather look upon this effort as the last remaining chance for the survival of Western civilization." Preserving Western civilization had been one of Eisenhower's cherished war aims. The leader of the crusade in Europe and the author of *Crusade in Europe*, Eisenhower was named the first Supreme Allied Commander of Europe, "this land of our ancestors," as he characterized it in a January 1951 radio broadcast. Eisenhower took up his post in April 1951. In that same year, the Supreme Allied Commander from America spoke to a London audience about the "march of human betterment that has characterized Western Civilization." Eisenhower spoke of Western civilization as most Democrats did. The cause of Western civilization was calmly bipartisan and transatlantic, civilian and military, practical and sentimental. It was not limited to the ivy-educated Europhiles clustered around Dean Acheson.[25]

As a president, Truman had to convert the prior internationalism of Wilson and FDR into a global policy for containing communism. He did not have to convert the Democratic Party to internationalism. Congressional support for the Marshall Plan and NATO notwithstanding, the Republican Party was not unequivocally Atlanticist in 1952. In fact, Eisenhower sensed a movement away from internationalism in the GOP. The Republicans were an opposition party in 1952. Perhaps it was in their interest and perhaps it was prudent for the Republicans to set themselves against the alliance-forming Democrats, to avoid foreign entanglements and to diminish the massive financial outlays for others' security. By fiscal year 1953, the United States was spending 12 percent of its GNP on defense. This kind of statistic alarmed Ohio's Senator Robert Taft, a Republican presidential candidate in 1952. A protégé of Herbert Hoover, Taft was elected to the Senate in 1938. He opposed a political economy of individualism to FDR's New Deal. There was an analogy in Taft's mind between the New Deal at home and the growth of foreign-policy ambition abroad: both forced the government to get bigger and bigger. Before Pearl Harbor, Taft had objected to the lend-lease program of aiding Britain. Then he objected to the NATO alliance, as had the last Republican to serve as president, Herbert Hoover, not only because it was costly but also because NATO was provocative to the Soviets, or "the Russians," as Taft liked to call them. He felt that NATO would "give the Russians the impression, justified at least to themselves, that we are ringing them about with armies for the purpose of taking aggressive action when the time comes." Taft did not endorse the foreign-policy status quo of 1952. Neither did many of his supporters.[26]

By contrast, Eisenhower ran for president to lead his country and to lead the West. He also ran for the sake of leading the Republican Party: foreign policy was either bipartisan or it was hamstrung, in his judgment. With little to prove in 1952 and within the range of retirement at age sixty-one, Eisenhower was not personally bent on becoming president. He was also convinced of the need for internationalism, for deepening the NATO alliance, for retaining what he had fought for in the war and for pursuing the foreign policy of Truman. On economic policy, as well, Eisenhower stood closer to Truman and FDR than to a GOP still skeptical about global free trade. And so, to block what Taft represented, Eisenhower let himself be drafted, ensuring that the Democrats would lose the presidency after a twenty-year run. The White House opened its doors to the first Republican Wilsonian in January 1953, the Republican Party united behind him. The survival of Western civilization was among Eisenhower's agendas. Throughout his presidency he would take note of Western civilization, equating it with the United States and the United States with Western civilization. Speaking at an October 1958 news conference, for example, he declared that "we are very apt, by focusing our eyes on some geographical point, to neglect the great principles for which a country such as ours has stood, for all these years, and for which Western Civilization has largely stood."[27]

In not neglecting Western civilization and in putting the Soviets off balance, Eisenhower had the unusual instrument of two brothers, Allen Dulles, Eisenhower's CIA director, and John Foster Dulles, his secretary of state. Allen and John were both graduates of Princeton, class of '14 and class of '08, respectively. John Foster Dulles had actually studied under Woodrow Wilson at Princeton and was with the American delegation at the Paris Conference in 1919. Allen and John Foster alike wound their way through corporate law to high political office. They were Republicans in the tradition of Elihu Root and his Council on Foreign Relations, internationalists in the East Coast foreign-policy establishment. John Foster Dulles had at times represented Harry Truman at international meetings, and he was also an advisor to Truman's opponent in the 1948 election, Thomas Dewey. The Dulles brothers knit together many different worlds—academia, business, law and politics. John Foster was the more religiously devout of the two brothers, channeling the Cold War piety of the Eisenhower administration, to which a rhetoric of light and darkness, good and evil, God and the Marxist-Leninist abyss came naturally. In this, John Foster Dulles was not the same as Acheson, who would give his memoirs the winking title of *Present at the Creation* and who was not one to associate either the United States or himself with godliness. John Foster Dulles sincerely believed in the Cold War as a crusade against communism, against the atheism that had given communism to the world and against the atheism that the Soviet Union and China were disseminating internationally.

The Dulles brothers served the anticommunist West through a foreign policy heavily reliant on covert maneuver. They enjoyed being Cold War shadow boxers, and their boxing ring was the whole globe. Eisenhower felt that covert action was cheaper and often more effective than outright war, which was a suicidal proposition given the Soviets' nuclear capacities. The U-2 reconnaissance aircraft, flown by the CIA in the 1950s, were a valuable hidden asset until one was shot down by the Soviets in May 1960. Policy-wise, Eisenhower gave the Dulles brothers the green light to coordinate the priorities of the State Department with those of the CIA, to embed covert action in American diplomacy. The results were breathtaking. The United States was able to encourage coups in Iran in 1953 and in Guatemala in 1954. These initiatives were deemed Cold War triumphs at the time. They were certainly consequential actions, and it was only later that the fallout— or blowback—would come to be felt back in Washington. In a different kind of covert action, Khrushchev's initially secret speech of 1956, in which he criticized Stalin's legacy and spoke openly about the crimes of the Soviet state, was obtained by the CIA and then broadcast around the world, contributing to the 1957 uprising against Soviet rule in Hungary and to the long-term demystification of Soviet power throughout Eastern Europe. John Foster Dulles's name was lent to the international airport in Washington, DC, honoring the secretary of state who had set the record for travel at the time. Already ill, Dulles made his last trip to West Germany to meet with Konrad Adenauer. As had the previous secretary of state, John Foster Dulles recognized Germany as the most important piece of the Cold War puzzle. For his relentless service to the American-led West, John Foster Dulles was accorded a funeral service at Washington's National Cathedral.

Allen Dulles, John Foster Dulles and Eisenhower served the West through culture as well as through diplomacy and espionage. Aware that the Soviet Union was burnishing its cultural reputation in Europe via classical music and ballet performances, Europe's communist parties and its own well-funded efforts at covert action, Eisenhower and the Dulles brothers felt duty-bound to do the same from the other side of the Iron Curtain. Often through murky funding and shell institutions, the CIA funneled resources into the cultural Cold War. It was especially interested in augmenting the autonomous postwar cultural and intellectual life that was either noncommunist or anticommunist. There were artists and intellectuals who believed sincerely in the anticommunist West, as it were, but who would never have agreed to be agents of the CIA or to accept CIA money openly. Although they thought of themselves as unbought, it was within the CIA's powers to support them, which it generously did. The Committee for Cultural Freedom, founded by intellectuals to diminish communist influence in Europe and the United States, was one such assembly of anticommunist intellectuals. Sidney Hook, a philosopher and leading figure within the committee, described it in his memoirs as "a nucleus for a Western community of intellectuals, who . . . felt embattled against the virus of neutralism that was spiritually disarming the West against Communist aggression." (Hook's image of the Cold War as political and spiritual matched that of British foreign minister Bevin.) Tasked with arming the West against communism, the CIA secretly propped up a number of high-quality intellectual journals in Europe that were fighting Sidney Hook's fight. It was one way to inoculate the West against the virus of Cold War neutralism.[28]

BACK IN EUROPE in 1951 to serve as NATO's Supreme Allied Commander, Dwight Eisenhower had to take a leave of absence from another job. Since 1948, Eisenhower had been the president of Columbia University, which refused to accept his resignation when he was tapped to lead NATO. Hence, Eisenhower was on leave from Columbia until he became president of the United States in 1953. (Woodrow Wilson was the other president who had previously been a university president.) Eisenhower at Columbia reinforced the Western civilization frame at American universities, Western civilization having been the golden thread of Eisenhower's military career. Eisenhower at Columbia also underscored the West's proximity as an academic ideal to the cause of the West within American foreign policy. The Columbia president's curriculum vitae documented a journey from the military to the academy, from the academy back to the military (NATO) and from the military to the White House: a bit of George Washington, a bit of Thomas Jefferson, a bit of Ulysses S. Grant, a bit of Woodrow Wilson. Another transatlantic pattern of the midcentury United States unrelated to Eisenhower's career concerned the artists and refugee scholars from Europe who had migrated to the United States in the 1930s and 1940s. Predominantly Jewish, many of the so-called refugee scholars became American citizens. As writers, teachers and citizens, they lent a gravitas and erudition entirely their own to the transatlantic relationship. Their rigorously Euro-American lives were punctuated by the turmoil of twentieth-century Europe, while their talent and mid-life transitions added a modern European layer to twentieth-century American intellectual life.

Europe's refugee scholars were learned cosmopolitans of the West who projected no one political or foreign-policy idea onto the United States. A group of philosophers, sociologists and political theorists, the Frankfurt School applied Marx's thought to the culture of capitalism, moving from Germany to Columbia University in 1935. Over time, Frankfurt School theories would inform the New Left of the 1960s and its efforts at a systematic critique of America's capitalist economy (and foreign policy). The political philosopher and historian of ideas Eric Voegelin taught in the United States from 1938 to 1958, and his books flowed into the postwar American conservative movement. His warnings against "eschatological" thinking provided young American conservatives with an improbable mantra in the 1960s. Out of deference to Voegelin they sported buttons and bumper stickers against "immanentizing the eschaton"—that is, against building heaven on earth as Voegelin accused the Bolsheviks and other zealots and ideologues of attempting to do. The political scientist Carl Friedrich had already been shifting between Heidelberg and Harvard in the 1920s, helping to launch the study of public policy in America. In 1936, he was among the founders of what would become Harvard's JFK School of Government. During the Cold War, Friedrich's elitist notions of democracy and of a Euro-Atlantic intellectual aristocracy confirmed the image of the United States as leader of a democratic West, with Harvard at the center of the intellectual-political web. At Harvard, making good on his notion of a Euro-Atlantic intellectual aristocracy, Friedrich was a mentor to two future national security advisors, Henry Kissinger and Zbigniew Brzezinski, both of whom were born in Europe.

Albert Einstein was the most conspicuous icon of these wondrously talented exiles from Central Europe. Somewhat less well known was another German-Jewish intellectual, Hannah Arendt. Having narrowly escaped the Holocaust, she moved to New York in 1941. Educated at various German universities, Arendt had a mastery of ancient and modern thought, of philosophy and literature and history, that was sui generis on the American scene. She relied upon it to conceive one of the pivotal Cold War books, *The Origins of Totalitarianism*, published in 1951. Her nuanced thinking accorded more with the decline than with the rise of the West à la William McNeill. Instead of applauding American democracy as the mirror opposite of Nazi-Soviet totalitarianism, Arendt traced a general tendency of modern society everywhere toward uprootedness and loneliness, "the curse of modern masses since the beginning of the industrial revolution." Totalitarianism was a modern rather than a European phenomenon. It surged upward from the gutters of modern life. Imperialism, racism and anti-Semitism were the rotten fruit of a misbegotten modernity, words of warning to the industrialized mass society omnipresent in the United States. As Arendt wrote in a Preface to *Origins* (dated 1950), "The subterranean stream of Western history has finally come to the surface and usurped the dignity of our tradition," the West at odds with itself. The Western tradition was dignified, and for Arendt it was our incomparable civilization, but it had been dirtied by its own subterranean streams. An American citizen as of 1950, Arendt cultivated a traditionalist radicalism that made her an advocate of ancient thought. She was a frequent critic of American politics, from McCarthyite authoritarianism to the Vietnam War to what she saw as the worrisome anarchy of the 1960s.[29]

Arendt's dialogue with classical antiquity was one of several ongoing Europe-inflected great-books dialogues with American democracy. Leo Strauss, a German-Jewish philosopher who made his way to the United States a few years before Arendt, had been similarly educated in ancient and modern philosophy. Strauss shared Arendt's dismay with mass society and with many of the typical traits of modern politics, and like Arendt, Strauss returned to the Greek polis as the foundation stone of Western politics. Strauss became an American citizen in 1944 and settled at the University of Chicago, where for decades he held the Robert Maynard Hutchins Distinguished Service Professorship. The living embodiment of the great-books ethos that Hutchins had impressed on the University of Chicago in the 1930s, Strauss inveighed against "historicism," the tethering of philosophical texts to their historical moment. Much as Columbia's John Erskine had, Strauss believed in the ongoing and essential vitality of the great books, which is how he read them, wrote about them and taught them, presenting himself as a twentieth-century Socrates. Strauss was the man with the questions, which was already the basic attitude of the Columbia and University of Chicago great-books programs. In his scholarship and teaching, Strauss also emphasized statesmanship, an aristocracy of wisdom that could balance out the follies and dangers of egalitarian democracy and of Arendt's homeless modern masses. Aristotle had tutored Alexander the Great. Shakespeare's plays and the King James Bible had tutored Abraham Lincoln. Politics without a philosophically elevated statesmanship was barbarism, in Strauss's view. Strauss's esoteric style and pedagogic charisma raised a devoted circle of students around him. He spent the last four years of his life, until 1973, teaching at St. John's

College in Annapolis, by then the epicenter of the great-books movement that had taken root at Columbia in the 1920s.

The refugee scholars lent their exceptional knowledge and exceptional biographies to the study of Western civilization in the United States. The study of the West might be an academic requirement, it might be conducted glibly or at a great distance, a dull museum exhibit of Greek and Roman busts. But the Frankfurt School, Voegelin, Friedrich, Arendt and Strauss were clearly at the cutting edge of political thought. They magnified the revelatory force of the Western civilization curriculum that McNeill had experienced at Chicago long before the arrival of the refugee scholars. One might take the example of Norman Podhoretz, a public high school graduate who came to Columbia from a working-class Brooklyn family. His Jewish immigrant background was not an impediment to the Bachelor of Arts he would earn in 1950. At Columbia, he could study with a Jewish professor like Lionel Trilling, an early alumnus of the Columbia great-books experiment who went on to teach it. The job of Trilling and his colleagues was to induct students like Podhoretz into the arts of Western civilization. As Podhoretz later recalled:

> It was the heritage of Western civilization to which we were being introduced. And yet the idea of Western civilization seemed so broad and generous, so all-embracing of whatever might be important or good or great in the world, that most of us thought of the adjectives as merely a polite tautology, a kind of elegantly liberal nod at the poor old Orient. To our minds, this culture we were studying at Columbia was not the creation or possession of a particular group of people; it was a repository of the universal, existing not in space or time but in some transcendental realm of the spirit.

THE ALLIANCE BETWEEN the study of Western civilization at the American university and the West of the Marshall Plan and NATO could be informal. The atmosphere of the universities might imply that to study the West was to perpetuate or to defend it along the rigidly East-West lines of the Cold War. Or it could be formalized in individual institutions. One such was founded by Elizabeth and Walter Paepcke, a Chicago businessman. Inspired by Robert Hutchins, Paepcke acted on the two-hundredth anniversary of Goethe's birth, in 1949, to summon artists and intellectuals to Aspen, Colorado, for a three-week music and ideas festival. Paepcke enlisted the University of Chicago's Mortimer Adler to present various strands of Western culture at periodic meetings of the like-minded. These strands were great books, music, design and politics. In 1950, the Paepckes created the Aspen Institute for Humanistic Studies, developing an Executive Seminar in which academics met with distinguished figures from business and government. On the government side, a cofounder of the Aspen Institute was Elizabeth Paepcke's brother, Paul Nitze, who served from 1950 to 1953 as director of the State Department's Office of Policy Planning and who was among the primary authors of NSC-68, a 1950 policy document that argued for the rapid mobilization of Western resources and spirit against the Soviet menace. William Nitze, Paul and Elizabeth's father, taught Romance languages at the University of Chicago from 1909 to 1941. He was an expert on the legend of the Holy Grail.[30]

The Aspen Institute's academic-policy bridge was emblematic of the Cold War university. Carl Friedrich's student Henry Kissinger was not of Hannah Arendt's or Leo Strauss's generation. He was younger, but he, too, had been a German-Jewish refugee, arriving as a teenager in New York in 1938. Kissinger had Walter and Elizabeth Paepcke's knack for amalgamating academic and government talent, which he did through the Harvard International Seminar starting in 1951 and which he would continue doing as a consultant to the State Department. He was the foreign-policy advisor to Republican Nelson Rockefeller in his hapless 1960 presidential campaign. As a student and then a professor of history and politics at Harvard, Kissinger scrutinized the nineteenth-century European diplomatic record. His 1950 undergraduate thesis had a marvelously portentous title—"The Meaning of History: Reflections on Spengler, Toynbee and Kant"—a study of three leadings theorists of modern history and civilization. To comment on the Cold War, Kissinger held up the concert of Europe, the long stretch of relative peace from the Napoleonic Wars to the outbreak of World War I, an enduring balance of power fashioned by gifted diplomats such as Prince Klemens von Metternich and Otto von Bismarck. An increasingly prominent participant in the foreign-policy debates of the 1950s, Kissinger considered the United States "the embodiment of mankind's hopes [and] . . . the bulwark of free peoples everywhere." He was a partisan of the West who did not necessarily believe it was on the rise. Later on, he would urge Richard Nixon to read Spengler and thus to explore the all too real possibility of a declining West.[31]

The joining of the academic and policy enterprise under the rubric of the West achieved a different synthesis in the career of Walt Whitman Rostow, the son of Russian-Jewish immigrants to the United States. A Rhodes Scholar in the mid-1930s, Rostow served in the Air Force and the Office of Strategic Services, the intelligence unit that would become the CIA during the war. A precocious academic economist, Rostow helped to draft pieces of the Marshall Plan, and he was both an advisor and a speechwriter for President Eisenhower. Rostow pushed Eisenhower to recognize the Cold War promise of economic aid, highlighting its political and military functions. He also promoted economic aid to needy nonaligned or friendly countries. Economic aid could be an index of capitalism's appeal, given the danger that "the underdeveloped countries will develop along lines hostile to the West and Western tradition," Rostow wrote in a 1957 book, *A Proposal: Keys to an Effective Foreign Policy*. For the government and the university, Rostow looked intently for Soviet economic vulnerabilities, doing what he could to inform the makers of American foreign policy about them. For much of the 1950s, Rostow taught at MIT. For a while, he was a visiting professor of American history at both Oxford and Cambridge.[32]

Rostow celebrated the rise of the economic West in *The Stages of Economic Growth: An Anti-Communist Manifesto*, which he published in 1960. (The book began as lectures to Cambridge undergraduates in 1958.) Rostow was not only rewriting Marx's legendary *Communist*

Manifesto of 1848 but also turning it inside out, outlining a response to Soviet foreign policy in the Third World in 1960. Since the rise of Chinese communism in 1949, the Soviet Union had been making strides in Asia, Africa, the Middle East and Latin America. On the one hand, Rostow wanted to warn Washington about the perils of ignoring the non-Western world. "There may not be much civilization left to save unless we of the democratic north face and deal with the challenge implicit in the stages-of-growth [outside the democratic North]," he wrote, "at the full stretch of our moral commitment, our energy, and our resources." On the other hand, Rostow's thesis about stages of economic growth was optimistic. The West's capitalist path from agricultural poverty to take-off (a signature Rostow turn of phrase) to modernity and industrial wealth could and should be replicated around the world. Economic growth was modernization and modernization was economic growth. Western Europe and the United States—the West—outdid the Soviet Union both in modernization and economic growth. Their economic turnaround since 1945 had been nothing short of miraculous, and because of the Cold War the West had to do more to popularize its winning model.[33]

Rostow's was a redrawing of the argument for the West made by Kennan, Acheson, Truman and Eisenhower, a redrawing or a thinning out. Rostow's theses recalled Herbert Hoover and his conviction that commerce was "the life blood of modern civilization." Rostow preferred civilization to Western civilization, though he acknowledged a "democratic north" and something he called "Western society" or "the West." Culture and history fell into the background for this social scientist's social scientist. Antiquity, the Enlightenment, kinship with Europe were either secondary or irrelevant to the economic and technological sophistication of the West: religion was likewise absent from his analysis. If these factors were secondary or irrelevant, the Western model could be universally applicable in the way that communism (in theory) was universally applicable. Many Western or capitalist formulas were—for Rostow—better suited to the world's poorest agricultural zones than was the Soviet Union's lumbering command economy.

Rostow's hope was that the Third World would choose the West and that the United States would facilitate this prudent choice:

> It is they [the postcolonial leaders] who, having helped achieve independence under the banners of human freedom, appealing to those values in the West which they share, must now accept a large part of the responsibility for making those values come to life, in terms of their own societies and cultures, as they complete the preconditions and launch themselves into self-sustained growth.

A Westernized modernization was appealingly flexible, according to Rostow. It would guarantee prosperity, and if Western political values were duly honored, it would guarantee freedom. Best of all, the ascent to growth could be pursued in the local terms of the ascendant societies and cultures. It was a destination to which there could be many journeys.[34]

Rostow's vision of a modern West defined by technological innovation and economic growth suited the State Department of the 1960s. In 2000, the State Department building would be named—very appropriately—in honor of Harry S. Truman. Its cornerstone was laid in January 1957 by President Eisenhower and Secretary of State Dulles. The building was dedicated in January 1961, after which it was the main building of the US Department of State. Over the decades, the physical State Department had migrated through Washington, and in 1961 it acquired a permanent home of its own in Foggy Bottom. Behind its construction was a shift in American diplomatic architecture whereby Assistant Secretary of State Edward Wailes's 1953 injunction to "discontinue modern architecture in favor of Georgian" was ignored. In the late 1950s, the Georgian style was discontinued in favor of a more modern architecture. The State Department adopted an architectural modernism alert to local detail and intended to signal openness, optimism and democratic potential. The Chicago firm of Skidmore, Owings and Merrill built glass-and-steel consulates in Frankfurt, Bremen, Düsseldorf, Stuttgart and Munich. Comparably modernist embassies arose in Accra (1958), the Hague (1959), Athens (1961), Baghdad (1961), Karachi (1961) and Dublin (1964).[35]

The Harry S. Truman Building deviated from the neoclassical precedent of civic architecture in Washington. It deviated from the marble structures with their porticos and columns and friezes that conveyed reverence for antiquity and told a distinct civilizational story. Architecturally, the State Department broke away from the White House, Congress, the Library of Congress, the Lincoln Memorial, the Jefferson Memorial, the National Archives and the Supreme Court Building. Like many of the high-prestige embassies of the late 1950s, the Harry S. Truman Building was designed in the International Style. Its clean lines, its sober refusal of statuary and ornament, its lack of text were the hallmarks of its streamlined midcentury modernity. The same was true for the stylish Dulles Airport outside Washington, DC, built between 1958 and 1962 and designed by Eero Saarinen, who was also responsible for US embassies in London (1960) and Oslo (1959). Dulles Airport honored the future of air travel, not the heavy hand of history, as had Daniel Burnham's 1907 Union Station. (The 1941 National Airport terminal, which is still standing, if a bit neglected, was a modern building that referenced the neoclassicism of George Washington's nearby Mount Vernon estate.) On C Street in Washington, DC, the State Department's cavernous lobby made no reference to the past, American or European or ancient. The flags of those countries with which the United States had diplomatic ties were its only decoration, a blanket of wavy color amid the lobby's somber play of gray squares and rectangles. The building's massive size showed the stature of American diplomacy. Its enormous (interior) windows implied a diplomacy unfettered and open to all the world.

One other architectural development circa 1963 marked the passage of the McMillan Plan and of related neoclassical projects into history. It entailed Charles McKim's Pennsylvania Station in New York City, the demolition of which began on October 28, 1963. There were solid business and real estate reasons to construct a taller building on this Manhattan spot. The original Penn Station had fallen into semi-disrepair by

1963, a sign that rail travel had been eclipsed by the automobile and the airplane. Saarinen's Dulles Airport was modern in 1963, whereas Penn Station was a crumbling landmark from the past. Nevertheless, the destruction of the old Pennsylvania Station was a cruel act of erasure, and the buildings that were put up in its place, the current Penn Station and Madison Square Garden, had none of the cultural significance and none of the civic grandeur that McKim's building had so proudly communicated. The disappearance of the neoclassical Penn Station sparked a movement to preserve historic buildings in the United States that was quite different in intent from the McMillan Plan, from the Chicago World's Fair and from the City Beautiful movement. McKim's Penn Station, backward-looking as its architectural style was, was still the epitome of a forward-looking modern building when it went up. So too was the National Mall a modern public space as it evolved, designed as a step on the advance of modern civilization, as the visible evidence of progress. Penn Station's destruction reminded Americans of the need to preserve a pre-modern architecture, and by 1963 the neoclassical style was no longer acceptably modern. Even in Washington, DC, a modern building was no longer supposed to be neoclassical in 1963. Smooth and functional, the Harry S. Truman building was a perfect artifact of its cultural and political moment.

It was in the auditorium of the recently built State Department that John F. Kennedy gave his first presidential press conference on January 25, 1961. The modernism of the building was innately Kennedyesque. A few days before the press conference Kennedy had devoted his inaugural address to a generational torch being passed and to the thrill of change. Even if the forty-four-year-old president's Cold War conviction harmonized with Eisenhower's, it was youth that was winning out (in Kennedy's eyes) in an America as ambient and enterprising as the early republic. Kennedy had met W. W. Rostow at a garden party in Cambridge, Massachusetts, hosted by the historian Arthur Schlesinger Jr., and Rostow had been a campaign advisor to Kennedy, coining phrases like "New Frontier" and "let's get this country moving again" that capitalized on Kennedy's style and youth. Kennedy appointed Rostow his director of policy planning at the State Department. There, Rostow could try to synchronize American foreign policy with the stages of economic growth. Rostow was one of many high-flying academics to turn up in the Kennedy administration. Harvard alone handed over Arthur Schlesinger Jr., Henry Kissinger (briefly) and McGeorge Bundy to the White House. In the crosshairs of the Cold War, the university and the government would stride hand in hand into the 1960s.[36]

Kennedy parted ways with Eisenhower by being more cosmopolitan or by wishing to be. Kennedy would modernize the United States and the West just as the architecture of American diplomacy had been modernized prior to his election in 1960. As the Rostow appointment indicated, Kennedy took a strong interest in the question of decolonization in the underdeveloped countries, many of which he had visited as an affluent young man. In 1957, Senator Kennedy gave a controversial speech in the Senate, "Imperialism—the Enemy of Freedom," on the wrongness of French and other kinds of colonialism. Kennedy's inaugural address had been a statement of the American creed in an ever more global cold war. Many of its pressure points were in Asia, the Middle East, Africa and Latin America. Kennedy founded the Peace Corps to channel the activism of American youth and to meet the imperatives of a global cold war, which, as Rostow knew, was as much a matter of economic development and creating an inviting image of the United States as it was of missiles and troops and spycraft. The Soviets and the Chinese were busily sending their doctors and engineers and teachers out into the world, personifications of their communist idealism. On June 10, 1963, Kennedy gave a commencement address at American University that reversed the expected Cold War antagonisms. He dismissed a "Pax Americana enforced on the world by American weapons of war." "We all inhabit this small planet" was the American president's banal and shocking admission to American University's graduating students.[37]

Kennedy the cosmopolitan inhabitant of this small planet could not escape the kind of Cold War interventions and covert activity that the Dulles brothers had cooked up for Eisenhower. Whatever he had said in the Senate about assisting decolonialization, a string of overseas disasters disturbed President Kennedy's leadership of the West. An ill-planned invasion of Cuba's Bay of Pigs was not merely a military set-back for the Kennedy administration. It was ready-made propaganda for Cuba's Fidel Castro, proof that the United States had not changed its ways since the US-Mexican War or the Spanish-American War or the neocolonial intrusions involved in the construction of the Panama Canal. For Castro, Kennedy was just another Yankee imperialist. More complicated was the situation in Vietnam, where the United States was assisting the anticommunist South. In the summer of 1963, Kennedy allowed a US-approved assassination plot to go forward in South Viet-nam, a sloppily made decision that left Washington with two unpalat-able options—to cut its losses and leave the Vietnamese domino to fall to communism, or to support a government that was corrupt, unpop-ular and in chaos. This was not what W. W. Rostow had predicted for places like Vietnam in his anticommunist manifesto.

Despite his misadventures in the Caribbean and Indochina, Ken-nedy relished American leadership of the West. He took on the cause in his inaugural address, a call to Americans to do with fervor what they had always done—to fight for liberty. A few months into his presidency, Kennedy met with Nikita Khrushchev in Vienna, and in notes to himself he could have been drafting an outline for Wil-liam McNeill's *The Rise of the West*, which had yet to appear in print. Kennedy instructed himself to "repeat the theme of confidence of the West—anti-Spenglerism. The West on the rise. All we have to do is hold together." His upbeat notes notwithstanding, the meeting went badly for Kennedy—Khrushchev did not agree with him about the rise of the West—but Kennedy's notes are a window into his mind. The fundamentals are strong, the West *is* on the rise, it must simply remember that it is rising. Kennedy's program for concerted action is "anti-Spenglerism," by which he must have meant the refusal of de-spair, fatalism, anxiety and pessimism. The inaugural address had al-ready been an instance of Kennedy's "anti-Spenglerism." We can hold together because we have reason to be confident in ourselves: World War II and Cold War themes, these political sentiments would have been thoroughly familiar to FDR, Truman and Eisenhower. Kennedy's message—to himself and others—was that the West had nothing to fear but fear itself.[38]

Where Kennedy could most credibly point to the rise of the West was in Europe. He gave his preeminent anti-Spengler speech on Western liberty in Germany. Dean Acheson had long ago won the debate on US-German policy: West Germany had not been put to pasture or turned into a demilitarized zone. Fourteen years old in 1963, the Federal Republic of Germany was genuinely a country, rearmed and in NATO. Greater Germany was also divided anew during Kennedy's presidency when, at Khrushchev's behest, a wall was put up in Berlin. Construction began on this Cold War symbol in August 1961, and, as everyone knew and none in East Germany could say, the wall was built to keep East Germans in, to lock them in, so attractive was the world on the wall's western side. Even before the wall went up, the American association of West Berlin with liberty was instinctual. A replica of the Liberty Bell had been installed in West Berlin's Schöneberg Rathaus (city hall) in 1950, part of a CIA-funded "Crusade for Freedom." In 1954, Herbert Hoover found his way to Berlin and to the Athenian and imperiled liberty of its residents: "thanks to the spirit and courage of men under the leadership of two great mayors you can, like the men of ancient Athens, hold your heads high and say: 'I am a Berliner,'" this unbeliever in the NATO alliance declared. The Berlin Wall matched American rhetoric of a Germany trapped between East and West, communism and capitalism, walled-in authoritarianism and unwalled freedom. These contrasting tensions were obviously worsening in 1962 and early 1963.[39]

And so, Kennedy scheduled a trip to West Berlin, "the testicles of the West," as Nikita Khrushchev loved calling the city. En route to Berlin in June 1963, Kennedy was worried not just about the Soviets' wall but also about French president Charles de Gaulle's recent attempts to decouple Germany from the transatlantic alliance and to undermine NATO. Under de Gaulle, France would withdraw its troops from NATO in 1966. De Gaulle had visited Berlin in September 1962, whereas no sitting American president had ever visited this city. Of course, Berlin was not the capital of West Germany, though it had been the capital of the Third Reich and before that of the *Kaiserreich*. The mayor of Social Democratic Berlin, Willie Brandt, was delighted to have Kennedy visit. The event showcased Brandt himself, strengthening his pro-Western wing of the Social Democratic Party. West Germany's Christian Democratic chancellor, Konrad Adenauer, would have preferred to keep Kennedy in Bonn, in the leafy capital on the right (Western) side of the Rhine, but Adenauer's priority was to have the American president commit as fully as possible to West Germany's defense. Where Kennedy made this commitment mattered less. At a June 23 press conference, Kennedy voiced the following affirmations: "your safety is our safety, your liberty is our liberty, and any attack on your soil is an attack on our own." Adenauer had gotten what he wanted.[40]

Kennedy got what he wanted as well, a public affirmation of American leadership from grateful European citizens. He delivered his Berlin speech from the balcony of the Schöneberg Rathaus, having just seen Khrushchev's wall on his procession through Berlin, which led him to qualify the pacifism and empathy of his gentle American University speech. The American and the West German had the same enemy just across the wall in the East, and Europeans seeking to know what liberty was in June 1963 did not have to go all the way to Philadelphia or Washington. "Let them come to Berlin," Kennedy recommended. There they could see what Western liberty was in reality. Gone was the Second World War, unmentioned was the Holocaust, Hitler's Berlin nowhere to be seen or spoken of. West Berlin was the real protagonist of Kennedy's speech, and the crowd in Berlin was glad to be heroic. So complete was Kennedy's identification with his audience that he slipped—casually almost—into their language, "*ich bin ein Berliner.*" He also slipped into another language as well. *Civis romanus sum,* "I am a Roman citizen," was an expression Kennedy had already used in a 1962 speech in New Orleans, but the phrase meant something very different in West Germany. There the Latinate bond of civilization, the updated *Pax Romana* and the shared classical legacy—the West, in short—lit up the German-American relationship as nothing else could. Americans and Germans were not just friends; they were fellow citizens, fellow communicants of political liberty, civilizational equals deserving of one another's protection. Under American leadership, West Germany had redeemed itself. That was Kennedy's message, all the more eloquent for being made indirectly. He let his audience fill in the blanks, which it did by roaring its approval.

After Kennedy's assassination only a few months later in November 1963, the German paper of record, the *Frankfurter Allgemeine Zeitung*, returned the compliment an American president had paid to Berlin and to all West Germans. "While a student at Harvard," the *Frankfurter Allgemeine Zeitung* stated approvingly in its obituary, "he [John F. Kennedy] became a European."[41]

PART II

The Abandonment
of the West

4

Questions, 1963–1979

We didn't land on Plymouth Rock, my brothers
and sisters—Plymouth Rock landed on *us*!
—MALCOLM X,
THE AUTOBIOGRAPHY OF MALCOLM X, 1965

A YOUNG MAN, Malcolm Little moved from Michigan to Boston in the 1930s. He worked at a dance hall, learned how to hustle on the city streets of Roxbury, a Boston neighborhood, and had various jobs on the railroads, going mostly between Boston and New York. One of those jobs brought him to Washington, DC. It was not the National Mall or the design of the McMillan Plan that impressed Little, not Union Station or the statues and streets of the grand representative city. Instead, it was the city's juxtapositions that shocked him, especially the acute poverty at its center. In *The Autobiography of Malcolm X,* as told to the writer Alex Haley, Malcolm recalled being:

> astounded to find in the nation's capital, just a few blocks from Capitol Hill, thousands of Negroes living worse than any I'd seen in the poorest sections of Roxbury; in dirt-floor shacks along unspeakably filthy lanes with names like Pig Alley and Goat Alley. I had seen a lot, but never such a dense concentration of stumblebums, pushers, hookers, public crap-shooters, even little kids running around at midnight

begging for pennies, half-naked and barefooted . . . just a few blocks from the White House.

WHATEVER THE CITY was supposed to tell its visitors about liberty and self-government, whatever claims there were to be made about a twentieth-century *Pax Romana, translatio imperii* or American leadership of the West, was turned upside down by Pig Alley and Goat Alley. The poverty and desperation on display in this Washington—"a Southern town with a strong Jim Crow tradition," in the historian Thomas Borstelmann's words—were right around the corner from the National Mall.[1]

The racial contradictions of Washington, DC, prompted Malcolm Little to rethink American foreign policy. Little was later arrested, and in prison he converted to Islam and to new ways of looking at the world. In conversation with another prisoner, Malcolm realized "that the white man was fast losing his power to oppress and exploit the dark world; that the dark world was starting to rise to rule the world again, as it had before; that the white man's world was on the way down, it was on the way out." Malcolm's realization was a realization about the West. He came to believe that history's greatest crime was slavery, the monstrous act of bringing Africans "to the West in chains, in slave ships," he wrote. The West's crimes were continuous and far-reaching: slavery, the racism that governed slavery and the separate-but-unequal tenets of segregation. The United States was a country built by slaves, its wealth and power the product of unfree African American labor. With such a legacy, it was logical that the United States would want to join its tainted foreign policy to that of Britain, France, Holland and Portugal. Empire had overrun the New World. Empire had engendered slavery. Of course, the United States was an empire among empires, and not just since the Spanish-American War of 1898. The United States was a republic born with the mentality of an empire.[2]

Malcolm X, as he would come to be known after becoming a Muslim, reread history in order to recalibrate the lines of American foreign policy. "I took special pains to hunt in the library for books that would inform me on details about black history," he recalled. Black history pointed to a sharp conclusion: that "the American black man is the world's most shameful case of minority oppression." Malcolm X was pessimistic about Washington, DC. It was lost to a romance of power inseparable from the romance of white supremacy, though this did not mean that African Americans were powerless to pursue another kind of foreign policy. Malcolm X, for one, was not going to wear the "white man's uniform"—that is, serve in the US military. To the contrary, he urged a union among "the independent nations of Africa and the American black people." He also pointed out that "the aroused black man can create a turmoil in white America's vitals—not to mention America's international image." That was one lever in a Cold War contest between the attractiveness of the Soviet Union and the attractiveness of the United States. The rest was truth telling and education, "telling the white man about himself," as Malcolm X tried to do. He was hopeful about the universities. A frequent speaker on college campuses, he felt that "the whites of the younger generation, in the colleges and universities, will see the handwriting on the wall and many of them will turn to the *spiritual* path of *truth*."[3]

Changes were coming not just to the universities. American foreign policy was opening up, and some of the old barriers were breaking down. These changes retraced the problem W. E. B. Du Bois had ascribed to African American politics in 1947, the dilemma of traveling further into the American mainstream or of standing as a group apart. The "Anglo-Saxon" grip on the American political elite was weakening. John F. Kennedy was at the cusp of this transition, the first president of Irish immigrant background, the Irish impediment having been as strong as the accompanying Catholic impediment from a nineteenth-century or eighteenth-century American point of view. (Thomas Jefferson had referred to Catholics as a "priest-ridden people [incapable of] maintaining a free civil government.") American Jews like W. W. Rostow were entering into government as well, as they had been since the Roosevelt administration. Rostow rose to the position of national security advisor in 1966, one hurdle overcome. Against much greater resistance, African Americans, too, were advancing within the halls of American foreign-policy power. Carl Rowan was named the director of the US Information Agency in 1964, making him the first African American to hold a seat on the National Security Council. To the extent that all of these minority group members endorsed the West in the Cold War contest—the thrust of American foreign policy, of course—they contributed something crucial. American leadership of the West did not have to be a racial proposition, and American foreign policy was not the sole preserve of Achesonian aristocrats, not restricted to those who were white and Protestant. American leadership of the West was not simply a recycling of Rudyard Kipling's white man's burden or of France's *mission civilisatrice*. It had the potential to be more broad-minded.[4]

And then there were Malcolm X's questions. How could the United States call itself the West and declare itself a child of Europe when the American population had such important non-European roots? What was the relationship between the West, the neoclassical heritage, the alleged European patrimony of the United States and patterns of exclusion and prejudice in American life? To what degree did slavery and segregation depend on the equation of the West with whiteness and of whiteness with white supremacy? Had the United States not betrayed democracy with the conquest of Native lands, the persecution of Native peoples and the Spanish-American War? Was the very European settlement of the Americas not the first page in the book of American imperialism, from Christopher Columbus and the conquistadors through to the imperialist orgy of the Chicago World's Fair and on to the high-tech soldiers and spies of the Cold War? The African American frame was only one of several possible frames for these questions, which could be posed with Native Americans, Asian Americans, Hispanics and many other groups in mind. The marriage of liberty and the West could be reworked just as Malcolm X had reworked it into the marriage of slavery and the West. If so, the Western orientation in American foreign policy was the source of unfreedom. These questions were radical in 1963, as they had been in 1947, and they were mostly asked by American radicals. As the Vietnam War drove these questions to the fore in the late 1960s, they would lead to something other than the Left of Harry Truman and JFK.

Among antiwar Americans of many backgrounds, the Vietnam War posed the West as a foreign-policy burden for the United States. A conflict that dated back to the Eisenhower administration, the Vietnam War had imperceptible beginnings. Without fanfare, Kennedy thickened the American military presence in Vietnam. Had he not been assassinated, he might have pulled back from Vietnam, but at the time of his assassination Kennedy's administration had an unconsidered policy; South Vietnam was highly unstable; and North Vietnam was far from defeated. An impending disaster in November 1963, the Vietnam War would become Lyndon Johnson's unshakable disaster when Kennedy was killed in Dallas, corroding the original and simpler terms of the early Cold War. It was one thing to guarantee the freedom of West Berlin and to stand near a replica of the Liberty Bell at Berlin's Schöneberg Rathaus, defending liberty where the Soviet Union threatened liberty. It was entirely another to pick up where the French colonialists had failed in Vietnam, to claim that one's anticommunist partners in South Vietnam were valiant democrats when they were not and to oppose a charismatic figure from North Vietnam who, at one point, had been an admirer of the American Revolution. Ho Chi Minh fancied himself the Thomas Jefferson of Indochina, and yet he was America's enemy. The Vietnam War's terrible bloodshed, its costs to the Vietnamese and to the American people, pressurized questions about American foreign policy and its claims to leadership of the West. Perhaps this vaunted civilizational ideal was itself a part of the Vietnam War's unfolding tragedy. The war also popularized questions that had previously been asked (by Du Bois and others) but that had often gone unheard, and the questions were not especially abstract. They were very real. They bristled with political consequences.

From the Vietnam War, questions radiated out about all aspects of the American Cold War. If a seductive ideal of the West had led the United States into imperialist temptation in Indochina, then the same might be true across the Cold War chessboard. The Korean War had stalemated in 1954, but in the Middle East, Africa and Latin America, the Cold War was costly and turbulent in the 1960s and 1970s. American advisors, American troops, American intelligence, American arms and American aid were flowing in every direction. What separated the United States of 1965 or 1975 from the French and British empires? These empires had been staffed by legions of ideologues, colonial administrators, experts and artists (Kipling, most memorably) who sang the beauties of empire, while the American Cold War university blended the study of the West with the celebration of the West and the celebration of the West with the advising of presidents and government institutions. These universities were proudly beholden to the responsibilities of the West, drawing the ire of the antiwar movement, which was itself prominent on university campuses. At Berkeley and Columbia and many other universities, the responsibilities of the West were interrogated, and the bonds that had connected the study of the West with the defense of the West began to break. Ultimately, William McNeill's *The Rise of the West* belonged more to the 1930s, the 1940s and the 1950s than to the decade in which it was published. Popular as it was upon publication, McNeill's 1963 book arrived at the end of an era in American politics and American foreign policy.

THE LONG, SLOW work of diversifying the American national security elite began at the end of the Second World War. Truman desegregated the US military in 1950, making it an African American ladder for professional advancement in the second half of the twentieth century. Reform of the State Department was more piecemeal. The reform had a prewar intellectual foundation. To take one example: the philosopher Alain Locke contributed to the notion of the New Negro, intellectual and self-aware and engaged in social and political change. Locke formulated his ideas at the height of segregation, in the years after World War I. A 1907 graduate of Harvard College and the first African American Rhodes Scholar, Locke taught at Howard University. He applied the New Negro's angle of vision to interracial—and to international—relations in a series lectures given at Howard between 1915 and 1916. They were titled "Race Contacts and Interracial Relations." In them, the ongoing overseas war in mind, Locke attacked imperialism as racist and exploitative. He identified a "science" of race that was really a mask for political and economic domination, a philosophy of the dominant groups:

> We should expect naturally that race theory should be a philosophy of the dominant groups. That is natural. That is inevitable. Further than that, we should expect that it would [make] some sort of brief for the prevailing types of civilization. But that is the utmost concession we can make to a study of race that professes to be scientific.

To clarify the self-serving notions of race is the first step to ending imperialism. Later, Locke saw some potential in the ideas Woodrow Wilson articulated in Paris, despite Wilson's own neglect of the peoples living under colonialism. Locke regarded Article 22 in the League of Nations' charter, which established a mandate system for the European empires, as the impetus for a new kind of international relations. If the empires could cede political power to mandates, imperialism would weaken and independence for previously colonized African (and other) peoples could be approached. Locke knew these ideas were peripheral to the mainstream foreign-policy thinking of the 1920s, not to mention the 1930s, but that only enhanced their salience in his eyes.[5]

Within Locke's idea of a New Negro was the potential for a new kind of American diplomacy and a new kind of American diplomat. Since the turn of the century, Du Bois had been promoting a "talented tenth" of African Americans educated in the liberal arts and destined to be leaders inside the United States; he had leadership on civil rights and domestic politics in mind. Where foreign policy and the talented tenth were concerned, Du Bois was predicting the future. Elite university education was the first step for the entry of African Americans into the halls of foreign-policy power. From outside the US government, Harriet Tubman had battled against the slave trade, hoping to shift

American policy. Between 1865 and the 1920s, the State Department was modestly receptive to hiring African Americans. Self-educated and a self-emancipated slave, Frederick Douglass had served (unhappily) as US minister to Haiti from 1889 to 1891, and Du Bois himself had a brief diplomatic posting in Ghana. By contrast, Ralph Bunche was a career diplomat. He had followed in Du Bois's educational footsteps, studying at UCLA and then going to Harvard, where he completed a PhD in political science in 1934. Already in 1929, Bunche had joined Locke as a colleague at Howard University. Bunche developed his dissertation, "French Administration in Togoland and Dahomey," a critique of European imperialism, into a book, *World View of Race,* which was published in 1936. In 1937, Bunche joined the Council on African Affairs, an organization founded by the activist Max Yergan to lobby the US government on workers' rights and independence movements in Africa. W. E. B. Du Bois, the activist and performer Paul Robeson and the politician Adam Clayton Powell were fellow members of the council. An Africa analyst for the Office of Strategic Services during World War II, Bunche worked with the Swedish sociologist Gunnar Myrdal on *An American Dilemma* (1944), a widely read sociological study of race and racism and a scholarly boost to the civil rights movement.[6]

Bunche put parts of Locke's new foreign policy into practice. He became the US ambassador to the United Nations in 1950, reviving a tradition of African American diplomatic distinction from the Civil War to the First World War that the astringent racial dynamics of the 1920s had derailed. In the twentieth-century State Department, there was a narrow-minded tendency to limit African American diplomats to symbolic postings in Africa or to exploit skin color for certain kinds of postings. A 1949 State Department report was titled *Countries to Which an Outstanding Negro Might Appropriately Be Sent As an Ambassador.* Bunche chipped away at this patronizing mind-set in his career and in his scholarship. *A World View of Race* was a hymn to Enlightenment rationalism. "I rely on reason, candor and truth," he explained of his political work. "They stand firm enough without support from emotion." In his capacity as an American diplomat, Bunche advocated education as the vehicle of a postcolonial African elite, a talented tenth abroad with which the United States could collaborate on international problem solving. Referencing cosmopolitan universalism rather than of East-West division, Bunche helped conceptualize a new American foreign policy for Africa and the Middle East. For his work on Arab-Israeli issues and for his other achievements, Bunche was awarded the Nobel Peace Prize in 1950, the first American who was not a secretary of state or a president to receive the prize: he was a principal negotiator at the UN and director of UN peacekeeping operations. In 1997, the State Department named its library, founded by Thomas Jefferson, after Ralph Bunche the scholar-diplomat.[7]

After Bunche's breakthrough, two other African American diplomatic careers took shape in the 1960s and 1970s more along classical Cold War lines than in the spirit of cosmopolitan universalism. Colin Powell was born in 1937 and graduated from the City College of New York in 1958. He later served as an army officer in multiple Vietnam tours. He had a White House Fellowship in the 1970s and after that a rapid rise in military and foreign-policy positions, culminating in his appointment as Chairman of the Joint Chiefs (during the First Gulf War) and as secretary of state from 2001 to 2005. A fellow Republican, Condoleezza Rice was the second African American secretary of state after Powell. Born in 1954, she was a 1974 graduate of the University of Colorado, where she earned her PhD, finishing in 1981, with State Department work along the way. (At age seventeen she had attended a summer music camp in Aspen, Colorado, and would later have a continuing affiliation with the Aspen Institute.) Powell and Rice broke out of a box that pegged African American diplomats as Africa specialists or as liaisons to the United Nations. Rice was a student of Joseph Korbel, an émigré from interwar Czechoslovakia whose daughter Madeleine Albright would become secretary of state in 1997. Indeed, it was one of Korbel's lectures on Stalin that attracted Rice to international relations generally and to Soviet studies in particular. When Rice went from national security advisor to secretary of state in 2005, she hung four portraits on her office wall—Thomas Jefferson, George Marshall, Dean Acheson and William Seward (who negotiated the purchase of Alaska). Representatives of the talented tenth, if not quite as Du Bois had intended it, Powell and Rice were conservative refutations of the segregationist mentality. The same year Rice received her doctorate at the University of Colorado, an African American student at Occidental College in Los Angeles gave his first public speech. It picked up (indirectly) on Alain Locke's old subject of race and international or interracial relations. This California undergraduate proposed divesting money from the South African economy because of South Africa's practice of segregation, or Apartheid. With this collegiate speech, Barack Obama began his political career.[8]

DESPITE THE ACHIEVEMENTS of a few, the Washington, DC, that Malcolm X visited as a young man did not change much after World War II. It was still a heavily segregated city when *The Autobiography of Malcolm X* was published in 1965. The laws were being altered, but most of the old barriers and the old attitudes were still in place. Like Malcolm X, Du Bois had come to believe that Western civilization had crushed African Americans—Plymouth Rock had landed on them. Du Bois had witnessed the American rise to superpower status between 1890 and 1947. Black soldiers fought valiantly in World War I, discovered new liberties in France and returned home to worsening repression. The European empires went back to business as usual after the Great War without any purposeful objection from the United States. The 1920s was the decade of the collegiate gothic and of the neo-gothic Ku Klux Klan. Teutonic civilization appeared no less heedless, no less emblematic of the national selfishness in the 1920s than it had in 1890 when Du Bois gave his Harvard commencement address on Jefferson Davis. Du Bois took an academic and a political interest in Africa, attending pan-African conferences between 1900 and 1945, trying to get his Encyclopedia Africana published and seeking out political bonds outside the United States. He published his book *The World and Africa* in 1947 and ran for the US Senate in 1950. Formal influence on American foreign policy eluded him, leaving him with protests like the 1947 National Association for the Advancement of Colored People (NAACP) appeal to the UN. In Du Bois's view, postwar American foreign policy was hopeless and getting worse. White Americans would not accept the message hidden in Negro blood—that a truly democratic foreign policy could only begin with full citizenship for African Americans, and that African Americans might have unique insight into the civilizational complexities of a decolonizing world. What was left, Du Bois concluded, was the imperative of saying no.

To Du Bois and others appalled by the midcentury racial status quo, two movements of the 1920s and 1930s were prior examples of African American dissent. Pan-Africanism was pioneered by Marcus Garvey, who moved from Jamaica to Harlem in 1916. Garvey not only oriented African American political life toward Africa but also tried to bring African Americans home to Africa with the Universal Negro Improvement Association. "Africa for the Africans at home and abroad" was his rallying cry. If the Association's effect was numerically marginal, Garvey's effect on consciousness was powerful. (Malcolm X's father was a follower of Marcus Garvey.) A dividing line between African Americans and the West could and should be drawn. Thus could the dictates of the white, imperial West be kept at bay. The other way of rejecting the dictates of the West or at least of the capitalist-imperialist West was to pay sympathetic attention to the Soviet experiment, though not necessarily to join the Communist Party. American communists were early supporters of the civil rights movement and outspoken defenders of the Scottsboro boys, for example, in a 1931 incident that pitted African American teenagers against the American legal system. In tandem with Moscow, American communists studied and critiqued race and empire globally, as well as racism and inequality within the United States, arguing for an autonomous African American region, a black belt, within the American body politic. Especially in the 1930s, the Soviet Union appeared to have answers to the crisscrossing dilemmas of poverty and racism. Although the African American athlete, musician, actor and film star Paul Robeson did not join the Communist Party, he lent his celebrity to communist causes and to the person of Joseph Stalin in the 1930s and 1940s, to immensely controversial effect.

Neither an enthusiast of Marcus Garvey nor a Communist Party member, James Baldwin was a young African American writer of the 1950s who applied his literary genius to many of Du Bois's questions. Born in 1924, Baldwin grew up in Harlem, was educated by New York City and made it over to France in 1948. He was not a scholar. He was a novelist whose *Go Tell It on the Mountain* (1953) was an excursus in African American history and a translation of *The Souls of Black Folk* into fiction. It built upon a prior architecture of fiction, on novels such as Jean Toomer's *Cane* (1923) and Zora Neale Hurston's *Their Eyes Were Watching God* (1937) that capitalized on African American milieus and vernacular African American speech. James Baldwin was also a widely read essayist whose first essay collection, *Notes of a Native Son* (1955), coincided thematically with a stirring civil rights movement. Baldwin was not the organizer Du Bois was, not the institution builder, but in his fiction and his nonfiction Baldwin was melding American audiences and genres in a way that was distinctively his. He did so at a moment when racial inequality was attracting ever more attention from white Americans: Supreme Court decisions such as *Brown v. Board of Education* (1954) were forcing a reconsideration of race in American politics and society. Like Du Bois, Baldwin was preoccupied by the question of the West. Baldwin was not inclined—as, say, William McNeill was—to associate the West with law, innovation and creativity. He was not a believer in the Columbian Republic that had disgusted Frederick Douglass by relegating Africans to the exotic sideshows of the Chicago World's Fair and by hiding African American history and culture from view. Baldwin analyzed the West as personally unassimilable and at the same time as the pivotal variable for American foreign policy in the early Cold War. Non-Western peoples and countries were rejecting colonialism and distancing themselves from Europe, in their politics and in their consciousness. Globally hyperactive, the American superpower was caught in the middle of decolonization, painfully mired its own ongoing (and very public) racial contradictions.

In *Notes of a Native Son,* Baldwin avoided the graceful synthesis of Western and African American culture for which Du Bois had reached for in *The Souls of Black Folk.* Baldwin did not sit down effortlessly and summon Aristotle and Marcus Aurelius. The void of not possessing the culture of Aristotle, Shakespeare and Aurelius was the void with which Baldwin had matured as a young man. For him, "the most crucial time in my own development came when I was forced to recognize that I was a kind of bastard of the West; when I followed the line of my past I did not find myself in Europe but in Africa." His African origins redirected the European lineage said to define American culture. The West's cultural monuments resisted Baldwin such that "I brought to Shakespeare, Bach, Rembrandt, to the stones of Paris, to the cathedral of Chartres, and to the Empire State Building a special attitude. These are not my creations; they were not my creation; I might search in them in vain forever for a reflection of myself." The music and architecture of this powerful civilization, from the gothic cathedral at Chartres to Fifth Avenue's Empire State Building, was a cultural mirror that was not Baldwin's mirror. The music and architecture would not let him see his face in their forbidding, whitened edifices. Europe was not Africa, Europe had enslaved Africa, and America had been derived from these simple, terrible facts. In an essay from *Notes of a Native Son,* "Encounter on the Seine," Baldwin wrote of "our history, which is the history of the total, of willing, alienation of entire peoples from their forebears." What is ours, Baldwin concluded, is the alienation. That was the line of *his* past.[9]

The essay in which Baldwin queried the West most profoundly appeared in *Harper's* in 1953. Baldwin included it in *Notes of a Native Son.* Titled "Stranger in the Village," it parallels Du Bois's search for a new American role in the world, one that would take into account the African and European foundations of American culture. Baldwin had spent a winter living in Switzerland. A remote alpine village, Baldwin realized, "is the West, the West onto which I have been so strangely grafted." The villagers, residents of the West, "have made the modern world." This recalls William McNeill's industrial metaphor of the West as a "world-girding" civilization. Westerners have power and they have an inheritance "related, as I am not, to Dante, Shakespeare, Aeschylus, Da Vinci, Rembrandt and Michelangelo, Heine." Baldwin's list is much like the list of names on the façade of the Boston Public Library or Columbia's Butler Library or the reading room of the Library of Congress. Western culture is a received ornament for Europeans and for white Americans, the record of a decorous and successful history. It is something sinister for the black-skinned man in its midst: "out of their [the Europeans'] hymns and dances came Beethoven and Bach. Go back a few centuries and they are in their full glory—but I am in Africa, watching the conquerors arrive." The Teutonic conquering civilization does not spare those whom it conquers. The conquered ended up as bystanders to the progression of other people's history, though a history that is also menacingly theirs.[10]

At the end of the essay, Baldwin unexpectedly turns isolation into integration or into a hypothetical integration reserved for a better future. Swiss homogeneity cannot match American heterogeneity, not in 1953. A first principle of the West may be racism, "the very warp and woof of the heritage of the West, the idea of white supremacy," as Baldwin writes. Because of centuries of American life, however, the African American is "not a visitor in the West, but a citizen there, an American." Forced to conform to the West and its idea of white supremacy, Baldwin's African American has what Du Bois called second sight: "his survival depended, and his development depends, on his ability to turn his peculiar status in the Western world to his own advantage and, it may be, to the very great advantage of the world." If white Americans can look beyond the idea of white supremacy, they will not only see themselves for the first time. They may also see their way to foreign-policy excellence in the 1950s or later, a foreign policy of color-blind citizenship. Because of their complicated history, "Americans are as unlike any other white people in the world as it is possible to be," Baldwin argues persuasively. More than synthesis, Baldwin finds a strand of progress in "Stranger in the Village." "It is precisely this black-white experience which may prove of indispensable value to us in the world we face today," he points out. "The world is white no longer, and it will never be white again." Baldwin was not rejecting the West, as such. He was affirming African American belonging—through a multicultural America—in the West. To see this in the 1950s was to see the agency of African Americans in American culture and potentially in American foreign policy, as well.[11]

Baldwin's fiction and nonfiction were the barometer of a changing West. Watched by Baldwin, the 1955 Bandung Conference of non-aligned nations emphasized a new zone of international politics dominated neither by the West nor by Soviet-Chinese communism. Bandung signified postcolonial autonomy coupled with a desire for international action based on this autonomy. Unlike the United Nations, the Bandung Conference had not been convened by Western powers. It was more autonomous. Fiction writers working in Western languages were claiming a postcolonial autonomy of a similar kind in the 1950s. Baldwin acknowledged the civilizational destiny of the English language, "which America had inherited from England, that is, from Greece and Rome." That was a part of the language's power, especially for those whose medium was English but whose ancestry did not descend from Greece and Rome, as it were. For Baldwin, "the American Negro is probably the only man of color who can speak of the West with real authority, whose experience, painful as it is, also proves the vitality of the transgressed Western ideals." The African American is "the connecting link between Africa and the West, the most real and certainly the most shocking of all African contributions to Western cultural life." The Bandung Conference did not redirect the Cold War overnight. It was the recognized autonomy of the postcolonial, nonaligned voices that mattered. Previously neglected or suppressed voices were coming forward, and Western audiences were gathering to hear them. As in Bandung itself, there were vast non-Western audiences, as well.[12]

Baldwin's shifting West and his inclusion of African American themes in English-language fiction had an analogue in one of the pivotal postwar English-language novels, *A House for Mr. Biswas*. Published in 1961 by V. S. Naipaul, an Oxford-educated writer of Indian background who had grown up in Trinidad, *A House for Mr. Biswas* was a milestone in Western cultural life. Naipaul knew the power of the English language as Baldwin knew it, a Western and a global language, by default the lingua franca of the twentieth century. Yet if the English language had been a tool of empire and of writers who graced empire with phrases like "white man's burden," English could be put to other purposes as well. *A House for Mr. Biswas* was a comedy of manners as subtle, quiet and slyly comic as a Jane Austen novel, and at the same time its milieu was radically new to canonical English literature, as was its protagonist Mr. Biswas, an impoverished Indian-heritage intellectual living on the margins in Trinidad. Loosely based on Naipaul's own father, Mr. Biswas carries the novel's full empathy, leaving it to the reader to find this empathy normal or abnormal. Naipaul did not write protest fiction, not overtly, and his nonfiction travel writings reflected a Western condescension toward the non-Western world, but *A House for Mr. Biswas,* Naipaul's tale of a valiant stranger in a strange land, was a revolution in literary perception. It was a fiction writer's Bandung.

Four years before *A House for Mr. Biswas* was published, Louis Armstrong voiced his dissent from the East-West orthodoxies of the Cold War. In September 1957, he reacted publicly to the intimidation of African American schoolchildren in Little Rock, Arkansas, by canceling a tour of the Soviet Union. These children were being denied their constitutional right to integrated schooling. Not previously known for political activism, Armstrong publicly criticized President Eisenhower for the travesty of Little Rock. "The way they treat my people in the South," Armstrong said, "they can go to hell." He called Eisenhower an "uneducated plow boy" and "two-faced," lamenting "the downtrodden situation" of his fellow African Americans in Arkansas and elsewhere. "I think I have a right to get sore and say something about it," declared one of the most famous men in the world in 1957. Armstrong knew perfectly well the Cold War stakes of his decision not to travel to the Soviet Union and not to play along with the cultural Cold War Allen and John Foster Dulles were perfecting. In the historian Thomas Borstelmann's words, Armstrong's decision *not* to go to the

Soviet Union "displayed America's racial dilemmas to a fascinated international audience." Washington's Cold War preoccupation, with its international image, created opportunities for somebody as famous as Armstrong, and he used it to criticize the hypocrisy of the American-led West.[13]

Not quite the celebrity Armstrong was, W. E. B. Du Bois was moving beyond criticism and toward exile in the 1950s. To be sure, his outrage with the transgression of Western ideals dated back to the late nineteenth century. In the 1950s, the American-led West continued to fail, in his view, by imposing on itself and others the detritus of its racist civilization. Segregation remained mostly intact at home. The tacit alliance with European imperialism remained intact as well, while white Americans proved incapable of understanding the connection between domestic racial prejudice and the ugliness of their foreign policy. In part for practical reasons, the United States supported the white Afrikaner government in South Africa. The America military needed its manganese, chrome and uranium. Revolted, Du Bois drew closer to the Communist Party in the 1950s, running into problems with the US Department of State, which revoked his passport from 1953 to 1959. Du Bois joined the US Communist Party in 1957 and met with China's Chairman Mao in China's Lake Country shortly before he became an expatriate in Ghana, the first African nation to detach itself from colonialism (in 1957) under President Kwame Nkrumah and the country in which Du Bois would die. His meeting with Mao yielded a famous photograph of the two men, both in overcoats and standing at ease. Mao is smiling, Du Bois doubled up in laughter. They were not comrades in arms, but together they form a Chinese-American image of mutual understanding, parity, commonality. This recreational photo was taken at a time when the United States had no diplomatic relationship with China and when the Korean peninsula was divided into American and Chinese spheres of influence. Snapped in 1959, the Du Bois–Mao photograph dates back to the very early stages of the Vietnam War. In this brewing conflict, Du Bois did not find himself on the side of anticommunist South Vietnam.

A FEW YEARS after Du Bois and Mao met in China's Lake Country, Lyndon Johnson decided to expand the Vietnam War. Eisenhower's domino theory was the pretext for war. If Vietnam fell, so too would the neighboring countries of Indochina, the theory promised. A communist Indochina would endanger the strategic position of Japan and Australia, essential American allies, possibly submerging nonaligned India in the communist wave. Sequentially, collapsing anticommunist resolve in Asia might invite Soviet aggression in Europe. That had been Eisenhower's and Kennedy's worst fear. Johnson inherited it the day Kennedy was assassinated. American credibility in Asia was believed to underwrite American credibility in Europe. Such was the argument of the Cold War's "wise men," seasoned diplomats like Dean Acheson and Averell Harriman who had devised the Marshall Plan, the NATO alliance and the many other instruments for containing Soviet expansion in Europe. Having urged Truman to support imperial France's position in postwar Vietnam, the wise men counseled LBJ to escalate in Vietnam. The Soviet Union had to be blocked from converting its many global advantages into a European campaign, and so, remarkably, LBJ was defending the West in Vietnam. American soldiers could be told that they were upholding the Western value of liberty in South Vietnam, but Johnson's White House was literally guarding the West in Asia, protecting a Europe condemned to live with Moscow's conventional military superiority.

Long before Johnson became president, the entire Vietnam tragedy had been eerily foreshadowed by Graham Greene, a British writer. Greene's 1955 novel, *The Quiet American,* featured Alden Pyle, an idealistic Harvard graduate and CIA agent stationed in Vietnam. Pyle mistakes the country around him for a piece on the game board of global democracy. In the novel, Pyle is seen through the disappointed eyes of an older British man, Thomas Fowler, the European who has been pushed to the margins. Pyle is cloaked in Fowler's cynicism: "perhaps only ten days ago he [Alden Pyle] had been walking back across the common in Boston his arms full of the books he had been reading on the advance of the Far East and the problems of China. He didn't even hear what I said; he was absorbed in the dilemmas of Democracy and the responsibilities of the West. He was determined—I learned that very soon—to do good, not to any individual person, but to a country, a continent, a world. Well he was in his element now with a whole universe to improve." In a few sentences, Greene exposed the inner direction of American foreign policy as it would play itself out in Vietnam. Books run the world. They outline and glamorize the responsibilities of the American-led West, furnishing the dilemmas of democracy to those fortunate enough to wield power. The scholar is a patriot gladly carrying out the nation's self-imposed duty, and the patriot is a scholar at heart. The folly of American policy is compounded by the earnestness of those who make it. Beware those in a hurry to aid a continent, a world and a universe, Greene was saying. Because of how they had been taught, Pyle and his fellow Americans had fallen victim to the siren song of the West.[14]

If Lyndon Johnson ever read *The Quiet American,* he did not take its warnings to heart. Never very quiet, he was yet another American who did not hear what either Graham Greene or Thomas Fowler had to say. Johnson raised the Vietnam War from a second-tier military and geopolitical project to a war that only the US government would not declare a war. He staked his presidency on the military action he ordered in Indochina, without fathoming the perils of guerilla warfare or what could plausibly be called a colonial war—such as the one France fought and lost in Algeria by 1962 (before Johnson became president). Johnson's military goals were impossible to realize. The United States would not directly invade the communist North, as it had in Korea, lest that provoke a war with China. Somehow Washington had to persuade North Vietnam not to interfere in the South. Yet the more American soldiers, planes and materiel were sent to South Vietnam, the more the communist North was convinced—and motivated—to intervene in the South. Even if LBJ had doubled his generals' requests for troops and hardware, the North would have kept on infiltrating the South, sabotaging its diminutive normalcy. The North assessed the overall American willingness to fight in Vietnam, and in the winter of 1968 it came near to finding the threshold. North Vietnam's Tet Offensive of January 1968 was a military setback for the North that nevertheless defeated LBJ within the United States. Johnson had been unable to improve the universe.

The Vietnam War catastrophe undermined overall American Cold War strategy. American military power was unsuited to Vietnam, and the credibility LBJ wanted so much desired was in fact shattered by the war. The war proved that a nuclear superpower could not defeat a poor, mostly agricultural and non-Western country. The Vietnam War fell in line with the Japanese victory over Russia in 1905 and the North Vietnamese defeat of France in 1954; it challenged the Western military mystique. Massive bombing of civilian areas and the use of chemical exfoliants like Agent Orange strengthened the accusation that Americans waged one kind of war in Europe and, as with Japan during World War II, another kind in Asia. American credibility suffered again when the events at My Lai, the killing of Vietnamese civilians by American soldiers in March 1968, came to light. The long-haul Cold War was a competition of attraction between the communist East and the anticommunist West. In the contested developing world, the United States began the Cold War with the advantages of American victory in World War II and American prosperity and with the lingering postcolonial élan of early American history. George Washington and Thomas Jefferson could be counted among the first postcolonial heroes. John F. Kennedy certainly saw them in this light, though no president after Kennedy could associate American foreign policy with an innocent anticolonialism; none, with the possible exception of Jimmy Carter, would really try. The United States was too caught up in the Cold War complexities.

The American Cold War complexities extended far beyond Asia. In theory, the ideal Cold War partner for the United States was an anticommunist or noncommunist democracy. Japan and West Germany fell within this attractive category. Other countries were strategically crucial for one reason or another, and they may have been anticommunist or noncommunist, but they were not American partners because they were democracies. During the Cold War, the United States aligned itself with a range of authoritarian regimes and outright dictatorships: Indonesia under General Suharto, which was as repressive as it was bloodthirsty; Pakistan, which blended military and religious rule into a unique kind of authoritarianism; South Africa, which with apartheid continued the worst traditions of colonialism; Argentina's right-wing dictatorship, which received American military aid; and the Shah's Iran, which was an ostensibly modernizing American ally in the Middle East until it was overthrown by the region's first Islamist revolution in 1979. These myriad American deals with the authoritarian devil were not the work of Democratic or Republican presidents. They were not unique to the 1960s. They ran from the start to the finish of the Cold War. Strategically defensible as it was in some of its particulars, the American record of hard-knuckled Cold War *Realpolitik* was long, and it compromised the reputation of the United States as a Jeffersonian sponsor of liberty. Nothing compromised the United States as conspicuously and as grievously as the Vietnam War.

Johnson's escalation of the Vietnam War also had unintended consequences within the United States. Johnson considered himself a progressive president. He had come to Washington in the 1930s, a Texas foot soldier in FDR's New Deal army. As president, Johnson hoped to complete the unfulfilled mission of the New Deal. He sponsored an ambitious legislative agenda, the Great Society, intended to remake American society through government initiative and to harness the country's wealth to its administrative acumen. In 1964, Johnson's landslide victory against the cartoonishly antiprogressive Barry Goldwater left him with as much of a mandate as any president has ever had (upon election). Yet by 1968, Johnson had lost the Left and he had lost the country's progressive youth to a rebellion that was not only about Vietnam. In the late 1960s, "the movement" was a rejection of Johnson's personality and his generation's cultural style and political attitudes. Part of this generational style was the decades-old rhetoric of Western civilization. In May 1964, for example, Johnson had spoken at the dedication of a George C. Marshall library, pronouncing on the value of opening "the mind of a new generation to the values and the visions of the Western civilization from which they come and to which they belong." This was standard presidential language in 1964, blandly normal. For the new generation to which LBJ wanted to appeal, such language was grating only a few years later. It was grating because it could not be disassociated from the American crimes in Vietnam and from the generational obtuseness of LBJ and others that had led to and sanctioned these crimes. Between 1964 and 1968, the gap widened immeasurably between the antiwar students and the World War II generation that had waged a crusade in Europe; Johnson and Kennedy were both of the older generation. Very quickly on the Left, Johnson went from hard-core New Dealer and JFK's genial Texan sidekick to a partner in the crimes of Western civilization.

At its height, the Vietnam War had a galvanizing effect on the civil rights movement. The movement's leader, Martin Luther King, was born in 1929 and he studied at Morehouse College, class of '48, at the Crozer Theological Seminary in Pennsylvania and at Boston University, where he finished his dissertation in 1955. In his education, King was drawn to the social gospel, to the application of Christian ethics and scripture to inequality and injustice. King also absorbed the new waves of theological thinking associated with Reinhold Niebuhr, a prominent Protestant intellectual of the 1950s. Niebuhr pressed the smugness of American politics through the mesh of irony and tragedy in his popular books, essays and lectures. Humility and tragedy had much to teach the ascendant superpower, and Niebuhr had a serious interest in the pathways of American foreign policy. Niebuhr's appeals to humility and tragedy left their mark on King the student.

Martin Luther King took inspiration as well from the nonviolent civil disobedience of Mahatma Gandhi, finding implicit parallels between colonization abroad and the perpetuation of racism and segregation at home. These were precisely the parallels Malcolm X had derived from studying African American history in prison. The African American struggle for equal rights was a kind of internal decolonization, in King's eyes. Around the time of Ghanaian independence in 1957, for which King traveled to Africa, he penned some notes to himself under the title "God's Judgment on Western Civilization." Because of segregation and racial prejudice, he stated, the United States "is not fit to be the leading country in the world"—not morally fit regardless of the power at its disposal. By 1960, Martin Luther King was the national leader of the civil rights movement, and in that year he seemed to have an ally in the Democratic candidate for the presidency. In October 1960, while Martin Luther King was in prison, John F. Kennedy placed a call to King's wife, Coretta Scott King, expressing his not-quite-public sympathy for King and the civil rights movement.[15]

John F. Kennedy and Martin Luther King both delivered their signature speeches in the summer of 1963. In West Berlin, JFK updated the phrase *civis romanus sum* by claiming it as an American president: the rights and privileges of Roman citizenship were those that accrued to the Western alliance of 1963. King updated the melody of American patriotism, itself an update of Britain's "God Save the King," in his "I Have a Dream" speech. He stood before the same Lincoln Memorial that had been unveiled in a 1923 ceremony before a segregated crowd. In 1939, Marian Anderson, an African American opera singer, had protested segregation when she was barred from performing at Washington's Constitution Hall by performing instead at the Lincoln Memorial. King gave his 1963 speech fully appreciative of the site's nonlinear political symbolism, emancipation and segregation juxtaposed: Lincoln's Emancipation Proclamation dated from 1863, exactly a century before King's speech. Standing thus with Lincoln, King took the backbone of American foreign policy, sweet land of liberty, from the song "My Country, 'Tis of Thee" and bent it back to an "old Negro spiritual." King spoke of liberty denied in the United States rather than of liberty possessed and perpetuated. The United States as a land of liberty was conditioned on improvement, since King's dream was the eradication of segregation. "And when we allow freedom to ring, when we let it ring from every village and hamlet, from every state and city, we will be able to speed up that day when all God's children—black men and white men, Jews and Gentiles, Catholics and

Protestants—will be able to join hands and to sing in the words of the old Negro spiritual, 'Free at last, free at last, thank God almighty I'm free at last.'" In some ways, King and Kennedy were converging in 1963. Kennedy's Department of Justice authorized extensive FBI surveillance of King, and Kennedy selfishly agonized over the electoral politics of civil rights for African Americans, but Kennedy was slowly granting credence to the civil rights movement. There was at least the potential for convergence.

A few years later, Lyndon Johnson's big-souled aspirations for the civil rights movement foundered on the war in Vietnam. Legislatively, he would do more on civil rights than Kennedy, and Johnson would lose the leader of the civil rights movement. Johnson's war in Indochina impressed King with the complicity between domestic and international affairs that Du Bois had been studying since the 1890s: domestic racism's potential to feed into a misguided foreign policy. The age of empire had slipped ignominiously away, Du Bois noted, but the Cold War was reviving the old imperial reflexes. In King's judgment, the Vietnam War called upon poorer African Americans "in extraordinarily high proportions," forcing them to prosecute the wrong fight for the wrong reasons at the wrong time. It was an immoral and expensive crusade against Vietnamese communists when the battle for equality and civil rights in the United States was only beginning. In his person, his thinking and his speeches, Martin Luther King synthesized the ethics of the civil rights movements with the ethics of the burgeoning antiwar movement. "Advocacy of free elections in Europe by American officials is hypocrisy when free elections are not held in great sections of America," King had argued in an assault on one pillar of American Cold War strategy. King's opposition to the Vietnam War was directed toward another pillar. Martin Luther King received the Nobel Peace Prize in 1964, a critic rather than an expositor of American foreign policy, and a minister rather than a diplomat. Receiving a prize that previously had gone to presidents and to State Department officials added luster to King's eventual antiwar advocacy, and in 1965 King was already calling for a negotiated end to the Vietnam War. By

April 1967, Martin Luther King considered the United States "the greatest purveyor of violence in the world today."[16]

Horrified by what was happening in Vietnam, King offered an alternative vision of how the United States, the West and the developing world might be integrated. As with the younger Du Bois and with James Baldwin, King saw a special role for the African American, not just in American society or in American politics but in American foreign policy as well. Should the civil rights movement succeed in the United States, the African American or American Negro, as King put it, could pivot to the international cause of decolonization. As he wrote in his 1967 book *Where Do We Go from Here:*

> Ghana, Zambia, Tanganyika and Nigeria are so busy fighting their
> own battles against poverty, illiteracy and the subversive influence of
> neo-colonialism that they offer little hope to Angola, Southern Rho-
> desia and South Africa, much less to the American Negro. The hard
> cold facts today indicate that the hope of the people of color in the
> world may well rest on the American Negro and his ability to reform
> the structure of racist imperialism from within and thereby turn the
> wealth and technology of the West to the task of liberating the world
> from want.

THE WEST HERE is not the West of liberty and self-government. Nor is it the West of the Cold War burdened with the fight against communism in the colonial and postcolonial domains. It is a force for technological good, which can lift Americans and Africans out of poverty. The crux of King's argument, though, is not the eradication of poverty but the African American ability to reform the structure of racist imperialism from within; it was the achievement of dignity. That was King's struggle precisely, and local as the American civil rights movement might be—its advances signified often by the names of places such as Birmingham, Montgomery, Selma and Little Rock—the hope of the people of color in the world might depend on what was happening in these provincial Southern cities. That was King's argument.[17]

King's "Beyond Vietnam" speech at Riverside Church in New York City was among his most public dissents from the war. Given on April 4, 1967, the speech featured King's critique of foreign policy and domestic policy during the Vietnam War. Having taken the civil rights movement to the North in the mid-1960s, King saw in military spending the ruin of the American economy. Chicago and other cities to which African Americans had migrated from the South were not solving the problem of poverty in the 1960s. They were slipping into lower and lower stages of poverty. Noting this, King said in his speech that he "was increasingly compelled to see the war as an enemy of the poor and to attack it as such." This was one of the war's twisted priorities. Another was the American government's refusal to see independence and decolonization for what they were. King argued for a return to first principles and for a return to the West of liberty rather than a West of empire. Precisely because the Marquis de Lafayette had given George Washington the key to the Bastille, "we in the West must support these [developing world] revolutions . . . the Western nations that initiated so much of the revolutionary spirit of the modern world have now become the arch anti-revolutionaries." Finally, the obscenity of the war needed to yield to spiritual decency in America, which could only be realized through the true elimination of slavery and its aftermath. Here, King turned to the poet Langston Hughes, "that black bard of Harlem," as King put it, who had written:

> *O, yes,*
> *I say it plain,*
> *America never was America to me,*
> *And yet I swear this oath—*
> *America will be!*

America would be America if it found a way out of the war and a way to racial equality. The path beyond Vietnam led out from a poem poised between a segregated past and an anticipated alternative future.[18]

Other political figures, branching out from the civil rights movement of the early 1960s, journeyed in more radical directions. Martin Luther King had couched his criticisms of American society and foreign policy in the familiar vocabulary of Christianity and the Enlightenment, of rights and righteousness. He was a pastor, an activist and a citizen. Like Malcolm X, the globally renowned boxer Muhammad Ali would not serve in Vietnam. His was an act of conscience and of profound disaffection with the direction of American foreign policy. "No Vietcong ever called me a nigger," Ali explained. The Vietcong were not his enemy, and the US government did not have the moral authority to enlist Ali in its overseas empire. Ali's audience was not simply American: it was certainly global. Ali's friend Malcolm X was no bastard of the West experimenting with syntheses of African, American and Western elements. Refusing to see African Americans as a unique voice in Western civilization, Malcolm X was a fiery critic of the West, that nexus of civilization and crime. Consistent with the Nation of Islam that he joined from prison, Malcolm X accepted the thesis that African Americans "were produced by the white man," he said in a January 1965 speech. "Whenever you see somebody who calls himself a Negro, he's a product of Western civilization—not only Western civilization, but Western crime. The Negro, as he is called or calls himself in the West, is the best evidence that can be used against Western civilization today." Malcolm X was moving away from such stark categories, though not toward an embrace of Western civilization, when he was assassinated in 1965.[19]

Malcolm X's best-selling autobiography coincided with a general uncovering of non-Western foundations to American culture and history. Alex Haley, Malcolm X's interlocutor and coauthor, published the novel *Roots* in 1976, a story that traces an African American family from Africa to the United States. It was made into a popular television miniseries a year later. Between the appearance of *The Autobiography of Malcolm X* in 1965 and *Roots* in 1976 there was an explosive repositioning of the European, the ethnic, the White Anglo-Saxon Protestant (WASP) and the non-European in American culture. Non-Western, non-Anglo-Saxon roots were apparent everywhere, in a myriad of civil rights movements and in cultural initiatives that stemmed from the electric radicalism of the antiwar movement. One such initiative of the late 1960s, the Black Power movement, turned official Cold War strategy on its head. Whether it was Cuba's Castro or Vietnam's Ho Chi Minh, communism did not make an inevitable enemy of a postcolonial leader. Postcolonial leaders might be potential movement allies and the US government the adversary of black empowerment. International partnerships arose around a shared skepticism or shared hostility toward the American-led West, with Vietnam as shorthand for the evils of American foreign policy and for the white-supremacist impulse that described America's role in the world. The darkness of American foreign policy was the same under Republicans and Democrats, under Richard Nixon and Lyndon Johnson, for the heart of darkness was the West itself. "When you talk of Black Power," the Black Power leader Stokely Carmichael pointed out, "you talk of building a movement that will smash everything Western civilization has created." In October 1968, at the Olympics in Mexico City, two American athletes raised their fists in a Black Power salute. They were not commenting on Western civilization so much as offering high-profile dissent from pro forma rallying around the flag, just as Louis Armstrong had done in 1957.[20]

THE PROLIFERATING CHALLENGES to the West in the late 1960s and early 1970s left their imprint on American intellectual life and on American universities. Vietnam compelled many intellectuals not just to oppose the war but also to reexamine the foundations of American foreign policy. It was their duty to scrape away the rusting mythologies of American liberty. Their preferred framework was more the perfidy than the rise of the West. An initial wave of critical questioning was the "Wisconsin school," named after students and scholars affiliated with the University of Wisconsin at Madison. Two classics of the Wisconsin school were William Appleman Williams's monograph *The Tragedy of American Diplomacy* (1959) and Gabriel Kolko's *The Politics of*

War (1968). The Wisconsin school sought a demystification of American foreign policy. The drive for liberty was analyzed as ideological subterfuge, cover for the profit motive of the American business and governing elite: the truth of American foreign policy was economic and exploitative, while the rhetorical smokescreen was Jeffersonian and democratic. A linguistics professor from MIT rather than Wisconsin, Noam Chomsky raised the political temperature in a burst of writing and public speaking about Vietnam and American foreign policy. In *American Power and the New Mandarins* (1969), he turned his gaze on the evils of the West and on the evils of the Cold War university in the era of the Vietnam War, attacking the twisted politics of knowledge through which expertise had been put into uniform and sent into battle. If Cold War foreign policy was at fault for Vietnam and for other betrayals of democracy, the universities had to be at fault as well.[21]

None other than former academic administrator Dwight Eisenhower had predicted the travails of the Cold War university, and this was in 1961, when college campuses were relatively unperturbed. Eisenhower devoted a portion of his farewell address, in which he condemned the "military-industrial complex," to the threat of co-opted universities. His was very much a Cold War worry: "the free university, historically the foundation of free ideas and scientific discovery, has experienced a revolution. The prospect of domination of the nation's scholars with Federal employment, project allocations and the power of money is ever present—and is gravely to be regarded." The Vietnam War strained each of Eisenhower's points: the nation's scholars who sought and found federal employment administering the war; university projects underwritten by the government, some involving the latest in modern weaponry; and the loss of autonomy and ethical compass that proximity to power and money can induce. Many of Chomsky's academic colleagues in Cambridge—MIT's own Walt Whitman Rostow and seemingly half the Harvard faculty—had rushed to the side of Presidents Kennedy, Johnson and Nixon, whispering soothing words in the emperor's ear and camouflaging American military power in Vietnam and elsewhere as the responsibilities of the West. Eisenhower would not have seen it this way, but Chomsky and a legion of antiwar students did. The Cold War university and the Vietnam War were a deadly combination, which meant that Eisenhower had been on to something. The Cold War combination of power and knowledge was gravely to be regarded.[22]

American universities themselves responded vociferously to the war in Vietnam. At first, American universities were resisting themselves. David Halberstam's blockbuster 1972 history of the Vietnam War, *The Best and the Brightest,* offered an indictment of the war—the war as a massive policy failure—that was common enough in 1972. More to the point was his indictment, beginning with the book's title, of the universities of the 1950s. Himself a Harvard graduate, class of '55, Halberstam accused the Cold War university of stoking the vanity of American policymakers, flattering the Kennedys and the Bundys and the McNamaras, each of them a quiet American along the lines Graham Greene had anticipated. Academia's best and brightest started to break ranks in the 1960s. Showing the way, Berkeley erupted in 1964. Vietnam was not yet the flash point for Berkeley's students in 1964. The oppressiveness of Cold War anticommunism was the problem, and so too was the industrialized, capitalist society that protesting students accused the university of appeasing. Columbia blew up in 1968; race relations in New York City, race relations on campus and the ongoing war in Vietnam resulted in days of violent protest in Morningside Heights. Since 1964, Vietnam had come to occupy center stage. In May 1970, no end to war in sight, four students were killed and nine wounded at Kent State University when the Ohio National Guard fired upon a group of antiwar protestors. Not just the universities but the country at large seemed to be divided into enemy camps and at war with itself.[23]

When the Vietnam War terminated in 1975 (for the United States), the universities refused to turn back the clock to the 1950s. Many professors observed an apolitical inwardness on the part of their students in the late 1970s, an exhaustion with politics and a drifting back to the conventional worries about graduation and career. The killings at Kent

State were the end of one chapter, the nadir of the conflict between universities and the government, students and police. Away from the headlines and away from the protests, the academic transformation of the American universities did not wind down in 1975. It was slow and unspectacular at first, issuing from the ferment of the 1960s, and at its core was an altered view of the United States and of the West. The Western civilization curricula of the 1920s were aging. William McNeill had published *The Rise of the West* at a time when universities were a comfortable appendage of state power, happily inside the West, a legacy of the Cold War and World War II. All this West and all this Western civilization were viewed through a different lens in the 1960s. Back in the late nineteenth century, Charles Eliot Norton had justified the study of classical antiquity as the study of the commanding races: perhaps one studied command so that one might be in command; very likely any notion of a commanding race in the United States was a notion of the white race. In the 1970s, a critical interrogation of the previous generation's academic-political coordination was begun and nowhere with such force as in the humanities. The study of the West that had been synonymous with the defense of the West, some decades in the making by the 1960s, was to be put on trial.

In this trial, Edward Said was among the most hard-driving litigators. The son of an American citizen who lived in the Middle East, Said was born in 1935 to an Arab family. The father who held the American passport was a Protestant. With the establishment of the state of Israel out of mandate Palestine, Said's Jerusalem-based family lost its property and moved to Cairo. That was one dissonance in young Edward's life. Another was his education at an elite Cairo school generative of "the basic split in my life . . . between Arabic, my native language, and English, the language of my education and subsequent expression as a scholar and teacher," Said wrote in his 1999 memoir, *Out of Place*. Living outside of Europe, Said was schooled in the culture of the West, as if there were no other kind of education. Even his musical education—he was a gifted pianist—immersed him in "the rationale of the history of Western music with its schools, periods, developing genres." Across

Cairo, Said was witness to "the replacement of the [colonial] British institutions and individuals by the victorious Americans, the old empire giving way to the new." Such was the cultural-historical-political window through which Said came to know the Middle East after the Second World War. He was an insider with the vision of an outsider.[24]

The confusion of East and West sharpened for Said when he moved overseas. Having been sent to study in the United States in 1948, Said's sensation of "always being out of place" had a precursor in the veil depicted by Du Bois in *The Souls of Black Folk*. James Baldwin the stranger in the Swiss village believed, as did Said, that he was unable to escape the West and unable to feel at home in it. Said was not American born and his roots were Arab rather than African: he did not suffer from the same exclusions Du Bois and Baldwin did. Said was out of place in his own way. He completed his Bachelor of Arts at Princeton in 1957 and his doctorate at Harvard in 1975, a student of comparative literature. He began teaching at Columbia soon after, a scholar who had mastered the Western canon but whose assimilation of this canon set him apart from his older-generation teachers at Princeton and Harvard. Said wrote his dissertation on Joseph Conrad, a novelist of Polish descent who had been born in the Russian Empire. Conrad had to appropriate the English language before he could write his decentered fiction in it. An itinerant life among empires confronted Conrad with modern politics in his maritime career and with the human consequences of imperialism, which gave him his great fictional themes. Conrad the fiction writer was an ideal object of scrutiny for Said the critic and scholar. Conrad's 1899 novella *Heart of Darkness* laced the conquering, unsettling West with ambiguity, making interchangeable parts of civilization and barbarism, and as for so many late-twentieth-century readers, *Heart of Darkness* was commentary on the Vietnam War for Said. In 1979, Conrad's literary-political parable was reworked into the archetypal Vietnam film *Apocalypse Now*.[25]

Said published his own deconstruction of the West, *Orientalism*, in 1978. It was a detailed study of British and French colonialism, of Western imperialism, though anything but a standard history of empire or a standard work of literary criticism. In *Orientalism*, Said did not write military or economic history. He did not tally up Western gunboats or plumb the archives of the East India Company. Nor did he limit himself to the study of plot and symbolism in literary texts. As a graduate student, he had taken up new bodies of philosophy and theory on the discursive nature of power—that is, on the encapsulation of power relationships in language and images. For Said, literature and language were the weapons of French and British colonialism, which depended on a certain image of the East and a certain image of the West to achieve its practical ends. Economic and military power assisted in the elaboration of the relevant language and images, while colonially minded language and images reinforced the material power of the West and the basic subordination of the East. There was a political point to coding the West masculine—strong, active, dominant—and the East feminine—weak, passive, submissive. (And some of these dichotomies went all the way back to ancient Greece.) Culture almost decreed that in international politics the masculine West was destined to colonize the feminine East. *Orientalism* laid all of this out in demanding and impassioned prose.

For much of *Orientalism*, the Orient is Asia or the Middle East and the Occident, or the West, is Europe. Orient and Occident were figments of the scholarly or literary imagination, according to Said, and they were the fig leaves of Western imperialism. Said emphasizes "the *strength* of western cultural discourse" in and outside of the West. In modern history, Europe's military-technological assets—its hard-power strength—helped it to define the Orient, "and knowledge of the Orient, because generated out of strength, in a sense creates the Orient, the Oriental, his world." Much like Graham Greene's Alden Pyle, the West conquers because it feels entitled to conquest: "the essence of Orientalism," Said contends, "is the ineradicable distinction between western superiority and Oriental inferiority." Napoleon invaded Egypt, and with the spoils of his conquest he sponsored the academic study of the Middle East in France and in Europe. Unsurprisingly, this stilted academic endeavor "proved" the inferiority of the Orient.

In *Orientalism,* Said offers a patchwork quilt of East-West contrasts. One is the warlike zeal of us versus them. For the Orientalist scholar or writer, "the apocalypse to be feared was not the destruction of Western civilization but rather the destruction of barriers that kept East and West from each other." Then there is religion and "the Christian West," the crusading West. In the binary of Christianity versus Islam, Islam is "the very epitome of an outsider against which the whole of European civilization from the Middle Ages was founded." Another East-West barrier is racial, that of "white Occidentalism and colored Orientalism." In *Orientalism,* Said frequently reaches out to his readers in the present tense, past and present converging. He writes, for example, that "a white middle-class westerner believes it his human prerogative not only to manage the nonwhite world but also to own it." In many cases, as Said of course knew, this white middle-class westerner was the person reading *Orientalism.*[26]

Had *Orientalism* been only a book about Europe, its impact would have been mostly retrospective and scholarly. Said would have added a literary dimension to the enormous scholarship on empire building. In the mid-1970s, when Said was putting *Orientalism* together, France and Britain had dropped back from the imperial scene, their major colonies long gone. Only a handful of formally European colonies still remained. What gave *Orientalism* its savor and its political punch was Said's inclusion of the United States with France and Britain: "since World War II America has dominated the Orient, and approached it as France and Britain once did," Said writes. The American separation from Europe, the Wilsonian attempt to democratize European foreign policy, and the Cold War contrasts of Western liberty versus Soviet tyranny—Truman's contrasts, Eisenhower's contrasts, Kennedy's contrasts—were a nonsense version of modern history to Said. They were a fairy tale that Americans told themselves, or they were worse than that. The gift of liberty was, in fact, the serpentine discourse of empire. The military and financial power, the loyal scribes and the tropes of empire had simply emigrated from Europe to the United States, and under the dark star of American leadership, the West was still its ancient disrupting, mercenary and domineering self. The United States was the exact synthesis of the Christian West and the white West with "the conquering West" of Christopher Columbus.[27]

Said's most devastating indictment was of the American-led West. Europe had swallowed the world whole between 1815 and 1914. Its scholarship and literature and philosophy told this sordid tale. Then, as Said had sensed in his Cairo boyhood, the United States took the baton from Europe. Or, as Said wrote in *Orientalism*, "the period immediately following World War II [arrived] when the United States found itself in the position recently vacated by Britain and France." American foreign policy reflects the ruthlessness of the white middle-class westerner who wants both to manage and to own the nonwhite world. Writing in the first-person plural, Said condemned "our leaders and their intellectual lackeys." Writing as a US citizen and emissary from the Middle East, "as an American and as an Arab I must ask my reader not to underestimate the kind of simplified view of the world that a relative handful of Pentagon civilian elites have formulated for U.S. policy in the entire Arab and Islamic worlds." The scandal of Orientalist thinking is that it drives American universities and serves at the behest of American power. Once a European malady, Orientalism in America is happening in real time, with global repercussions.[28]

Edward Said's *Orientalism* was not the typical essay on American foreign policy. Said suggested no coherent alternative path on specific foreign-policy questions. He did not write about American Cold War strategy in the Middle East or elsewhere. His aim was bigger and more general. It was to unravel the identification of the United States with the West, to criminalize this identification and at the same time to prove that the West is nonexistent. The West was the product of a sickly imagination, and a monstrous West had summoned into being a monstrous East. The misdeeds of American foreign policy will cease only when there is no longer a West or an East. This was Said's policy prescription: "terrible reductive conflicts that herd people under falsely unifying rubrics like 'American,' 'the West,' or 'Islam,' and invent collective identities for large numbers of individuals who are actually quite diverse, cannot remain as potent as they are, and must be opposed." A professor at the university that had first fashioned the Western civilization curriculum, Said waved farewell to Western civilization in *Orientalism*, bidding this hateful anachronism good riddance. The West was, as Said wrote in a 2003 afterword to *Orientalism*:

> an ideological fiction, implying a sort of detached superiority for a handful of values and ideals, none of which has much meaning outside the history of conquest, immigration, travel and the mingling of peoples that gave the western nations their present mixed identities . . . this is especially true of the United States, which today cannot seriously be described except as a palimpsest of different values and cultures sharing a problematic history of conquest, exterminations, and of course major cultural and political achievements.

{NoIndent}SAID WAS TEARING down the ideological fiction of the West, detaching the West from its self-declared values and ideals. These are the ideological fictions. In place of the West and its shared history of achievement, conquest and exterminations, Said was offering the history of immigration, travel, the mingling of people and mixed identities. He wanted nothing black and white and no falsely held values and ideals. He wanted an endless rewriting, a moveable palimpsest of names and problem-ridden cultures rather than a leather-bound collection of stable and beloved traditions. What Columbia's Butler Library said the West was, was not what Said said it was. Said's impact on the humanities in the 1980s and 1990s is hard to exaggerate. *Orientalism* permanently dethroned books like William McNeill's *The Rise of the West*, and it permanently undermined the prestige of Western civilization curricula at American universities.[29]

ON THE AMERICAN Left, the Cold War policies of Truman, Kennedy and Lyndon Johnson did not survive the Vietnam War. Or if these policies survived, their cultural underpinnings did not. LBJ decided not to run for reelection in 1968, leaving the Democratic Party rudderless, and at the Chicago nominating convention antiwar protestors clashed with police on the city streets. They were clashing with the Cold War heritage of the Democratic Party. Between 1945 and 1968, Democrats held the White House for fifteen years, Republicans for eight, and by 1968 the Democratic Party was the party of the Cold War, a source for many Democrats more of shame than of pride. In November 1968, Eisenhower's former vice president won the election, and for eight tortuous years Vietnam was Richard Nixon's headache and that of his successor Gerald Ford. In the 1970s, the Democratic Party altered its foreign-policy mind-set, introducing a universalistic doctrine of human rights, without giving up on the Cold War. It was a doctrine attuned to a global era, a cause free from the prejudices and hierarchies of civilization and of Western civilization. Meanwhile, at the sharper edges of the antiwar movement, Edward Said's theses echoed in the critiques of American foreign policy. The critique was never accepted in full by the Democratic Party, but it began to transform the universities that had once propelled the idea of the West into American foreign policy. More immediately, Vietnam polarized American foreign policy. The moderate, continuity-oriented Republicans of Eisenhower's day were losing their hold, while Democrats were eager for a new departure. For years, the curse of the Vietnam War was there be exorcised from American politics and from American foreign policy alike.

Before the Democrats could retake the White House, once Lyndon Johnson had lost it, they were forced to reckon with the foreign policy of Richard Nixon. Nixon was hated on the Left for perpetuating the Vietnam War and for his personality and cultural style, but Vietnam was only one part of his foreign policy, and it was the one most predetermined by the decisions of Johnson and Kennedy. Skilled at diplomacy, Nixon was as much the Republican internationalist as he was the fire-breathing anticommunist of the Eisenhower era. In the 1940 election, he had cast his vote for Wendell Willkie, the Republican advocate of one-world internationalism. Running for Congress in a California district strongly opposed to the Marshall Plan, Nixon had supported the plan anyway, and in his mind's eye he was a "peacemaker," the son of a Quaker family. (In the eyes of the antiwar movement, he was of course the exact opposite, a warmonger with fascist leanings.) Yet it was Nixon who in February 1972 went to China and in 1971 and 1972 achieved some significant diplomatic progress with the Soviet Union— the Quadripartite Agreement that resolved the status of Berlin, and then two arms-control agreements that were hashed out between Nixon and General Secretary Leonid Brezhnev. Nixon had none of Kennedy's talent for speaking poetically about Western liberty. He could not have moved a crowd in Berlin as Kennedy had in 1963, and since 1963 the Vietnam War had changed the attitudes of Berliners to the United States, but Nixon was also aware of the price foreign-policy messianism could exact, as were Lyndon Johnson's critics. Nixon was a president, as many had been before him, eager to see the United States in the role of mediator, inching international relations away from conflict through deliberation. Whatever the contradictions of his Vietnam policy, Nixon's achievements in this regard were nontrivial.[30]

The Democratic politician able to capture the post-Vietnam political spirit, the Democrats' anti-Nixon, was Jimmy Carter. Winner of the 1976 presidential election, Carter pursued a global rather than an East/West foreign policy without at all giving up on the West. The man from Plains, Georgia, who was elected president in the republic's bicentennial anniversary year was an avid Cold Warrior even if he was not always recognized as such. He was a graduate of the Naval Academy, an engineer on nuclear submarines, and nowhere did he favor surrender to the Soviet East. The Vietnam War had been lost long before Carter came to the White House. The policy of détente, of relaxing relations with the Soviet Union, which Carter was not unhappy to maintain, had been pioneered by Richard Nixon and Henry Kissinger. Nixon had been the one to go to China some thirteen years after W. E. B. Du Bois posed with Mao. Détente's set-piece achievement, the Helsinki Final Act, was negotiated pre-Carter in the early 1970s. It guaranteed Europe's borders, which had been contested since 1945, and committed an unbelieving Soviet Union at least nominally to human rights. Helsinki was a surprising oasis of agreement between the

United States and the Soviet Union in the desert of Cold War violence, deception and one-upmanship. (Henry Kissinger found the wording and the provisions of the Helsinki Final Act and the act itself so ridiculous that its authors "can write in Swahili for all I care.") The Helsinki Final Act was signed by the Republican President Gerald Ford in August 1975. To the extent that Carter tolerated pragmatic engagement with the Soviet Union, he could rightly say that he was acting within the fold of his Republican predecessors, Ford and Nixon.[31]

President Carter's scholar-patriot of the West was Zbigniew Brzezinski. Brzezinski had been born in Warsaw in 1928. His diplomat father brought the family to Canada ten years later. After studies at McGill University in Montreal, Zbigniew Brzezinski made his way to Harvard University. There, he wrote a dissertation on Sovietology and in 1956 coauthored *Totalitarian Dictatorship and Autocracy* with the German-born political scientist Carl Friedrich. Brzezinski worked briefly at the State Department's Office of Policy Planning in 1966, in the midst of the escalating war in Vietnam, and he was the anticommunist anchor of Carter's National Security Council. As national security advisor, Brzezinski was neither opposed to détente and to some level of diplomatic engagement with the Soviets nor willing to condone the Soviet-dominated status quo in Eastern Europe (despite Helsinki). Nonacceptance of Soviet rule in Eastern Europe was long-standing American policy—notwithstanding Gerald Ford's career-ending assertion of Eastern European independence in a 1976 presidential debate with Carter. For the Soviet Union and for the United States, events were starting to move unpredictably in the late 1970s. The arrival of a Polish pope in Rome, John Paul II, in 1978 coincided with the fact of a Polish-born national security advisor in the White House, both of them enthusiasts of a postcommunist Eastern Europe. Ripples in the deceptively placid surface of Eastern European politics were starting to appear.

Carter's foreign-policy innovation was not détente, per se, but to take seriously a preexisting investment in human rights. He pursued a preexisting aspect of détente that had never much moved Nixon or

Kissinger. A candidate who rode a surge of moral purity to the White House, a modern president uncommonly open about his Christian piety, Carter had been elected to cleanse American foreign policy of Vietnam and domestic politics of Watergate. He was supposed to make things better. Human rights appealed to Carter the idealist and to Carter the Sunday-school teacher. They were God-given and consonant with the highest ideals of the American republic, one of the truths that had been declared self-evident in the 1770s (without the qualifying adjective *human*). Best of all, Jefferson's inalienable human rights were close at hand in the 1970s. With the Helsinki Final Act, the West promised noninterference with Europe's borders, including those Stalin and Churchill had penciled in at Yalta. This was a great accomplishment for Soviet diplomacy, and Moscow could interpret Helsinki as the final acceptance of a Soviet sphere of influence in Europe, which it was not. But from East Berlin to the Baltics, from Stettin to Trieste, the Soviet Union's sway would not be militarily challenged. The West had made a serious concession and in return received a Soviet promise about honoring human rights, a promise made in bad faith. Once it was on the books, however, the promise of human rights behind the Iron Curtain took on a life of its own.

If the Carter administration hit upon a human rights bonanza in Eastern Europe, the application of human rights was by definition global. These were the rights of the human race after all. They could not only be applicable in the West. Otherwise, they would have been Western rights—*civis romanus sum*. The concept of human rights helped Carter to thread a policy needle. Human rights were a provocation to communism more moral than proxy wars and espionage. They were an affront to the Soviet Union and to communist China. Neither political system could survive the adoption of a free press, freedom of speech and assembly, freedom of religion. Human rights were thus a tool of influence within communist countries and a bridge to dissident movements. Human rights also promised an American foreign policy liberated from LBJ's and Nixon's quasi-imperial defense of the West. Carter focused less on the military containment of communism and more on decency and solidarity as universal imperatives. For Carter, the beatitudes—from the Sermon on the Mount, the call to help the poor and the downtrodden—had a practical meaning in the exercise of foreign policy. A modest example was Carter's shift on South Africa in which he endorsed "majority rule" over Apartheid, in part because of African American advocacy on the issue and in part because Apartheid was such a stark repudiation of human rights. Without giving him any observable foreign-policy victories between 1976 and 1980, Carter's advocacy of human rights had a second life after 1992, underscoring the foreign policy of Democratic and Republican administrations alike (until 2016). For his human rights and his efforts at conflict resolution, as president and after his presidency, Carter won a Nobel Peace Prize in 2002.

Carter's first and only term as president concluded in a minor key. The long twilight struggle Kennedy had called the Cold War was by no means brightening in the late 1970s, even if the Vietnam War was over. Vietnam was one point on the narrative of Western decline that haunted the 1970s. Another was the energy crisis, the spike in costs that disrupted the economies of the United States and Western Europe. The transition away from the broad-based middle-class economic growth of the 1950s and 1960s was traumatic, and the energy crisis, which was willed in part by countries in the Middle East, gave the impression of a West unable to control its own destiny. Carter waged a losing political battle to correct this impression. A nervous president, he struggled to reverse the impression of decline, making him not so much the anti-Nixon as the anti-Kennedy. He could not get the country moving again. He could not locate a new frontier. Stagflation and foreign-policy humiliation converged on a word that was vaguely Spenglerian—*malaise*. The Carter presidency evoked the malaise of the West. Environmental degradation and the alleged death of New York City in 1975, among many other American cities, including Washington, DC, could be easily added to the roster of all that was going wrong. The overstretched West seemed unsustainable in the 1970s, a verdict with which Carter appeared to agree. He turned down the thermostat in the White House and wore sweaters to demonstrate his humility and thrift in hard times.

International events filled in the portrait of a faltering West. Revolutionaries in Iran were openly defiant of the United States. The 1979 Iranian Revolution was incomprehensible to most Americans, though it was transparently anti-American and anti-Western. The US Embassy was overrun, its employees taken hostage and made into mass-media monikers of revolutionary propaganda. Also in 1979, the Soviet Union invaded Afghanistan. Dogged diplomacy had secured the Cold War borders for Europe in 1975. Elsewhere borders were still in flux and the Soviets on the prowl. The American Left did not fault Carter for leading the West poorly. If anything, Carter was too much the old-type Cold Warrior for the Left, too much the alumnus of the Naval Academy. He had decent instincts but had not been creative or effective enough to change gears. On the Right, Carter was not enough of a Cold Warrior, symbolizing liberal weakness and a will to surrender that amounted in the 1970s to a collective failure of nerve. The election of 1980 pitted Jimmy Carter against Ronald Reagan, the former scourge of the antiwar radicals in Berkeley when he had been the governor of California and a conservative defender of the West.

The 1980 election would by no means retire the questions that had held center stage in the 1960s and 1970s. There would be no going back to the early Cold War, when the country had a single, containment-driven foreign policy, a sizable political center and a high degree of bipartisan consensus, upheld by the Asiatic enemies in the East. There would be no going back to the simplistic historical narrative whereby the United States had sprung from Europe's loins, a fortunate child of the West. There would be no going back to the time before the hard questions Malcolm X had learned to ask in Washington, DC, to research in prison and to convey to bigger and bigger audiences through the spoken word. There would be no going back to John F. Kennedy's ease of communication in Berlin, a hero among heroes, and his reduction of American foreign policy to the rise of the West. To too many people the American-led West was troubling, strange, wicked and had either gone far off course in Indochina or displayed its true colors in the jungles of Vietnam. Nor were the worried questions about the West confined to the Left and to the critics of the Vietnam War. Many American conservatives had spent the 1960s asking questions, too. Not even Reagan's victory in 1980, welcome as it was on the Right, could quiet the conservative premonition of a West on the verge of self-destruction.

5

The Suicide of the West?
1963–1992

> . . . family, community, church, country and, at the farthest
> remove, civilization—not civilization in general but this
> historically specific civilization, of which *I* am a member.
>
> —JAMES BURNHAM, *THE SUICIDE OF THE WEST*, 1964

RONALD REAGAN WAS never anything other than optimistic about the West. In this he could draw on a long presidential tradition. Reagan was sure that American foreign policy should promote liberty and self-government and equally sure that liberty and self-government were the wave of the future. A devout Jeffersonian. Reagan also shared the mediating and the messianic leanings of Teddy Roosevelt and Woodrow Wilson, seeking enhanced military strength as the elder Roosevelt had, seeking to display this strength and at the same time affirming a negotiated peace as Wilson had tried to do at Versailles: Wilson's Fourteen Points inform Reagan's foreign policy. Reagan adored FDR precisely because FDR had been such a fearless warrior for democracy, the savior of Western liberty at its moment of maximum peril. Reagan sympathized with Truman, Eisenhower and JFK—with the Truman who contained Soviet expansion, with the Eisenhower who kept up containment around the globe and with the Kennedy who youthfully captured a rising West in Berlin and at home. For Reagan's electorate, his optimism about the West was a return of sorts, a welcome erasure of Vietnam and the 1960s, a restoration of the strategic clarity that had imposed itself on American foreign policy on December 7, 1941, that day of infamy and transformation. One of the reasons Reagan beat Carter in 1980 was Carter's characteristic worry, his dogged intuition that the America of the 1970s had gone terribly astray. Reagan had learned from FDR's mantra: happy days are here again.

Reagan's optimism acquired a retrospective legitimacy from events that occurred after he left the White House in January 1989. The course of events was circuitous. In 1981 and 1982, the United States and the Soviet Union were in mutual peril, with the United States pressuring Moscow and with the Kremlin a revolving door of geriatric (and hard-line) leaders. Mikhail Gorbachev's arrival in 1985 was an opening for Reagan and for those in Eastern Europe and the Soviet Union who sensed the weakening of the old order. Reagan's unexpected receptivity to diplomatic engagement with Gorbachev gave Gorbachev political cover back in Moscow, but Gorbachev could not balance a declining Soviet economy with the maintenance of control over Eastern Europe and the many restive populations of the Soviet Union. What happened in 1989 shocked everyone—from the streets of Poland, to the corridors of power in Moscow, to the cubicles of the CIA. Eastern Europe broke away from a Soviet Union too passive and too confused to act, and overnight a unified Germany was in NATO. A moment later the Soviet Union was no more. This was not the rise of the West: it was something more consequential. It was the unconditional surrender of the East (minus China) and the ideological victory of the West, or perhaps it would be more accurate to say civilizational victory, even if civilization was far less common a cultural and political category in 1989 than it had been in the 1940s and 1950s. A Reagan administration official would equate the end of the Cold War with the end of history itself.

Reagan's optimism obscured much history that was not triumphant. It obscured the political divisions over Vietnam, which by the 1970s were divisions about American politics, American culture, American society. Reagan was a polarizing president in the 1980s, just as he had been a polarizing governor of California in the late 1960s and early 1970s. At the Reagan-era universities, the culture wars signaled the discontents of many students and professors. They would not to endorse Reagan or the Cold War as the United States had learned to fight it. They would not flatter the overzealous ego of the West. Academics did not own the culture of the 1980s by any means, but the multiculturalism of the sixties-era rights revolutions and the questions about the West that had been asked by Du Bois, Baldwin, King and many others flashed through American culture at large in the 1980s—its music and its literature, its movies and television shows, its sense of history and the common good. Partially in response to a culture in flux, the conservative movement from which Reagan's thinking and his campaign had emerged thrilled to Reagan's presence in the White House while despairing about the direction of Reagan's America, which was ever drifting away from the ideals and the hierarchies of the Columbian Republic. Unlike Kennedy's or Truman's, Reagan's optimism about the West was conservative. It was not a bipartisan affiliation, and it was everywhere contested.

Unifying a figure as he was for conservatives, Reagan was also anomalous as an American conservative, and to a degree he was anomalous in his attitude toward the West. He was an optimistic internationalist who had been a New Deal Democrat well into his twenties. The American Right, however, had a long shadow history of anti-internationalism. Eisenhower had quelled it in the 1952 presidential election, World War II and the Cold War having altered the strategic calculus across the political spectrum. By 1992, a semiserious contender for the Republican nomination was Pat Buchanan. At the convention that nominated President George H. W. Bush, Reagan's vice president, as the Republican candidate running for a second term, Buchanan gave a barnstorming speech about the depravity of American culture and of American liberalism. Buchanan's chief object of scorn was internationalism: he wanted a West not so much of liberty and self-government as of Christian piety and ethnic Europeanness. Buchanan's political anger had roots in the postwar conservative despair, in the conservatism that was not Reaganesque and in all the conservatism that was Spenglerian, nostalgic and declinist. The most interesting twentieth-century conservative book on American foreign policy and the West was titled not *The Rise of the West*, as McNeill had dubbed his academic monograph, but *The Suicide of the West*, and *The Suicide of the West* was published in 1964. On the Left, it was the very power of the West that came to rankle. (See Edward Said's *Orientalism*.) On the Right, the decline of the West, the long predicted final sunset lodged in the very word *west*, was often the most disturbing scenario, if not to the Californian who promised morning in America on the campaign trail and who promised still more improbably a new dawn for the West, were he to be elected in the 1980 election.

PESSIMISM ABOUT THE West was rampant in the postwar conservative movement. The book that inspired the movement, passages of which Ronald Reagan would memorize, was Wagnerian in its gloom. Like so many other big twentieth-century conservative books, *Witness*, which was published in 1952, was a book about the West. Its author, Whittaker Chambers, had fallen into communism as a Columbia undergraduate, having been among the first students in the Columbia great-books program. Chambers was a communist believer long before the Great Depression. In the early 1930s, he was confident that the capitalist West was collapsing. When he agreed to be an agent of Soviet espionage, he was tasked with aiding the revolution from Washington, DC. Starting with FDR's election in 1932, Chambers directed a network of Washington-based American spies. All the while, as Chambers recounts in *Witness*, he was suffering the moral contradictions of Stalin's Soviet Union. Then his eyes opened to the truth of communism and its murderous pursuit of equality. *Witness* narrates his turning from communist conviction as an act of Christian devotion: Chambers patterned *Witness* on the *Confessions* of Augustine. In the late 1930s, having broken away from Moscow and having become a Quaker, he resurfaced as a journalist in Henry Luce's *Time/Life* media empire. His beat was culture and foreign affairs. By then a political and cultural conservative, Chambers went to work for *Time* in Rockefeller Center. He assigned himself the Herculean job of educating an unreceptive American public in the evils of communism.

Par for the course in the late 1940s, Chambers saw the Cold War as a stridently East-West conflict. Yet for Chambers, the military configurations, the balance of forces and the nuclear logic for this conflict were all secondary. As he had been trained to do at Columbia, Chambers explored modern life through the lens of civilization, which is the lens he applied to the Cold War. On the one side was a communist civilization armed and predatory and eager to disperse the poison gas of revolution, the false promise of proletarian virtue, the dangerous allure of international brotherhood. On the other was a Western civilization capitalist and democratic. It was also Christian or Judeo-Christian, which for Chambers was the heart of the story. Civilizations inspire devotion and sacrifice, in his view, and people must be willing to fight and die for them. In the 1930s and 1940s, with a victorious Soviet Union and Mao's newborn communist China, communist civilization had this power in abundance. Communism had overtaken imperial Russia in 1917 and China in 1949. The West had communist sympathizers, often more educated than working-class, of the kind Chambers himself had been in the 1920s and 1930s. Ideas in the communist orbit were fashionable, while intellectual conservatism was moribund in the 1940s. To Chambers, this meant that the West had lost confidence in its itself, that its Christian faith had dissipated in the nineteenth century and evaporated in the twentieth. The West's own secularism and materialism were the agents of its decline. As goes the spirit, so goes the civilization.

Chambers used his position at *Time* to diagnose the disease and to evangelize for the cure. The West needed to restore itself, and the United States needed to restore the West. With these premises in mind, Chambers was the primary author of a seven-part series of opulently illustrated historical sketches for *Life* magazine. A history of Western culture, it was among the most popular items the Luce press ever published, coming out in 1947 and 1948. Because of their popularity, these articles appeared in book form as well. A subheading to the series title read "America is heir and hope of the West's civilization," which was Chambers's core polemical point. He narrated the rise of the West in a manner similar to McNeill's *The Rise of the West:* an enterprising, entrepreneurial civilization that spanned the commercial flowering of the Venetian Republic and the advent of American democracy. This was the vigorous, restless West, and unsurprisingly one of Chambers's heroes was Christopher Columbus. Much more than McNeill, though, Chambers put religion in the foreground of the West's story. The West had been fueled and held together by faith. Chambers gave pride of place to Protestantism, and despite his private reservations about capitalism, which Chambers disliked as much as an anticommunist as he had as a communist, he attributed creativity to the West's skill at trade and commerce. There was more than an echo of the Columbian Republic in the review of Western culture for *Life* written by this alumnus of Columbia University. It was a portrait that would have been acceptable—standard fare in many ways—in the 1890s.[1]

Chambers's hopes for a conservative movement followed from his despair about a weakening of Western culture in the 1950s. Despair gives *Witness* its thematic architecture, which is probably the most Spenglerian book an American could ever write. In it, Chambers referred to the West as sick, asking "whether this sick society, which we call Western Civilization, could in its extremity still cast up a man whose faith in it was so great that he would voluntarily abandon those things which men hold good, including life, to defend it." The West had been ravaged by the anonymity of the modern city, a claim that dominated Spengler's *Decline of the West* (and Hannah Arendt's *The Origins of Totalitarianism*), by an obsession with buying and selling and by the barbarism of unbelief. The Christian West had already been reduced to a wasteland, "The Wasteland" being a 1922 poem of T. S. Eliot. What had once been bright and beautiful and whole in Europe was "a heap of broken imagines" in Eliot's unforgettable language. Chambers could not have agreed more, and for this reason he was convinced that the Soviet Union would be victorious in the Cold War. It believed so fervently in Stalin and in the communist creed. *Witness* was a Dosto-evskian conversion narrative, overwrought with piety and ideas, and an eight-hundred-page political pamphlet. Chambers retraced the epis-tles of Paul, another convert and martyr, by contrasting the light of Christianity with the darkness of communism. Much as Paul's epistles presumed a faltering pagan world, Chambers's spiritual melodrama re-quired a faltering West, and Chambers rushed to get *Witness* out in 1952. Even if he disliked Eisenhower, which he did, Chambers still wanted his much-anticipated book to tip the scales in the Republicans' favor. In Chambers's maximalist reasoning, a vote for Adlai Stevenson, Eisenhower's Democratic opponent, was a vote for communism.[2]

A despairing Chambers instilled the conservative movement with his total antipathy to the Left. An ex-communist at war with the Soviet Union, he was no less at war with the American Left. In his opinion, the Left was traveling the road from socialism to communism. The true spirit of the New Deal inclined toward communism. One of Cham-bers's American partners in espionage had been Alger Hiss, a distin-guished New Dealer and rising star at the State Department. Dean Acheson and Harry Truman had been supportive when Hiss was first accused of being a spy for the Soviet Union. For this and other reasons, Chambers did not consider FDR, Truman and their foreign-policy teams the gallant protectors of the West. They may have gone through the motions. They may have been superficially anticommunist, but as figureheads of the American Left they had knowingly or unknowingly undone the lock, thrown open the gate and let Stalin's Trojan horse into the Western citadel. The American Left had done the same, mak-ing it into an enemy of the Christian West more local and lethal than the Soviet Union, Chambers thought. The American Left had access to the government, to the media, to the universities: its gurus were cele-brated on college campuses, its writers had infiltrated Hollywood, its folk singers played to adoring crowds in Carnegie Hall. By weakening these crucial institutions of culture and governance, the Left was engi-neering the breakup of the West from within. Unknowingly, perhaps,

Truman and Acheson were assisting in the death of the West. Marginally preferable to a Democrat, Eisenhower was nevertheless a politician and foreign-policy president in Truman's and Acheson's image.

Chambers was as gloomy as he was because of his unusual definition of the West. Anything but a Jeffersonian, he stood on the margins of the American political tradition, thoroughly suspicious of the Enlightenment. In his view, the Enlightenment had brought an arid secularism in its wake. It had mocked religion, eviscerated scripture and elevated the arrogance of scientists above the humility of the pious. Secularism, the forgetting of God, was responsible for Marx and for the Bolshevik Revolution. With the Cold War battle of faith, a creeping secularism was taking over even those quarters of American life that claimed to be conservative. Moderate Republicans like Eisenhower or Nelson Rockefeller were really liberals in disguise. They were too at ease with "the enlightened, articulate elite which, to one degree or another, has rejected the religious root of the civilization—the roots without which it is no longer Western Civilization, but a new order of beliefs, attitudes and mandates," Chambers wrote in a 1954 letter to the conservative intellectual William F. Buckley Jr. In the second year of the Eisenhower administration, everything for Chambers was still going wrong. As he had from his teenage years and student days, Chambers breathed "the vapors of the perishing West" throughout the 1950s. He died in 1961 no less despondent than he had been in 1952 or 1929.[3]

Chambers and the conservative movement were condemned to semipeaceful coexistence with Eisenhower in the 1950s. The movement did not like Ike, and Ike had little need for a conservative movement and little interest in one. Eisenhower aspired to a national unity beyond party, and the parochialism of movement politics was anathema to him. His military background, his service in World War II, placed him somewhere outside the Republican Party. In foreign policy, Eisenhower could draw on a bipartisanship of the willing for which the relevant division was more internationalist-isolationist than Republican-Democrat or liberal-conservative. A Republican internationalist like Eisenhower could harken back to the Republican internationalists of the 1920s and the Nobel Prize–winning secretary of state Elihu Root, a conservative and a spirited internationalist. Or Eisenhower might look to William Howard Taft, Philander Knox, Henry Cabot Lodge, Charles Evans Hughes, Frank B. Kellogg, Henry Stimson and Elihu Root's beloved Council on Foreign Relations, which had preserved a Wilsonian internationalism after World War I, helping to make internationalists of the country at large. Eisenhower's secretary of state, John Foster Dulles, was an active member of the Council on Foreign Relations while a corporate lawyer in the 1930s and 1940s. So too was his brother Allen prior to his job as Eisenhower's CIA director. Eisenhower may have been more willing to threaten the use of nuclear weapons and more amenable to covert action than Truman, but he agreed entirely with the twin responsibilities of containing the Soviet Union—to hold the line and to show restraint, to prevent the spread of communism and to respect certain Soviet interests in order to prevent nuclear war. Eisenhower calmly equated containment with the survival and flowering of Western civilization. It could all be done in a moderate, bipartisan fashion.

Thus, in the 1950s, the conservative movement was fighting communism and fighting for a post-Eisenhower, post–New Deal America. The conservatives around Chambers and Buckley worried greatly about the geopolitical weakness of the West. Too often the West had capitulated to the Soviet Union, they thought. The most damning examples were the Yalta and Potsdam conferences through which the Soviet Union had imposed a sphere of influence in Europe. This made the West complicit in the unjust division of Central Europe and the Soviets' enslavement of such Central European capitals as Prague, Budapest and Warsaw. With this enslavement came the massive persecution of Christians—Protestant, Catholic and Orthodox alike. American conservatives rallied behind Hungary's Cardinal Mindszenty, whom the communist regime had tortured. From 1956 to 1971, József Mindszenty was granted political asylum at the US Embassy in Budapest, a martyr to Soviet communism and a conservative hero in the United States. Another conservative hero was John Birch, an American Baptist missionary and US Army captain killed by communists in China in 1945, a much mythologized life and a much mythologized death. The hard-right anticommunist John Birch Society was founded in 1958. For many conservatives, the "loss" of China was a political tragedy, the grievous disruption of decades of American investment and missionary activity. Onward marched the conquering and godless communist soldier. With the British and French European empire retreating after the war, communism was advancing in Asia, claiming China, dominating one-half of Korea and expelling the French from North Vietnam. In these places, the recessional of the West was obvious. When Hungarians rose up against the Soviet occupation and for inclusion in the West in 1956, the United States confirmed conservative fears by doing nothing to help them. Eisenhower was as weak as the Democrats he so cheerfully resembled.

The second front for the conservative movement was the home front. Whittaker Chambers had outlined the basic conservative position: that the entire American Left was either so naive or so socialistic that it was a fifth column. The West's string of defeats—in Europe and in Asia—could only be explained by internal failure. The turncoat Alger Hiss had staffed President Roosevelt at Yalta. He and how many other communists had bored in at the State Department? At the White House? At the Department of Defense? Wisconsin's Republican senator Joseph McCarthy may have been crude, but if an ignoramus he was a useful ignoramus in the eyes of the conservative movement, and a necessary one. He would clear the Aegean stables of a compromised American government. He and others would have to sweep away the detritus of the New Deal and of the Alger Hiss–type bureaucrat with New Deal platitudes on his lips and treason in his heart. For four years, from 1950 to 1954, McCarthy railed at the Truman and Eisenhower administrations. When the McCarthyite net fell on Eisenhower himself, the conservative intellectual Russell Kirk rushed to Eisenhower's defense. "He is a golfer," Kirk explained about the president—and therefore (in Kirk's syllogism) incapable of being a communist. Political lines were sufficiently tangled, however, for Richard Nixon, an unknown congressman who committed himself to Chambers's version of events—that Alger Hiss was a spy for the Soviet Union, that Chambers was an honorable anticommunist—to rise to the vice presidency in 1952. Nixon's national career began in the trenches of the domestic anticommunist combat.[4]

A separate though related strand of 1950s American conservatism, libertarianism, had its origins in Europe. In the 1930s, a group of renegade economists in Vienna broke from the left-leaning orthodoxies they attributed to their profession and to the big-government spirit of the times. The so-called Vienna school disdained statist direction of the economy. With the totalitarian Soviet Union and Nazi Germany as cautionary examples, they celebrated individual and market freedoms not just as the catalysts of economic growth but also as the pillars of Western liberty, which was capitalist rather than socialist. They had happened on a new way to defend the West: the preservation of liberty through free-market economic policy was another. Several members of the Vienna school emigrated to Britain in the late 1930s, and over time their ideas and several of the school's most gifted exponents emigrated to the United States. One of these refugees from Vienna, Friedrich Hayek, published the *Road to Serfdom* in 1944, its title true to Hayek's alarming argument. Hayek worried about the "entire abandonment of the individualist tradition which has created Western civilization." His manifesto on Western liberty captivated conservative readers in the United States, merging the global problem of communism with its local manifestations, the Sino-Soviet bloc abroad with the welfare state at home. How was the United States to get off the road to serfdom and get back on the road to freedom? That was the question. Hardly mainstream in the 1950s, even on the Right, libertarianism was destined to have a profound influence on American foreign policy and on American norms of globalization in the 1990s and the early twenty-first century. What Hayek considered the genesis of Western civilization, the market's freedoms and the individual's rights, would have its global moment after 1991.[5]

Back in the 1950s, the locus of the conservative movement was *National Review,* an idiosyncratic magazine, saturated in discussions of the West. Ronald Reagan was a very early subscriber. Whittaker Chambers's correspondent and friend William F. Buckley Jr. founded *National Review* in 1955. However much he admired Chambers, Buckley was not a naysayer aghast at the sickness of Western civilization. He was enamored of Western civilization and enjoyed defending it in politics and culture, in public debate, in his prolific writing and on television. Buckley was a Catholic graduate of Yale, class of '50, whose undergraduate immersion left him cold. He documented his miseducation in a 1951 memoir-polemic titled *God and Man at Yale: The Superstitions of "Academic Freedom."* It was a book that lamented the lazy secularism and New Deal chic of America's elite universities. These universities should be teaching students the Western tradition, Buckley believed, which was faith in God and an appreciation of economic and political liberty. Yale's alumni agreed with him on this elementary point, Buckley was sure. The not especially big problem, Buckley contended, was the left-wing professoriat. Here, the alumni should band together to reorient Yale—to bring the real West back, as it were. Put in such stark terms, Buckley's argument could seem somehow un-American, a reduction of free speech to superstition, but in one sense Buckley was right about the past. Since the seventeenth century, fostering civilizational commitments in students had been the common practice of most American universities, mixing classical antiquity, Christianity and the modern West (broadly construed). The Western civilization curricula of the 1920s were a variation on an old theme. In *God and Man at Yale,* Buckley subordinated academic freedom to the university's right (not without historical precedent) to teach its students the traditions of a single civilization.

Via *National Review,* Buckley planned a Republican Party more capable of defending the West. He followed *God and Man at Yale* with *McCarthy and His Enemies* in 1954, an apologia for the marauding Wisconsin senator. McCarthy was not tilting at windmills in Buckley's view. The communist disease had to be excised if domestic American politics was to be mended and if American foreign policy was to exchange failure for success. To the conservatives gathered around

National Review, Buckley sketched a foreign policy beyond the compromises of Eisenhower and his fellow Democrats. The West needed
to push harder against Soviet and Chinese power. It could shore up its
internal strength by replacing the welfare state with economic liberty,
by standing up for itself culturally and by acknowledging and celebrating its Judeo-Christian heritage. Buckley's conservative defense of the
West entailed a rejection of the civil rights movement of the 1950s
and of decolonization overseas. A 1957 *National Review* editorial proclaimed "the cultural superiority of white over Negro," and a 1960
editorial defended white rule in South Africa, proof of the historian
Thomas Borstelmann's point that "the tradition of white supremacy in
the United States was embedded in a broader global pattern of white
control of people of color." Western civilization connoted whiteness
for Buckley. When he argued that the West should be more assertive
about its mission, during the Cold War and during decolonization,
he meant that the West should avoid apologies and concessions. The
segregated American South and the white South African government
were allies in the battle against communism, and they were cherished
outposts of Western civilization in Buckley's understanding. In 1965,
Buckley took up these themes in a televised debate with James Baldwin
at the University of Cambridge. The students sided with Baldwin.[6]

When Eisenhower left the White House in January 1961, the
conservative movement had the solace of a Democratic president to
oppose, but it also had to contend with the death of conservative leadership. The New Deal was establishment consensus, and establishment
consensus was the New Deal. Even the mainline Protestant churches
had adopted the era's ambient progressivism, conservatives feared.
Long-held national security doctrines set the tone: containment plus a
ritualized US-Soviet diplomacy, the summitry of presidents and Soviet
general secretaries shaking hands and sitting down together. Stalemate
in Korea was emblematic—to movement conservatives—of a stalled
Cold War. Continuity had decreed that Richard Nixon run on the
Republican ticket in 1960, the Eisenhower administration in perpe-
tuity. Continuity took on another shape when John F. Kennedy won

the election, vowing to preserve the spirit of Truman, FDR, Wilson—and Eisenhower. Kennedy consulted with Eisenhower on how best to conduct foreign policy: they understood one another well. Conservatives worried that Kennedy, with his magical youth and his golden tongue, would define liberty as some mix of the welfare state, of a secular (modern) culture and of a Cold War posture conditioned more to compromise than to confrontation. Thus would he lead a supine West untutored in Soviet evil. The conservatives had already lost the universities by 1960. God and Western man were invisible on Ivy League campuses, and these same universities were the wholesale suppliers of Kennedy administration officials. McGeorge Bundy, JFK's national security advisor, a Yale alumnus and a Harvard dean, had written one of the most savage reviews of Buckley's *God and Man at Yale*.[7]

Conservative anxiety contrasted with the official triumphalism of the early 1960s. In 1963, William McNeill might applaud the rise of the West in print and be applauded for his learning and enthusiasm. Kennedy could remind himself of a rising West before meeting with Khrushchev, articulating this ascendancy once again in his remarks in West Berlin, but to many *National Review* conservatives these attitudes were delusional, an understatement of communist strength that betrayed an unawareness of Western weaknesses. The same Russel Kirk who chided the John Birch Society for confusing Eisenhower with a communist called the automobile "the ultimate Jacobin" and pined for the leadership of Randolph of Roanoke, a Virginia politician of the 1820s and 1830s, so at odds was Kirk with modernity. The author of *The Conservative Mind*, Kirk was a connoisseur of modern America's pathologies. He lived a reclusive life of quasi-aristocratic and low-tech remove in rural Michigan. Every step toward bipartisan consensus could be construed by such conservatives as a step toward the modern abyss. Eisenhower, Kennedy and William McNeill had it backward: the decline of the West was the active and pernicious process whereby the West murdered itself. The suicide of the European West had already happened, as F. Scott Fitzgerald had a fictional character observe in his novel *Tender Is the Night* (1934). Touring the World War I battlefields years after the war, the novel's protagonist, Dick Diver, so-liloquizes: "this Western front business couldn't be done again . . . this took religion and years of plenty and tremendous sureties and the exact relation that existed between the classes. . . . You had to have a whole-souled sentimental equivalent going back further than you could re-member." (*Tender Is the Night* finishes with Dick Diver, having seen the ruin of the West, ruining himself.) Whole-souled sentiment was now gone as were the sureties and the religion. The West was hollowed out, midcentury conservatives sensed, and it was at war with a ferocious enemy—not just with itself. By the 1960s, conservatives were asking whether the suicide of the West was destined to be Euro-American.[8]

James Burnham, a conservative intellectual and editor at *National Review*, was the magazine's foreign-affairs pundit. Like Chambers, Burnham had been a communist in the 1930s, though a follower of Trotsky rather than of Stalin. Of affluent background, Burnham was a philosophy professor at New York University. He had studied at Oxford—under J. R. R. Tolkien, among others—before becoming a revolutionary in Manhattan. Ex-communists like Burnham and Chambers brought worldliness to the conservative movement when they came over to it. The intellectual Left had applied Marxist presuppositions to the turbulence of the 1930s with wondrous sophistication, capturing the rush of events in history and theory. Indeed, no one did this better than Lenin and Trotsky, the Bolsheviks with leather jackets and golden pens. In the era of the Spanish Civil War, the Left had learned to think globally—Moscow, Madrid, London, Beijing, Tokyo and New York belonged to a single geopolitical narrative. In the United States, radicals learned to express themselves in the quicksilver debates and fabulous expository prose of magazines like *Partisan Review*. To spend time in this milieu was to be trained in dialectical argument, in arguments that dipped and pivoted and startled. It was to be trained in the dramatiza-tion of politics and political ideas, a quality not overabundant in con-servative letters before *National Review* came on the scene.

In good prose, James Burnham's *The Suicide of the West* drama-tized several sweeping foreign-policy ideas. *The Suicide of the West* was published the same year Barry Goldwater, a politician partial to the conservative movement, upended the Republican Party. Goldwater was libertarian in economic policy and unaccepting of the Cold War status quo in American foreign policy. Buckley and many others at *National Review* contributed to Goldwater's campaign and ghostwriting his campaign book, *The Conscience of a Conservative*. In *The Suicide of the West*, Burnham took a step back from parties and campaigns and focused on the lost imperatives of American foreign policy. The perfidy of the Soviet Union did not need to be demonstrated to a conservative candidate. Far more interesting was the perfidy of American liberals and of those under-the-radar liberals who had co-opted the Republican Party. Suicide and decline are not the same. Decline happens over time. It can occur against the will of the entity in decline. Unlike Spengler's German phrase, *das Untergang des Abendlandes,* in English "the decline of the West" evokes Edmund Gibbon's *The Decline and Fall of the Roman Empire* (1776–1789) and Gibbon's notion of decadence, the overripeness of a civilization, its gradually going soft. The virtuous republic based on the renunciation of appetite—Cincinnatus giving up power and returning to the plow—can always yield to the Oriental luxuries of tyranny, of an empire awash in wealth and power but incapable of doing what it must to protect itself. Once decadence insinuates itself into a civilization, the local barbarians can initiate destruction at their leisure, as they did when they sacked Rome, though annoyingly for American conservatives Gibbon attributed the decline of the Roman Empire to Christianity (in addition to imperial overreach) rather than to pure luxury or to the unancient phenomenon of secularism. Contrasted to decline, suicide is sudden. It is conscious, willed, and its wounds can only be self-inflicted.[9]

Burnham's *The Suicide of the West* traces the rise of the West and its imminent suicide. Burnham concludes by speculating about the possible survival of the West. He moves quickly through the rise of the West, the origins of which lay not in classical antiquity but in Charlemagne's Europe. "Liberty, Freedom and Justice are the three primary social values or goals that have been approved or at least professed by nearly everybody . . . in Western civilization, whatever the philosophy or program, since the Renaissance," Burnham writes. Like McNeill, he has no doubt that "the United States is both the offspring and organic part of Western civilization." (The University of Chicago had taught William McNeill to regard the United States as an "offshoot" of the West.) Burnham's map of the West is large. Western Europe is the heartland, and the United States a beacon in the Western Hemisphere. Poland, Hungary, Bohemia and the Baltic Republics had been "an integral, and very important, part of the West" until the Red Army forcibly installed them in the East. Burnham characterizes Russia and Japan circa 1914 as "major non-Western power centers." The Soviet Union is a non-Western power in the geopolitical company of China, the Middle East and the countries of Latin America.[10]

The rise of the West was some twelve hundred years in the making, Burnham argues, but in the twentieth century its decline has been precipitous. From 700 to 1914 CE, the West took shape, gathered its energies and projected them outward. Writing with pride, Burnham states that "there before your eyes you can see at once that in AD 1914 the domain of Western civilization was, or very nearly was, the world." This was McNeill's world-girding civilization, though McNeill had begun his story in ancient Greece and Rome. Since 1914, however, the West has been pared down, a function of two world wars and of "communism's anti-Western enterprise." The paring down, self-imposed at first, then a project of Moscow's and of Beijing's, led to the tragedy of decolonization, the dismantling of the West in Burnham's view as it was for the magazine he helped to edit in the 1950s and 1960s. The Suez crisis of 1956, in which France and Britain were made to back down, was the death knell of Western power in the Middle East. It was postcolonial Egypt's victory and, for Burnham, a microcosm of a global development whereby either communism or postcolonial nationalism or some combination of the two was curtailing Western civilization. In the Suez crisis, as Burnham was well aware, Eisenhower came down on Egypt's side, bringing American power to bear *against* Britain and France. This was one of many examples of how President Eisenhower was unable to defend the West.[11]

Though communism and decolonization appear throughout *The Suicide of the West*, the subject closest to Burnham's heart is American liberalism, the toxin that will one day kill the West. The West depends ultimately on the United States, and the United States finds itself in thrall to liberalism, "the ideology of Western suicide," Burnham writes. He glances back to a primordial American liberalism, the attitudes of a George Washington or a John Quincy Adams who "believed in self-government, independence and sovereignty of their country, and also in the right of other nations and peoples to be independent and self-governing." This was a liberalism of the West. Woodrow Wilson and Franklin Roosevelt presided over the perversion of liberalism, a liberalism of "glittering abstractions." The simple fact that their liberalism is "anti-traditional" proves that twentieth-century liberalism is beholden to "principles that are internationalist and universal rather than local or national." Whether it is W. W. Rostow's stages of economic growth or JFK's foolish speculations about world peace or the disturbingly transnational United Nations, a liberal American foreign policy is running aground because of universalism. Burnham dreads a "world state having no roots in human memory, feeling and custom, [which] would inevitably be abstract and arbitrary, thus despotic, in the foreseeable future, if it could conceivably be brought into being." Wilson's and Roosevelt's aspirations will end either in despotism or they will collapse beneath the weight of their own folly.[12]

Identifying liberals as the active enemies of the West, Burnham indicts liberalism for more than its abstraction and internationalism. On the one hand, liberals are deficient in patriotism, secular and alienated from "Christianity, the traditional religion of Western civilization." Liberals have also been hypnotized morally by the civil rights movement and by decolonization, having elaborated an ethics of self-hatred. With James Baldwin in mind, Burnham writes that "the liberal community not only flagellates itself with the abusive writings of a disoriented Negro homosexual, but awards him money, fame, and public honors." Listing liberal publications in the United States and Europe—*The Nation, Dissent, Der Spiegel, New Statesman, L'Express*—Burnham condemns the internationalist liberal for developing "a generalized hatred of Western civilization and of his own country as a part of the West." Interestingly, Burnham sees national belonging (his own country) as a bridge to civilizational belonging. Hence, the bond between the conservative's patriotism and the conservative's love of the West, whereas liberals vacillate between shame for their country and shame for this Western civilization. They can belong only to that which is not real and therefore not corrupted. For Burnham, an internalized loathing of the West explains the flight of liberals into glittering abstractions like the world state. It is the softest, subtlest way to push for the dissolution of the West. It is the softest, subtlest way to prepare for the suicide of the West.[13]

Burnham offers a method for avoiding suicide. It is conservatism, for the conservative knows and loves Western civilization. Dedicated to the life of the West, the conservative prizes "family, community, church, country and, at the farthest remove, civilization—not civilization in general but this historically specific civilization, of which *I* am a member." These organically rooted conservatives are spiritually equipped to nourish rather than to undermine the West. Their world is ordered from the particulars of the *I* to the particulars of the civilizational *we*. To get the West off life support, conservatives will have to reassert "the pre-liberal conviction that Western civilization, thus Western man, is both different from and superior in quality to other civilizations and non-civilizations." Compromise and apology are liberal errors, admissions of inferiority. The conservative is by definition proud of Western civilization's superiority and must strive to convey this pride. Only because Western civilization is superior, which Burnham believed it was, is it "worth preserving."[14]

In tune with nineteenth-century discussions of civilization and with the postwar conservative movement, Burnham's was a white West. In 1947, Burnham had published *The Struggle for the World,* an essay on American foreign policy and a "Western-based, American-led world strategy." He had since been cheered by the fate of West Germany. It had "resumed its place as an organic part of the Western whole."

This was a bright spot in the overall trajectory of Western defeat, the drumbeat of concessions to the Soviet Union from Yalta onward, the removal of the courageous anticommunist General MacArthur in 1951, the inability to protect the "pro-Western but right-wing Batista" in Cuba. Cuba's President Fulgencio Batista had been deposed by the pro-Soviet Fidel Castro in 1959. Burnham's "I" and his "we" are white, and surrender to communism dovetailed with surrender to the uprisings of the nonwhite and formerly colonized world. So too was the West white: "now that the white Westerners—we are mostly white, and it is an inescapable fact—are climbing down, it is time for asserting not the empty illusion of brotherly equality but a new reality of changed priorities on the global scale," Burnham writes, leaving unexplored the American part of this equation. It is not clear whether the United States is home to biracial Westerners, as James Baldwin had wondered in "Strangers in the Village," or whether only white Americans belong to the West. Burnham skirts this question by labeling the West "mostly white." If there could be nonwhite Westerners, as Burnham's language seems almost to admit, they were left to at the side of the majority white West.[15]

The Suicide of the West reflects Burnham's bottomless disaffection for the liberal country. He had much more of Whittaker Chambers's looming pessimism than of William F. Buckley Jr.'s puckish optimism. The West had lost its soul for Burnham, since "all secular goals are in the last analysis subordinate to the ultimate moral or religious goal of the citizens composing the community." The problem with American foreign policy was the secular and civilization-less goal of internationalism, "the vague Globalism in place of a serious world outlook" in Washington and in other centers of decision making. Such globalism will never come to pass. It will merely distract from the actual challenges and prevent them from getting solved. Liberals' adherence to globalism marks the republic's loss of direction, "with the decay of religion and with an excess of material luxury." For Burnham, liberalism itself must begin to fade, after which a serious outlook can first be entertained and the West embraced for its particular excellence as well as for its superiority to other civilizations. Then communism and decolonization could be repelled and the Batistas of the postcolonial world supported, and the Hungarian and other indigenously Western freedom fighters would know that Washington was with them. Only the restoration of Western civilization in the country that leads the West can halt "the drift of U.S. foreign policy and put the West out of its Cold War jeopardy."[16]

AFTER 1964, ALTHOUGH the conservative movement would gain momentum, it was slow to achieve influence on foreign policy. After Barry Goldwater's loss to Lyndon Johnson, Burnham, Buckley and their circle would have to keep waiting for the restoration of the West. Some hope focused on a former Hollywood actor who gave a vivid speech—"the speech," as it would come to be known in conservative circles—at the 1964 Republican nominating convention. Having outshone Goldwater as a public speaker, Ronald Reagan became governor of California in 1967. Richard Nixon, the man who emerged in the mid-1960s as a presumptive leader of the Republican Party, attempted a rapprochement with Buckley and the conservative movement. Hoping to woo Buckley to his side in 1968, Nixon served him South African brandy at a meeting, a sign of his conservative credentials. Always an A-list anticommunist, Nixon could be unpredictable on foreign policy. He could be pragmatic, and he was not a zero-sum negotiator. His conservatism was thin, his opportunism thick. In 1968, Nixon devised a "Southern strategy," a rightward move intended to flip the Southern states from Democratic to Republican only a few years after major civil rights legislation had upended the racial status quo nationally and especially in the South. A national realignment shaped by his Southern strategy, and not so by Johnson's bad decisions in Vietnam, put the White House within reach for Nixon.[17]

Nixon's presidency, followed by Gerald Ford's two-year tenure in the White House, was an intriguing interlude in the development of a postwar conservative foreign policy. Nixon's primary foreign policy advisor was Henry Kissinger, who shifted American foreign policy away from the Wilsonian fervor of the early Cold War at a time when Wilsonian fervor was already overburdened by Vietnam. With Indochina in disarray and communism advancing in the developing world, Kissinger aimed for equilibrium and order in the late 1960s. His strategy for serving the West was not to bang the drum of war, or to assert Western values globally, but to face up to the West's relative decline and to exploit diplomacy in such a way as to disadvantage (without provoking) the Soviet Union. More of a European than an American conservative perhaps, Kissinger was no student of James Burnham. Having been mentored by the moderate Republican Nelson Rockefeller and having made his career in Cambridge, Massachusetts, Kissinger did not harbor a burning hatred of liberalism. (Neither in his domestic policies did Richard Nixon.) Kissinger also dismissed the conservative movement's penchant for rollback, the dynamic revision of the military balance of power in Europe. In practice, Kissinger's and Nixon's adherence to the West wavered between the pragmatic and the transactional. Ideology was a secondary concern for both of them.

Despite or because of their shared pragmatism, Nixon and Gerald Ford changed the shape of the Cold War. It was their lot to live through the final stages of the Vietnam War and the initial stages of a global economic downturn. Very quickly after Kennedy's death, the war had divided the American population, and the division would never heal. The internal polarization and frustration served as checks on American action in the Cold War. Aware of the reigning limitations, Nixon and Kissinger both went to China, which proved a masterstroke of Cold War diplomacy, opening new options to the United States and complicating the old East-West competition. It was not sufficient for the West to condemn China from afar. The West had to deal with China. In the weakness of the West's inability to impose its terms on China lay a diplomatic opportunity. Nixon and Kissinger were willing to endure the disapproval of James Burnham and the *National Review*. Meanwhile, a long, intricate diplomatic process was playing out in Helsinki, Finland. Its result, the Helsinki Final Act of 1975, ended any thought of rollback and showed that the United States and the Soviet Union could conduct real diplomacy. It was nuts-and-bolts negotiating, a cascade of bundled concessions following from a relationship between General Secretary Brezhnev and President Nixon that verged on friendship. The loss in Vietnam, the opening to China and the strange success of US-Soviet diplomacy in Helsinki implied a stabilizing Cold War rather than a resurgent West. The GOP of Nixon and Ford seemed able to live with a West in semi-decline.

Nevertheless, in the 1970s, the out-of-power conservative movement had not given up on influencing Washington. Chambers and Burnham had jumped from communism to conservatism before the Cold War. Another group jumped in a similar direction in the early 1970s, going from socialism to liberalism to moderate conservatism. As such, they were new to conservatism or *neoconservative,* an adjective that, like the adjectives *Quaker* and *Puritan,* started as a slur until it was taken up as a label. The neoconservatives had a group profile: from the New York area, from working-class backgrounds, these were academic stars mostly from "ethnic" or minority backgrounds (Jewish American, Irish American, Italian American). FDR, Truman and JFK had been *their* presidents when they were liberals, and this was a clue to the neoconservative mind. The welfare state, the civil rights movement, the relative secularism and modernity of Truman and Kennedy were building blocks, especially so since they were compatible with a strenuous anticommunism and with all that Truman and Kennedy had done to set an American Cold War foreign strategy. In other words, the neoconservative West was not at all the West of Chambers, Buckley and Burnham. It was not irrational or illiberal or irreducibly Christian. The neoconservatives' West was democratic above all. It had Enlightenment pedigree. Neither was it the guilty, exploitative West of Noam Chomsky and the more radical tip of the antiwar movement. Rebelling against these antiwar celebrities had been the founding act of the neoconservatives whose West was Harry Truman's West *after* the Vietnam War. In the 1970s, the neoconservative's standard-bearer was the Democratic senator from Washington State, Henry "Scoop" Jackson, the force behind the Jackson-Vanik amendment of 1974, which employed trade to pressure the Soviet Union and other nonmarket economies, an assertive exception to the spirit of détente.

The neoconservatives' intellectual vehicle was *Commentary*, a magazine edited by Norman Podhoretz. Educated in Western civilization at Columbia in the 1940s, Podhoretz published many of the pivotal essays of the neoconservative movement in the 1970s and its signature memoir, *Breaking Ranks: A Political Memoir* (1979). In foreign-policy debates, Podhoretz and the neoconservatives were in constant conflict with the Left. Vietnam had made the Left so one-sidedly critical of the United States that, if listened to, it would hand the world to the Soviet Union on a silver platter: that was the neoconservative fear. Podhoretz and the neoconservatives were also at odds with Kissinger and the realists of the American Cold War. Nixon was decently anticommunist, in their judgment, but what he had forgotten was the moral matrix of the Cold War, the established and obvious reality that the Soviet Union was an interventionist tyranny and the United States an arsenal of democracy. Nixon had forgotten Thomas Jefferson and the ball of liberty rolling around the world, its pace consistently quickened by the American example. Nixon had forgotten about the Statue of Liberty in New York's harbor and the immigrants' angle of vision when they first sighted this statue, a gift from the French Republic dedicated in 1886 and a figure derived from Libertas, the Roman goddess of liberty. (A similar 1863 statue stands atop the US Capitol.) Together with George Washington's possession of the key to the Bastille, the Statue of Liberty is as luminous a symbol of the transatlantic West as there is. The neoconservatives wanted the liberty represented in the statue to be better represented in American foreign policy. They were sure that surviving and one day winning the Cold War depended on it.[18]

In the 1970s, a host of talented and courageous Eastern European dissidents and intellectuals augmented the American neoconservative movement and the Cold War West. These Eastern Europeans were the victims of various communist governments. They had a moral authority that anticommunist intellectuals in the United States had lost because of Vietnam, and they were the often humorous poets of liberty and self-government, principles that were the opposite of hard, humorless communist repression and authoritarianism. Czechoslovakia's Vaclav Havel and Poland's Adam Michnik were admirers of the West, of which they felt themselves a part. Havel was a playwright, and Michnik, a political thinker and activist. They and their Eastern European colleagues loved the West's atmosphere of liberty. To build a ladder up and out of Soviet-style tyranny, they scrutinized interwar, precommunist Central Europe and especially the democratic Czechoslovakia that Neville Chamberlain had handed over to Hitler. They upheld the individual, the individual's rights and the individual's conscience in opposition to the collective authorities of the communist state, which were in practice the dictatorial authorities of the corrupt ruling party. For Havel and Michnik, an America and Europe amalgamated into a liberty-loving West had the necessary reservoir of ideas and traditions to restore liberty in all of Europe. In the wake of Vietnam, their sincere, searching voices could revivify a faltering American foreign policy. For the neoconservatives, Poland and Czechoslovakia occupied the place of Greece for the Europhilic Americans of the 1820s. Prague and Warsaw were themselves a suppressed West struggling to free themselves from the chains of an Eastern despotism.

The human rights provisions in the Helsinki Final Act emboldened Michnik and Havel in their affinity with the West. Both Michnik and Havel had frequent run-ins with the secret police and served time in jail. They did some of their best thinking and writing in jail, a chronic problem of dictatorial regimes. In 1976, Michnik finished writing *The Church and the Left,* a treatise on a possible Catholic-democratic transformation of communist Poland. Arrayed against a reactionary communism were the church and the Left—not the church versus the Left. Michnik's prophetic meditation on the coming collision between the Catholic Church and the Soviet Union was not published until 1981. Two years after he had written his anticommunist how-to book, the first Polish pope, John Paul II, was ordained, while in 1978 Vaclav Havel wrote "The Power of the Powerless," homage to civil society and to the irrepressible workings of the individual conscience. Havel turned communist ideology inside out: the proletariat had not been liberated according to Marx's plan. It had been rendered powerless by communism, but even the disempowered have bits of power, Havel noted. Minor acts of resistance, simple assertions of word and deed and a stubborn adherence to the truth were the seedbed of a postcommunist democracy. When Havel and Michnik looked to the United States, they still saw liberty in practice rather than a disturbing source of foreign-policy hubris, prejudice and error: the United States was the key to their Bastille. The neoconservatives of the 1970s felt the same way about the failures of communism in the East and the contrasting virtues of liberty in the post-Vietnam West.[19]

Topsy-turvy as ever, events between 1970 and 1980 favored the neoconservatives. Nixon was an accomplished foreign-policy president whose personal paranoia was his undoing. The Watergate scandal was the climax of his presidency, a domestic attempt to subvert democracy that was accompanied by Kissinger's close cooperation with antidemocratic forces in Chile and elsewhere. Could it be that the chiseled pragmatism of Nixon and Kissinger was not so much a strategic coup de grâce as a negation of the country's best foreign-policy instincts? Watergate put this question in a punishing light, and not just for the neoconservatives but for the nation at large. The neoconservatives felt vindicated in their desire for a president other than Nixon. Then came Jimmy Carter, the proponent of that which was geopolitically impossible in the neoconservatives' estimation, a childlike moralist lost amid the rough verities of twentieth-century international affairs. Nixon had encouraged détente, a posture of relaxation toward the Soviet Union. Carter deepened détente and seemed anxious about the moral fiber of post-Watergate America. He never seemed far away from an apology, the neoconservatives feared, until the Soviet Union invaded Afghanistan in 1979 and the foreign-policy disarray of the Carter White House was revealed for all the world to see. First the misery of Vietnam; next the disgrace of the energy crisis; and to top it off the incursion of Soviet tanks, helicopters and troops into impoverished Afghanistan. How much worse was it going to get on Carter's watch? the neoconservatives repeatedly asked. The simultaneous outbreak of revolution in Iran and the ongoing humiliation of the US Embassy staff there suggested a grim set of answers. The neoconservative desire for a president other than Nixon shaded into an acute desire for a president other than Carter.

Ronald Reagan's affection for *Commentary* was one of many attributes that pleased the neoconservatives. Like them, Reagan had begun his political life as a Democrat. When he read them, Reagan associated the neoconservatives' anticommunism with political orthodoxy, a tendency stretching from Woodrow Wilson through FDR to JFK— idealistic and optimistic and when necessary assertive. World War II was one point of pride in Reagan's understanding of the United States and the West, and the Cold War was another. In the 1950s, many of Reagan's opinions began to coincide with those of the conservative movement. In the 1960s, Reagan was appalled by changes on the American Left and especially by the bubbling up of an antiwar movement in Berkeley and elsewhere. Clashes between the pro-war Republican governor in Sacramento and the antiwar radicals in San Francisco were the essential political theater of the 1960s, each side pushing the other to sharper and sharper political formulations, greater and greater enmity. If the antiwar movement viewed American power as a threat to liberty and a tool of empire, Reagan drew the opposite lesson from Vietnam. Since communism was liberty's implacable foe, it was the West's implacable foe, Reagan reasoned. Whether in Indochina or in Europe, only American power stood in the way of communism's secularizing and enslaving armies. Reagan also shared James Burnham's sense that the Cold War was geopolitical and domestic. There were the communists over there *and* the liberals here at home. For the West to win the contest, Berkeley, too, would have to be defeated. This was no longer Harry Truman's Cold War.

Reagan was a vigorous culture warrior. After Vietnam, he would not find a common point around which to rally the whole country. To the disgust of the Left, Reagan would continue to argue that the Vietnam War, had it been more resolutely fought, could have been won. Reagan did, however, have a gift for synthesizing the Republican Party with the conservative constituencies around it. He commanded the conservative culture of the Cold War, channeling its not exactly compatible designs for a libertarian political economy and an activist foreign policy. In 1980, conservative political culture was strongly religious. With an indistinct religious profile—not Catholic, not mainline Protestant, not quite evangelical—Reagan represented a Judeo-Christian ethos. FDR had represented this ethos, but the battles of the 1960s had introduced new divisions. Reagan himself themed religion conservative, drawing from his literary hero, Whittaker Chambers, a right-wing theology of the Cold War in which the Soviet Union was evil and the West was good. The antithesis of communism, for Reagan as for Chambers, was God, and as president, Reagan would appoint William Casey his head of the CIA. A devout Catholic with a Manichean view of the Cold War, Casey gave secret briefings on international affairs to Pope John Paul II. Standing before an audience of evangelical Christians, Reagan labeled the Soviet Union an evil empire in 1982. Anti-Soviet barbs were nothing new in American politics, but the president's departure from diplomatic politesse and the religiously tinged word *evil* were novelties that were definitely Reaganesque. The Judeo-Christian God versus godless communism was one axis of the East-West struggle for Reagan and for his conservative supporters.

Reagan's version of Western liberty was enthusiastically capitalist as well as Judeo-Christian. Through *National Review* and other sources, he had grown familiar with the thinking of Friedrich Hayek, Milton Freedman and other libertarian thinkers. The very rise of the West, in the libertarian schema, was owed to individual talent, to an unencumbered public sphere and marketplace and to a set of laws that safeguarded the economic initiative of those with the will and the ability to succeed. Communism was the exact opposite, Reagan thought: it abolished private property, subordinated everything to a communal "social justice" and invited the state to envelop the individual in tyranny. Whether Asiatic or Oriental or Germanic, communism did not belong to Ronald Reagan's and the libertarians' West. Even Europe's social democracies were suspect, and Reagan's natural ally on the other side of the Atlantic was Margaret Thatcher, the British prime minister who was similarly inclined to scale back government and let slip the engines of entrepreneurship and the market. For Thatcher and Reagan, it was a replay of the Franklin Roosevelt–Winston Churchill partnership—far apart as FDR and Reagan were on the welfare state—the United States and Britain once again the stalwart soldiers of the West. Yet FDR had the Depression and the war to mobilize the nation behind him; he and Churchill had been virtuosos of wartime unity. Reagan and Thatcher were divisive in their ideals of economic freedom as they were in their foreign policy.

On foreign policy Reagan was as elusive as he was divisive. The conservative movement had despised Eisenhower for his reserve and his acceptance of certain Cold War limits. Regan, who might be a conservative FDR, would be no second Eisenhower. Reagan honored the conservative movement by decrying stasis in the Cold War, having inherited a Cold War that he wanted to revolutionize, a Cold War stalled by Nixon's baby steps and Carter's malaise. Against the will of the State Department, Reagan tried to make the Soviet Union publicly uncomfortable by denying any moral parity between the United States and the Soviet Union. That was the point of the evil empire reference. Reagan used invective and anticommunist jokes (often of Soviet vintage) to point out the unsustainable absurdities of Soviet atheism and Soviet political economy. This cannot last—that was his message to the Soviet leadership in the early 1980s, when one elderly and reactionary general secretary after another was dying in office. Because it was superior, the West would prevail, Reagan believed (influenced surely by Burnham and others at *National Review*). To bolster this superiority and to demonstrate it, Reagan massively increased defense spending when he came to office. He pressured the Western Europeans, many of them still in thrall to détente or *Ostpolitik*, West Germany's efforts to extend a hand across the border to the East, to accept more nuclear missiles on their territory. It was not rollback of the kind Burnham might have preferred, but the enhanced spending and the covert operations William Casey cooked up for a receptive Eastern Europe were not intended to calm down the Cold War. After the defeats and despair of the 1970s, they were supposed to signal renewed Western self-confidence. They were an attempt to intimidate Moscow on the assumption that some unspoken momentum favored the West.

A messianic evangelist of American liberty, Reagan was also a skilled mediator. This less visible, less stylized Reagan was a diplomat rather than a general or a missionary, and a diplomat in search of a structured end to the Cold War. Reagan once described his grand strategy as "we win, they lose"; but he did not have the Soviets' unconditional surrender in mind. A nuclear superpower could not be defeated. Reagan could, however, find justification for negotiating with the Soviet Union when Mikhail Gorbachev, a buoyant statesman and the least cynical of Soviet politicians, came to power in 1985. Gorbachev had studied law at Moscow State University and was a practicing Leninist. He retained Lenin's desire to plant real, existing socialism in Europe and to reclaim the Western possibilities the Soviet Union had sacrificed to brutal leaders like Stalin and Khrushchev. Reagan maneuvered Gorbachev toward the preferred American outcomes without humiliating the Soviet general secretary. It helped that Gorbachev administered Eastern Europe in such a way as to undermine Soviet legitimacy—without Reagan or the United States having to lift a hand. Gorbachev could not promote *glasnost* (openness) and *perestroika* (restructuring) without risking the Soviet Union's empire. Since the creation of the Soviet Union, Moscow had been ruling European populations that did not want to be ruled from Moscow: the more *glasnost* there was, the more this open secret would be exposed. James Burnham had identified Bohemia, Hungary, Poland and the Baltic States as organically Western and therefore in shackles as communist states. In precisely these countries rebellions stirred against Soviet domination under Gorbachev. While investing in weaponry and unsettling the Cold War balance of power, Reagan could work with Gorbachev's preference for the peaceful resolution of conflict. A fire-breathing anticommunist since the 1950s, and a joyful ideologue, Reagan was a surprisingly capable diplomat in office.

Reagan gave his most ideological speech on Western liberty and Eastern despotism in June 1987. He gave it on the fortieth anniversary of the Marshall Plan and in Berlin, very much aware of the precedent John F. Kennedy had set in this city. In his speech, Reagan spoke at the wall, before the Brandenburg Gate, rather than at the Schöneberg Rathaus. He was not there to repeat Kennedy's speech. Reagan's West was, for one, more economically defined than Kennedy's had been. Reagan made reference to a sign placed before the devastated Reichstag—"the Marshall Plan is helping here to strengthen the free world." In Reagan's eyes, this was a sign celebrating "a strong, free world in the West" where "that dream became real," freedom through prosperity. In the Berlin of 1987 Reagan could outline his economic idea of Western liberty and contrast it with the poverty of communism: "in the West today, we see a free world that has achieved a level of prosperity and well-being un-precedented through all human history. In the Communist world, we see failure, technological backwardness, declining standards of health, even want of the most basic kind—too little food." For JFK, the Cold War was defined by military and ideological competition. West Berlin's were political and civic freedoms—*civis romanus sum*—and the com-munist world was not so much poor as threatening, and nowhere as im-mediately as in Berlin. Whatever Kennedy's religious emotions were in Berlin in the summer of 1963, his audience did not hear about them.[20]

Reagan wanted to restore Christendom to the West and to do so in Berlin. Stunted in so many ways, "the totalitarian world produces backwardness because it does such violence to the spirit, thwarting the human impulse to create, to enjoy, to worship," Reagan informed his Berlin audience. Standing before the Berlin Wall, a necessary prop for the speech, Reagan compressed freedom of worship into an anecdote, the story of a "secular structure," the Alexanderplatz television tower in East Berlin, the tallest structure in East or West Berlin. According to Reagan, the East German authorities kept trying and failing to cor-rect a design flaw in the tower. "Even today when the sun strikes that sphere . . . the light makes the sign of the cross." The tower served Reagan as a metaphor for the Christian West, persecuted and irrepress-ible. Yet Reagan was not simply more religious than JFK had been or more overtly so. He was more conciliatory than Kennedy had allowed himself to be when the Berlin Wall was all of a year old. "We in the West are ready to cooperate with the East to promote true openness, to break down the barriers that separate people, to create a safe, freer world," Reagan said, though the conciliation was to be on American terms, of course. After November 1989 when the Berlin Wall fell and the Cold War effectively evaporated, Reagan's 1987 speech would be remembered not for the call to create a safe, freer world in cooperation with the Soviet East—and still less for its call to make Berlin the air transportation hub of Europe. It would be remembered for one simple phrase: "Mr. Gorbachev, tear down this wall."[21]

REAGAN WAS NO hero to academics, and in the 1980s American academia and the White House were as out of sorts as they had been in the late 1960s and early 1970s. American academia was outgrowing the West. In November 1968, San Francisco State College students protested for a School of Ethnic and Area Studies. In the following year, some 524 colleges and universities witnessed similar protests. In the words of the historian Matthew Jacobson, "knowledge itself became a Civil Rights issue [after the 1960s], as students and less traditional faculty members began to theorize and contest the ways in which the 'apartheid curriculum' of the liberal tradition reinforced the white supremacist patterns endemic to American life." The liberal tradition might mean one thing in Italy or France, relatively homogeneous countries that were physically connected to classical antiquity. The United States was different, and American universities had to educate students in their own society, preferably in ways that did not entrench white-supremacist patterns: that was the newfound challenge. Curricula had been opened to African American writers, Hispanic writers and female writers because their exclusion from academic consideration was akin to cultural apartheid. If academics cared to end white supremacy, they would have to see that their teaching and scholarship were free from white supremacy and recalibrate from a Western or liberal tradition to one that was more multicultural. As Matthew Jacobson rightly observes, students and less traditional faculty led the way.[22]

New academic programs in ethnic studies and black studies were created throughout the 1970s and 1980s. What had been less traditional became more traditional or more common as most universities felt the need to open up and to alter the preexisting balance in American academic culture between majority and minority, valued and not valued, elite and non-elite. The new knowledge of multiculturalism had been inhibited by the lingering prestige of Greek and Latin, by the academic obsession with Europe or Eurocentrism and by an internally American elitism that placed Europe on a pedestal and denigrated non-European cultures. To this end, black studies, Chicano studies and postcolonial studies were the foundation for popular academic programs in the 1980s and 1990s. Meanwhile, American history was to be written "from the bottom up," incorporating groups that were not exclusively white, male and powerful. Monticello was a house that belonged to Thomas Jefferson, for example, but Jefferson was not its only historically significant inhabitant. A history from the bottom up would shed light on the slaves as well as the masters who lived at Monticello, the men and the women. American history flowed from the complexity of a Monticello and a University of Virginia, both of which had been homes to liberty and to slavery. The British scholar Paul Gilroy's landmark history, *The Black Atlantic: Modernity and Double-Consciousness* (1993), reconfigured Atlanticism, changing it from a purely European creation to a creation in which Africa and Africans played a central role. Instead of a diplomatic history obsessed with the likes of FDR and Churchill, American studies often championed groups that had suffered at the hands of the British and American governments, from the persecution of Native Americans to the establishment of slavery to the internment of Japanese Americans during World War II. American studies scholars tended to view the Cold War through the lens of Vietnam, doctors gathered to diagnose the illness of American hegemony, the Orientalist or imperial bent of policymakers in and after the Cold War or all the way back to the American Revolution and European settlement of the Americas.[23] Engagement with the world beyond the West could also arise directly from the Cold War university.

Government funding and general demand had put area studies on the academic fast track in the 1940s, and even more so in the 1950s. National security required nothing less: the State Department and the intelligence community needed Russian speakers, Arabic speakers and Chinese speakers. It needed good academics to train them: it needed wide-ranging expertise. These academics and experts created programs and departments that were a conduit for international academic talent in the history, politics, literature and art of the non-Western world—programs broader in scope than the contributions of the refugee scholars Hitler had sent from Europe to the United States. Professor Halil İnalcik, to take one of many examples, opened the American mind to Ottoman history through academic appointments at Harvard, Columbia, the University of Pennsylvania and the University of Chicago from the 1950s to the 1980s. His students would bring Ottoman studies to many other American universities. To take another example: while William McNeill was working on *The Rise of the West* at the University of Chicago, his colleague Marshall Hodgson was writing a three-volume history, *The Venture of Islam: Conscience and History in a World Civilization* (1974). The American university was increasingly receptive to world civilization and less and less narrow-minded because of its extensive Cold War investments. There was more to the world than the West, as had already been true for the contents if not for the title of McNeill's 1963 book.[24]

Though area studies might be linked to government priorities and government funding, a newly critical interpretation of the Western heritage often accompanied the decentering of Europe. A scholar of empire and of the color line, Du Bois had been writing in this vein already in the 1890s. Edward Said had devoted *Orientalism*, his 1979 historical-literary study, to the relationship between power and knowledge, academia and foreign policy, contending that Western knowledge was the handmaid of Western imperialism. Permeating the humanities, the critical methods Said applied to the literature of Western imperialism were applied to Western history, philosophy and politics: power in all its cultural forms was to be approached suspiciously; in particular, the power of the West was to be approached suspiciously. In 1985, a scholar of philosophy and literature, Gayatri Spivak, published a seminal essay, "Can the Subaltern Speak?" Born in India in 1942, Spivak had studied at Cornell, after which she taught at several American universities, joining Said at Columbia in 1991. In "Can the Subaltern Speak?" Spivak queried a West that brashly spoke for the world it had conquered or aspired to conquer, enacting "the asymmetrical obliteration of the trace of that Other in its precarious Subjectivity," that precariously subjective Other being the person living under colonialism. Who had the right to speak? And whose view was objective? Whose was subjective? As did many of her academic colleagues in the 1980s, Spivak identified not with the powerful protagonists of the West like Columbus, but with their disempowered victims, those who had been relegated to subaltern status and who in the service of Western triumphalism had also been rendered voiceless.[25]

Columbus himself could be central to these debates. In 1984, the Bulgarian scholar Tvetan Todorov published *The Conquest of America: The Question of the Other*, a Saidian study of American origins. Todorov delved into the story of Columbus, not to erect yet another monument to this excessively famous man, but to see him from the perspective of the non-Europeans who first encountered him. Todorov's title was indicative, placing *conquest* where *exploration* had previously been. In the hagiography, Columbus had been the man of discovery. In Washington Irving's popular nineteenth-century biography, Columbus had embodied Christian piety. The various paintings in which Columbus and his voyage were depicted in the US Congress and in the Library of Congress presented and flattered Columbus as an agent of American liberty. Todorov put no stock in this Columbian triad of discovery-piety-liberty. Nor did Todorov see a scientist or entrepreneur in Columbus. For him, Columbus was an agent of power and violence, violent because he was powerful, and for his world-historical arrogance there were real "others" who paid the price. These were the native peoples or subalterns the European and American historians had overlooked for centuries and whom the painters and the sculptors had romanticized into inhuman caricature. Columbus's voyage was pretext for genocide, and throughout his book Todorov merges analysis of the European Holocaust with analysis of Columbus's American career, a concordance of Western history that did not occur to McNeill. Published eight years before the five-hundred-year anniversary of 1492, *The Conquest of America* commemorated the loss of liberty. Columbus, who cannot be detached from the American narrative, is a kind of switch conductor. His heroism sends the story down one track. His villainy sends it down another.[26]

International recognition of the historical-cultural ferment in the United States came in 1993 when Toni Morrison was awarded the Nobel Prize for Literature. Born in 1931, Morrison was a graduate of Howard University, class of '53. At Cornell University, she wrote a master's thesis on alienation in the novels of Virginia Woolf and William Faulkner and then worked as an academic and an editor, in which capacity she encouraged both African and African American writers. Morrison published her first novel, *The Bluest Eye*, in 1970, and her best-known novel, *Beloved*, in 1987. *Beloved* is a historical novel that circles the Civil War, going back and forth in time, with the experience of African American women at the novel's center. *Beloved* draws on European and American modernism, on the time-bending devices of writers like Woolf and Faulkner to capture the lives-in-time and lives-in-history of its African American characters. Morrison is also very different from Faulkner, who could not escape the myth of the lost cause, of the South's defeat in the Civil War, or the curse of its faded romance. History itself is the curse in *Beloved*, as is racism, and both are relentless. Morrison diagramed the aftereffects of slavery in her characters, male and female, their paths to recovery and what it was they were trying to recover from. As literature, *Beloved* was either outside the traditional canon of Euro-American literature, in a separate category, or it redrew the canon—precisely the kind of question that was debated by the literary critics and scholars of the 1980s and 1990s. In 2015, the Columbia faculty voted to add Toni Morrison's fiction to its "Literature Humanities" or great books of Western civilization course.

The two major academic trajectories of the 1980s, the crossing of the color line and the critique of the West, met on the campus of Stanford University a year after Toni Morrison published *Beloved*. In the assessment of the historian Lawrence Levine, what fizzled out in the 1960s and 1970s "was a certain arrogance, an unquestioned assurance that Western Civilization embodied all the culture and history and literature we needed to know to live our lives and comprehend our past and present." A 1976 American Historical Association conference session on Western civilization courses yielded the verdict of Amherst professor Frederic L. Cheyette—that these courses were "truncated and provincial." Too old-fashioned, they overlooked popular culture and visual culture. As early as 1968, the Stanford faculty had started to feel uncertain about its Western Civilization course. In the words of the course's director, "many of us faculty are no longer convinced that there is a standard or specifiable body of knowledge or information necessary for a liberal education." It was the students, however, who forced the university to reconsider the merits of its Western Civilization program in the mid-1980s. According to William King, president of Stanford's Black Student Union:

> I know Professors . . . are simply preserving that tradition which they consider correct and which guided their life in a positive way. But by focusing these ideas on all of us they are crushing the psyche of those others to whom Locke, Hume, and Plato are not speaking, and they are denying the freshmen and women a chance to broaden their perspective to accept both Hume and Imhotep, Machiavelli and Al Malgili, Rousseau and Mary Wollstonecraft. . . . The Western culture program as it is presently structured around a core list and an outdated philosophy of the West being Greece, Europe, and Euro-America is wrong, and worse, it hurts people mentally and emotionally in ways that are not even recognized.

KING MADE ONE further point about Stanford's Western Civilization program. In his view, the approach to the West that Stanford's program took was too cloistered. As a student, King had hoped to see "the acknowledgement that the West as we know it is not European but international in its origin and tradition," but that acknowledgment had not been made in his education. So high-profile was the issue of cultural tradition and attitude that Ronald Reagan's secretary of education, William Bennett, visited Stanford in 1988 and debated its president on the relative merits of the West. Bennett contended that Stanford must have its students "study, nurture, and defend the West," and that is because the West "is good." Presumably, he was speaking for the White House on the goodness of the West.[27]

As these debates took their course nationally, American students continued to wrestle with the West in their coursework and in their reading. On the side of those supportive of studying, nurturing and defending the West was the conservative *Dartmouth Review*. One of its editors, Dinesh D'Souza, stood in the limelight for a while with his scathing 1991 book *Illiberal Education: The Politics of Race and Sex on Campus*. Other reckonings were more private. A student at Howard University in the mid-1990s, Ta-Nehisi Coates, born in Baltimore in 1975, recounts in his 2015 book *Between the World and Me* the distance between himself and a West that was omnipresent, foreign and unwelcoming. "Serious history was the West," he writes, "and the West was white. This as all distilled for me in a quote I once read from the novelist Saul Bellow. I can't remember where I read it, or when—only that I was already at Howard. 'Who is the Tolstoy of the Zulus?' Bellow quipped. Tolstoy was 'white,' and so Tolstoy 'mattered,' like everything else that was white mattered." There were "many Malcomites" at Howard when Coates was a student there, many avid readers of Malcolm X, and many books like Chancellor Williams's *The Destruction of Black Civilization* (1971) to be discovered. There was no shortage of available courses on African and African American history, but these two worlds—the world of Howard and the world of Saul Bellow—were at odds with one another. The problem, for Coates, was the West, a dividing line between what mattered and what did not in American intellectual culture and a dividing line between white and black in a rigidly unintegrated country.[28]

Nobody captured Secretary Bennett's pro-Western side of the argument more explosively than Allan Bloom did in his 1987 *succès de scandale*, *The Closing of the American Mind*. This thorny book spent thirty-one weeks on the *New York Times* Best Sellers list. Its author was a product of the University of Chicago great-books program. He had taught at Cornell, the site of a campus uprising in 1968, which Bloom experienced firsthand. He returned to teach at the University of Chicago outraged by the radicalism he had encountered in Ithaca, New York. *The Closing of the American Mind* intentionally evokes Spengler's melancholy, with Bloom taking on the decline of the West in the American university. In the beginning were "the Western nations, i.e. those influenced by Greek philosophy," he writes. The West had been summoned by "civilization-constituting figures like Moses, Jesus or Achilles," and it was both religious and secular. There was "the West's common faith, Christianity," which shared its grandeur with the secular Enlightenment. Bloom was himself Jewish, not the pious type and uninterested in religious advocacy. Yet he admired the Anglo-Saxon strain in the American academic tradition and the imprint the Protestant elite had left on American culture. They had given the country "its traditions, its literature, its special claim to know and supervise the language, and its Protestant religions." He must surely have loved the National Cathedral in Washington, DC, though Bloom's own church was the university, and especially the gothic University of Chicago campus. For him, the university "as we know it, in its content and aim, is the product of the Enlightenment."[29]

Bloom's book is part outraged monologue and part stand-up comedy. It was a takedown of the university Edward Said had helped to build. *The Closing of the American Mind* was also a foreign-policy book published at a time when foreign policy was in the headlines. When Bloom's colleague William McNeill was writing *The Rise of the West*, the university and the civilization around it were healthy, from Bloom's perspective. For Bloom, "the fifties were one of the great periods of the American university." In the 1960s, this health was destroyed. What was lost was "the wisdom of Europe" and "the longing for Europe."

The American university had nurtured a civilization "that was never a native plant. We were dependent on Europe for it." In a country preoccupied with business and the practical arts, sixties-style assaults on university tradition amounted to a void: "everything has tended to soften the demands made on us by tradition," Bloom wrote; "this simply dissolves it." To forget the West was to forget the responsibilities of the West, however much sarcasm Graham Greene may have dumped upon these responsibilities in *The Quiet American*. Bloom turned to Winston Churchill to elaborate this particular idea. The outcome of the Second World War had hung on a slender civilizational thread reaching from England back to ancient Greece:

> Churchill was inspired by his ancestor Marlborough, and his confidence in his own action is inconceivable without the encouragement provided by that model. Marlborough said that Shakespeare was essential to his education. And Shakespeare learned a large part of what he knew about statesmanship from Plutarch. This is the intellectual genealogy of modern heroes.

Bloom was proposing that, hero or villain, democrat or fascist, you are what you study. You are what you hold dear. At moments of war or of potential tyranny when the storm is gathering, you either believe in your course of action or you do not believe in it. Education can foster a Churchillian resolve, or it can leave its recipients lacking all conviction. Everything essential comes from education. There is nothing the least bit trivial about reading Plutarch at age eighteen, in Bloom's view. No less trivial is it not to have read Plutarch by age forty-five.[30]

The gerund in Bloom's title lent the book its present-tense immediacy. The American mind was *closing*, Bloom argued, much as the German mind had closed to such horrendous effect in the 1930s. For Bloom, "what happened in the universities in Germany in the thirties is what happened and is happening everywhere" around him in America. Were the United States a small country, this loss—of Europe's wisdom, of the Enlightenment, of the whole heroic Western genealogy—might matter less. As it was, the United States was the world's mightiest country. Its failures and its successes, the openings and closings of its mind, would affect the international order. One way or another, they would be conveyed outward by American foreign policy, which encompassed more than the country's economic and security interests. For Bloom, American foreign policy had civilizational causes and effects just as the university's ability to teach its students to be civilized had foreign-policy consequences. Bloom referred to "civilization, or the same thing, education." He had the Cold War in mind in his book's final sentences, and Gorbachev or no Gorbachev, the American-led West was attenuating before his eyes:

> This is the American moment in world history, the one for which we shall forever be judged. Just as in politics the responsibility for the fate of freedom in the world has devolved upon our regime, so the fate of philosophy in the world has devolved upon our universities, and the two are related as they have never been before. The gravity of our given task is great, and it is very much in doubt how the future will judge our stewardship.[31]

IN 1981 AND 1982, Francis Fukuyama, a thirty-year-old holder of a bachelor's degree in classics and a former student of Allan Bloom's at Cornell (class of '74), held a position at the State Department's Office of Policy Planning. He spent the following six years at the Rand Corporation working on Cold War strategy while the Cold War was rushing through its final phases. In 1989, after Reagan's vice president George H. W. Bush had become president, Fukuyama went back to Policy Planning as its deputy director. Around this time, he was invited by the University of Chicago's Olin Center for Inquiry into the Theory and Practice of Democracy to lecture on politics and history. The lecture must have gone well, for it resulted in an article. "The End of History?" was published in the summer 1989 issue of the *National Interest,* a neoconservative foreign-policy magazine founded in 1985. Fukuyama's article could be compared in its impact only to

George Kennan's 1947 *Foreign Affairs* piece—"The Sources of Soviet Conduct." Kennan's tour-de-force proposal for containment had been written from the same office where Fukuyama was working in 1989, and in which W. W. Rostow had ended up after writing *The Stages of Economic Growth*. Rostow's study had some remarkable similarities to the book Fukuyama elaborated from his *National Interest* article. In the words of the journalist Charles Krauthammer, who blurbed *The End of History and the Last Man* (1992), which had gained a clause and lost a question mark from the article, Fukuyama's theses were "bold, lucid, scandalously brilliant. Until now, the triumph of the West was merely a fact. Fukuyama has given it a deep and highly original meaning."[32]

An intervening event between the 1989 revolutions in Eastern Europe and the appearance of Fukuyama's book was the release of the anti-Apartheid activist Nelson Mandela from a South African prison in February 1990. The pernicious legacy of European imperialism had been fallen on Mandela's shoulders, and throughout the Cold War the United States had stood with the practitioners of Apartheid. The CIA may even have assisted the South African government in Mandela's arrest in August 1962. The geopolitics of the Cold War had engendered many such alliances. The freeing of Mandela and the simultaneous unwinding of the Apartheid regime in South Africa, just when the Cold War was ending, added to the mood of Western jubilation after 1989. Without Soviet meddling to worry about, alliances could be newly contemplated. Perhaps the agony of the Cold War compromises could be retired and true democracy and human rights could be the guiding light of American foreign policy. At last, Washington was able to place itself unequivocally on the side of the Mandelas. Coming when it did, Mandela's liberation from the South African past allowed two political trends to merge—the absorption of Eastern Europeans into the West, and the final throwing off of colonialism by its former victims—to Western applause. Perhaps the victorious West could absolve itself of its own guilt, of American misdeeds in Vietnam or of Europe's misdeeds in Africa, in a new birth of freedom outside of Europe. Simplified story lines in Eastern Europe

and Africa alike, these simultaneous liberations were the most capti-
vating news of 1989 and 1990.[33]

Liberation had great currency for the author of *The End of History
and the Last Man*. From the nineteenth-century German philosopher
Hegel, Francis Fukuyama adopted the notion that all people seek
recognition in addition to physical well-being. Tracking this notion,
Fukuyama regarded much human history until the Renaissance as de-
formed by a master-slave dynamic. A few masters robbed the many
slaves of recognition. Then came the bourgeois revolution of the seventeenth century, from which grew the tree of liberal democracy. The
pioneer was the British Empire, which furnished "the Anglo-Saxon
version of liberal theory on which the United States was founded."
An "Anglo-Saxon liberal tradition" granted political and economic
recognition to those who fueled its success, expanding upon "the objective historical relationship that existed between Christian doctrine
and the emergence of liberal-democratic societies in Western Europe."
Fukuyama's historical patterns were—not accidentally—the building
blocks of Reagan's Cold War outlook. In fact, Fukuyama's history was
basically what Whittaker Chambers had put together for *Time* in the
1940s, with somewhat more political economy and less religion in the
civilizational mix. In *The End of History and the Last Man*, political
liberty demands economic liberty (capitalism): Ronald Reagan had hit
each of these themes, including Christian doctrine, in his 1987 speech
in West Berlin. As Fukuyama put it in the language of social science
rather than of sentimental anecdote, "the growth of liberal democracy,
together with its companion, economic liberalism has been the most remarkable macropolitical phenomenon of the last four hundred years."[34]

Fukuyama's opponent in *The End of History and the Last Man* was
not the Left. His opponent was pessimism about the West, which was
the problem of America's educated classes (Right and Left). "We in
the West," he wrote in *The End of History*, "have become thoroughly
pessimistic with regard to the possibility of overall progress in democratic institutions." In this "we" he included those who deconstructed
the political tradition of the United States and Europe—the academic

climate at Edward Said's Columbia and other such universities. (Before joining the Reagan administration, Fukuyama had gone as a graduate student to Paris, where he studied with the philosopher Jacques Derrida and contemplated an academic career in Said's discipline of comparative literature.) By "we in the West," Fukuyama was also hinting at the hangover from the Carter presidency, the sense that progress was over and decline around the corner, a loss of faith in democracy in Fukuyama's judgment. He wanted to refute the theorists of malaise, decline and suicide. He could not sympathize with Spenglerian modes of thinking, "the profound pessimism . . . born of the truly terrible political events of the first half of the twentieth century." He recognized the "suicidal self-destructiveness of the European state system in two world wars," but that was a previous era and that was the European state system. Even in the dismal 1970s, right-wing governments had begun to topple in Europe. With the exit of Portugal's António Salazar and Spain's Francisco Franco, the Iberian peninsula was finally giving up on its dictators. Then, in the 1980s the dictatorships started to fall in Latin America and Eastern Europe: Samuel Huntington, one of Fukuyama's graduate-school teachers at Harvard, published a book in 1991 on the overall advance of democracy in the 1980s, *The Third Wave: Democratization in the Late Twentieth Century.* By the end of the 1980s, the left-wing authoritarian governments were dissolving, outlining "a common evolutionary pattern for *all* human societies," Fukuyama wrote. The masters were in retreat, and the erstwhile slaves were gaining in recognition.[35]

Amid the liberal-democratic fiesta, Fukuyama sounded two cautionary notes. He predicted that the greatest challenge to political liberalism would come "from those societies in Asia which combine liberal economies with a kind of paternalistic authoritarianism." This might be Lee Kuan Yew's Singapore or it might be China, where a tremor of revolution had been felt in May 1989. Students fashioned a papier-mâché goddess of democracy and shouted antigovernment slogans on Beijing's Tiananmen Square without accomplishing what their counterparts were accomplishing in Poland, East Germany and

Czechoslovakia. The Chinese Communist Party survived 1989 intact. It did not make its peace with democracy, although it had long ago made its peace with aspects of capitalism. China threatened the integrity of Fukuyama's argument, in which political culture and economics were shared expressions of political liberalism, with democracy and capitalism destined to be twins. In a world falling over itself to become the West, there was still an East. Finally, there was the "last man" who surfaced in the title of Fukuyama's book, the slightly pathetic beneficiary of history's having come to a harmonious end. The last man was no slave: democracy had already lifted him above slavery. He was not quite a master either, as "the fundamental transition that has occurred in modern life was the domestication of the master, and his metamorphosis into economic man." Fukuyama was right about "the allure of modern Western European consumer civilization." It was world-girding in the 1990s, a prosaic *consumer* civilization, decreeing that the last man would not be another Christopher Columbus. He would not explore, conquer and convert. He would vote, compromise and shop.[36]

Many, perhaps most readers of *The End of History and the Last Man* ignored the last man altogether. They latched onto the title's delirious termination. Western Europe and the United States had won the unwinnable contest. They were freer and richer than the communist East. Their military posture was more sustainable, and liberal democracy had won because it was the superior civilization, consumer or otherwise. Fukuyama did ask whether it is "possible that political liberalism is simply a cultural artifact of European civilization and its various off-shoots," as William McNeill had more or less argued in *The Rise of the West*. McNeill had highlighted civilizational magnetism, and that in sum was Fukuyama's argument about the West in circa 1992. Political liberalism owed much to the West and to "the Western philosophical and historical tradition started in Greece." Yet this was merely a historical detail. Because it resolved the dilemma of recognition so handsomely and because its resolution bestowed liberty and prosperity, the Columbian West would know no competitors. Between 1989 and 1991, the Eastern Europeans and the Russians had given up communism for democracy, Fukuyama was convinced. "Western confidence in the stability of Soviet communism rested on a belief, conscious or not, that the Russian people were not interested in or ready for democracy," Fukuyama pointed out, and this confidence had been misplaced. The Russian people *were* interested in democracy, and they *were* ready for it. In 1991, the Russian people had taken to the streets in the name of democracy, and Boris Yeltsin, a communist turned democrat, was their prophet. The magnetism of the West was restructuring the international order. "What is emerging victorious," Fukuyama wrote, "is the liberal *idea.*" *Time's noblest offspring is the last.* Suicide was nowhere in sight.[37]

Fukuyama's measured melancholy was inadequate to the political situation in the United States. He took cohesion much too much for granted, understating the complexity of American politics as the Soviet enemy was slipping away. On the Left, Fukuyama's book was mostly reviled. It was entirely out of sync with American academia, with little to say about the race-class-gender inequalities in which the West had been complicit for centuries and in which the West was still complicit, in the verdict of many humanities and social science professors. If the last man (man!) would be living in Western-style capitalism forever, the non-West having vanished and socialism having been left behind, then Fukuyama's book was less a political science treatise than a dystopian novel, a rewrite of Orwell's *1984* for the twenty-first century. Many professors, and even more graduate students, read *The End of History* as the road map of the coming capitalist catastrophe. On the Right, Reagan's and Fukuyama's optimism was mainstream in 1989, but just beneath the surface were James Burnham's fears about Western suicide. Perhaps the rights revolutions of the 1960s, the creeping secularism and the ceaseless technological change had deprived the West of its soul. Conservatives could read *The End of History* as the road map to the coming liberal catastrophe. In 1964, Burnham's *Suicide of the West* had been a defense of nationalism and the West, of a distinct and superior Western civilization, a kind of Western nationalism. The very internationalism Fukuyama championed in 1992, all the world converging on a single model, peacefully sharing in liberal democracy and a liberal international order, might lead to the suicide of the West by other means—the death of Western civilization through the triumph of global cosmopolitanism. One place at least where history had not come to end was the United States.

6

The Post–Columbian Republic,
1992–2016

Well, the last I heard of Arab
He was stuck on the side of a whale
That was married to the deputy
Sheriff of the jail
But the funniest thing was
When I was leavin' the bay
I saw three ships a-sailin'
They were all heading my way
I asked the captain what his name was
And how come he didn't drive a truck
He said his name was Columbus
and I just said, "Good luck"
—BOB DYLAN, "BOB DYLAN'S 115TH DREAM," 1965

AS THE FIVE-HUNDREDTH anniversary approached, William Mc-Neill was asked to join the Christopher Columbus Quincentenary Jubilee Committee. In the commemoration of Columbus, McNeill was a natural choice. His distinguished scholarly name was connected to *The Rise of the West*, published some seven decades after the World's Columbian Exposition of 1893—and some three decades before the five-hundredth Columbian anniversary. Columbus and the rise of the West were natural companions, fellow travelers of modern history. Yet McNeill had a hard time with the committee, which could not agree on the meaning of Christopher Columbus's voyage. The committee was, as McNeill recalled in his memoirs, "polarized between persons of Italian descent and Latinos." It selected a theme that would have been unremarkable a few decades earlier, "Columbus and the Age of Discovery." Even after its internal debates, the committee did not foresee "the storm of criticism the quincentenary provoked" from the general public. McNeill's own sympathies were divided between honoring and dissecting the European legacy encoded in the Columbian Republic. He had never wanted to be a cheerleader of the United States, a trait he attributed to his having been born in Canada. He had been educated at Chicago to be a communicant of Western civilization, but he was receptive to nonheroic takes on Columbus. For this reason, in part, McNeill had been moving since 1963 from the West and toward world history.[1]

In 1992, McNeill was well aware that historians were casting a critical eye on Columbus and the West. He tried not to be too stridently old guard, as when he reviewed a 1990 book—*The Conquest of Paradise* by Kirkpatrick Sale, a nonacademic author—for the *New York Times*. In the review, titled "Debunking Columbus," McNeill objected to a vilification of Columbus, not because Columbus is so transparently world-historical but because he is in so many ways unknowable: "no doubt this [*The Conquest of Paradise*] is a useful corrective to the hero worship Columbus has often been accorded," McNeill wrote. "But uncritical adulation and the lambasting that Mr. Sale administers are both ahistorical, in the sense that they select from the often cloudy record of Columbus's actual motives and deeds what suits the researcher's 20th-century purposes." Whether McNeill liked it or not, the anti-Columbus books kept coming. Jan Carew published *Rape of Paradise: Columbus and the Birth of Racism in the Americas* in 1994. These critical studies were only one-half the story at the time of the five-hundredth anniversary. In 1992, the Australian director Ridley Scott released *1492: Conquest of Paradise,* a B movie with Gerard Depardieu as a swashbuckling Columbus, a Renaissance man of will and curiosity, friendly to the Native populations and at odds with the imperial zeal of the Spanish nobility. Even in 1992, with some reconfiguration of the earlier legend, the nineteenth-century Columbus was still visible.[2]

Columbus Day stayed on the books as a holiday, but Columbus was a source of strife in the 1990s. For many, to celebrate Columbus was a travesty. The academic John Sanchez argued circa 1992 that "while Columbus didn't actually insert the sword in the millions of people who died he started the process of enslavement, murder, disease, pollution and racism that came after exploration and conquest. . . . To us he's Hitler." In 1990, the National Council of the Churches of Christ expressed its condolences "for the descendants of the survivors of the subsequent invasion, genocide, slavery, 'ecocide,' and exploitation of the wealth and land." A celebration is "not an appropriate observation of this [five-hundredth] anniversary," the National Council stated. For these observers, a Pandora's box had been opened in 1492. Out of it came the intended murder of the Native population (genocide), the theft of territory (invasion) and the sins of slavery. Ecocide might seem an incongruous accusation on this list, but it was true to an image the Columbian Republic had spun from Columbus's life story. This was the man of science, the explorer, Columbus, the fifteenth-century industrialist. The Columbian mastery of nature had reached a high point at the 1893 Chicago World's Fair, and for many in the environmental movement, the West had industrialized and monetized the world to disastrous effect. That was what the National Council of Churches had meant by ecocide. In 1992, the University of California at Berkeley renamed Columbus Day as Indigenous Peoples Day, as have many American communities since 1992. Rather than the achievements of the Christian explorer, for some it was the harm done to indigenous peoples that deserved to be remembered every Columbian autumn.[3]

Arguments about the West that had been confined to seminar rooms in the 1970s and 1980s were roiling the public sphere in the

1990s. (Tvetan Todorov's brilliant book on Columbus had come out in 1984.) These culture wars were more like the Korean War than World War II. Neither side could ever win. Both sides had to comfort themselves with local and at times Pyrrhic victories. An Indigenous Peoples Day in Berkeley, California, did not overturn the national holiday, while the national holiday gave rise to Indigenous Peoples Day. Columbus Day might also be understood as it was in the 1890s, among Italian Americans and for those on the right side of the political spectrum. In 2002, the HBO series *The Sopranos* aired an episode titled "Christopher" that dramatized Columbus Day, with Italian Americans and Native Americans coming to blows on the streets of Newark, New Jersey. With culture and politics stalemated, the bipartisan foreign policy that had extended from Pearl Harbor to the assassination of John F. Kennedy was similarly a thing of the past. Reagan's West was already a partisan, a conservative West. With the loss of the Soviet Union in 1991, the internal enmities advanced and bipartisanship receded. For much of the Right, Bill Clinton's presidency was illegitimate in some way. He faced a Congress in revolt in 1994 and was impeached by the House of Representatives in 1998. For much of the Left, the presidency of George W. Bush was illegitimate in other ways. It had been stolen in Florida in 2000 and perpetuated by a deceitful war on terror. Such was the narrative of Michael Moore's popular 2004 documentary film, *Fahrenheit 9/11*. Then came the illegitimate Barack Obama whose key political opponent on the Right did not so much challenge his policies as his very personhood, routinely questioning whether Obama had been born in the United States. The collapse of bipartisanship was about much more than the West, but disagreements about the West and about figures like Columbus added to the cultural brinksmanship of a polity at odds with itself.

However mired in partisanship, however agitated by the culture wars, the post–Columbian Republic was also the unrivaled leader of the West in the 1990s. That was Fukuyama's point: the splintering of the Soviet Union had been an unblemished triumph of America and the Western idea, which for Fukuyama were one and the same.

America's wealth had helped it through the Cold War, had given it the world's preeminent military. After 1991, with the Soviet Union no more, the United States had been cut free from the Cold War constraints. Vietnams would be easy to avoid from now on. An absent Soviet Union eliminated the need for proxy wars and for propping up rotten regimes just because they were or claimed to be anticommunist. Thus liberated, the United States could project power with suppleness and empathy—in the Middle East, in Asia, in Europe. It could reject once and for all the rivalry of powers for the community of powers. Whatever he might have envisioned for the future, Woodrow Wilson had been condemned to live in a world of European great powers. So too had FDR. Then Truman and Reagan and all the presidents in between had to live with China and the Soviet Union (and until the mid-1960s a Chinese-Soviet partnership). Presidents Bill Clinton, George W. Bush and Barack Obama faced far less resistance. Fukuyama prophesied that Westernization would be indefinite. It was not a policy but a progression that resembled the settlement of the American West, the image with which Fukuyama closed *The End of History and the Last Man*, with the pioneers gliding from East to West. The world's countries were like "a long wagon train strung out along the road," Fukuyama wrote. Accidents are possible. "Several wagons, attacked by Indians, will have been set aflame and abandoned along the way"—a Nazi Germany, say, or a Soviet Union—"but the great majority of wagons will be making the slow journey into town." And now the American West was the world, its inhabitants rushing westward, as in Emanuel Leutze's 1860 mural for the House of Representatives, *Westward the Course of Empire Will Take Its Way*, their horizon full of Californias.[4]

The post–Cold War presidents solved the problem of a preeminent if culturally riven United States by universalizing American foreign policy. They universalized what Truman, Eisenhower and Kennedy had referred to as the West. Clinton, Bush Jr. and Obama believed that the underlying patterns of international politics were what Fukuyama had discerned, a mechanism for increasing democracy and openness. None was eager to tether the West to a single, unique civilization, or none tied the benefits of liberty and self-government to the single, unique civilization of the West. Clinton, George W. Bush and Obama foresaw conciliation flowing from the Western virtues of liberty and self-government, and by downplaying particularism, they could welcome new peoples and new constituencies to the democratic fold. Their universalization of the West was not without Cold War precedent. Paraphrasing Jefferson, possibly, Eisenhower had written in his memoirs (circa 1965) about a Western civilization for all: "I have unshakable faith that the ideals and way of life that Western civilization has cherished . . . will flourish everywhere to the infinite benefit of mankind." Such was Eisenhower's faith in the midst of the Vietnam War, though he was not commenting on the 1960s or on his tenure as president. He was articulating his faith in the ultimate triumph of Western civilization, from which everyone everywhere stood to benefit. Starting in the 1990s, Eisenhower's good cheer was much easier to come by in Western capitals, easier to maintain and easier to pin to the present moment.[5]

Clinton, Bush and Obama represented three different kinds of internationalist optimism. Clinton was an economic optimist; Bush, a geopolitical optimist; and Obama, an institutional optimist. Clinton began the "Washington consensus" whereby free trade and the elaboration of economic rules were to be the levers for prosperity and political-economic integration. The Washington consensus built on American advantages in business and technology, summing up the end phase of the Cold War. The Soviet Union had destroyed itself through economic inefficiency and by building mental and physical walls. To lower the barriers of economic and intellectual exchange was to open the world to creativity and, over time, to democracy: Clinton could make good on the economic liberties and the gospel of prosperity that Ronald Reagan had put before his Berlin audience in 1987. George W. Bush surely agreed with each of these points, but the September 11 attacks goaded him into a series of foreign-policy gambles. His working assumption was that liberty, a universally held good, was the antidote to fanaticism and terrorism. If so, the United States should roll the ball of liberty once again, by force if need be. After initiating the 2002 war in Afghanistan, Bush focused on the Middle East. As he had been advised at Camp David right after September 11, removal of the autocrat Saddam Hussein was the necessary next step. The residents of the Middle East would find their way to democracy and economic freedom, and Bush's freedom agenda was wider even than the Middle East. Obama substituted the liberal international order for the Washington consensus and for wars of choice. Law, institutions, education, charismatic leadership and order were his long game, the lifting of people from poverty and the multilateral cultivation of political dignity and shared decision making. Liberty and self-government were living ideals for these three presidents. For different reasons, each of them consigned a self-conscious and crusading West to the past.

Yet, from 1992 to 2016, the West was not universalized. The consensus on political economy and international affairs in Washington was supposed to blossom into a global consensus. This never came to pass. Liberty did not overtake the Middle East. In 2011 and 2012, the Arab Spring yielded to a winter of armed conflict and repression. A war-weary United States and a risk-averse European Union found themselves without leverage in the Syrian Civil War. Washington and Brussels stood by helplessly as bloodshed led to the mass migration of some eleven million Syrians, though when an Islamic State and Caliphate were proclaimed in Syria and Iraq in 2014, the United States and an international coalition rose to the occasion. Meanwhile, Vladimir Putin returned to the Kremlin in 2012, having come to power in 2000 and having partially given up the Russian presidency from 2008 to 2012, in no mood to concede anything to Washington or to any community of powers. Russia showed itself an imaginative and cagy opponent of the liberal international order. Perhaps the most glaring problem with the liberal international order, from 1992 to 2016, was that it did not include China. China profited greatly from the economic order of the 1990s and early twenty-first century—the general stability and the attendant chances to modernize and to invest—which was largely guaranteed by the United States. Without doing too much to antagonize Washington, China pursued a foreign policy and an order of its own. Beijing had no reason to concede to the West when it could harness the liberal international order for the sake of aggrandizing China. In Beijing's assessment, the liberal international order would be eclipsed at some point by an order of Chinese design.

Other setbacks for the Washington consensus and the liberal international order were more local. The shifts registered in Europe first. Southern Europe's economic stagnation sparked anger at alleged German domination of the European Union. In Central Europe, nationalism led some political leaders to defy Brussels and to thumb their noses at the liberal international order. In 2015, a migrant crisis destabilized the entire European continent in mood if not always in fact. In the summer of 2016, Britain voted to leave the European Union, reversing a twenty-five-year trend in Europe toward greater institutional integration and greater internationalism. The political rhythms in the United States were similar. Year by year, the culture wars had been sharpening. After September 11, intractable battlefield wars in Afghanistan and Iraq made Americans wary of intervening abroad, while the entire era was one of gaudy prosperity and Dickensian inequalities. The 2016 election was won by Donald Trump, an advocate of an ethnonationalist West, a skeptic about Europe and the transatlantic relationship, a nonbeliever in international order and international institutions. Trump was a man at odds with both the American foreign-policy elite and the entire Wilsonian heritage in American foreign policy. Only in 2016 did the scope of the actual cultural and economic tensions—so long in the making—come fully into view. With Trump's election, an American-led West was becoming an object of nostalgia. It might still be a rhetorical figuration or a future option, but it was no longer the point of orientation for American foreign policy. The Washington consensus had unraveled most spectacularly, not in Beijing or Moscow or Damascus but in Washington, DC.

A DECADE BEFORE the new millennium, George Herbert Walker Bush announced a "new world order." Watching on television, he saw the

Soviet flag above the Kremlin was lowered for the last time on December 31, 1991. Washington's excitement and sense of validation could not have been more expansive. This was a (brave) new world order for Europe in which the East-West divisions had been redefined seemingly overnight—redefined or simply erased. East was not East: East Germany was no more, the Eastern Bloc was no more, and therefore West was not quite West either; it was not the same West. The formerly communist states of Eastern Europe were in theory no less European than France or Britain. In 1992, the most overt European affirmations of the transatlantic West came from those who had once been anti-communists and dissidents. Vaclav Havel went from internal exile to the Czech Republic's presidential palace. Adam Michnik exchanged imprisonment for the position of public intellectual and newspaper editor in an independent, postcommunist Poland. Enamored of Europe, enamored of the United States, Havel and Michnik continued to make an eloquent case for "civil society," for political liberalism as Fukuyama had defined it, after 1989. Civil society realized the liberties codified in the US Constitution and Bill of Rights. Havel and Michnik were not on the CIA's payroll, and they had not been invented by the Dulles brothers. Nor were they the disappointments the South Vietnamese "democrats" had been in the 1960s. Havel and Michnik were the political and intellectual protagonists of the West, Churchill's and Truman's children. Freed from Soviet interference, these architects of civil society would have allies to the democratic West (Europe) and to the democratic East (Russia), in a Europe without borders. So it was hoped at the time.

The new world order was evolving outside of Europe as well. Of cautious disposition, George H. W. Bush relaxed the Reaganite march to liberty and tried to manage it. No American president ever had as much foreign-policy magic happen on his watch: the peaceful resolution of the Cold War; the surrender of the Soviet competitor in Asia, Latin America and the Middle East; the dismantling of Apartheid in South Africa; the realistic prospect of a Europe "whole and free," as President Bush had put it in a May 1989 speech in West Germany.

When Iraq's Saddam Hussein challenged the regional order in the Middle East by invading Kuwait in August 1990, the United States could respond without having to deal with Moscow, a miraculous sign of the times. The Unites States was also under no obligation to wage a proxy war in Iraq. Suddenly, Iraq was the issue in Iraq, and not the distribution of power between the West and the communist East. In concert with his national security advisor Brent Scowcroft, a Kissinger protégé inclined to see stability as a high ideal of American foreign policy, President Bush did not try to democratize Iraq after defeating it in war. The United States had every military advantage over Iraq, but in the Middle East President Bush was serving as the regional guarantor of order, not as Iraq's liberator. A tacit hierarchy set the priorities. In Europe, liberty and self-government were to advance within and near the NATO alliance, within and near the European Union. In Russia, the aura of liberty and self-government was good enough. In the Middle East, order alone was sufficient. Bush and Scowcroft valued order in the Middle East to such an extent that they cooperated with Saudi monarchs and Egyptian strongmen and let an anti-American dictator stay in power in Iraq. The new world order was not a new birth of freedom everywhere.[6]

In ways W. W. Rostow and Ronald Reagan would both have appreciated, Bill Clinton added more economic heft to the new world order. "It's the economy, stupid," was a Clintonian maxim about domestic American politics, and it carried over into his foreign policy. Globalization's impresario, Clinton was not especially tied to the West. In 1993, he found an already unifying Europe, an ailing Russia and an open terrain for American global influence. Clinton was twenty-two years younger than George Bush Sr., a World War II veteran who had been a contemporary of John F. Kennedy's. An antiwar protestor in his youth and the first Rhodes Scholar president, Clinton accepted that American power had a dark side. He regretted the mistakes that had brought the United States to Vietnam and accepted that racism marred both American history and the history of American foreign policy: Toni Morrison went so far as to call Clinton America's "first black president." Clinton sought a fresh approach on race and politics, one less burdened by the cultural hubris of the West. His America would enjoy a power never before possessed, the power of system building and human rights, and the power of an economic globalization that had been anticipated in the 1960s, derailed in the 1970s and lightly approached in the 1980s. Rostow the academic had calculated the stages of economic growth. In the 1990s, Clinton could watch them proceed, as American universities, American businesses and American technology rebuffed all accusations of a closing American mind. To the contrary, American ingenuity sheltered by the rule of law would spearhead global economic development. It was a tapestry of win-win arrangements for Washington. Markets, talent, ideas, technologies and commerce were all flowing through new channels in the 1990s, symbolized best of all by the Silicon Valley enclave that was the wealth-creating epitome of the American model. The Washington consensus applied as well to postcommunist Russia as it did to the developing economies of Asia, Africa and Latin America. If Bush alluded to order of a new kind, Clinton perceived a world that was new and a world that was gradually being emptied of East and West. In his speech at the 1992 Democratic convention, he promised "an America that will not coddle dictators from Baghdad to Beijing"—and that was just the autocratic countries whose capital cities began with the letter *B*.[7]

In Europe, Clinton aligned this new order with NATO expansion and the growth of the European Union. The EU was the center-stage political experiment of the 1990s, a transnational venture driven by a recently unified Germany, for which "Europe" or "more Europe" was the fill-in-the-blank solution to the problems of history and nationalism. With the Cold War winding down, George H. W. Bush had helped to integrate Europe by not antagonizing a Soviet Union in its death throes. As chronicled in *Germany Unified and Europe Transformed: A Study in Statecraft*, an exuberant 1995 book by two of the president's top national security advisors, Philip Zelikow and Condoleezza Rice, Bush's first priority was Germany. George Bush Sr. supported a vision of Germany within Europe and of a Europe with Germany, much as

Dean Acheson had after 1945. Clinton agreed with both Bush and Acheson on Europe and showed himself to be a skilled diplomat in Europe, a friend to other center-Left leaders such as Britain's Tony Blair and Germany's Gerhard Schröder and a friend of a different sort to Boris Yeltsin, who served as Russia's president in the 1990s. Yelstin was an exotic European leader, neither inside nor outside of the Western club. His grand strategy was to enable a "Greater Europe" from Lisbon to Vladivostok, a concept of Mikhail Gorbachev, a Eurasian zone of peace and commerce. Meanwhile, within Europe the Schengen Agreement, which was put into practice starting in 1995, removed many borders for Europeans. The euro was introduced in 1999 and Berlin restored to its capital-city status in 2000, a German and a European capital. From an American and from a European and for a while from a Russian point of view, the EU was an institutional nucleus around which a greater Europe could form. Informal partnerships and the unrestricted movement of ideas would allow the EU's vision of the future to supersede the hemmed-in, on-edge, tragic Cold War.[8]

Compared to the EU's growth in the 1990s, NATO expansion was a less idealistic venture. It was a project driven by Eastern European fear, Russian weakness and an American desire to do something. Bill Clinton convinced an initially reluctant foreign-policy establishment in Washington to support NATO's enlargement beyond East Germany. His strongest critic was George Kennan, who predicted a catastrophic counterreaction from Russia. (Paul Nitze and Robert McNamara were also skeptics about NATO expansion.) Poland, Hungary and the Czech Republic were invited into NATO in 1997. Membership completed their path from Soviet domination to Euro-American liberation, absolving France and Britain from having failed to protect Eastern Europe from either Nazi Germany or the Soviet Union. Eastern Europe had escaped the unwanted East: if Europe's geography could not be physically altered, a Central Europe could still be extracted from what had been the Warsaw Pact countries. NATO expansion coincided ideologically with the expansion of the EU. Europe's artificial separations and twentieth-century wounds were to heal in the same way France and Germany had mended their ancient wounds after 1945—by integrating their economies and by giving up elements of national sovereignty for institutionalized peace and cooperation. By adding to NATO membership in the 1990s, Clinton set in motion the diplomatic process whereby the Baltic Republics, Slovakia, Slovenia, Bulgaria and Romania might join NATO, which they did in the "big bang" of 2004. Clinton's goal was to fuse peace and stability. There would be no American retreat from Europe: instead, there would be more international order for the United States to lead. Bill Clinton was present at the creation of a new Europe.

NATO expansion was also Clinton's method of consolidating democracy across Europe. Warren Christopher was Clinton's first secretary of state, a lawyer and World War II veteran who wanted to see the countries of Central Europe rooted in the West. The way forward was to transcend the Cold War divisions, as Secretary Christopher described his approach to NATO expansion in his memoirs: "I reasoned that if we did not enlarge the alliance, we would permanently endorse the dividing line that Stalin had drawn across Europe in 1945. Countries sitting on or near that line—the Central European nations—were naturally fearful of a resurgence of Russian imperialism. To leave them in fear, I thought, would make them resentful of the West, more cautious, and reluctant to embrace democratic change." Bill Clinton's second secretary of state, Madeleine Albright, had a biography that was a history of the European twentieth century in miniature. Albright's father had been a diplomat in interwar Czechoslovakia. A graduate of Wellesley College, class of '55, Albright's thesis was "The Subversion of Czechoslovak Democracy by the Communists." After graduate work with Zbigniew Brzezinski at Columbia, she joined Jimmy Carter's National Security Council together with Fukuyama's graduate-school teacher, the political scientist Samuel Huntington. Albright cherished the multilateral legal traditions of American foreign policy. As secretary of state, she advocated for "broad-based coalitions, multinational sanctions, internationally approved use of force [that] will prove to be the key for dealing with those who threaten their neighbors with weapons of mass destruction." NATO expansion very much fit within Albright's view of Europe, an American responsibility and a building block of world order. Having become the first female secretary of state in January 1997, Albright hung the photos of two American Europeanists, George C. Marshall and Dean Acheson, in her seventh-floor office. (Marshall and Acheson looked down from these same office walls later when Condoleezza Rice was secretary.) Secretary Albright wished to extend Marshall's and Acheson's legacies beyond the Cold War.[9]

The economic scene of the 1990s gave President Clinton further confidence in NATO expansion. The Cold War had everywhere produced parallels, perimeters and lines of separation: us against them, communism against anticommunism, North against South, East against West. It was the grand strategist's chessboard par excellence. Without the Cold War, integration was plausible for all of Europe because integration was breaking out everywhere in the 1990s. China was projecting itself into the global economy at tremendous speed. Russia had integration with the West as an explicit foreign-policy goal in the 1990s. Where countries fell short in this cycle of geopolitical integration, technology was building webs and networks whether politicians wanted them or not. Author of the popular 1999 book, *The Lexus and the Olive Tree: Understanding Globalization*, Thomas Friedman was a *New York Times* journalist who celebrated technology much as President Clinton celebrated technology. Technological change made possible a light-touch American foreign policy. The United States could incentivize integration in Europe by being an example of the networked country. On the basis of economic and political liberty, mutual attractions would form between the United States and the outside world. In the process, markets for American goods would emerge, and the universities and business centers of the United States could be global magnets for talent and entrepreneurship: New York and the San Francisco Bay Area and all the other hubs would flourish under these circumstances. The "Washington consensus" was not just Woodrow Wilson's League of Nations in action. It echoed Teddy Roosevelt's and Elihu Root's will to construct the Panama Canal as well and thus to have the United States a Pacific and an Atlantic power, a commercial center to the world at large. A pacified Europe and an expanded NATO, with mirrored alliances in Asia and Latin America, fit into a global template. Clinton's Washington gladly underwrote the security commitments necessary for the global economy to prosper.[10]

The vogue for integration and globalization was less win-win in practice than in theory. It ignored troubling nuances. The West had been enlarged to global proportions, as Fukuyama had predicted. This was the more original meaning Fukuyama had attributed to the triumph of the West. If the very idea of the West was triumphing, then an expanded NATO would only be a first step. NATO might be necessary while there was still the wreckage of the Cold War to contend with and while a country like Russia was not yet Western, not yet a liberal democracy. Once Russia and China followed the West, all the world would belong to the same family. Conflict would end, leaving NATO a comforting anachronism that could be replaced by a properly global security architecture. That was the hope. At the same time, a great many of the old divisions and problems could still be detected beneath the surface. China was steadfastly refusing to democratize: it rejected liberty and self-government in favor of one-party rule. Reading between the lines, an expanded NATO was (among other things) a wedge against Russia, as Warren Christopher admitted in his memoirs, a hedge against resurgent Russian imperialism. NATO had only one majority Muslim member state, Turkey, which would not be invited to join the EU. Globalization and integration had their unspoken protocols, and an irony of NATO expansion into Eastern Europe was a political and security culture in Poland, Hungary and the Baltic States based on civilizational borders, whatever Thomas Friedman or Francis Fukuyama might contend about unbound Westernization. These countries defined themselves against the Muslim Middle East in the South and against Russia in the East. Russia was still the unregenerate East in Warsaw, Vilnius and Tallinn. The Ministries of Foreign Affairs and even more the Ministries of Defense in Eastern Europe greeted NATO expansion as a full-throated affirmation of Western civilization and as the line of division between themselves and an Asiatic Russia. Clinton's foreign policy called forth complexities that globalization would not be able to resolve. Over time they were complexities that globalization would exacerbate.

DURING BILL CLINTON's first term, Madeleine Albright's former National Security Council colleague Samuel Huntington was winding his way to a dissenting view on globalization and American foreign policy. Huntington was "a lifelong Democrat," in the journalist Robert Kaplan's words, who had been a speechwriter for Adlai Stevenson, an advisor to Hubert Humphrey and a speechwriter for Jimmy Carter and who contributed to several of Carter's speeches on human rights. If he had been an establishment profiler, he was anything but an establishment thinker. Like his student Fukuyama, Huntington devised a larger-than-life thesis with the assistance of the right-leaning Olin Foundation, giving the Bradley Lectures at the American Enterprise Institute in 1992. Huntington's "Clash of Civilizations?" article in *Foreign Affairs* (summer 1993) was as seminal as Fukuyama's "End of History?" essay had been three years earlier. Also like Fukuyama, Huntington had transposed his article into a book, *The Clash of Civilizations,* which came out in 1996. Huntington took in the long line of books about civilization and the West, going back to the nineteenth century. He adopted a bit of Spengler's pessimism and shared robustly in Spengler's faith in civilization as a category of international relations analysis. Huntington took in as well the American conservatives' connection between civilization and foreign policy, a nontechnocratic view of foreign policy to which culture and especially religion were integral. From Edward Said, Huntington acquired a flexibility of perspective and a distaste for the conceit that Western civilization was in fact world-girding. Huntington faulted academia for confusion about the West, but not Edward Said, per se. Huntington was well aware of Fukuyama, of course, and Huntington disagreed completely with the end-of-history hypothesis. Even if the Cold War was over, there was and would be no diminution of cultural conflict, Huntington was sure.

Post–Cold War culture was the opposite of boring, and the listless, overfed last man a fabrication. Civilizations were real, belief was real, cultural competition was real. No amount of economic growth, technological change and American success would reduce the likelihood of clashes among the world's rival civilizations.[11]

In a blurb for *The Clash of Civilizations*, Henry Kissinger described Huntington as "one of the West's most eminent political scientists." Kissinger's wording was telling—Huntington not a leading American political scientist but a political scientist "of the West." The Cold War over, the West was being simultaneously forgotten and flattered, Huntington thought, overestimated and underestimated. He could see economic "modernization" around him, economic and technological change, but he cautioned his readers against the overinterpretation of this circumstance "after the Cold War." Reaching back to W. W. Rostow and rejecting the conventional wisdom that Fukuyama represented (in Washington, DC, at least), Huntington emphasized that "modernization is distinct from westernization and is producing neither a universal civilization in any meaningful sense nor the westernization of non-Western societies." The era of ideologies, from the Bolshevik Revolution to the East-West competitions of the Cold War, was passing. The era of civilizations was either beginning or returning. Fukuyama was right about the defeat of communism and an ideological victory of sorts for liberal democracy, but Huntington's student was wrong about the convergence of trend lines into one international system. After the Cold War, "global politics began to be reconfigured along cultural lines," Huntington wrote. Ethnicity, religion and civilization had not been subsumed into pure economics. They were obstreperously alive, now more than ever, when "local politics is the politics of ethnicity [and] global politics is the politics of civilizations."[12]

Having cast off the primacy of economics, Huntington elevated religion as a variable in international affairs. Civilizations grow out of religions, and in foreign policy religion matters because of civilization: "of all the objective elements which define civilizations . . . the most important is usually religion." Huntington tallied up seven major civilizations composed of religion, history, geography and sensibility—Sinic, Japanese, Hindu, Islamic, Orthodox Christian, Western Christian and Latin American. Hindu and Muslim civilizations are monolithic, whereas Huntington broke Christianity into three distinct civilizations, separating Western Christian from Latin American and Orthodox Christian. One of the earliest geopolitical definitions of the West had been the world of Western or Latin Christianity versus the Orthodox East. Huntington revived this pedigreed definition in *The Clash of Civilizations*. Latin America, however Catholic, is not the West. Orthodox Christian Greece falls outside the West, together with Serbia, Bulgaria, Romania, Ukraine, Belarus and Russia. Huntington's map complicates any equation of NATO with the West. Indeed, NATO straddles a fault line of civilizations in Huntington's scheme, given its one Muslim and several Orthodox Christian member states. The leading country of NATO is, however, solidly of the West: "until the end of the nineteenth century America had only limited contacts with non-Western civilizations. Once the United States moved out into the world scene, however, the sense of a broader identity with Europe developed . . . twentieth-century America had defined itself as part of and, indeed, the leader of a broader entity, the West, that includes Europe."[13]

In 1996, one of the West's most eminent political scientists was worried about Western overconfidence. Though "democracy is the political form of Western civilization," Huntington wrote, and though democracy was in its giddy heyday in the mid-1990s, the West had a past as fraught and controversial as Edward Said had contended in *Orientalism*. Huntington was a devout but unsentimental westerner: "the West won the world . . . by its superiority in applying organized violence. Westerners often forget this fact; non-Westerners never do." Huntington cited Said approvingly in *The Clash of Civilizations* vis-à-vis the stability and the homogeneity of the standard East-West divisions. "These myths," Huntington wrote, "suffer the defects of the Orientalism which Edward Said appropriately criticized for promoting 'the difference between the familiar (Europe, the west, 'us') and the strange (the Orient, the east, 'them')' and for assuming the inherent superiority of the former to the latter." No advance of the West was possible without a commensurate backlash. Convinced of its own superiority and therefore of the inevitable spread of its civilization, the West was losing sight of other civilizations, of the anger they might have toward the West and of their will to power as civilizations. The world is "multicivilizational," and within it, civilizations are struggling for prestige, power and influence. Competition among the seven major-league civilizations was more Huntington's model than some Spenglerian libretto of rise and fall, growth and decay, but Huntington did share a cyclical frame of reference with Spengler. For Huntington, Fukuyama's error resided in the linear neatness of his argument, the rise of the West followed by the rise of the West *ad infinitum*. The actual future was far more uncertain.[14]

As his title promised, Huntington sketched the coming threats to the West. He kept his eye on religion, observing that "the revival of non-Western religions is the most powerful manifestation of anti-Westernism in non-Western societies . . . a rejection of the West and of the secular, degenerate culture associated with the West." Islam stood at the center of this problem, in Huntington's view, but Hinduism and Orthodox Christianity in tandem with nationalism had their own potential to menace the West. Huntington listed Russia and Turkey as societies unsettled by their belonging and nonbelonging to the West. The belt of Orthodox Christian countries running from Greece through the Balkans to Ukraine and Russia, many of them newly independent in 1996, worried Huntington. Where civilizations merged, interacted and collided was where conflicts—clashes—were bound to arise. This was a problem NATO could not solve, though it was a problem to which NATO might contribute, because "the success of NATO has resulted in large part from its being the central security organization of Western countries with common values and philosophical assumptions." NATO had housed the West during the Cold War, but it was moving far afield from the traditional West. The zone of conflict, Huntington predicted, would be Ukraine, the borderland between two civilizations, although Russia and Europe presented second-order threats.

For civilizational conflict, the global flash points would be in Asia and the Middle East, Huntington predicted, the clashes stemming from the "interactions of Western arrogance, Islamic intolerance, and Sinic assertiveness."[15]

The most memorable passages in *The Clash of Civilizations*, which was advertised as an investigation into world order, laid bare the West's internal crisis. At the height of the West's power, in the 1990s as in the 1890s, decline was imminent. Overextension or hubris was half the story, the other half being the secular, relativistic, degenerate culture the West's enemies accurately detected in the West. Looking back to the nineteenth century, Huntington concluded that "the most successful protagonists of Western culture are . . . Christian missionaries." (Whittaker Chambers would have wholeheartedly agreed.) They extended the West because they believed in it. When "the American phase of Western domination began" in the 1940s, something started to go wrong. A new vulgarity set in, leading Huntington to the revealing quip—a parodic reply to the decade's economic-minded optimists, its Tom Friedmans and its Francis Fukuyamas—that "the essence of Western civilization is the Magna Carta not the Magna Mac." Yet it was McDonald's Big Mac, as well as Pizza Hut and Kentucky Fried Chicken, that represented Western civilization in the former Soviet Union and elsewhere. Too much Magna Mac and too little Magna Carta could only spur Russians over time to assert the non-Western civilizational lineage that came more naturally to them anyway. The religious extremists of the Middle East would react to the Magna Mac with even greater outrage. Here, Huntington's book harkened back to the midcentury conservative literature about the West, retracing James Burnham's 1964 anxieties about the emptiness of the West. Whittaker Chambers's designation of the West as "this sick civilization" was not quite Huntington's, but neither did Huntington look at the West in the 1990s and see a picture of civilizational health.[16]

When writing on the health of the American university, Huntington's language darkened further. The hour was already late, and as far as the academic vocation was concerned Huntington doubted that the

West could renew itself, wondering whether its "sustained moral rot [will] simply accelerate its end [inviting] subordination to other economically and demographically more dynamic civilizations." Muslims in Europe and Hispanics in the United States were altering the West's social fabric, but it was those in the elite universities who were most at fault for expelling the West. Huntington decried a "concentrated and sustained onslaught from a small but influential number of intellectuals and publicists. In the name of multiculturalism they have attacked the identification of the United States with Western Civilization, denied the coexistence of a common American culture, and promoted racial, ethnic and other subnational cultural identities and groupings." Huntington did not agree with the Edward Said who wrote with pain about his hybrid identity and believed that the United States would benefit from a humanistic purview larger than East and West, larger and less encumbered by the West's extensive history of imperialism. Huntington wanted American universities to produce believers in the West, secular missionaries, perhaps, whose common culture was vibrant and strong enough to be shared with others. Absent the libertarian emphases, there was a bit of William F. Buckley's *God and Man at Yale* in Huntington's *Clash of Civilizations.*[17]

The Clash of Civilizations also picked up where *The Closing of the American Mind* left off. World order was being hashed out not so much on the playing fields of American schools and universities as in their curricula and syllabi. The multiculturalists are in charge, and they "wish to create a country of many civilizations, which is to say a country not belonging to any civilization and lacking a cultural core. A multicivilizational United States will not be the United States; it will be the United Nations." Higher education and foreign policy, as pursued in the United States, were the lifeblood of the West, but without the Western ideal, higher education and foreign policy alike would sink into "a global Dark Ages." The defenders of the West were in retreat. Their war with the multiculturalists was, "in [political scientist] James Kurth's words, 'the *real* clash' within the American segment of Western civilization." Huntington felt himself trapped between the West-diluting multiculturalists and the West-loving universalists like Fukuyama. He feared that although "multiculturalism at home threatens the United States and the West; universalism threatens the West and the world. Both deny the uniqueness of Western culture." Bill Clinton was misleading the United States, and the multicultural Left was encouraging him. So was the libertarian and neoconservative Right, all of them enemies of uniqueness, of the local passions and enduring faiths that would never be melted into a single world order. The West's economic and military power was a chimera, a distraction conducive to excess, blinding the West to its cultural and spiritual needs. Huntington's West was grievously disunited in 1996, and "whether the West comes together politically and economically . . . depends overwhelmingly on whether the United States reaffirms its identity as a Western nation and defines its global role as the leader of Western civilization." Huntington did not seem to expect that it would.[18]

IN THE 1990s, the contest among Huntington, Fukuyama and Said was an intellectual duel to the death. If one of them was right, the other two had to be wrong. The clash was coming. The clash was not coming. The end of history was at hand. The sins of Orientalism, of Western imperialism, would have to be repented before East and West could be forgotten and something more enlightened put in their place. Clinton stood nearest to Fukuyama: the end of history was the Washington consensus, and there could be consensus blossoming out from Washington precisely because history had come to a satisfactory end. For the Clinton administration, Said was too critical and Huntington too curmudgeonly to inform policymaking. September 11 and its aftermath dramatically rearranged these arguments and positions. With greater and greater frustration, Fukuyama watched the war in Iraq unfold, and without abandoning his commitment to democracy promotion he publicly parted ways with the neoconservative movement. In 2006, he published an elegiac book-length essay, *America at the Crossroads: Democracy, Power and the Neoconservative Legacy,* a lament for all that had been lost in Iraq, after which his pessimism would only deepen.

September 11 had not invalidated the beauty of the Western idea for Fukuyama. The fanaticism behind the attack could be interpreted as an upside-down tribute to this beauty: the mighty West versus a vestigial and enraged non-West. But the Iraq War, conducted in the name of liberty and self-government, was a real problem for the West as it was for Fukuyama's youthful optimism about liberty and democracy. Shock and awe rained down on Baghdad, leaving chaos instead of democracy and a bitter conundrum of American power, awesome enough to move mountains, but not in the direction that Washington wanted.[19]

For Said, the Iraq War was the usual Western disaster and further proof of a wanton, thuggish and ill-informed West. This Anglo-American adventure in the deserts of Mesopotamia was Orientalism redux, the kind of thing Cecil Rhodes or Teddy Roosevelt or Winston Churchill would have enjoyed doing, guns and bibles in hand. As Said wrote in a preface to the twenty-fifth-anniversary edition of *Orientalism* (2004), the Iraq War was nothing other than "an imperialist war confected by a very small group of unelected U.S. officials . . . [and] urged against a devastated Third World dictatorship having to do with world dominance, security control, and scarce resources, but disguised for its true intent, hastened, and reasoned for by orientalists who betrayed their calling as scholars." Here, Said was on the edge of interpreting the Iraq War as the fault of American academics—of the orientalists who had betrayed their calling as scholars. Whatever the universities were teaching, those students who had gone on to become policymakers, Said's small group of unelected officials, had learned nothing from the West's horrific past. They had learned nothing from him. Those in thrall to such self-confident ignorance were condemned to repeat the mistakes of the past. So construed, the West was irredeemable.[20]

More than Said's anger or Fukuyama's faith in the future, *The Clash of Civilizations* came closest to capturing the national mood after September 11. Huntington had put the word *clash* in his very title, and a clash had come. Against the academic grain of the 1990s, he had presented religion as a catalyst of geopolitical conflict, which was undeniable on and after September 11. (The year before 9/11, Huntington released *Culture Matters,* an edited volume that was a prophetic investigation of culture and international affairs.) Culture and identity were as salient as religion in the aftermath of the attacks on New York and Washington, DC. When members invoked Article 5 of NATO's founding charter and pledged their military support to the United States, when a French newspaper headline read "We Are All Americans" on September 12, 2001, a Western and not just an American response to this event was sounded. The German historian Heinrich August Winkler retrospectively wrote in a history of the transatlantic West that "there was an almost universal awareness after the terror attacks of September 11 in New York and Washington that this had been an attack not only on America but on the West as such." At issue was not just the security of the West, the NATO alliance and the capacity of the United States to defend itself and its allies in the wake of the attack. For many Americans and Europeans, September 11 amounted to an attack on liberty and therefore on the West. The Princeton historian Bernard Lewis, Edward Said's favorite *bête noire,* channeled these emotions into a series of books and essays after September 11, inquiring into the pathologies of the Muslim world. Chronicler of a despotic East, Lewis gladly sided with Europe and the United States, the liberty-loving West. He published *What Went Wrong? Western Impact and Middle East Responses* in 2002.[21]

Between September 11 and the invasion of Iraq in spring 2003, Vice President Dick Cheney consulted with Bernard Lewis about the Middle East, but George W. Bush played down the rhetoric of civilization and the rhetoric of East-West conflict that had fueled the Cold War. After September 11, Samuel Huntington himself insisted that *The Clash of Civilizations* was a study of international politics and not a user's manual for getting civilizations to clash: it predicted but did not endorse civilizational tension. Huntington challenged the presumption that a Huntingtonian would favor war in the Middle East. Moving toward war in the Middle East, Bush remained in the end-of-history fold, seeking a translation of Ronald Reagan's foreign policy, in which Fukuyama had been involved directly, from the late twentieth to the twenty-first century. Reagan had stood before the Berlin Wall, he had called upon Mr. Gorbachev to tear it down, and as if he were Joshua, the wall had come tumbling down. Reagan had soliloquized about Western liberty and the Christian cross in Berlin, whereas George W. Bush detached liberty from any qualifying adjective. Liberty was neither American nor Western. If Bush had to supply an adjective for liberty, it would be "God-given," and not by the Judeo-Christian God alone. Western interests, not the rhetoric of the West, were involved in the Iraq War. As the Bush administration defined them, these interests were the imperative of counterterrorism, the shattering of authoritarianism in the Middle East and the guaranteeing of energy flows from the Middle East into the global economy. The shattering of authoritarianism was a universalist venture, a freedom agenda, which would place the Middle East on the right side of history. The Cold War was a modest affair compared with the messianic project George W. Bush outlined in his Second Inaugural Address. Kennedy had promised merely to fight for liberty and to bear any burden on its behalf. Forty-four years later, George W. Bush spoke as an Old Testament prophet who lived in an impure world but whose eyes could see the end of tyranny, the end of history after the end of history. Bush was not to be pinned down to hemispheric or civilizational or national categories. "The best hope for freedom in our world," he proclaimed in his inaugural address, "is the expansion of freedom in all the world."[22]

THE TRANSATLANTIC RELATIONSHIP was conspicuously the collateral damage of the Iraq War. The Soviet threat was long ago and by 2001 had been forgotten. After September 11, we were all Americans for a while, but European skepticism about American foreign policy picked up in 2002 and 2003. NATO did indeed fight a war in Afghanistan, where European soldiers died because of the September 11 attack. Transatlantic tensions concentrated on the next forever war caused by September 11. Some in Europe supported George W. Bush's will to invade: Britain's Tony Blair was one ally, as was Spain's prime minister José Maria Aznar. Partnership with the United States was a foreign-policy sine qua non in Eastern Europe, and a war in Iraq could be tolerated for the sake of sticking with the United States. A handful of the formerly anticommunist dissidents, like Adam Michnik, believed that the elimination of Saddam Hussein's dictatorship resembled the elimination of Soviet dictatorship in 1989. By contrast, many in Western Europe approached war in Iraq through the lens of the Vietnam War. Whether the United States was constructing an empire of liberty or behaving like an old-school empire lay in the eye of the European beholder. Unsurprisingly, the France that had never loved NATO or American leadership doubted that America's war in Iraq was a good idea. Unsurprisingly, Germany valued pacifism above war in 2003. Surprisingly, Germany's foreign minister publicly questioned the Bush administration's forthcoming war. "I am not convinced," Joschka Fischer told Secretary of Defense Donald Rumsfeld at the 2003 Munich Security Forum. An outspoken critic of the Vietnam War in his younger years, Fischer was unconvinced by the case for the war the United States was making. In 2004, the German philosopher Jürgen Habermas published *The Divided West*, an indictment of American foreign policy for its betrayal of international order, its repudiation of Wilsonianism and its deviation from the Enlightenment ideal of peace through deliberation. In the opinion of Habermas and many Germans, there was more hope for the West in Berlin, Paris and Brussels than in George W. Bush's Washington, DC.[23]

The US-Russian relationship was the inconspicuous collateral damage of the Iraq War. In 2000, Vladimir Putin had come to power in mysterious ways, with a stated interest in integrating Russia into the West. He presented himself as a modernizer, and in the first years of his presidency he broached the possibility of Russia joining NATO, while Kennan's old office at the State Department, the Office of Policy Planning, floated the idea, as well, in a 2003 memo titled "Why NATO Should Invite Russia to Join." Russia offered the United States material support after September 11. Yet the partnership to which Putin aspired, and about which the Office of Policy Planning was bold enough to speculate, collapsed beneath the weight of US-Russian differences and beneath the weight of the Iraq War. A paradox of Bush's universalist yearning was the unilateral style of his diplomacy. In December 2001, Bush pulled the United States out of the Antiballistic Missile Treaty with Russia, which had been signed by the United States and the Soviet Union in 1972. The death of this treaty coupled with Putin's misgivings about the Iraq War were small cracks in the edifice of a Europe whole and free—to the degree that Bush Sr. had Russia in mind when he coined this phrase at the end of the Cold War. US-Russian relations were the least of Washington's worries at the time. They were not the least of Putin's worries, and he would openly break with the idea of an American-led West some four years after the Iraq War began. At the Munich Security Conference in 2007, by which time the Iraq War was synonymous with American foreign policy for Putin, the Russian president gave a fire-breathing speech denouncing the depravity of American foreign policy and of American-style democracy promotion.[24]

The key American text on the transatlantic parting of ways after September 11 came from Robert Kagan. Kagan was the son of a Yale classics professor. From 1984 to 1986, he had served on the State Department's Policy Planning staff, one of several jobs he had in the Reagan administration. Kagan was Reaganesque in his conviction that liberty and American military power were twinned—indeed, that only American leadership and American power were sufficient to the task of widening liberty's global scope. In the lead-up to the Iraq War of 2003, Kagan wrote *Of Paradise and Power: America and Europe in the New World Order* in which he agreed with Habermas about the peaceful nature of European foreign policy. With a wink, Kagan compared European strategic culture to the goddess Venus, a love fest. Europe for Kagan was effectively Western Europe: whether Russians were from Venus *Of Paradise and Power* did not say. Somewhat unusually, Kagan aligned American foreign policy not with the Enlightenment rationalists but with the seventeenth-century philosopher Thomas Hobbes and with the adjective *Hobbesian*. The world, in Kagan's eyes, was Hobbesian and inclined toward the state of nature. It was a dark forest, and

if there were gleams of Enlightenment, if there were law and cooperation, it was because these goods had been brought to the forest by force
of arms. It was the United States that had subdued Hitler. It had been
a military venture, and with pride Kagan affiliated American grand
strategy with Mars, the god of war. Americans were from Mars and
Europeans from Venus. In the spring of 2003, Kagan wanted a martial
Washington to reach into the Middle Eastern forest and assert its will
in the metastasizing chaos over there.[25]

IN 2004, HAD Habermas been able to vote for an American politician,
he would surely have voted for Barack Obama. A senator from Illinois, Obama was selected to give the nominating speech at the 2004
Democratic Convention in Boston. He startled his audience with his
eloquence and with a vision of postpartisan unity. In the midst of the
Iraq War, he was also the rare politician to doubt the decision to invade. Senator John Kerry, the party's presidential nominee in 2004,
had voted for the war, a vote he defended on the campaign trail. Senator Hillary Clinton had voted for the war. The courage not to join
the pro-war bandwagon was crucial to Obama's political success, to his
improbable journey from the Illinois State Senate to the US Senate to
the White House in 2008, while from 2004 to 2008 the war went from
debatable disaster to objective disaster. "In the quarter-century-long
struggle to define American leadership after the Cold War," as one of
Obama's senior foreign-policy advisors, Derek Chollet, put it, Obama
favored multilateralism, restraint and a culturally neutral principle of
liberty. His ideal was an order embedded in international institutions.
If he was recoiling from the Iraq War, Obama did not at all reject the
American foreign-policy heritage. A presidency that foregrounded the
transatlantic relationship and the Wilsonian tradition, Obama's was
the last twenty-first-century presidency framed by liberty as a foreign-
policy ideal. After eight years of acting on these commitments, Obama
had to watch them disintegrate into Donald Trump's 2016 victory.[26]

Well versed in the West and its discontents, Obama was as educated
a man as has ever made it to the White House. He is in the company

of Thomas Jefferson, John Adams, John Quincy Adams, Abraham Lincoln and Woodrow Wilson, all presidents who were seriously moved by ideas. The idea of the West had been present but diminishing in the intellectual world the young Obama entered. He was born in 1961. In high school in the 1970s, Obama took a popular "Ideas in Western Literature" class at Hawaii's elite Puna School, in which he read Sartre, Camus, Borges, Hesse and Kafka. (All of these brooding high-modernist writers would have loathed the Western-progress ethos of the Chicago World's Fair.) Obama had also lived in Indonesia as a child, and his father was from Kenya. Mixed-race parentage and a childhood outside the mainland United States added to Barack Obama's awareness of a world beyond the United States and Europe. His childhood and young adult years gave him many contradictions to consider: the distance between white and black in American life; the proximity between white and black; the distance between Europe and the places it had colonized; and the postcolonial World's globalized proximity to the West. By experience, disposition and education, Obama was prone not to endorse or reject the West but to move fluidly in and out of it. His teenage reading in the African American literary and intellectual canon—W. E. B. Du Bois, James Baldwin, Toni Morrison and many others—refined the questions of belonging and not-belonging that haunted his adulthood. As an undergraduate at Columbia, Obama had the chance to study with the scholar who had titled his memoir *Out of Place* and whose monograph, *Orientalism,* was a study of the Western ambiguities. Amusingly, Obama was unimpressed by Edward Said's class on modern fiction at Columbia. He found it too theoretical and considered Said a "flake."[27]

As president, Obama struck a balance between criticism and defense of the West. In one of the most important speeches of his presidency, given in Cairo in June 2009, he decried the "legacy of colonialism." This was one tonality. He struck another tonality in a speech to an African audience. "It is easy to point fingers," the American president noted in this July 2009 speech, "and to pin the blame for these problems on others. Yes, a colonial map that made little sense bred conflict, and the West often approached Africa as a patron, rather than a partner. But the West is not responsible for the destruction of the Zimbabwean economy over the last decade, or wars in which children are enlisted as combatants." That was another tonality, imputing responsibility to the non-West and establishing a limit to historical grievance. Over the last decade, Zimbabweans had managed Zimbabwe, and they needed to face up to the results. In Accra, where W. E. B. Du Bois is buried, Obama spoke of the need for "strong institutions" (also in 2009). He was advocating for government as it existed in the EU and the United States—advocating not for their export to Africa through force or other means but for the value of Western-style institutions, per se. They could be imported effectively by a sovereign African state and adapted to local tradition and circumstance. Or perhaps the West was not the model for Africa, and there were more internally consistent ways of building up effective legislative and judicial institutions. This was a question for Africans to decide.[28]

Coming after George W. Bush and the Iraq War, Obama sided instinctively with the legalistic version of American liberty and kept his distance from the messianic version. At Harvard Law School, Obama had been president of the Law Review; he spent some time as a young man teaching law at the University of Chicago. He was a peacemaker who believed, as had Teddy Roosevelt and Woodrow Wilson before him, in the mediating capacities of American diplomacy. He drew inspiration for these capacities in the founding documents of the American republic, regularly citing the never-ending work of establishing a more perfect union, regularly placing "we the people" at the center of his national and international narratives. As Derek Chollet notes of Obama the person, "he prizes deliberation." Democracy in practice was the peaceful resolution of conflict, and because the United States had come so far with its own union, from the eighteenth century to 2008, the next step was to push for a more perfect union abroad, to roll the ball of liberty forward with all deliberate speed. What he did not want was democracy promotion through military force or *Making War to Keep Peace*, a book posthumously published in 2007 by Jeane

Kirkpatrick, the neoconservative thinker and Reagan's ambassador to the United Nations from 1981 to 1985. Making war to keep peace is an impeccably Orwellian concept, and Obama had campaigned against this kind of shoot-first-think-later foreign policy. He owed his election not just to the course of the Iraq War but to the financial crash of 2008, which limited Washington's ability to make war. Obama had the examples of Europe, Asia and Latin America to consider as well. Rescued from the Cold War pressures, many countries in these regions had moved toward more cooperation, more democracy, more trade, more peace since 1989. So had large parts of Africa, where the Cold War burdens had once been perilous. George W. Bush had made his African policy a priority, and on the pillars of democratic and economic success a new house could be erected for the international community. The Obama administration called this house the liberal international order. It may have been of American make, but within the nonimperial liberal international order countries were at liberty to chart their own course.[29]

Obama's notion of liberal international order did not exclude military action. The first Democrat to be elected after September 11, Obama profited politically from the foreign-policy failures of his Republican predecessor, but he could not rest his laurels on the mistakes of others. He had to prove himself as commander-in-chief. When receiving the Nobel Peace Prize in 2009, in effect for winning the 2008 presidential election, Obama spoke in Oslo about the necessity of war. He held both Eisenhower and George Bush Sr. in high esteem, Eisenhower for his ability to restrain military spending, and Bush Sr. for his diplomatic aplomb. The victor of World War II and the victor of the First Gulf War were not the foreign-policy heroes of a pacifist. For Democrats of Obama's generation, the Kosovo War of 1998 had been a turning point, consigning Vietnam to ancient history and consigning even the Cold War to history. Humanitarian intervention practiced by Democrats like Bill Clinton and his hard-driving negotiator-in-chief Richard Holbrooke were an admirable new departure for American foreign policy, many around Obama believed. Holbrooke was a twentieth-century

Teddy Roosevelt, a diplomat thoroughly convinced that with the right degree of imagination military force could enable mediation. The Dayton Accords of 1995 mirrored the 1905 Treaty of Portsmouth, both of them overseas conflicts brought to a diplomatic end on American soil. (Holbrooke held the negotiations in a hangar full of American military planes, lest the negotiators lose sight of the connection between war and peace, force and negotiation.) As Derek Chollet notes of Holbrooke's diplomatic legacy and of humanitarian intervention more generally, "once America acted through a combination of force and diplomacy, it ended a war and renewed US leadership." One of Obama's closest national security advisors, Ben Rhodes, admiringly labeled Holbrooke "a towering figure in the Democratic Party's foreign policy establishment."[30]

The Obama administration considered Clinton's achievement of international order in the Balkans an instructive precedent. There had been a policy bridge between the Kosovo War and the Iraq War as well, humanitarian intervention having been among the justifications for the Iraq War. But Obama interpreted the Iraq War as George W. Bush's deviation from international order and humanitarian intervention. For Obama, the right relationship between humanitarian intervention in the late 1990s and the twenty-first-century liberal international order was set out in a Pulitzer Prize–winning book, *A Problem from Hell* (2002), by the journalist and human rights activist Samantha Power. Power juxtaposed multiple examples of genocide—in Ottoman Turkey, in Europe, in Rwanda—with the foreign-policy question of when and whether to intervene, openly arguing for certain kinds of military intervention: the responsibility to protect, even across the lines of national sovereignty. Power's arguments were in tune with the Truman National Security Project, a consortium of hawkish Democrats, which was founded in 2004 and whose members were prominent in the Obama administration. One appreciative reader of *A Problem from Hell* was Barack Obama, who appointed Power to a position on his National Security Council staff. Ben Rhodes, who saw a role model in Samantha Power, wrote that "to my generation of liberals, she offered an alternative to the neoconservative views that dominated the debate after 9/11: She supported an interventionist America that promoted human rights and prevented atrocities, yet she'd opposed the war in Iraq." As for their generation, Power was born in 1970, Rhodes in 1977. In 2013, Obama made Power a member of his cabinet by appointing her the US ambassador to the United Nations, a position she held until January 2017. The conscience of the liberal international order, Power prodded the president to intervene militarily in Libya, which he did, and in Syria, which he did on a small scale.[31]

Much broader than humanitarian intervention or the responsibility to protect, the Obama administration's ideal of liberal international order can be traced as far back as the seventeenth century. An early-modern theorist of international relations, Hugo Grotius (1583–1685), philosophized about an international society rooted in law and based on agreement rather than coercion. In the 1970s, the international relations scholar Hedley Bull reworked Grotius's ideas in a series of influential books. He published *The Anarchical Society* in 1977, in which he looked at preexisting international societies through a civilizational lens: "a common feature of these historical international societies is that they were all founded upon a common culture or civilization or at least some of the elements of such a civilization," Bull wrote. Fascinated by civilization and order, Bull examined the future of international society and its legal underpinnings in *The Expansion of International Society* (1984) and *Justice in International Relations* (1984). William Burns, deputy secretary of state from 2011 to 2014, was an influential participant in Obama administration foreign-policy debates, and in the late 1970s, Burns had been a student of Hedley Bull's at Oxford. What Burns learned from Bull flowed into the liberal international order— the international society—President Obama was eager to encourage. For Burns, Hedley Bull's *The Anarchical Society* "remains as clear and compelling a framework for thinking about international order as I have ever read. Bull's thesis was straightforward: Even in a Hobbesian world, sovereign states have a self-interest in developing rules and institutions to shape their interactions and enhance their chance for security and prosperity." Obama wanted his State Department to focus on precisely these rules and institutions.[32]

President Obama also wanted to calibrate American power with the liberal international order and not to get bogged down in war as he believed his predecessor had. Obama sought a truly global purview. Limiting as the prerequisite of a common civilization might be, Hedley Bull's international society had been pioneered in Europe and had come to acquire global application. It was a Western proposition into which the non-West could be invited. The preeminent American exponent of international society served in Fukuyama's old office at the State Department at almost the same time as Fukuyama. This was John Ikenberry, who was at the Office of Policy Planning from 1991 to 1992, after which he embarked for Princeton University, where he wrote *Liberal Order and Imperial Ambition* (2006) and *Liberal Leviathan* (2011), among many other books. Elaborating upon Bull's earlier ideas, Ikenberry argued for an international order led by the United States and dedicated to rules and norms, strengthening the legal and institutional sinews of an international order that would run on deliberation. Professor Ikenberry was the patron saint of the Obama administration.[33]

Ikenberry's West is the lynchpin of an almost mechanical international order. His is not a West shaped by culture or religion, Bull's common culture or civilization. Ikenberry's 2002 essay, "Democracy, Institutions, and American Restraint"—from an edited volume he titled *America Unrivaled,* very much a 2002 turn of phrase—foreshadows the policy outlook of the Obama administration. It was a paean to "strategic restraint" along the following lines. "Western order has a structure of institutions and open politics that bind major states together," Ikenberry writes. Germany and the United States could be examples, and in addition to their open style of politics Germany and the United States are bound together in the NATO alliance. This internationalism arose after World War II, Ikenberry explains, both in Europe and in Asia. For the system to thrive, the United States must exercise restraint and not attempt to dominate its partners. By showing restraint, the United States encourages its partners to support the system that was built out by Washington in the 1940s—an explicitly American-led order. Such give-and-take is necessary for the institutions of domestic politics: international institutions are no different. Cooperative institutions generate further cooperation, from which further institution building ensues, giving momentum to the liberal international order and grounding it in balance and stability. This shows the *"increasing returns to institutions"* (Ikenberry's italics), the benefits of the liberal international order as opposed to anarchy or to the zero-sum competition outside of institutions. A member of President Obama's National Security Council staff and later his ambassador to Russia, Michael McFaul writes of President Obama as "a 'liberal institutionalist,' believing that American support for international rules, norms and organizations strengthened America's influence in the world in the long run." Ben Rhodes uses the same word to describe the president: Obama "is at his core an institutionalist." Obama in the White House was not a student of Edward Said. He was a student of John Ikenberry.[34]

For the Obama administration, the liberal international order was mostly preferable to the West. It acknowledged a world of which Europe and the United States were not necessarily the center, which was undoubtedly the world of the twenty-first century. President Obama charted a pivot or rebalance to Asia, indicating that European conflicts were at a comfortingly low boil and that the center of economic gravity was shifting over to Asia. After the Cold War obsession with Europe and the war-on-terror obsession with the Middle East, Asia demanded more attention from the makers of American foreign policy, whether "Asia" meant China's geopolitical rise or the vibrant economies and polities that stretched from India to Japan to Australia. Pivoting to Asia would enhance the role of the United States as a Pacific power, and as a Pacific power the old-fashioned rhetoric of the West had always been confusing. It had been confusing *during* the Cold War. In China, India, Vietnam and many other countries, emotional expressions of Western affiliation were likely to recall the West's imperial legacy. Obama was aware enough of Edward Said's thinking to know this. He did not want to refight the Spanish-American War, and appeals to the liberal international order were appealingly neutral. Furthermore, the liberal international order had political value within the United States in 2008. As a foreign-policy motif, it suited the post–Columbian Republic that the United States was five hundred years after Columbus's arrival in the Americas; it was open to all the world. The liberal international order did not dispense with liberty, self-government or American leadership. But the liberal international order's exponents were glad to dispense with the racial, ethnic, religious and cultural baggage of the West. Those of them educated in the 1980s and 1990s—Samantha Power graduated from Yale University in 1992 and Ben Rhodes from Rice University in 2000—had been trained to identify and to question this baggage. Obama's presidency raised fascinating questions about "the end of white America" or "The End of White America?" as the cultural critic Hua Hsu put it in a 2009 *Atlantic* article. Domestically and abroad, the crystalline cultural openness of the liberal international order had political salience both for the Obama administration and for its electorate.[35]

Hillary Clinton, Obama's first secretary of state, was a committed believer in the liberal international order. A senator from New York and the First Lady from 1992 to 2000, Clinton was not identical to Obama in foreign-policy outlook. She was more hawkish, having traveled a long political road from the antiwar protests of the late 1960s. Clinton graduated from Wellesley in 1969, making national news with a progressively themed commencement speech, but by the 1990s she and her husband Bill were the centrist spirit of the Democratic Party. A constant in Hillary Clinton's thinking was the commitment to rights, and if Obama's approach to foreign policy revolved around institutions, Clinton's revolved around rights. At the Fourth World Conference of Women in Beijing in September 1995, Clinton gave a memorable speech on human rights. "If there is one message that echoes forth from this conference," she contended, "let it be that human rights are women's rights and women's rights are human rights, once and for all." In this speech, Clinton was aligning two trajectories, the national movements for women's rights (for suffrage and equality under the law) and the international campaign for human rights, into a single universalist trajectory. Giving the speech in China reinforced its universalism. The message could be expressed by an American political figure in Asia, or it could be just as plausibly expressed by an Asian activist in the United States. As secretary of state, starting in 2009, Clinton "was determined to put this 'unfinished business' at the top of America's diplomatic to-do list," she wrote in her memoir *Hard Choices*. She meant the unfinished business of human right and women's rights, as identified in her 1995 speech in Beijing. To this to-do list she added gay rights, and she directed the State Department to launch "a wide range of global and regional initiatives" on human rights, women's rights and gay rights. She used her unusual celebrity status as secretary and the related media attention to advance these agendas, doing so in concert with White House policy initiatives. Clinton put rights at the center of American diplomacy, not for the first time but with an urgency that was sui generis. It was her distinctive contribution to advancing the liberal international order.[36]

Hillary Clinton's director of policy planning from 2009 to 2001 was Anne-Marie Slaughter, an academic versed in international law and eager to translate the idea of a liberal international order into policy reality. A 1980 graduate of Princeton, Slaughter did her Doctor of Philosophy at Oxford, where she, too, was influenced by Hedley Bull. As dean of Princeton's Woodrow Wilson School, Slaughter was responsible for hiring John Ikenberry, with whom she would collaborate on multiple publications such as *The Crisis of American Foreign Policy: Wilsonianism in the Twenty-First Century*. In an interview, she described a vision of international affairs she shared with Ikenberry—and with Immanuel Kant and Thomas Jefferson. (Slaughter spent much of her childhood in Charlottesville, Virginia, and in 2007 was awarded the Thomas Jefferson Foundation Medal in Law by the University of Virginia School of Law.) "A large part of what we are getting at with that concept [liberty under law] has been American policy since Jefferson—that for moral and instrumental reasons a world of mature liberal democracies would be a better and safe place," Slaughter explained. "That's Kant and Jefferson both," progenitors of the American foreign-policy tradition. For Slaughter, as for many in the Obama administration, an emphasis on rights and on international law was a new departure after the Iraq War, and at the same time it was a return to the basics, to the constitutional process and to the spirit of the Declaration of Independence. Crisis-ridden as the aftermath of the Iraq War was, Slaughter was clearly committed to a Wilsonianism for the twenty-first century, a Wilsonianism as ripe for reinterpretation as it was for perpetuation. What Slaughter believed as an academic she believed as the director of policy planning. The next two directors of policy planning after Slaughter, David McKean and Jon Finer, both held law degrees; both were versed in the failures of the Iraq War; and both followed Slaughter in her ideal of liberty under law.[37]

Through the liberal international order and by seeking to scale back military action, President Obama reoriented American foreign policy. The Iraq War had undermined faith in American leadership, in Washington's competence and in its capacity to set achievable foreign-policy objectives. Tyranny would not be wiped from the face of the earth in 2004, 2008 or ever. The Iraq War also undermined faith in the idealism for which the revolutions of 1989 were an effortless metaphor, in part because the Iraq War had been fought in the name of democracy. The Iraq War muddied the end of history, as Fukuyama himself had admitted. In office, Obama chose not to withdraw entirely from the wars in Iraq and Afghanistan, but his personal charisma and his start-no-wars foreign policy repositioned the United States after the acrimonious Bush years. In his Cairo speech, Obama avoided Western liberty as the key to international politics and outlined a liberalism of understanding and empathy. Preparing the speech with Ben Rhodes, Obama sought a middle way. "The West . . . has to reeducate itself about Islam and the contribution it has made to the world," the president instructed his speechwriter, "and Islam has to recognize the contributions that the West has made to articulate certain principles that are universal." In the speech itself, Obama implied that Western norms and Western culture were not to be imposed: "it is important for Western countries to avoid impeding Muslim citizens from practicing religion as they see fit," he stated. Differences have to be accepted: "We cannot disguise hostility towards any religion behind the pretense of liberalism." In Cairo, Obama lent material support to international institutions and to multilateralism, the alpha and omega of the liberal international order. His low-key liberalism, a liberalism without hubris, coincided with a reinvigoration of America's standing in the world—in Europe, Asia, Africa and Latin America (less so in the Middle East). Though it varied, of course, from country to country and from region to region, the overall direction was positive. According to Pew polling, Obama finished his presidency with global confidence in the United States at 64 percent and with the same percentage of global confidence in the American presidency.[38]

In President Obama's two terms, the liberal international order made considerable advances. A rules-based community of consensus, the EU existed because nationalism and balance-of-power approaches to diplomacy had been set aside. Two of the main initiatives of the Obama administration, pursued in tandem with the EU, were the Paris Climate Accords and the Iran nuclear deal. Both involved intricate negotiation; both required the highest degree of multilateralism; and both were proof that an international society could be used to address policy challenges on par with global warming and nuclear proliferation. Many of the Europeans who had opposed the Iraq War were delighted to encounter a different style of leadership in President Obama, one that seemed intrinsically more European, though it was as much Wilsonian or Achesonian as it was twenty-first-century European. Another sign of European attraction came from Ukraine, in which massive protests arose in favor of moving closer to Europe. President Viktor Yanukovych's November 2013 decision not to sign an association agreement with the European Union—"a step that would have helped cement Ukraine's ties with the West," as Ben Rhodes put it—triggered the protests that led to his downfall. (The activist whose Facebook posting began the Maidan uprisings, Mustafa Nayyem, went in the summer of 2014 to study with Francis Fukuyama, who encouraged Nayyem to launch a political career, which he did.) In Kyiv, young Ukrainians waved EU flags at the protests. In the eyes of American policymakers, the battle between Russia and the West that ensued was a battle for a Russian sphere of influence, on the one hand, and Ukraine's "Euro-American integration," on the other. "Since 2014," Derek Chollet (then the assistant secretary of defense for international security) wrote, "Ukraine's new leadership has wanted to develop a military oriented toward the West." More than a few echoes of the Cold War were audible on both sides of the conflict, but in Washington and in Brussels the support for Ukraine was never articulated as a struggle for Western civilization. Many Ukrainian politicians were fond of describing Ukraine as a bulwark of Western civilization separating Europe from an Asiatic and barbaric Russia, whereas for Washington the Ukraine crisis was a crisis of the liberal international order. It would be resolved by more liberal international order: a reformed Ukraine would be a victory in which Russia was to be punished for its hostility to the liberal order and Ukraine rewarded for its support. On this strategy, President Obama and Germany's chancellor Angela Merkel were in perfect agreement—"there was no foreign leader he [Obama] admired more," according to Ben Rhodes. They were the self-conscious protagonists of the liberal international order.[39]

The diplomatic subtleties of maintaining the liberal international order suited John Kerry, who became Obama's second secretary of state in 2013. Kerry's father had been an American diplomat, and as a boy John Kerry had lived for a short while in Cold War Berlin. Educated in Europe and at Yale, which he attended with George W. Bush, Kerry was elected to give the class oration in 1966. He argued that "what was an excess of isolationism has become an excess of internationalism" and that "the United States must, I think, bring itself to understand that the policy of intervention that was right for Western Europe does not and cannot find the same application to the rest of the world." The Cold War had led to overreach, especially in Asia. Kerry later fought in Vietnam and returned home an antiwar activist.

A senator since 1985, he ran for president unsuccessfully in 2004. As secretary of state, Kerry was a superb mediator, a key figure in both the diplomacy to limit Iran's nuclear program and in global efforts to deal with climate change. Once the Ukraine crisis began, Kerry was an engine of Euro-American unity vis-à-vis Russia. He kept the twenty-seven EU member states and the United States behind economic sanctions that had been levied against Russia for its 2014 annexation of Crimea and its simultaneous invasion of Eastern Ukraine. True to his undergraduate self, Kerry did not seek a single recipe of intervention or nonintervention: geography, history and local politics demanded a regional application of American power and influence. As far as the transatlantic relationship was concerned, Secretary Kerry left office in January 2017 on a very high note.[40]

President Obama gave his most stirring speech on the West and the liberal international order not in Berlin but in Athens. On November 16, 2016, he spoke at the opening of the Stavros Niarchos Foundation Cultural Center, a cultural grant-giving foundation. In Athens, Obama sketched the story of the West from antiquity to the Enlightenment to the phrases of Thomas Jefferson: "the flame first lit in Athens never died. It was ultimately nurtured by a great Enlightenment. It was fanned by America's founders, who declared that 'We, the People' shall rule; that all men are created equal and endowed by our creator with certain inalienable rights." Edward Everett, the secretary of state from the 1850s, who had sung the glories of a reviving Greek democracy in the 1820s, might have sung the 2016 story of liberty in exactly the same cadences. This was the old-time religion of Western liberty made American and American liberty made Western. Then President Obama changed gears:

> Now, at times, even today, those ideals are challenged. We've been
> told that these are Western ideals. We've been told that some cultures
> are not equipped for democratic governance and actually prefer au-
> thoritarian rule. And I will say that after eight years of being President
> of the United States, it is absolutely true that every country travels

its own path, every country has its own traditions. But . . . the basic longing to live with dignity, the fundamental desire to have control of our lives and our future . . . these yearnings are universal. They burn in every human heart.

These valedictory words of Obama's do not deny a degree of Western provenance for democracy—the flame first lit in Athens. The president was speaking in Greece, after all, but dignity and self-government rather than culture or civilization are the heart of the matter, and they are hardly limited to the West. The democratic hunger for agency is universal, an idea that was fundamental to Obama's foreign policy, as it had been to American foreign policy since 1992, if not since 1893 or 1776. What was surprising for a speech given in November 2016 were the two qualifiers—"at times" and "even today"—when it came to the relevant challenges. By late 2016, this was to understate the scope of these challenges, both in Europe and elsewhere. The argument for democratic governance had not been settled for all in the fall of 2016.[41]

Starting in 2011, Obama's liberal international order began to collide with multiple stumbling blocks. Ben Rhodes described 2010 as "the last year when foreign policy felt somewhat routine" in the White House, the feeling of routine punctured by chaos in the Middle East. The end of history came closest to occurring in the Middle East in 2011, when grassroots protest and social media combined to generate the Arab Spring, popular uprisings against dictatorships and authoritarianism that recalled the millennial language of George W. Bush's Second Inaugural Address. Perhaps the expression of freedom in all the world was pulsating at last through the Middle East. Then it came to dust. New autocrats emerged, and in Syria a civil war led to mass destruction, millions of refugees, a vacuum of power and great-power tensions reminiscent of the Balkans before the First World War. Syria became the Hobbesian underbelly of the liberal international order. Meanwhile, Putin's Russia was not only autocratic. It was autocratic and expansionary, having gone to war with Georgia in 2008, having rearranged the borders of Europe in 2014 and having sent its military into the Syrian conflict in 2015, blithely disregarding American admonitions not to do any of these things. Russia was also implementing new tactics of disinformation intended to destabilize Europe and the United States. It was actively ignoring the liberal international order, which came easily to Russia, for the Kremlin believed in a very different order—hierarchical, confrontational and subordinate to the power, the vanity and the interests of a few great powers. China was the liberal international order's most formidable enemy because it could be construed by some as an attractive alternative to this order. Illiberal China was growing in wealth and international clout, its rise both an affront and a challenge to an American-led liberal international order.[42]

THE MOST DEVASTATING enemies of the liberal international order were those that came from within. The Obama era finished with a double shock. First came the British "Brexit" referendum on leaving the European Union, which passed in the summer of 2016, a referendum on British concerns that took on more than British meanings. Another way for Fukuyama to ponder the end of history was to write about "getting to Denmark," a turn of phrase from his 2011 book, *The Origins of Political Order*. To get to Denmark was to arrive at the right political destination for Fukuyama. But what if the Danes themselves no longer wanted to get to Denmark? Or, substituting Denmark for Britain, what if getting to Denmark required leaving the European Union and latching on to Europe's recrudescent nationalism? Prior to the Brexit vote, President Obama had signaled his support for "remain." Either his support was insufficient or the weighing-in of an American president was a misstep in a referendum that played so sensitively on national identity. Part of Brexit's popularity came from a dormant West defined not as liberty but as an ethnonationalist entity, one defined in opposition to the liberal international order, in opposition to secular universalism, in opposition to the migration and immigration that make nation-states less homogeneous. Across Europe, the 2015 migrant crisis had brought back this West from (relative) obscurity. The popularity of an ethnonationalist West was often said to be conservative or populist, but in actual fact it crossed party lines. Its fans drew from the Far Right and the center Left, as a segment of voters migrated from conservative and social-democratic political parties to populist-nationalist parties in France, Britain, Germany and elsewhere. These voters sought and were promised a new world order of revitalized nation-states alive with sovereignty, protected by definite borders, and less culturally and demographically various. Compromise with Russia and the curtailment of immigration, not the spread of liberty, would define the foreign policy of the Brexiteers and of their disparate colleagues across the European continent.[43]

The second shock of 2016 was Donald Trump's election. Trump was himself an occasional Brexiteer and in rhetoric a natural companion to the European populists. He certainly preferred them to the foreign-policy establishment in the United States or Europe and to anything that President Obama represented or favored on the international stage. The clearest thread in Trump's foreign policy was loathing of what the previous two presidents had done. In particular, he hated their universalism. In an April 2016 foreign-policy speech, candidate Trump noted "the dangerous idea that we could make western democracies out of countries that had no experience or interests in becoming a western democracy." That was a dig at George W. Bush. Trump continued with a dig at Obama. He promised to work with allies to "reinvigorate Western values and institutions. Instead of trying to spread universal values that not everybody shares or wants, we should understand that strengthening and promoting Western civilization and its accomplishments will do more to inspire positive reforms around the world than military interventions." Obama would have agreed about the unattractiveness of military interventions, but Trump was more than hinting here at dismantling the liberal international order, reinvigorating institutions that were specifically Western (presumably in need of reinvigoration out of neglect) and promoting one unique civilization in a world of other unique civilizations. The affirmation of human rights, humanitarian intervention, the responsibility to protect and the liberal international order had all been premised on universal values, on the way in which women's rights in the United States were a subspecies of human rights the whole world over, and vice versa. To deny universal values, to pair them with decay and their rejection with national recovery, was to deny the liberal international order.[44]

Trump's illiberal West was not without historical roots in the United Sates. It was most directly anticipated by Pat Buchanan, a dissenter from foreign-policy orthodoxy of the Left and the Right. In 1960, Buchanan completed a BA in American studies at Georgetown University. Before a career of punditry, he was a speechwriter for Richard Nixon, thriving on the culture-war invective that Nixon and his vice president, Spiro Agnew, relished using. Buchanan was the aggrieved tribune of the silent majority, the true patriot because he was the typical American, in his eyes and a humble servant of the forgotten nation. Long after Nixon's demise, Buchanan did not interpret the Cold War as a bracing challenge for American foreign policy. He considered it a curse because the Cold War corrupted the national purpose that Buchanan designated "republican," compelling the United States to act against its nature as an empire. Buchanan pinned internationalism and universalism and globalism on a snobbish and unpatriotic American elite. The evolution of his thinking can be glimpsed through the titles of his books: *The Great Betrayal* (1998), *A Republic, Not an Empire* (1999), *The Death of the West* (2002), *Where the Right Went Wrong* (2004) and *Suicide of a Superpower* (2011). After a decent run in the 1992 Republican presidential primaries, Buchanan grudgingly gave his support to George Bush Sr. Into the 1990s, Buchanan continued to define himself against neoconservatism on the Right and internationalism on the Left, judging both a violation of the American national interest and a sign that the United States had lost the homogeneity previously given to it by Western civilization. Buchanan looked with nostalgia to the organically European (white) and Christian heritage he attributed to a lost American nation-state.[45]

Trump's 2016 campaign had its surest ideological foundation in Pat Buchanan's *The Death of the West: How Dying Populations and Immigrant Invasions Imperil Our Country and Civilization*. As had *Suicide of a Superpower,* Buchanan's 2002 book pays self-conscious homage to *The Suicide of the West,* written by "the ex-Trotskyite and geostrategist James Burnham," in Buchanan's words. Buchanan could not stand George Bush Sr.'s son, George W. Bush. In his assessment, "the political differences between the Beltway parties were inconsequential" in the 2000 election. An affluent elite culturally alienated from the nation and in thrall to globalization had taken over both parties, Buchanan argued, unperturbed by the anti-Semitic tenor of his argument. Buchanan was endlessly horrified by the post–Columbian Republic and by its very loss of faith in Columbus: "not long ago, every American child knew the names of all the great explorers—Magellan, da Gama, de Soto, Cortes, Henry Hudson—but the greatest of all was Columbus, for he had discovered America in one of the greatest events of world history." The policy issue that most upset Buchanan in *The Death of the West* was not Columbian amnesia but US policy on immigration and by extension demography—the decreasing whiteness of the United States. He praised Eisenhower for sending "illegal aliens packing in Operation Wetback" and was baffled by the Republicans of 2002 who "will not even demand that we seal a border that 1.5 million aliens attempt to breach every year." Buchanan was cheered by the thought that "poor whites are moving to the right" and saw in this move the salvation of conservatism, because "the global capitalist and the true conservative are Cain and Abel."[46]

More than a footnote to *The Death of the West* was Buchanan's disgust with the European Union. The 1991 Maastricht Treaty was a decision to convert Europe's "free-trade zone into a political union and [to transfer] their sovereign powers to a socialist superstate." If anything, the cultural revolution Buchanan laid at the feet of "the 1960s" had wreaked greater havoc in Europe than in the United States. At any rate, "this revolution is not unique to us [Americans]; it has captured all the nations of the West. A civilization, a culture, a faith, and a moral order rooted in that faith are passing away and are being replaced by a new civilization, culture, faith, and moral order." In fact, "the moral rot is even more widespread in Europe." (Huntington, too, had been preoccupied with the moral rot of the West.) The passage from the age of empire to the European Union was pure decline in Buchanan's view. Contradicting himself, he could endorse an activist foreign policy so long as it was forthrightly imperial and so long as it was forcing the West upon a non-West, but in 2002 "all the Western empires are gone" and "Western man [has been] relieved of his duty to civilize and Christianize mankind." Without this duty to fulfill, Western man had grown decadent, Buchanan felt. Buchanan's admiration for European imperialism seems to be of a piece with his admiration for the Confederacy and his contempt for the American cultural elite who are "almost slavishly on the side of those who wish to dishonor every banner and disgrace every leader associated with the Confederate States of America." The political constructs of the old moral order were, for Buchanan, preferable to such typical constructs of the new order as the European Union.[47]

Buchanan's 2002 book, a *New York Times* best-seller, has a polemic's classic mix of pessimism and optimism, the problem sensationalized and the problem solved. It stokes fear in order to stoke action of a certain kind. The situation in 2002 is disastrous, Buchanan affirms. The West is dying. Multiculturalism, immigration, godlessness, homosexuality and decadence are winning out, but Buchanan's goal in writing about the death of the West and in anatomizing its decadence is awakening. In the imbalance between elite internationalism and popular and populist nationalism, the death of the West can be reversed, and the West reborn. As Buchanan put it, "because it is a project of elites, and because its architects are unknown and unloved, globalism will crash on the Great Barrier Reef of patriotism. That is our belief, and that is our hope." These sentences are a pun on the sociologist Werner Sombart's prediction that socialism in the United States would crash on "the reefs of roast beef and apple pie." Just as socialism lost out in America, Buchanan reasoned, the West will win out. Whether or not Donald Trump read *The Death of the West*, Buchanan's book was the script for his campaign: the hostility to immigration, the anxiety about American greatness fading away, the mockery of perceived elites, the hatred of liberals and liberalism, the rejection of internationalism and military interventions abroad and the undisguised fear that a once predominantly white population was about to lose control. It would take a lot to make America and the West great again.[48]

For his campaign slogan, Trump selected a two-word commentary on American foreign policy. Though it goes back to President Harding, "America First" had been more memorably coined in opposition to American entry into World War II. It was the rallying cry of Charles Lindbergh and others who prioritized the defense of fortress America above the defense of liberty in Europe. In a 1939 *Reader's Digest* article, Lindbergh explicated "America First" as a civilizational mission. To be against foreign-policy internationalism was to be in favor of the West as Lindbergh understood it, without using the word *West*. In Lindbergh's view:

> Another barrier between the teeming millions of Asia and the Grecian inheritance of Europe [is] . . . the priceless possessions which permit the White race to live at all in a pressing sea of Yellow, Black, and Brown. . . . We, the heirs of European culture, are on the verge of a disastrous war, a war within our own family of nations, a war which will reduce the strength and destroy the treasures of the White race.

Lindbergh's racial panic was widely shared in the 1920s, not least by *The Great Gatsby*'s Tom Buchanan. By 1941, the likes of Lindbergh had lost out to the likes of Dwight Eisenhower and George Marshall, at least where party politics and electoral politics were concerned. (Eisenhower was no friend of the civil rights movement, but he did not base his idea of the West on racial panic; he based it on liberty and self-government.) By 2004, Charles Lindbergh was a figure so seemingly peripheral to the history of the United States that it was left to writers of fiction to imagine a world in which he was politically influential. In 2004, the writer Philip Roth released *The Plot against America*, a novel in which FDR loses the 1940 election and Lindbergh wins with a conspiratorial assist from Nazi Germany. Lindbergh was a fictional president and a counterfactual isolationist in power until his historical legacy was suddenly recast in 2016.[49]

Running against Hillary Clinton, the "America First" candidate did not merely repudiate Barack Obama's legacy in 2016. That would have been a standard campaigning tactic. Instead, Donald Trump repudiated the internationalist legacy of the Republican and Democratic Parties, Reagan no less than Truman, the messianic purveyors of liberty like George W. Bush and the legal-minded enthusiasts of liberty like Wilson and Obama: there would be no ball of liberty rolling anywhere under Trump. The American-led West was not eternal in 2016. With a long prehistory, it was a by-product of World War II—an accident of the 1930s and 1940s, one could almost say—and it had never lacked for critics. W. E. B. Du Bois and Malcolm X had accused the West and especially the American-led West of practicing a racially motivated colonialism without end. James Burnham had pinned the suicide of the West on John F. Kennedy and his ilk, on liberalism, in essence claiming the West for conservatives alone. Edward Said had pinned the terrifying rise of the West on a small group of policymakers in Washington, DC, too badly educated to see the world for what it is and to act humanely in it. The many pre-2016 critics had revealed two truths about the United States and the West. The culture had shifted in the last few decades of the twentieth century and the first few of the twenty-first. The West as such was out of fashion. The culture had moved past it, or fragmented around it, and nowhere more so than in American universities. Second, partisan rancor was acute, with intractable, polarizing disagreements about whether the United States should be the West and, if so, which West it should be. How Columbian should the United States be? Should it be Columbian at all? Should it be anti-Columbian? Not wanting to get impaled on these questions, the post–Cold War presidents tended to steer clear of the word *west*. They were better off politically if they could sidestep or muffle its innate contentiousness. In a sense they were leaving the West behind, but they also stayed firmly and sincerely within the Jeffersonian—or Western—tradition of American foreign policy. They agreed, each in his own way, on the value of liberty and self-government. It was no coincidence that by 2016 President Obama's closest ally was Chancellor Merkel, and for many real-time observers of the 2016 election it was self-evident that partnerships like the Obama-Merkel partnership would last for the foreseeable future, as would the international order they cherished; perhaps Obamas and Merkels of the world would continue to define the future. This expectation was mistaken. By January 2017, Angela Merkel was a strangely solitary figure, holding tight to the verities of an earlier age. The breakdown, the giddy rejection of past precedent and the precipitous collapse of consensus on the most basic terms and direction of American foreign policy, the willed abandonment of the West, hit the post–Columbian Republic on November 8, 2016.

Conclusion

The owl of Minerva begins its flight only with the
coming of dusk.

—G. W. F. HEGEL,
THE PHILOSOPHY OF RIGHT, 1820

A MERE TWENTY-FIVE years had passed since the Soviet East vanished politely into thin air, yet by 2016 the West found itself
mired in uncertainty. One source of uncertainty was the American
commitment to the ideals of the West—to liberty and self-government
in its foreign policy. A related source of uncertainty was the transatlantic relationship. Self-confidently growing in 1991, the transatlantic relationship could be identified as in turmoil in late 2016. This
was something larger and more comprehensive than the division of
the West Jacques Derrida and Jürgen Habermas had attributed to the
Iraq War, a Euro-American disagreement over George W. Bush's un-
sung crusade in the Middle East. In 2016, the dilemma was not of
disagreement but of dissolution, a fraying foreign-policy tradition in
the United States and as a result an insecure transatlantic relationship.
NATO was still in place. Even with Britain on the way out, the EU
was still in place. The ramparts had not been overrun. Neither Washington, DC, nor Brussels nor Rome had been sacked. The West would
not be defeated in war. It was not being upended in revolution, and yet

it still might go the way of the Holy Roman Empire or of the European monarchies, many of which lingered on in name long after they had ceased to be politically or militarily viable. Sketching the decline of the West around the time of World War I, Oswald Spengler may simply have been a hundred years too early.

In the transatlantic relationship of 2016, the party moving toward divorce was not Britain but the United States. Europe had its internal woes. These were financial, and they involved the political feasibility of the EU, but whatever Brexit and the related EU troubles were, they were not votes against the transatlantic relationship. Likewise, the crisis in Ukraine, very much ongoing in 2016, was a function of Ukraine's wanting to *join* the NATO alliance and to *ally* itself more closely with the United States and the West: in December 2014 the Ukrainian parliament voted to change Ukraine from a nonaligned country; the parliament's aspiration was membership in Western institutions. Since 2016, despite the unpopularity of Donald Trump among most European populations—and especially in Germany— Europe's countries have pursued a strategy of preserving transatlantic ties and of not openly breaking with the United States, hedging in hopes of a better future. Disagreements about trade, Middle East policy and climate change have not (yet) been overwhelming. France, Britain and Germany remain wedded to the liberal international order and to human rights, and through these principles to the core elements of the Euro-American West. European leaders like Chancellor Angela Merkel and President Emmanuel Macron continue to advocate for liberty and self-government in Europe, and where possible for liberty and self-government outside of Europe. The day after the election of Donald Trump, Merkel made the case for liberty and self-government in the United States. Her words of congratulation alluded to a German-American relationship sustained by democracy, freedom and rule of law. "I offer the next President of the United States close cooperation on the basis of these values," the German chancellor guaranteed, not knowing what the future would bring.[1]

In the absence of American leadership, however, France, Germany and other powers have struggled to defend Western principles even in Europe. Britain has been consumed with more local preoccupations. In the 1990s, liberty was overtaking Europe and its periphery. Leonard Bernstein had substituted the word *freedom* for *joy* in the choral finale to Beethoven's Ninth Symphony, performing it at the Berlin Wall on December 25, 1989. Together with Beethoven, he had set the West to music. Beethoven's ecstatic melody was appropriately the anthem of the European Union. Freedom and joy formed the anthem of the European future. In the 1990s, Yeltsin's Russia was a fledgling democracy and Turkey was maneuvering to join the European Union. Europe's former communist countries were desperate to be seen as the West, having recently been *liberated* from communism: their raison d'être as postcommunist states was liberty. In 2016, the political landscape was everywhere less conducive to Western liberty. Putin's Russia was skillfully exporting autocracy. Hungary and Poland were not exactly dictatorships. They were managed or illiberal democracies with curtailed media freedoms, manipulated judiciaries and rulers hungry for authority because they feared the operational dynamics of liberty. When Hungary shuttered the Central European University in the winter of 2018, the closure was met with little protest from Berlin, Paris or Brussels. The CEU had been brought into existence as a venue for scholarship and as a regional venue of political liberty, Jefferson's University of Virginia repurposed for Central Europe and intended to enact the Enlightenment marriage of learning and liberty. The CEU's closure spelled out the empirical abandonment of the West. In 2018, the university's struggles had the same claim on the future as did the EU's commitment to imperiled civil liberties in Central Europe.

Since 2016, transitions in Europe have paled beside those in Washington, DC. The statement of the US ambassador to Hungary on the CEU's unhappy fate described the new American diplomacy. "It doesn't have anything to do with academic freedom," Ambassador David Cornstein explained. The focus of President Trump's foreign policy is never on liberty, though the word pops up now and then in his speeches and in White House and State Department statements. Trump's emphasis is on reducing American expenditures in Europe. Europe must pay more, especially for security, and Trump's stated goal is to extract as much financial benefit from Europe as possible. The transatlantic West as a locus of values—that ball of liberty Jefferson had envisioned—has been a mistake in Trump's eyes. It has left the United States with the short end of the stick. To incur American costs for the sake of a European university closure would be folly. To impose costs on the EU in the perceived economic interest of the United States is wisdom. As candidate and president, Trump has argued for more sovereignty, more nationalism and more entrenched borders in Europe— in effect, for a Europe without the EU. Trump does not seem to know or care that the EU has been an asset to American foreign policy and a boon to the transatlantic relationship, adding to its efficiency and clout. The EU is not without its drawbacks where liberty and self-government are concerned, but Poland and Hungary illustrate the peril of a Europe surging with greater nationalism. The return of meaningful nationalism to France and Germany would be peril of another magnitude.[2]

Trump's foreign policy mirrors Trump's America. Liberty and self-government abroad cannot be credibly promoted if liberty and self-government are deteriorating at home. President Trump is trapped in the US Constitution, but left to his own devices he would move the United States in an authoritarian direction. So much is self-evident from his attacks on press freedom, his calls for the judiciary to punish his political opponents and his conviction that the judicial and legislative branches of government owe the chief executive their obeisance. That the government's legislative and judicial branches have not given the Trump White House their obeisance (with some exceptions) does not erase the fact of Trump's anticonstitutional aspirations, which are gradually permeating American foreign policy, minimizing alliances, elevating deals above values and alienating the countries of Western Europe that have been the historic backbone of the transatlantic alliance: a Fort Trump in Poland will not compensate for a ruptured US-German relationship. Trump's admiration for autocrats like Vladimir Putin is not an anomaly of his worldview. It is an expression of his worldview. In his indifference to liberty and contempt for self-government at home and abroad, Donald Trump is the first non-Western president of the United States.

THE CURRENT CRISIS in transatlantic relations cannot be pinned entirely on the person of Donald Trump and on the accidental nature of his election in 2016. The abandonment of the West has been long in the making, and on both sides of the Atlantic the rationales for codependence are gone. Europe is not destitute. Its military situation is not dire. So secure has most of Europe been since 1989 that a balance-of-power or a sphere-of-influence foreign policy is more a history lesson and a reminder of wrong turns than a living aspect of European diplomacy and strategic planning. Europeans are secure because they have resolved their internal rivalries, the contest for territory and the litigation of borders that has been so divisive throughout European history. A Europe at peace with itself is the wealthiest area of the world. It need not defer to the United States on anything, while for many Europeans the economic inequality, the cultural conservatism, the policies on the environment and gun ownership they see in the United States are as foreign as they are retrograde. American realities dictate a political culture from which a certain European distance is advisable. True before Trump, this is especially true under Trump. The United States is no longer the swing-dancing Mount Olympus of democracy that must be admired and studied so that it can be absorbed into a stratified Europe. In 2020, Europe's proportionally low defense spending, its relative military weakness and its reliance on American security guarantees are peculiarities of the postwar era. Europeans could choose to declare their independence from Washington by constructing either a European military alliance or a European army that would answer to European politicians alone. Such distancing is possible in theory. Dwight Eisenhower had argued for a single European state, army and currency back in the 1950s.

Likewise, the United States has considerably less strategic dependence on Europe than it did in 1945. The first half of the twentieth century was determined above all by military conflict in Europe. Every American who lived through this period knew the terror of modern war. Yet the American enemy in these wars—Germany—is now a NATO ally of the United States. German pacifism has become as proverbial as German militarism once was. France and Britain remain the allies they have been for decades. In the 1940s, the American military had been left in Europe to forestall war, and world war in Europe is difficult to imagine in the twenty-first century. Even Russia, which has returned to an adversarial stance toward Europe, has an economy one-twentieth the size of the US economy and is highly reliant on the European energy market. Any invasion of NATO territory would be ruinous for Russia, which tries to subvert what it cannot conquer. War in Europe speaks to no living fear among twenty-first-century Americans whose immediate associations with Europe are with tourism, cuisine, fashion and the history of war, perhaps, but not with real-time military conflict. Hitler fascinates Americans in part because he is so exotic, a uniform-wearing mustachioed dictator, a mad German with a Napoleonic thirst to control all of Europe and as such the opposite of the contemporary European politician or bureaucrat. In sum, Europe is no longer the crisis zone it was from 1914 to the end of the Cold War. The United States has the means to lead the transatlantic West. Whether it will see a motive to lead the West is far from certain—with or without a President Trump.

The economic justification for stationing American troops in Europe is also less pressing than it used to be. Since the 1970s, the European integration has recast Europe, undoing the old-fashioned ties between economic and military power. Germany enjoys a privileged position within the EU, but even if it wanted to, it could not exchange its economic might for military advantage. Germany is too slight militarily and too tied to its neighbors to entertain the thought of war. For the United States, an economically joined EU is a satisfactory resolution to the strategic problem of Europe: it reduces friction and creates interdependence. (Of course, the survival of the EU is not a given, and among other things the collapse of the EU would be a sudden military headache for the United States.) In addition, the place of the West globally has been shifting. For much of the twentieth century, Europe was at the center of the global economy. Disorder in Europe meant economic dislocation everywhere. The twenty-first-century global economy is more diversified than was the international economy of the 1940s. For the United States or any other power, the Rhineland and the Ruhr Valley, European coal and steel are no longer the key to Europe and still less the key to the global economy. There are a thousand other keys to the global economy, infinitely decentralized and intertwined with the internet and modern transportation. In the twenty-first century, the United States will need to have a global foreign policy for a global economy. No longer do all financial roads lead to London or Frankfurt or Paris. Europe is only one piece of a vast and intricate puzzle.

The decentering of the West in international affairs goes well beyond economics. For American foreign policy, the ascent of non-European powers calls for a recalibration of the Cold War formulas that Truman and others had devised. As the Obama administration realized, Asia is likely to be the locus of twenty-first-century international affairs. In addition, many of the policy challenges of the twenty-first century, from terrorism to climate change to global pandemics, will be transnational. If they are to be solved at all, it will be only through collective and cooperative action that is global in scope. In 2008, the international relations scholar Charles Kupchan published *No One's World: The West, the Rising Rest, and the Coming Global Turn*. He was charting the new foreign-policy realities, and Kupchan would go on to serve as the National Security Council's senior director for Western Europe from 2014 to 2017. There, he could watch firsthand the dance between the West and the Rising Rest. In *The Post-American World*, the international affairs expert Fareed Zakaria, who completed a PhD under Samuel Huntington in 1993, updated Kupchan's up-for-grabs designation of no one's world. Zakaria's was not a world without American leadership. It was a world in which non-Western powers were establishing parameters within which the West (like it or not) would have to operate. Zakaria put out his book in 2012, four years before the election of Donald Trump.[3]

In addition, the West is not the organizing principle it once was in American politics and intellectual life. In 1965, US immigration policy was reformed, and at last the bias toward Europe was excised. The gates were opened to large-scale immigration from Asia and Latin America. The demographic patterns that resulted from this policy change confirmed an ancient truth: the European component was only one of several strands in the American social tapestry. The Columbian Republic had always been a fiction. It was destined to be replaced by the acknowledged diversity of a post–Columbian Republic. Early in his life, W. E. B. Du Bois had pictured a United States that was larger or better than the West, humanized by a democratic acceptance of racial difference that he never witnessed in his own lifetime. The American university, which had lionized the West in the first half of the twentieth century, took Du Bois's insights to heart in the 1980s and 1990s. A global purview could be acquired by provincializing Europe, to cite the title of a 2000 book by Dipesh Chakrabarty, *Provincializing Europe: Postcolonial Thought and Historical Difference*. Chakrabarty is a historian at the same department where William McNeill had once researched, taught and written about the rise of the West. To provincialize Europe was to reconceptualize the United States. In academia, its Native American past was brought into focus, its African American heritage explored, its long history of global migration and immigration folded into the history of immigration from Europe's North, South, East and West. These were valuable academic changes, much contested in the public sphere, and they were reflected in the intellectual posture of the Obama administration. An old American type, a man of mixed-race ancestry who could navigate multiple worlds, as Frederick Douglass had in the nineteenth century, Obama was certainly a new kind of American president. He enjoyed global popularity in part because he was not a white American man trumpeting the virtues of the West.[4]

In the new academic and intellectual landscape, gain has coexisted with loss. The culture wars, which made the West a constant reference point in the 1980s and 1990s, gave way in the twenty-first century to the plight of the humanities. If the Western Civilization programs are mostly dead, the humanities are dying. To argue over the West, to dispute the nature of civilizational inheritance, to ascertain whether the American mind is opening or closing, demands an awareness of history and philosophy. It demands that history and philosophy matter, and at the moment they matter less and less (in American culture). With a few exceptions, twenty-first-century American universities cannot agree on what their students should love, or if they should love anything at all, which grants students a real freedom. From their assignments and requirements, they can choose what if anything to love. Without being inducted into a tradition, however, students will pose pragmatic and punishing questions about the humanities. What are they good for? It can be hard to say. The earlier and imperfect justification for the humanities had been cultural. The universities were *telling* students who they were. "With the Greeks our lives begin," Charles Eliot Norton had written, as if his claim were self-evident or self-evident for Harvard's late-nineteenth-century student body: the Greeks are ours, and we are theirs. The eighteenth-century American affiliation with classical antiquity proceeded from this kind of claim, as did the twentieth-century Western civilization curricula. Students were told to love the West because it was their civilization. To remove this love and this self-love (Western-themed or not) may be to remove the very foundation of the humanities, which are expensive and time-consuming to study, and without the humanities there can be no West. There can be a NATO and there can be transatlantic commerce, there can be mutual interests, but without the humanities it will all be without historical and cultural purpose. Among young people on both sides of the Atlantic, such purpose may already be gone.

From another angle, political polarization has weakened the West. The Left side of the American political spectrum is culturally uncomfortable with the West. The West is too seemingly white, too male in its history, too elitist, too complicit in the Euro-American aggressions of less enlightened eras. Yet, theoretically Euroskeptical as it may be, the Left side of the political spectrum is quite Europhilic in practice, admiring of social democracy in Europe, bullish about the EU and generally solicitous of the transatlantic relationship (in part as a check on American nationalism). Such was the outlook—broadly speaking—of the Obama administration. To be progressive was to be cosmopolitan and as such to be pro-European. The Right side of the political spectrum sees greater value in the West, per se. It continuously frets about the suicide of the West, and it is at conservative colleges and universities where Western civilization is still enthusiastically taught. But Europe and the EU in particular are problematic for conservatives, as Pat Buchanan argued in the 1990s. They are too seemingly divorced from nationhood, too invested in the welfare state, too pacifist, too secular to be admirable. For the Far Right, Putin's Russia displays the national and Christian conviction that the EU has never had. Attitudes toward Europe do not unite Left and Right in America. Indeed, Europe is yet another object of partisan strife in which the actual enemy or problem is to be found on the other side of the aisle—with the Left's cosmopolitanism or with the Right's nationalism. Every one of these differences has been magnified by the Trump presidency. To find parallels to the acrimony of the present moment, one has to look back to partisan divisions over the post–World War I international order or to the depths of the McCarthy era, if not to the ill-omened 1850s. The bipartisan West of the 1950s and early 1960s belongs to the distant past.

Finally, the decline of the book haunts the contemporary travails of the West. From the very beginning, the West in America arose from texts that were read and reread, shared and then passed down to future generations. It was the classical texts that were revered in the eighteenth and nineteenth centuries, mastery of which made one educated: the Homer, the Plato, the Aristotle, the Cicero, and so forth. It was the King James Bible that supplied American politicians with phrases like "a city upon a hill" (Matthew 5:14–16) and justice rolling down "like waters" (Amos 5:21), immersing its readers in the Israelite and the Christian narratives. The King James Bible immersed its readers as well in the language of seventeenth-century England, a language at once bare and ornate, precise and metaphoric, economic and extravagant, and a tie that bound the Americans steeped in it to the culture of the European Renaissance and Reformation. These canonical texts were a common currency. The Euro-American world, the transatlantic West, was at its heart a textual community, truly more Magna Carta than Magna Mac. It was an intellectual tradition held in common, and its greatest book, Alexis de Tocqueville's *Democracy in America* (1835–1840), was European. De Tocqueville fashioned a compendium of American and European texts into a long meditation on liberty and self-government, stretching back to antiquity and forward to the American future. In its intelligent optimism and prescient pessimism, *Democracy in America* is the masterpiece of the Euro-American textual community and the book around which the twentieth-century West was destined to revolve.

This Euro-American textual community is mostly gone. The internet and social media have displaced the book. Nothing has been transformed as radically in the past twenty years as the status of the text. The Euro-American textual community is no more because the relationship of even the most educated American readers to expository prose, to literature, history and philosophy, has melted into the blinking textual communities of the internet. The eternal present equals constant writing and rewriting, word after fleeting word, commentary upon commentary, tweet upon tweet. Today's text will float into tomorrow's and tomorrow's and tomorrow's. Well suited to its cultural moment, the Trump White House is radically disconnected from books and thoroughly plugged into social media. This simple fact relates as much to President Trump himself as to his most vocal critics whose primary media is not books but the internet. Among the pro- and anti-Trump textual communities, there is precious little political or intellectual common ground and certainly no books held in common; what they have in common is their mutual enmity. Thus the chasm between present and past grows ever wider together with the chasm between Left and Right. In the contest between internet and book, the book cannot compete, a simple fact that is of enormous cultural consequence. Over time it will be a fact of political and geopolitical consequence as well.

A CURIOUS FACTOR in the abandonment of the West since 1991 was the success of the West. The abrupt and delightful end of the Cold War incited a dangerous triumphalism. Because the enemy had been vanquished without bloodshed, two misleading expectations ensued. One was that a world without enemies would perpetuate itself. Such a world was normal: the Cold War had been abnormal and that was why it had ended. The liberal international order was global and could be extended everywhere. The other error of judgment was more internal, and this was that the Western economic model was the measure of success. It promised riches because it had been so effective at delivering riches in the past. The welfare-state-oriented West of the 1940s and 1950s was an answer to the Great Depression as well as to the threats of fascism and communism. Economic uncertainty was the enemy of democracy, Franklin Roosevelt and others came to believe, so greater economic certainty (freedom from want, freedom from fear) would have to be guaranteed for democracy's sake. The West of the 1990s and beyond was much more sanguine about a deregulated economy and a deteriorating social safety net. Was the West not richer than everyone else? Even after the market crash of 2008, it took some time for inequality to impact the foreign policy of Britain and the United States, for the have-nots to associate the foreign-policy status quo with the haves. Eight years later, the have-nots made their voices heard in London and in Washington, DC.

Triumphalism had encouraged overreach. The expectation that the non-West was destined to resemble the West caused enormous for-eign-policy frustration after September 11. The most spectacular in-stance was the Iraq War. The 2003 invasion was supposed to replicate the events of 1989, oppressed citizens taking to the streets, a tyrant overthrown, his statues pulled down just as Lenin's statues had been across Eastern Europe. George W. Bush was to be Ronald Reagan re-dux, a destroyer of walls. That analogy was devastatingly wrong. Less immediately wrong were the hopes that Russia and China could be ushered into the liberal international order. China would one day be a responsible stakeholder, and Russia could be either pushed or pulled into realizing the lost democratic potential of the 1990s. Here, 2011 and 2012 were turning points. The Arab Spring of 2011 collapsed into anarchy and violence, yet another failed repeat of the 1989 playbook. With Putin's return to the Russian presidency in 2012, Russia's rejection of the West was decisive. The global turn away from the West was spinning faster than the White House could accommodate. Moscow and Beijing had little genuine interest in this international order, which they judged an odd and increasingly delusional fantasy of the West. China and Russia agreed on an international order defined not by global rules and still less by liberty. Authority, great-power jockeying, spheres of influence and the balance of power were the thing.

In the "no one's world" of Charles Kupchan's book title, China and Russia are looking for their place in the sun. China has an economy on target to being the largest of the twenty-first century, and China practices a step-by-step, year-by-year economic statecraft that is the envy of Europe and the United States. China is not out to topple the West: the economic interdependence is too great, as are the military risks. But to challenge the West in the South China Sea and wherever else the West might impede Chinese expansion is, for China, a historical-political pleasure. Russia is likewise attempting to contain the West. In Putin's assessment, the American-led order in Europe and the Middle East has been bad for Russia: since the Iraq War of 2003, the United States has pursued a reckless global strategy of regime change and fostered a liberal international disorder, Putin has many times argued. Washington was responsible for stirring up chaos in Iraq, Georgia, Libya and Ukraine. At some point, Putin feared, the democratizing arrow of American foreign policy would be pointed at Moscow. When the West imposed sanctions to get the Russian military out of Ukraine, Putin initiated a campaign of disinformation and political interference across the West.

In the race with the West, China is the disciplined long-distance runner and Russia the risk-taking sprinter. China and Russia are no longer geopolitical adolescents in a Western world, as they had been pegged in the 1990s. Together, China and Russia constitute a distinct and gathering challenge. They will continue to manipulate a pliable information landscape. They will tarnish the West and the Western model by amplifying actual shortcomings, by inventing nonexistent shortcomings, by presenting American foreign policy as the sum total of its failures, by portraying social divisions as more extreme than they are and by taking advantage of whatever crisis or opportunity comes their way—protests, referenda, contested elections. China and Russia bring formidable resources to bear on these tactics, integrating intelligence services, the military, state-sponsored media and diplomacy. (This is a mix that the big players of the Cold War, including the United States, had employed from 1945 to 1991, with the exception of state-sponsored media for the United States.) Strange perhaps by the standards of the West-dominated 1990s, these developments are by no means fatal to the West. They are the regular pattern of great-power rivalry—not "the rare occurrence of the expected," in William Carlos Williams's gorgeous phrase. China's and Russia's rise as non-Western powers was the predictable occurrence of the (un)expected. The West is not equivalent to international order, and the West will have to recognize this, learning to live in tension with other powers and for the first time in centuries to contend with non-Western schemes of international order and information flows.—International news services that do not originate in the West, a novelty when Al Jazeera was created in 1996, are and will remain a fact of life.

A subtler challenge is the lingering reality of Chinese and Russian authoritarianism. A premise of the 1990s was that liberty is smooth. It is the way to progress. It *is* progress, and it can subdue and even eliminate history, whereas authoritarianism or tyranny is rough and a recipe for political misfortune. A misreading of the Soviet Union's collapse, this was a misreading of politics per se. Authoritarian forms of government tend to stagnate, and they can be undone by leadership transitions and angry crowds, but empires, monarchies and dictatorships are more common historically and often more long-lasting than republics or democracies. Authoritarianism works. China and Russia are struggling to demonstrate the validity of authoritarianism—its coherence and efficiency, its integration of government functions, its promise of stability—in what could be an existential challenge to the West. No underlying historical rhythm guarantees that democracy is just around the corner in China or Russia or anywhere else. Beijing and Moscow have shown some ability to incite authoritarianism not just against the West but within the West. By contrast, liberty and self-government are fragile, as de Tocqueville and the Founders were well aware. Liberty and self-government demand vigilance, and self-government in particular demands an educated citizenry, which is hard to achieve and harder still to maintain. The Sino-Russian authoritarian challenge does not make liberty less relevant to international affairs or to American foreign policy. To the contrary, it makes liberty more relevant. The West as a self-contained or expanding venture in liberty and self-government is more relevant as well. The case for the West is more urgent now than it was on the November evening the Berlin Wall disappeared. Then, a compromised Soviet communism was on trial. Now, it is a wavering West that is on trial.

A TRANSATLANTIC WEST grounded in liberty and self-government has ebbed and flowed in American politics and in American foreign policy. Woodrow Wilson's presidency ended in the decline of the West or a vacuum of the West, which was followed by the protracted crises of the West in the 1920s and 1930s, very much crises of liberty and self-government. Lyndon Johnson mangled Kennedy's picture-perfect West by deciding to escalate in Vietnam, pledging the United States to the protection of a nonexistent democracy in South Vietnam and tying American foreign policy in knots. Sickened by the poison of the Vietnam War, Richard Nixon did not restore faith in the West between 1968 and 1974. In the Watergate scandal, Nixon's disdain for the art of self-government coupled with the stirrings of an American authoritarianism stained American leadership of the West. Thirty years later, the Iraq War divided the West, leaving an impasse in the transatlantic relationship. The Europeans, as the German foreign minister proclaimed at the 2003 Munich Security Forum, were not convinced. They were not convinced by the American rush to war. Yet after each of these downturns and each of these setbacks, the transatlantic relationship and a foreign policy oriented toward liberty and self-government could be salvaged. When Trump is no longer in office, the West may be consigned to some museum of American foreign policy, a thought-provoking instance of how things were back in the twentieth century, a punctuation mark ending the chapter that began with the Declaration of Independence. Or it can be revived.

The foreign-policy argument for reviving the West post-Trump is urgent. Blissfully reclaiming the pre-Trump status quo will be impossible. A rethinking is in order. First, liberty and self-government will need to be reasserted within the United States, and the spirit of the Constitution and Bill of Rights restored to the White House. That would be the foundation for a foreign policy geared not just toward order and the national interest but also to the traditional and long-held ideals of American foreign policy, the ideals that in the eighteenth century were revolutionary. The appreciation of these ideals demands a varied approach: a recommitment to the transatlantic relationship, an ongoing reconsideration of the balance between the messianic and the legalistic common to the Western ideal in American foreign policy, and a selective use of the West globally—neither burying the narrative and legacy of the West in an abstraction like the liberal international order, nor making the West the be-all-and-end-all of American foreign policy as it more or less was in the 1940s and 1950s.

The construction of the transatlantic West is quite probably the greatest achievement of American foreign policy. A peaceful, integrated Europe has been an enormous market for American goods, a source of investment in the United States and the precondition for countless joint ventures in business, culture and scholarship. European and American creativity fuel each other: on this point at least the Chicago World's Fair got it right. Geopolitically, Europe and the United States have the capacity to act together and, when they do, to synchronize massive economic and military resources. Euro-American cooperation on counterterrorism is often behind the scenes, but it is crucial. Going forward, the transatlantic relationship has great potential, and if the United States is to retain a foreign-policy commitment to liberty and self-government, it will have no more dedicated ally than the EU and the major powers of Europe (give or take the tenor of their leadership). Europe sounded the right cautionary notes vis-à-vis the Vietnam and Iraq Wars. It has often been a constructive critic of American foreign policy—and when the United States has been able to build consensus with Europe, its foreign-policy capacity has been much amplified. The Cold War would have been impossible for the United States without its European allies. The achievements of 1989 were Euro-American achievements. Wisely managed, the transatlantic relationship can double the foreign-policy effectiveness of the United States.

In the future, the United States should revive the transatlantic West in a more than technocratic fashion. John F. Kennedy's 1963 speech is the gold standard. More than an adventure in rhetoric, it was backed by studious diplomacy. Through the pageantry of JFK's procession through West Berlin and through the political drama of his visit to the Berlin Wall, the Cold War contrasts of 1963 were presented and clarified to European and American publics. Then came the speech in which Kennedy translated his private will to ensure "the rise of the West" and to defy Spengler's pessimism into a supple and poetic language. *Ich bin ein Berliner.* There he stood, his affiliations laid bare, an American president proud to be among friends in Berlin. *Civis romanus sum:* at the center of Western civilization was the citizen, the cardinal unit of political liberty, Kennedy reminded his postfascist audience. Future American presidents should take note of Kennedy's example, recalling the Marquis de Lafayette's gift to George Washington, the key to the Bastille at Mount Vernon. An abundance of history and culture can be referenced to articulate the legacy of liberty between the United States and Europe. American presidents can speak of this West in Europe, as President Obama did in Athens in late 2016, and they can still find the images and symbols to convey their preference for liberty over tyranny. A president other than Donald Trump could have given a great speech in Berlin about the abandonment of Budapest's Central European University. *I am a Budapester,* this president might have begun, or *an outraged Budapester.* No doubt there will be many occasions to speak on liberty's behalf in the future.

John F. Kennedy's messianic streak offers troubling lessons about the revival of the West, highlighting the importance of law and institutions. Messianism leads to overreach, excess, hubris: it led Kennedy and Johnson into Vietnam, a war that was fought (like World War II) in the name of the West and a war that was lost, one might say, in the name of the West. After phases of messianism, the door opens to politicians whose pragmatism or realism or isolationism or cynicism can militate against a foreign policy aligned with liberty and self-government. That was one of the cycles, going back to the Iraq War, that propelled the 2016 election in which cynicism and isolationism came perilously to the fore.

To keep messianism in check, a revival of the West should foreground its legal side. It is less stirring, less Kennedyesque or Reaganesque, but it is a treasure of American foreign policy. Since the 1890s, American presidents have sought (among other things) to be mediators and peacemakers. They and especially their secretaries of state have been mediators and peacemakers via treaties, laws and institutions, from the 1905 Treaty of Portsmouth to the well-intentioned if doomed Kellogg-Briand Pact of 1928 and the Dayton Accords of the late 1990s, which settled the war in Bosnia. So far, twenty-one American citizens have won the Nobel Peace Prize between 1906 and 2009, including four presidents, two vice presidents, five secretaries of state and two high-ranking State Department officials—not a bad record. Liberty without peace is not liberty, and the better angels of American foreign policy have tried to instill more self-government into international relations, more deliberation and more traction for human rights. The US government has a fraught relationship with the UN, but the UN stems in part from an American notion of international affairs, the New England town meeting and the Virginia House of Burgesses writ large, to which the balance of power and spheres of influence are either peripheral or problematic. Whether to address climate change or prevent armed conflict, American foreign policy needs to rekindle its love affair with the legalistic West and with its equivalent in international affairs so that international cooperation and institutions can continue fostering a community of powers, as Woodrow Wilson had put it in 1916, and inhibiting a rivalry of powers.

The hardest part of reviving the West in the twenty-first century involves the shock of the global. In Europe, the transatlantic West is a matter of history and friendship, or this is what it has been in the best of times. Outside of Europe, the West (transatlantic and otherwise) can be distant, alien and unwanted. The United States cannot indiscriminately define itself only as a Western power and an expositor of Western values. It can be both of these things, but to act globally it must be flexible, doing justice to its own internal diversity and to the non-West which is an increasingly wealthy and populous portion of the globe. A dual-track approach would be best, promoting the West when dealing with Europe and promoting the ideals of liberty and self-government when dealing with countries that are not European. After all, the essence of the West in American foreign policy has never been ethnic or racial. The president of Stanford's Black Student Union William King, who challenged the way Western Civilization was taught in the 1980s, was exactly right about the West being international and not exclusively European. What matter are the ideas and principles that have arisen from the West. Even Truman, Eisenhower and Kennedy, the great West-loving presidents of the early Cold War, had to wrestle with liberty and self-government not just in Europe but globally.

The geographic intricacies of the West and the non-West are as old as the word *West*. They are instructive for American foreign policy. Most elementally, the West is where the sun sets relative to where it rises. Bishop Berkeley's 1728 poem celebrates the planting of arts and learning in the far-away Americas, the place that will become the West, once the westward course of empire has taken its way. By placing arts and learning in the foreground of his West, Berkeley was raising ideas, principles and art above peoples and power, above geography even. By extension, liberty and self-government as ideas and as the art of politics are not the foreordained property of the Europeans or the British or the Americans. They are ideas on the move. They take their way and can be debated and argued for in the court of international opinion. Liberty's magnetic attraction should be the frame for democracy promotion American-style, whereas democracy promotion as a military venture is likely to fail. The grotesque idea that, to succeed, American foreign policy must sweep all peoples and all countries with it into the promised land of democracy has already led to multiple disasters. Instead, Western liberty can be planted where the soil is receptive and where the seeds are wanted. Some seeds will die out, some will be blown away, some will be uprooted and some will grow to maturity. Liberty and self-government are not universal, and they will never be. Neither are they limited to Europe and the United States.

Finally, a revival of the West will be necessary in an international system that China and Russia are actively shaping. The twenty-first-century triad of great-power politics is China, Russia and the West. At times, China and Russia appear more attuned to this reality than the West does. Beijing and Moscow seem to relish the competition and the prospect of pushing against what they feel was pushing against them in the past. In a nuclear age, the likelihood of direct confrontation is small. Nobody would survive it, leaving China, Russia and the West condemned to live with one another. This limiting factor heightens the importance of ideas and culture, for ideas and culture are more permeable than borders and military alliances: NATO may reign supreme in Europe, while the political cultures of the individual member states are all up for grabs; ideas and culture travel across borders, even Russian and Chinese borders. In the domain of culture and ideas, the West has a real advantage over China and Russia. Liberty and self-government are positive goods. Authoritarianism can only be dressed up as a positive good. It can be claimed as good for what it provides—order, stability or prestige—but in practice the deprivation of rights and the corruption on which authoritarianism rests are at least eventual debits.

The West should eschew messianism with Russia and China; it should not seek their political surrender; but there is nothing to stop the West from arguing for itself, from standing up for itself and from building coalitions and alliances among those countries that wish to move in the orbit of liberty and self-government. If the argument is not made, it will be lost. It should be made with precision, prudence and eloquence, and with a sense of the long, winding history that lies behinds the contemporary argument.

THE WEST'S CULTURAL resonance in a post-Columbian United States cannot be simple. To be viable, it must resonate with the cultural overtones of a happily diverse country. In the past, a West-oriented foreign policy could certainly dovetail with white supremacy, the theft of Native land, slavery, the formal imperialism of the early twentieth century, the brutality of American warfare in the Asia Pacific, the internment of Japanese Americans and the Cold War support for authoritarian and racist regimes. From Ralph Bunche to Colin Powell, however, a West-oriented foreign policy has not been implemented or believed in by white Americans alone. A foreign policy affiliated with liberty and self-government was no less rigorously espoused by Barack Obama than by Thomas Jefferson or by Obama's predecessor from Illinois, Abraham Lincoln. Within American foreign policy, liberty and self-government have had a European backdrop, but they have been absorbed into American life in ways consonant with the country's rich and intrinsic diversity. Just as self-government is neither a conservative nor a progressive cause, it is not the property of any one ethnic, racial or religious group. While threading African American sorrow songs through *The Souls of Black Folk,* the music of his people, W. E. B. Du Bois affirmed his right to sit with Shakespeare and Aristotle, an inheritance of his people. Du Bois appreciated all there was in Shakespeare's and Aristotle's civilization that was also his. A revitalized West of principle could be used to tamp down identity politics on the Left and the Right, offering a shared set of ideals rather than a plaything of conservatives, a synonym for empire or a cause for ethnonationalist chest thumping. Perhaps there lies within the idea of the West a civic commitment that can rise above the differences and divisions of our fractured political moment.

To be revived, the West will need institutional backing. Schools and universities are on the front lines. Not the servants of American foreign policy, they should be its critics, and American universities can follow no national blueprint on foreign policy or on curricula. Columbia and the University of Chicago have kept their great-books programs. Stanford will never bring back its Western Civilization program. Most professors and students have no desire to see Western Civilization programs up and running again, but universities are schools for citizens, and to the extent that they honor this responsibility they should teach the problems of liberty and self-government—they should teach this West—in the following manner. They should require students to know a handful of key texts: the Declaration of Independence, the US Constitution, the Gettysburg Address and Martin Luther King's "I Have a Dream Speech." They can require some knowledge of the philosophical and literary foundation for these texts, from the Book of Amos to the writings of John Locke to the eighteenth-century Enlightenment (Kant, especially) and beyond. A touch of Greco-Roman antiquity would not hurt. Universities could also train students in the foreign-policy initiatives that have been derived from liberty and self-government. They could scrutinize the pivotal American presidents who have handled these concepts, from Jefferson to Obama, together with their most trenchant critics. Universities should require study of Woodrow Wilson's Fourteen Points, the Atlantic Charter, John F. Kennedy's Inaugural Address and his 1963 speech in Berlin, and Ronald Reagan's complementary 1987 speech in Berlin. They could assign only one textbook, de Tocqueville's *Democracy in America*. Students would be taught to know and to remember these texts and to see them as a story (among other stories) to which they themselves belong. These students will, as citizens, vote and run for office. They will serve in the State Department, the Pentagon and the White House. When they govern, they can reach back into their education to communicate with their fellow citizens, grounding their thinking in the wisdom and idealism of the past, without forgetting that the history of East, West, North and South is "little more than the register of the crimes, follies, and misfortunes of mankind," as Gibbon rightly noted in *The Decline and Fall of the Roman Empire*. So oriented, universities would be, as they one way or another are, the bridge between ideas and politics, between thinking and policymaking.[5]

To be revived, the cultural West will have to have a place outside the university as well. Its ideas have long flourished in civic architecture. The McMillan Plan was an extraordinary specimen of political pedagogy. For all its sticking to neoclassical and European form, it made an original and permanent statement about American democracy. The National Mall is a public place, not a former aristocratic or monastic garden appropriated and handed over sheepishly to the public. The Mall was conceived as such by Thomas Jefferson, with a President's House and a Capitol that "were not to be joined by a plaza or boulevard, as was usually the case in large European cities at the time [1790s], but by a public walk along the Tyber, a small tributary of the Potomac," in the words of architectural historian Fulvio Lenzo. Jefferson handed his 1791 plan for a National Mall to the architect of the capital city, Charles Pierre L'Enfant. The Mall's beauty is not solitary and hidden behind Kremlin walls. When presidents are inaugurated, there is no limit to the number of people who can gather on the Mall. When in 1963 Martin Luther King spoke on the Western side of the National Mall, at the Lincoln Memorial, he spoke to the nation. That was television, and that was what it meant to speak to an audience assembled at this particular spot in Washington. In the McMillan Plan, the national and the civic, the nation and the citizen, were in dialogue. The buildings individually and in their ensemble were intended to educate, not just to impress, as the citizen who makes the nation must be educated in liberty and self-government—or so it was believed circa 1900. Thus a civilizational fabric unfolds at the center of Washington. The treasures of history, art, philosophy and law were the treasures that had given the United States its republic. They were the treasures this democratic republic would need in the future, self-education being the first step on the road to self-government. Depending on where you are in the city, the Library of Congress can loom larger than the US Capitol, first among equals in American civic architecture. These two neoclassical buildings depend on one another, the silent library and the unruly house of government. Democracy without a library would be anarchy, or through ignorance it will be turned to tyranny. The many museums on the National Mall advance this same stern thesis.[6]

Replicas of the McMillan Plan should not be superimposed onto the post–Columbian Republic. The Plan's Europhilia is an impediment, but a diverse and self-aware post–Columbian Republic can still learn from the McMillan Plan. Culture and politics combine into story. The story evolves, and the story changes. It ends only when it ceases to be told. This is precisely what happened in the 1961 State Department building, a stone's throw from the National Mall. It escaped the neoclassical strictures that were unsuited to 1961, that were too backward-looking and boring, and the building says next to nothing—apart from paying homage to the first Cold War president, Harry Truman. The Harry S. Truman Building tells us that American foreign policy requires immense office space. It has wiped clean any ornament, any text, any statue that might make the running of American foreign policy any less functional. On the building's first floor, there is a small bust of Montesquieu, who as the author of *The Spirit of Laws* (1748) is worth honoring in the US Department of State; but he is there inexplicably alone just outside a busy reception room. The Harry S. Truman Building affirms modernity rather than the West. The US Capitol, the Jefferson Memorial, the Lincoln Memorial, the Supreme Court building had done just the opposite: they had affirmed the West by bypassing the more modern architectural styles of their day. As does the Truman Building, the brutalist Hirshhorn Museum and Sculpture Garden (1974), the ugly National Air and Space Museum (1976) and I. M. Pei's marvelous East Building of the National Gallery (1978) aspire to a purity of form and function. They could stand anywhere in the world. Their architects got the commissions to put them on the National Mall, and so they did.

To be sure, neoclassicism is no longer the answer. The 1998 Ronald Reagan Building and International Trade Center stands near the Mall and is an entirely uninspired assertion of the neoclassical style. It completes the Federal Triangle Project of 1929 to 1938, which added a suite of heavy neoclassical buildings to the space between the White House and the National Mall. The enormous Department of Commerce occupies one point on this triangle. It was completed in 1932, and the 1934 Department of Justice grimly occupies another corner. The Ronald Reagan Building of Pei, Cobb, Freed and Parthers hints mutely at a presidential and diplomatic narrative. It contains a Woodrow Wilson Plaza and is home to the Woodrow Wilson International Center for Scholars. Its oversized, anachronistic neoclassicism could be said to underscore the West of Woodrow Wilson and the West of Ronald Reagan, putting them in close proximity to the West of the National Mall. (Wilson and Reagan were both fans of free and international trade.) If so, the Ronald Reagan Building makes these associations with the West without creativity, amounting to an architecturally elevated place for work, for conventions and for the tourists passing through en route to the city's true monuments and memorable set-piece buildings. It is not a real contribution to the iconic narrative downtown Washington was designed to convey. It lacks the stateliness of Daniel Burnham's Union Station and the spare loveliness of John Russell Pope's National Gallery. A troglodytic tribute to the West, the Ronald Reagan Building turns its back on the modern city around it.

If the civic architecture of the post–Columbian Republic is to maintain a connection to the West, it will need to steer clear of knee-jerk neoclassicism and generic modern buildings. It will need to retell the story of liberty and self-government, drawing upon the personalities and events that are a credit to American foreign policy. Washington's World War II Memorial is another missed opportunity in this regard, so inelegant that it evokes the totalitarian 1930s rather than Periclean Athens or the Roman Republic. Its neoclassicism is inferior to that of the nearby Lincoln and Jefferson Memorials, but in mistakes new paths can be uncovered. The Cold War is awaiting its memorials. They will arrive through controversy and disagreement, as all the major Washington monuments do, and they will be subject to the debate that surrounded Maya Lin's Vietnam War Memorial of 1982. In Lin's exceptional memorial future buildings may well find their inspiration—the way in which Lin reached a vast audience and created one of Washington's most moving civic spaces. Her memorial formed a new frame for the Lincoln and Washington Memorials, placing the names of those who died in Vietnam on the level of the mythic names commemorated on the National Mall. Lin's memorial is not, however, a story of liberty and self-government. It is agnostic on these two points, shrouded in ambiguity as to whether the Vietnam War deviated from Washington's and Lincoln's aspirations to liberty and self-government, or whether Lin's tombstone of a wall is the very tombstone of the American republic.

In fact, there is already one building on the National Mall that wonderfully speaks to the post–Columbian Republic and to the best principles of the West. It is the National Museum of African American History and Culture (NMAAHC). It could not have been imagined by the makers of the McMillan Plan or by the city they refashioned without in any way trying to desegregate, although the origins of the NMAAHC lie not too far from the McMillan Plan. In 1916, a Committee of Colored Citizens was formed to honor African American soldiers. This committee helped to generate the designs for a National Negro Memorial in Washington, DC. Had it been built, it would have contained a hall of fame, a museum, a library and an auditorium. It was to be a columned, neoclassical building presumably in the style of the Lincoln Memorial and as such an extension of the McMillan Plan. Congress approved a resolution in 1929 for a memorial building to go up, and President Coolidge signed it into law. President Hoover established a planning commission. The Great Depression set these plans back, and President Roosevelt let them languish. In the 1960s and 1970s, museums of African American history were built in Chicago, Cleveland, Boston and Detroit, but the hope for a museum in Washington had not been forgotten. In 1968, James Baldwin testified in Congress on the need to honor African American history in the nation's capital. The stranger in the Swiss village was not a stranger to Washington, DC, or not in the same way:

> If we are going to build a multiracial society, which is our only hope, then one has got to accept that I have learned a lot from you and a lot of it is bitter, but you have a lot to learn from me, and a lot of that will be bitter. That bitterness is our only hope . . . it is our common history. My history is also yours.[7]

The NMAAHC came closer to reality in the 1980s. The Democratic congressman and civil rights hero John Lewis introduced a bill for a museum in 1988. In Congress, Sam Brownback, J. C. Watts Jr. and Max Cleland joined Lewis, while President George W. Bush approved the idea in December 2003. A report, *The Time Has Come,* was also released in 2003, and the historian John Hope Franklin chaired a Scholarly Advisory Committee to the museum from 2005 to 2009. The museum was opened in 2016. It was designed by David Adjaye and Philip Freelon, whose achievement is on par with the Lincoln, Jefferson and Vietnam Memorials. This building has the shape of a Yoruba crown or corona, borrowed from the Yoruban sculptor Olowe of Ise, and its prodigious metalwork recalls the labor of African American slaves. The NMAAHC is emphatically not neoclassical. Its hue is between brown and golden, and that may be its most striking architectural detail. It is not white, not marble, not the US Capitol, not the White House, not the Washington Monument, not the Jefferson Memorial. In this it was anticipated by the National Museum of the American Indian (2004), which shattered the norm that a museum building on the National Mall has to be white. The National Museum of the American Indian is an off-white. In its collections, the nonwhite NMAAHC raises the necessary moral questions not just about the prior architecture of the National Mall but about the slaveholders, Washington and Jefferson, whose commemoration occupies the symbolic center of the Mall. These are the undying questions of the post–Columbian Republic, and their power and salience have attracted millions upon millions of visitors to the NMAAHC. Since opening in the fall of 2016, it has been Washington's most vital and important public space.

The exhibition spaces contrast slavery with freedom, and segregation with true self-government. The three history galleries follow three phases. The first is "Slavery and Freedom." The second is "Defending Freedom, Defining Freedom: The Era of Segregation, 1877–1968." The third is "A Changing America, 1968 and Beyond." It is not a museum of American foreign policy, but foreign policy and international affairs are a part of it. The Columbian themes of navigation and exploration occupy the first of the three history galleries. They are what enabled the fifteenth-century European encounter with Africa, which in turn fostered the transatlantic slave trade and the horrors of the Middle Passage, all of the history that the 1893 Chicago World's Fair deliberately ignored. Another exhibition room depicts African American participation in American wars, "Double Victory: The African American Military Experience." Most striking of all is the museum's juxtaposition of two historical objects. One is a large train wagon built to enforce the laws of segregation, immobile and on solid ground. The other is a brilliant blue-and-yellow Stearman Kaydet airplane, hung from the ceiling, as if still in flight. It was used by the Tuskegee airmen who had trained at Morton Field in Tuskegee, Alabama, and were the first African American combat pilots. Fighting from within a segregated military, some one thousand African American pilots served General Eisenhower's crusade in Europe. They earned 150 Distinguished Flying Crosses along the way. They, too, had saved the West.

Just above the NMAAHC's Stearman Kaydet is a line of poetry from Langston Hughes. It is from his 1926 poem, "I, Too," and it is the museum's dividing line, between past and present, between slavery and freedom, between the pressures of politics and the efflorescence of cultural accomplishment to which the museum's upper floors are dedicated. The poem in its entirety reads:

I, too, sing America.

I am the darker brother.
They send me to eat in the kitchen
When company comes,
But I laugh,
And eat well,
And grow strong.

Tomorrow,
I'll be at the table
When company comes.
Nobody'll dare
Say to me,
"Eat in the kitchen,"
Then.

Besides,
They'll see how beautiful I am
And be ashamed—

I, too, am America.[8]

HUGHES LETS IN echoes of Homer, the first lines of the *Iliad:* "Sing, Goddess, Achilles' Rage, Black and murderous . . . " He also enjoys the echoes of Walt Whitman and his "I sing the body electric." The poem gestures toward Homer and Whitman without imitating them. It is not only an "I" who sings. It is the "I, too" who sings, the darker brother who is excluded, relegated to the kitchen and whose beauty is unseen. Shame accrues to those who exclude, not to the excluded, and one day the practitioners of segregation will see themselves and be ashamed. The line of Hughes's poem that appears on the wall of the NMAAHC is its final line—"I, too, am America." The ambiguity, melancholy and affirmation of these four words are perfect for the museum as a whole.

The NMAAHC stands at the center of the National Mall. It qualifies but does not erase the celebratory narrative of liberty and self-government, the narrative of the West, that has animated the Mall ever since L'Enfant sketched the plans for Washington, DC, with the palace of Versailles in mind, and ever since the McMillan Plan conjured the National Mall from L'Enfant's original drawings. The NMAAHC is the unanticipated and proper realization of the McMillan Plan: the substance of American democracy and the history of African Americans can be separated only by an act of blindness. Adjaye's building had to match the proportions of the Mall's overall design and in its tiered geometry join it to the Mall's other buildings. When President Obama opened the museum on September 24, 2016, he struck an inclusive note. He combined the museum and its contents with the ideals of liberty and self-government communicated by the Mall: "It [the NMAAHC] is a monument, no less than the others on this Mall, to the deep and abiding love for this country, and the ideals upon which it is founded. For we, too, are America." Langston Hughes had made an impression on the president, who interjected a political text into his reading of Hughes's poem. "We the people" are the subjects of the US Constitution. We, too, are the American polity, Obama was saying, the Americanness of African Americans merging with the rights enshrined in the Constitution. Implicit to Obama's connective nouns and pronoun—*monument, Mall, country, ideals, we*—are the marvel of liberty and self-government and the president's belief that these ideals do not fall to the side of the NMAAHC. By being what it is and where it is, the NMAAHC fulfills these ideals.[9]

In Obama's affirmation a new West can be glimpsed, foundational and forward-looking. Looked at from the North, the NMAAHC modifies the Washington Monument. It is united visually with the Washington Monument, as the Washington Monument will be forever united with this building and with this museum. The museum's outside diagonals are at the same seventeen-degree angle as the triangles on the top of the Washington Monument. "Side by side, these two spots [the NMAAHC and the Washington Monument] are symbolic of our national journey," First Lady Laura Bush noted at the groundbreaking for the museum in February 2012. The museum's upper-level windows provide views of the Washington Monument and the US Capitol, an aesthetic power that borders on political power. The NMAAHC literally changes the way the US Capitol is seen. Within the museum's non-white exterior, liberty and self-government determine the arrangement of the exhibition rooms: self-government denied, self-government fought for, self-government expanded. The ramps and hallways configure the exhibition rooms, rising up from slavery to freedom, from disenfranchisement to the first African American president. The museum offers its visitors the progression from slavery to freedom—a more linear progression than American history warrants. The visitor then walks out onto the National Mall, having been invited to think about its full ensemble, about its will to educate and to remember, about its confidence in democracy, its open spaces set aside for recreation and protest, its ideal of liberty ancient and modern, and to think about the country just beyond this optimistic rectangle of lawns, text, statues, monuments and memorials.[10]

Acknowledgments

THE ABANDONMENT OF *the West* has been long in the making. It flickered to life twelve years ago with a conference, "The Idea of the West," Christof Mauch and I cohosted in Munich in 2008. Christof's early, continuing and energetic encouragement was invaluable. Over several years, this book took shape at the Center for Advanced Studies at the Ludwig-Maximilians-Universität in Munich, which hosted conferences on "Ideas and Images of the West," "The Enlightenment between Europe and America," "American Music and the Cold War" and "A Great Divide: Transatlantic Relations." I am immensely indebted to the Center for Advanced Studies for the westward-leaning conferences it made possible and for the camaraderie, the freedom and the intellectual buoyancy it radiates. These uncommon gifts were made more precious by the personal ties that formed on Seestr. 13. Annette Meyer and Sonja Asal helped with this book as much in their personal engagement and erudition and friendship as in their professional capacities.

I benefited in a thousand ways from invitations to discuss this book when it was a work in progress. These came from Jeremi Suri at the University of Texas at Austin; Jennifer Burns and the Bay Area intellectual historians; Andreas Buchleitner and the University of Freiburg; Allan Needell and the Smithsonian Institution Contemporary History Colloquium; Malachai Hacohen and Duke University (where Emily

331

Levine asked a transformative question); Marc Roseman and the University of Indiana at Bloomington; Nelson Lichtenstein and Elena Aronova and the University of California at Santa Barbara; Bernd Roeck and the University of Zurich; Michael Hochgeschwender and the Ludwig-Maximilians University in Munich; Meike Zwingenberger and the Amerikahaus in Munich; Jakob Köllhofer and the DAI Heidelberg Cultural Center; Jamie Gianoutso and Mount St. Mary's University; Saverio Giovacchini and the University of Maryland at College Park; Merecedes García Peréz and the Embassy of Spain in Washington, DC. The History Department at the Catholic University of America sponsored a very helpful colloquium on the draft of a draft of a first chapter. The Archbishop of Munich, Cardinal Reinhard Marx, hosted an unforgettable conversation about this book, among other things, in his lovely residence in Munich. Heidi Tworek kindly and incisively reviewed several chapters.

In addition to the Center for Advanced Studies in Munich, I would like to thank the Fulbright Foundation and the German Marshall Fund's Transatlantic Academy for fellowships material to the writing of this book. Steve Szabo was the most charming and learned of helpers on this project. Since 2017, the German Marshall Fund has granted me multiple fellowships and ideal conditions for thinking about the West. The GMF's Derek Chollet gave me a copy of his superb book on the Obama administration at just the right moment. If the West is truly being abandoned, it is not the fault of the German Marshall Fund. The Wilson Center's Kennan Institute and its director Matt Rojansky have been another source of inspiration for this book. The Catholic University of America has helped in material and nonmaterial ways. I have had the good fortune to work there since 2005 and to write alternately on history, on culture and on foreign policy—or in the case of this book to write about history, literature and foreign policy all at once. I am especially grateful to Catholic University's graduates and undergraduates for their questions and their enthusiasm, and to the Dean of the Graduate Studies for financial support.

I would also like to thank the Franklin Fellowship program at the US Department of State. Robert Dry and Mary Daly paved my way to the Office of Policy Planning, which happens to be one of the protagonists of this book. It was a privilege to serve for two years in this office. David McKean was generous enough to hire me (perhaps because he is a fellow historian). His integrity, acumen and wit are in the best traditions of American foreign policy. The same can be said of Jon Finer, whose quick curiosity is at the heart of good policymaking. My S/P colleagues amassed exceptional ability, decency and high spirits. This book flows directly from the two years of analysis and conversation, debate and deliberation, briefing and debriefing, affirmation and skepticism, memo writing and speech writing and email writing that took place on the seventh floor between 2014 and 2016. I would like to thank all those across the Department of State, from INR to EUR, who were willing to find a spot for the never-quite-forward-leaning professor from across town.

Basic Books has provided a wonderful home and vehicle for this book. Dan Gerstle was the crucial bridge and is an editor with vision and a very bright future ahead of him. Brian Distelberg took over midway and proved an editor of exceptional skill, clarity and attention to detail. He made this a much better book. Roger Labrie performed marvelous editorial surgery on the manuscript. Christina Palaia and Michelle Welsh-Horst helped to streamline, polish and copy edit this book. From above, Lara Heimert added her intellectual good cheer and a dash of her press's signature combination of academic rigor and public salience.

Thanks in a different register go to my East-West family. My Lithuanian relatives have a more-than-academic knowledge of the relevant distinctions. With their characteristic generosity, my parents-in-law helped give me time to write and tolerated the conversion of their sauna into an office. My parents are the ideal readers of this book as well as my teachers in the awesome power of ideas. Their own lives have crossed and continue to cross the borders between East and West—at times literally and more often in the terrain of reading and reflection. My brother, Daniel, and sister-in-law, Melinda, have deep experience in the divisions and connections between East and West. It was a happy serendipity that Daniel and I could address these themes not just as loquacious brothers but for a time as purposeful colleagues.

My wife, Alma, followed the progression of the manuscript and book with interest, insight and humor, even if humor is too sparsely present in the pages of this gloomily titled book. Having lived through the collapse of the Soviet Union, she knows what comes after the fall (not to mention the skyfall), a connoisseur of the quality that most of us historians discover only at the end of our labors: the irony of historical change. If the East would try to paint the moon red, and if the West would try to etch the words "coca cola" onto a red moon, it would come as no surprise to her. She has assisted with this book at every step. I hope my daughters Ema and Maya will one day read this book. If they do, they will recognize in it the Washington, DC, that we (inadvertent students of the McMillan Plan) explored on outings, field trips and often enough in the back-and-forth of daily life. But, more importantly, they should do what they can to retain the effervescence, the ebullience and the exuberance they so often demonstrated while it was being written. This book is dedicated to them.

Permissions

Notes

INTRODUCTION

1. On "His Eye Is on the Sparrow," see Elisabeth Bumiller, *Condoleezza Rice: An American Life* (New York: Random House, 2007), 87. Condoleezza Rice, "We have seen," quoted in Peter Baker, *Days of Fire: Bush and Cheney in the White House* (New York: Doubleday, 2013), 11.

2. Peter Baker, *Days of Fire*, 14.

3. "A crusader's shield" in Yuri Slezkine, *House of Government: A Saga of the Russian Revolution* (Princeton, NJ: Princeton University Press, 2017), 589.

4. A. G. Hopkins, *American Empire: A Global History* (Princeton, NJ: Princeton University Press, 2018), 304. Harry Truman, "that first crusade," quoted in David McCullough, *Truman* (New York: Simon & Schuster, 1993), 243.

5. See Dwight Eisenhower, *Crusade in Europe* (New York: Doubleday, 1948). Dwight Eisenhower, "this crusade," quoted in Stephen Ambrose, *Eisenhower: Soldier and President* (New York: Simon & Schuster, 1990), 543. See also Herbert S. Parmet, *Eisenhower and the American Crusades* (New York: Macmillan, 1972). Melany Ethridge, "increased consciousness," quoted in Francie Grace, "Billy Graham Is Back," CBS News, October 18, 2002, https://www.cbsnews.com/news/billy-graham-is-back/.

6. On the Canova statue of Washington, see Xavier F. Salomon with Guido Beltramini and Mario Guderzo, *Canova's George Washington* (New York: Frick Collection, 2018).

7. Henry Ware, "oh Greece," quoted in Caroline Winterer, *Culture of Classicism: Ancient Greece and Rome in American Intellectual Life* (Baltimore: Johns Hopkins University Press, 2004), 63. Edward Everett, "great and glorious

part," quoted in George Herring, *From Colony to Superpower: US Foreign Relations since 1776* (New York: Oxford University Press, 2008), 153.

8. See Asher Benjamin, *The Practical House Carpenter* (Boston: Asher Benjamin, 1830).

9. On Shakespeare and popular American culture, see Lawrence Levine, *Highbrow/Lowbrow: The Emergence of Cultural Hierarchy in America* (Cambridge, MA: Harvard University Press, 1988), 19; see also Lawrence Levine, *The Opening of the American Mind: Canons, Culture, and History* (Boston: Beacon Press, 1996), 35–102.

10. Examples of usage of the word *western* are taken from under "western," in *Oxford English Dictionary*, 2nd ed. (Oxford: Clarendon Press, 1989): R. Johnson, "our western world," in *Kingdom and Commonwealth* (1601); "India and the western nations," in *Penny Cycl.* (1839); "the Western Powers," *Times* (London), November 23, 1914.

11. Eric Ambler, *Cause for Alarm* (London: Holder and Staughton, 1938), 132.

12. Osama bin Laden, "chief crusader," quoted in Andy McSmith and Ben Aris, "Bin Laden War on 'Crusaders,'" *The Telegraph*, September 25, 2001, https://www.telegraph.co.uk/news/worldnews/asia/afghanistan/1341564/Bin-Laden-war-on-crusaders.html.

13. Thomas Jefferson to Tench Coxe, June 1, 1795, Thomas Jefferson Exhibition, Library of Congress, https://www.loc.gov/exhibits/jefferson/181.html.

14. Immanuel Kant, "the influence of Greek history," quoted in Brett Bowden, *The Empire of Civilization: The Evolution of an Imperial Idea* (Chicago: University of Chicago Press, 2009), 80.

CHAPTER ONE: THE COLUMBIAN REPUBLIC, 1893–1919

1. Phyllis Wheatley, "Fixed are the eyes," quoted in Claudia Bushman, *America Discovers Columbus: How an Italian Explorer Became an American Hero* (Lebanon, NH: University Press of New England, 1992), 42.

2. Timothy Dwight, "following crimes," quoted in Bushman, *America Discovers Columbus*, 51.

3. On the pledge of allegiance, see Hopkins, *American Empire*, 335.

4. Adam Tooze, *The Deluge: The Great War, America and the Remaking of Global Order, 1916–1931* (New York: Viking, 2014), 27.

5. House of Representatives Act quoted in Bushman, *America Discovers Columbus*, 161. On Woodrow Wilson in Columbus, Ohio, see Herring, *From Colony to Superpower*, 431.

6. Frederick Jackson Turner, "four centuries," quoted in Robert Muccigrosso, *Celebrating the New World: Chicago's Columbian Exposition of 1893* (Chicago: I. R. Dee, 1993), 124. Frederick Jackson Turner, "growth of nationalism," quoted

in David F. Burg, *Chicago's White City of 1893* (Lexington: University Press of Kentucky, 1976), 258–259.

7. Harriet Monroe, "dost thou hear?" quoted in Burg, *Chicago's White City of 1893*, 104. Grover Cleveland, "splendid edifices," quoted in Burg, *Chicago's White City of 1893*, 111. Henry Adams, "first expression," quoted in Burg, *Chicago's White City of 1893*, 340.

8. Frederick Douglass, "African savages," quoted in Muccigrosso, *Celebrating the New World*, 145. "White America's" quoted in Muccigrosso, *Celebrating the New World*, 143.

9. On the study of Latin, see Winterer, *Culture of Classicism*, 102. On W. Averell Harriman's education, see Walter Isaacson and Evan Thomas, *The Wise Men: Six Friends and the World They Made* (New York: Simon & Schuster, 2013), 47.

10. On Jane Addams and the classics, see Winterer, *Culture of Classicism*, 147. James Turner, "concocted Western civilization," quoted in *The Liberal Education of Charles Eliot Norton* (Baltimore, MD: Johns Hopkins University Press, 2002), 385. Charles Eliot Norton, "life begins," quoted in Turner, *Liberal Education of Charles Eliot Norton*, 385. Charles Eliot Norton, "fuller acquaintance," quoted in Winterer, *Culture of Classicism*, 135.

11. Levine, *Opening of the American Mind*, 58. On James Breasted's *Ancient Times*, see Bruce Kuklick, *Puritans in Babylon: The Ancient Near East and American Intellectual Life, 1880–1930* (Princeton, NJ: Princeton University Press, 1996), 184.

12. Charles Dickens, *American Notes for General Circulation* in *The Works of Charles Dickens*, Vol. 28 (New York: Scribner's, 1898), 138.

13. Karl Marx, "vigorous exponent," quoted in Herring, *From Colony to Superpower*, 179; Lucas Alamán, "most unjust war," quoted in Herring, *From Colony to Superpower*, 206.

14. Israel Zangwill, *The Melting Pot* (New York: Macmillan, 1911), 37.

15. See Max Nordau, *Degeneration* (Lincoln: University of Nebraska Press, 1993). See Thomas Mann, *Death in Venice: and Seven Other Stories*, trans. H. T. Lowe-Porter (New York: Vintage Books, 1963).

16. F. Scott Fitzgerald, *The Great Gatsby* (New York: Scribner's, 1925), 16.

17. W. E. B. Du Bois, *Dusk of Dawn*, in Nathan Huggins, ed., *Writings* (New York: Library of America, 1986), 55, 586–587, 570.

18. W. E. B. Du Bois, "Commencement Address," in Huggins, *Writings*, 812–814.

19. W. E. B. Du Bois, *The Souls of Black Folk*, in Huggins, *Writings*, 364, 365. "There are today no truer exponents of the pure spirit of the Declaration of Independence than the American Negroes."

20. Du Bois, *The Souls of Black Folk*, in Huggins, *Writings*, 438. George Schuyler, *Black No More* (New York: Negro University Press, 1969), 88–89.

21. Woodrow Wilson, "no war ever," quoted in Herring, *From Colony to Superpower*, 335. On ambassadors in Washington, DC, see Hopkins, *American Empire*, 335.

22. Townsend Harris, "our standards," quoted in Herring, *From Colony to Superpower*, 213; James Blaine, "the standard," quoted in Herring, *From Colony to Superpower*, 292. *Hawaiian Star*, "good bye to Western civilization," quoted in Hopkins, *American Empire*, 425.

23. Richard Olney, "fitting opportunity," quoted in Herring, *From Colony to Superpower*, 6.

24. William McKinley, "great trust," quoted in Michael H. Hunt, *Ideology and US Foreign Policy* (New Haven, CT: Yale University Press, 1987), 38. William McKinley, "civilize them," quoted in Herring, *From Colony to Superpower*, 323. Thomas Borstelmann, *The Cold War and the Color Line: American Race Relations in the Global Arena* (Cambridge, MA: Harvard University Press, 2001), 16. Theodore Roosevelt, "black chaos," quoted in Herring, *From Colony to Superpower*, 328. E. L. Godkin, "civilize Kansas," quoted in Herring, *From Colony to Superpower*, 323. Horace Greeley quoted in Hunt, *Ideology and US Foreign Policy*, 34.

25. Teddy Roosevelt, "the great civilized nations," quoted in Hopkins, *American Empire*, 336. Teddy Roosevelt "increasing interdependence," quoted in Greg Russell, "Theodore Roosevelt's Diplomacy and the Quest for Great Power Equilibrium in Asia," *President Studies Quarterly* 38, no. 3 (September 2008): 433.

26. Theodore Roosevelt, "years of their decay," quoted in Leroy G. Dorsey, *We Are All Americans, Pure and Simple: Theodore Roosevelt and the Myth of Americanism* (Tuscaloosa: University of Alabama Press, 2007), 22. On the staffing of the State Department circa 1898, see Foster Rhea Dulles, "John Hay," in *An Uncertain Tradition: American Secretaries of State in the Twentieth Century*, ed. Norman A. Graebner (New York: McGraw-Hill, 1961), 25.

27. See Woodrow Wilson, *Congressional Government: A Study of American Politics* (Boston: Houghton Mifflin, 1885); Woodrow Wilson, *The State: Elements of Historical and Practical Politics* (Boston: Heath, 1898); and Woodrow Wilson, *Constitutional Government in the United States* (New York: Columbia University Press, 1908).

28. Woodrow Wilson, "constitutional liberty," quoted in Christopher Nichols and Nancy Unger, eds., *A Companion to the Gilded Age and Progressive Era* (Oxford: Blackwell, 2017), 314; Woodrow Wilson, "the South American Republics," quoted in Edward Ayers, Lewis Gould, David Oshinsky, and Jean Soderlund, *American Passages: A History of the United States* (Boston: Cengage, 2009), 631.

29. Woodrow Wilson, April 2, 1917, War Message to Congress. https://www.archives.gov/historical-docs/todays-doc/?dod-date=402.

30. Hu Shi, "product of Western civilization," quoted in Erez Manela, "Imagining Woodrow Wilson in Asia: Dreams of East-West Harmony and the Revolt against Empire in 1919," *American Historical Review,* December 2006, 1340. On Robert Lansing and an Atlantic Union of Democracies, see Daniel M. Smith, "Robert Lansing," in Graebner, ed., *Uncertain Tradition,* 120. On Henry Cabot Lodge and security guarantees for France and Britain, see Colin Dueck, *Hard Line: The Republican Party and US Foreign Policy Since World War II* (Princeton, NJ: Princeton University Press, 2010), 19.

Chapter Two: The Case for the West, 1919–1945

1. Oswald Spengler, "the best Germans," quoted in John Farrenkopf, *Prophet of Decline: Spengler on World History and Politics* (Baton Rouge: Louisiana State University Press, 2001), 159.

2. Oswald Spengler, "maritime bases," quoted in Farrenkopf, *Prophet of Decline,* 160. Oswald Spengler, "Russia is the land of Asia," quoted in Jacinta O'Hagan, *Conceptualizing the West in International Relations Thought: From Spengler to Said* (New York: Palgrave, 2002), 67.

3. Adam Tooze, *The Deluge* (New York: Viking, 2014), 12. Theodore Roosevelt, "whiskered Wilson," quoted in John Chalmers Vinson, "Charles Evans Hughes," in Graebner, ed., *Uncertain Tradition,* 134.

4. Richard N. Current, "Henry L. Stimson," in Graebner, ed., *Uncertain Tradition,* 179.

5. Benito Mussolini, "Rome must," quoted in Slezkine, *House of Government,* 587.

6. Hanns Johst and Gottfried Benn, "Statement," quoted in Benjamin G. Martin, *The Nazi-Fascist New Order for European Culture* (Cambridge, MA: Harvard University Press, 2016), 15. Joseph Goebbels, "decisive hour," quoted in Martin, *Nazi-Fascist New Order,* 181; *Frankfurter Zeitung,* "cultural union," quoted in Martin, *Nazi-Fascist New Order,* 113.

7. Soviet manual on urban planning quoted in Slezkine, *House of Government,* 592. Leon Trotsky, *Literature and Revolution* (New York: Russell & Russell, 1957), 30.

8. Boris Iofan, "monumental decoration," quoted in Slezkine, *House of Government,* 590–591.

9. Thomas Jefferson, "our Saxon ancestors," quoted in Nell Painter, *The History of White People* (New York: W. W. Norton, 2010), 111. Painter, *History of White People,* 176.

10. Allan Bloom, *The Closing of the American Mind: How Higher Education Has Failed Democracy and Impoverished the Souls of Today's Students* (New York: Simon & Schuster, 1987), 243.

11. Henry James, "no cathedrals," quoted in Levine, *Opening of the American Mind,* 60.

12. Isaacson and Thomas, *Wise Men,* 270. Winston Churchill, *Secret Session Speeches* (New York: Simon & Schuster, 1946), 15.

13. Donald F. Drummond, "Cordell Hull," in Graeber, ed., *Uncertain Tradition,* 185. Cordell Hull, "spheres of influence," in *The Memoirs of Cordell Hull,* Vol. 2 (New York: Macmillan, 1948), 1314–1315.

14. Isaiah Berlin, "Roosevelt through European Eyes," *Atlantic Monthly,* July 1955, 67. William Leuchtenberg, *The FDR Years: On Roosevelt and His Legacy* (New York: Columbia University Press, 1995), 6.

15. Atlantic Charter, August 14, 1941, http://avalon.law.yale.edu/wwii /atlantic.asp.

16. Harry Hopkins, "grave predicament," quoted in Bill McIlvaine, "Harry Hopkins: President Franklin D. Roosevelt's Deputy President," *History Magazine,* April 2000, https://www.historynet.com/harry-hopkins-president-franklin -d-roosevelts-deputy-president.htm.

17. Borstelmann, *Cold War and the Color Line,* 31.

18. Lionel Trilling, "The Future of the Humanistic Ideal," in *The Last Decade: Essays and Review, 1965–1975,* ed. Diana Trilling (New York: Harcourt, Brace, Jovanovich, 1979), 164, 165. John Erskine, *The Delight of Great Books* (Indianapolis: Bobbs-Merrill, 1928), 16, 29.

19. See Jacques Barzun, *From Dawn to Decadence: 1500 to the Present: 500 Years of Western Cultural Life* (New York: Harper Collins, 2000).

20. Herbert Edwin Hawkes, "The Evolution of the Arts College: Recent Changes at Columbia," *Columbia University Quarterly* 29 (1937): 37.

21. See Mortimer Adler, *The Great Ideas; A Syntopicon of Great Books of the Western World* (Chicago: Encyclopaedia Britannica, 1952). Walter Lippmann, "In the future," quoted in William Haarlow, *Great Books, Honors Programs, and Hidden Origins: The Virginia Plan and the University of Virginia in the Liberal Arts Movement* (New York: Routledge, 2003), 2.

22. Stephen Ambrose, *Eisenhower: Soldier and President* (New York: Simon & Schuster, 1990), 186, 76. Dwight Eisenhower, "no other war in history," quoted in Ambrose, *Eisenhower,* 206.

23. Ambrose, *Eisenhower,* 334.

24. Dwight Eisenhower, "Dante," quoted in Ambrose, *Eisenhower,* 333. Dwight Eisenhower, "Londoner," quoted in Ambrose, *Eisenhower,* 412.

25. On Harry Truman and the KKK, see David McCullough, *Truman* (New York: Simon & Schuster, 1992), 64, 77. On Dean Acheson and Harry Truman, see Isaacson and Thomas, *Wise Men,* 371. McCullough, *Truman,* 164. On Bill Clinton and Marcus Aurelius, see Garry Wills, "Bill & the Emperor," *New York Review of Books,* October 8, 1998, https://www.nybooks .com/articles/1998/10/08/bill-the-emperor/.

26. Harry Truman, "this is a republic," quoted in McCullough, *Truman*, 771.

27. Winston Churchill, "saved Western civilization," quoted in McCullough, *Truman*, 875.

28. John Dower, *War without Mercy: Race and Power in the Pacific War* (New York: Pantheon Books, 1986), 164. Teddy Roosevelt, "I suppose I should be," quoted in Dower, *War without Mercy*, 151.

29. See Heinrich August Winkler, *Der lange Weg nach Westen* (Munich: Beck, 2000).

30. Melvin Leffler, *A Preponderance of Power: National Security, the Truman Administration, and the Cold War* (Stanford, CA: Stanford University Press, 1992), 23. Harry Truman, "if Western Europe," quoted in Leffler, *Preponderance of Power*, 12.

31. Franklin Roosevelt, "We have learned," quoted in Gideon Rose, "The Fourth Founding: The United States and the Liberal Order," *Foreign Affairs* 98, no. 1 (January–February 2019): 21.

Chapter Three: The Rise of the West, 1945–1963

1. William McNeill, *The Pursuit of Truth: A Historian's Memoir* (Lexington: University of Kentucky Press, 2005), 24, 10.

2. See Alfred Toynbee, *A Study of History* (London: Oxford University Press, 1946-); and Alfred Toynbee, *Prospects of Western Civilization* (New York: Columbia University Press, 1949).

3. William McNeill, *The Rise of the West: A History of the Human Community* (Chicago: University of Chicago Press, 1963), 215, 217, 260, 391.

4. McNeill, *Rise of the West*, 505.

5. McNeill, *Rise of the West*, 807.

6. Harry S. Truman, "Statement by the President on the 500th Anniversary of the Birth of Leonardo da Vinci," Public Papers, no. 89, https://www.truman library.org/publicpapers/index.php?pid=972&st=da+vinci&st1=; McNeill, *Rise of the West*, 668.

7. McNeill, *Rise of the West*, 558. McNeill, *Pursuit of Truth*, 75. McNeill, *Rise of the West*, 599.

8. McNeill, *Pursuit of Truth*, 39. John Hannah, "bastions of our defense," quoted in John Ernst, *Forging a Fateful Alliance: Michigan State University and the Vietnam War* (East Lansing: Michigan State University Press, 1998), 6.

9. Painter, *History of White People*, 23. Konrad Adenauer, "Asian steppe," quoted in Klaus Wiegrefe, "Adenauer Wanted to Swap Berlin for Parts of the GDR," *Spiegel Online*, August 15, 2011, https://www.spiegel.de/international /germany/secret-documents-released-adenauer-wanted-to-swap-west-berlin -for-parts-of-gdr-a-780385.html.

10. On the links between Stalinist terror and progress, see Barrington Moore, *Terror and Progress USSR: Some Sources of Change and Stability in the Soviet Dictatorship* (Cambridge, MA: Harvard University Press, 1954). For a CIA analysis of Nikita Khrushchev's 1961 "national liberation" speech, see "Analysis of the Khrushchev Speech of January 6, 1961," https://www.cia.gov /library/readingroom/docs/1961-06-16.pdf.

11. On US military assessments of Soviet military strength in Europe, see William Park, *Defending the West: A History of NATO* (Boulder, CO: Westview Press, 1986), 23. On the postwar despair in Germany, see Werner Sollors, "Introduction: Before Success," in *The Temptation of Despair: Tales of the 1940s* (Cambridge, MA: Harvard University Press, 2014), 1–20.

12. George Kennan, "The Sources of Soviet Conduct," *Foreign Affairs* 25 (July 1947): 582; Woodrow Wilson, "providence," August 13, 1914, letter to Edward M. House, quoted in Herring, *From Colony to Superpower*, 399.

13. George Kennan, *Memoirs* (New York: Pantheon Books, 1983), 19, 74, 116.

14. Nathan Haskell Dole, "Oriental neighbor," quoted in David Engerman, *Modernization from the Other Shore: American Intellectuals and the Romance of Russian Development* (Cambridge, MA: Harvard University Press, 2003), 57. Kennan, *Memoirs*, 119.

15. James Forrestal, "greatest crime," quoted in Isaacson and Thomas, *Wise Men*, 308; Averell Harriman, "unless we wish," quoted in Isaacson and Thomas, *Wise Men*, 248.

16. Kennan, *Memoirs*, 31. James Forrestal, "essentially Oriental," quoted in Frank Costigliola, *Roosevelt's Lost Alliances: How Personal Politics Helped Shape the Cold War* (Princeton, NJ: Princeton University Press, 2012), 372.

17. Harry Truman, "free peoples," quoted in Hunt, *Ideology and US Foreign Policy*, 157.

18. Ernest Bevin, "spiritual forces," quoted in Lawrence S. Kaplan, *The United States and NATO: The Formative Years* (Lexington: University Press of Kentucky, 1984), 51.

19. George Marshall, "left to their own resources," quoted in Debi Unger and Irwin Unger, *George Marshall: A Biography* (New York: Harper, 2014), 411.

20. Isaacson and Thomas, *Wise Men*, 514. Park, *Defending the West*, 55. Robert Schuman, "Germany has no army," quoted in Park, *Defending the West*, 16. Dean Acheson, *Present at the Creation: My Years in the State Department* (New York, 1969), 490. Isaacson and Thomas on Dean Acheson, *Wise Men*, 514. Dean Acheson, "Europe, we had always believed," quoted in Isaacson and Thomas, *Wise Men*, 697.

21. W. E. B. Du Bois in W. E. B. Du Bois, ed., *Statement on the Denial of Human Rights to Minorities in the Case of Citizens of Negro Descent in the United*

States of America and an Appeal to the United Nations for Redress (New York: National Association for the Advancement of Colored People, 1947), 5.

22. Du Bois, *Statement on the Denial of Human Rights,* 21–22.

23. McNeill, *Pursuit of Truth,* 152, 74. George Kennan, *The Kennan Diaries,* ed. Frank Costigliola (New York: W. W. Norton, 2014).

24. Midwestern senator quoted in Dueck, *Hard Line,* 71.

25. Dwight Eisenhower, "rather look," "land of our ancestors" and "march of human betterment," quoted in Ambrose, *Eisenhower,* 496, 501, 509.

26. Robert Taft, "give the Russians," quoted in James Patterson, *Mr. Republican: A Biography of Robert A. Taft* (Boston: Houghton Mifflin, 1972), 436.

27. Dwight Eisenhower, "we are very apt," quoted in Herring, *From Colony to Superpower,* 647.

28. Sidney Hook, *Out of Step: An Unquiet Life in the Twentieth Century* (New York: Harper & Row, 1987), 440.

29. Hannah Arendt, *The Origins of Totalitarianism* (New York: Harcourt, Brace and World, 1966), 475, xxxi.

30. On the history of the Aspen Institute, see "A Brief History of the Aspen Institute," https://www.aspeninstitute.org/about/heritage/.

31. Henry Kissinger, "embodiment of mankind's hopes," quoted in Hunt, *Ideology and US Foreign Policy,* 183.

32. W. W. Rostow and Max Millikan, *A Proposal: Keys to an Effective Foreign Policy* (New York: Harper, 1957), 8.

33. W. W. Rostow, *The Stages of Economic Growth: An Anti-Communist Manifesto* (Cambridge: Massachusetts Institute of Technology Press, 1959), 167.

34. On Herbert Hoover and civilization, see Melvyn P. Leffler, "Expansionist Impulses and Domestic Constraints, 1921–1923," in William H. Becker and Samuel F. Wells Jr., eds., *Economics and World Power: An Assessment of American Diplomacy Since 1789* (New York: Columbia University Press, 1984), 232–233. W. W. Rostow, *Stages of Economic Growth,* 144.

35. Edward Wailes, "discontinue modern architecture," quoted in Jane C. Loeffler, "The Architecture of Diplomacy: Heyday of the United States Embassy-Building Program, 1954–1960," *Journal of the Society of Architectural Historians* 49, no. 3 (September 1990): 257.

36. On John F. Kennedy's introduction to W. W. Rostow, see Nils Gilman, *Mandarins of the Future: Modernization Theory in Cold War America* (Baltimore: Johns Hopkins University Press, 2003), 198.

37. On John F. Kennedy's June 10, 1963, American University Commencement Address, see https://www.jfklibrary.org/archives/other-resources/john-f-kennedy-speeches/american-university-19630610.

38. John F. Kennedy, "repeat the theme," quoted in Christopher Browning and Marko Lehti, *The Struggle for the West: A Divided and Contested Legacy* (New York: Routledge, 2009), 65.

39. Herbert Hoover, "thanks to the spirit," quoted in Andreas Daum, *Kennedy in Berlin* (New York: Cambridge University Press, 2008), 49.

40. Nikita Khrushchev, "testicles," quoted in William Taubman, *Khrushchev: The Man and His Era* (New York: W. W. Norton, 2003), 396–397. John F. Kennedy, "your safety is our safety," quoted in Daum, *Kennedy in Berlin*.

41. *Frankfurte Allgemeine Zeitung*, "a European," quoted in Daum, *Kennedy in Berlin*, 193.

CHAPTER FOUR: QUESTIONS, 1963–1979

1. Malcolm X, *The Autobiography of Malcolm X* (New York: Ballantine Books, 1992), 84. Borstelmann, *Cold War and the Color Line*, 165.

2. Malcolm X, *Autobiography of Malcolm X*, 186, 187.

3. Malcolm X, *Autobiography of Malcolm X*, 201, 207, 309, 213, 392.

4. Thomas Jefferson, "priest-ridden people," quoted in Hunt, *Ideology and US Foreign Policy*, 58.

5. Alain Locke, see Jeffrey Stewart, ed., *Race Contacts and Interracial Relations: Lectures on the Theory and Practice of Race* (Washington, DC: Howard University Press, 1992), 3.

6. On State Department hiring practices, see Allison Blakely, "Blacks in the US Diplomatic and Consular Services, 1869–1924," in Linda Heywood, Allison Blakely, Charles Stith, and Joshua C. Yesnowitz, eds., *African Americans in US Foreign Policy* (Urbana: University of Illinois Press, 2015), 5, 13.

7. 1949 State Department report, "Countries to Which an Outstanding Negro Might Appropriately Be Sent As an Ambassador," cited in Michael L. Krenn, "Carl Rowan and the Dilemma of Civil Rights, Propaganda, and the Cold War," in Heywood, Blakely, Stith, and Yesnowitz, eds., *African Americans in US Foreign Policy*, 67. Ralph Bunche, "I rely on reason," quoted in Brian Urquhart, *Ralph Bunche: An American Life* (New York: W. W. Norton, 1993), 22.

8. On Condoleezza Rice and Joseph Korbel, see Bumiller, *Condoleezza Rice*, 58. On the four portraits in Condoleezza Rice's State Department office, see Condoleezza Rice, *No Higher Honor: A Memoir of My Years in Washington* (New York: Crown, 2011), xiii–xiv.

9. James Baldwin, *Notes of a Native Son* (Boston: Beacon Press, 2012), 6, 7, 136.

10. Baldwin, *Notes of a Native Son*, 171, 172.

11. Baldwin, *Notes of a Native Son*, 173, 175.

12. Baldwin, *Notes of a Native Son*, 170, 176.

13. Louis Armstrong, "I think I have a right," quoted in Lisa Davenport, "The Paradox of Jazz Diplomacy: Race and Culture in the Cold War," in

Heywood, Blakely, Stith, and Yesnowitz, eds., *African Americans in US Foreign Policy*, 148. Borstelmann, *Cold War and the Color Line*, 103.

14. Graham Greene, *The Quiet American* (London: Penguin Classics, 2004), 10.

15. Martin Luther King Jr., "God's Judgment on Western Civilization," in Clayborne Carter, ed., *The Papers of Martin Luther King, Jr.*, Vol. VI (Berkeley: University of California Press, 2007), 26.

16. Martin Luther King Jr., "extraordinarily high proportions," quoted in Adam Fairclough, *Martin Luther King, Jr.* (Athens: University of Georgia Press, 1995), 113. Martin Luther King Jr., "free elections in Europe," quoted in Borstelmann, *Cold War and the Color Line*, 107, 208.

17. Martin Luther King Jr., *Where Do We Go from Here: Chaos or Community?* (New York: Harper & Row, 1967), 57.

18. Martin Luther King Jr., "Beyond Vietnam" (audio speech), April 4, 1967, Martin Luther King, Jr., Research and Education Institute, Stanford University, https://kinginstitute.stanford.edu/king-papers/documents/beyond-vietnam.

19. Malcolm X, "On Afro-American History" (speech to the Organization of Afro-American Unity), New York City, January 24, 1965, Malcolm X, http://malcolmxfiles.blogspot.com/2013/07/on-afro-american-history-january-24-1965.html.

20. Stokely Carmichael, "Western civilization," quoted in Michael Kaufman, "Stokely Carmichael, Rights Leader Who Coined 'Black Power,' Dies at 57," *New York Times*, November 16, 1998, https://www.nytimes.com/1998/11/16/us/stokely-carmichael-rights-leader-who-coined-black-power-dies-at-57.html.

21. See William Appleman Williams, *The Tragedy of American Diplomacy* (New York: W. W. Norton, 2009); Gabriel Kolko, *The Politics of War: The World and United States Foreign Policy, 1943–1945* (New York: Random House, 1967); and Noam Chomsky, *American Power and the New Mandarins* (New York: Vintage Books, 1969).

22. Dwight Eisenhower, "the free university," in 1961 Farewell Address, "Military-Industrial Complex Speech," in Public Papers of the Presidents, Dwight D. Eisenhower, 1960, 1035–1040, https://avalon.law.yale.edu/20th_century/eisenhower001.asp.

23. See David Halberstam, *The Best and the Brightest* (New York: Random House, 1972).

24. Edward Said, *Out of Place: A Memoir* (New York: Knopf, 1999), xiii, 82, 97.

25. Said, *Out of Place*, 3.

26. Edward Said, *Orientalism* (New York: Vintage Books, 1979), 25, 40, 42, 263, 49, 70, 253, 108.

27. Said, *Orientalism*, 4, 80.

28. Said, *Orientalism,* xviii, xxvi.

29. Said, *Orientalism,* 347.

30. Richard Nixon, "peacemaker," quoted in Dueck, *Hard Line,* 150.

31. Henry Kissinger, "can write in Swahili," quoted in Dueck, *Hard Line,* 179.

CHAPTER FIVE: THE SUICIDE OF THE WEST? 1963–1992

1. *Life* magazine, "heir and hope," quoted in Michael Kimmage, *The Conservative Turn: Lionel Trilling, Whittaker Chambers and the Lessons of Anti-Communism* (Cambridge, MA: Harvard University Press, 2009), 158.

2. Whittaker Chambers, *Witness* (New York: Random House, 1952), 4.

3. Whittaker Chambers to William F. Buckley Jr., April 6, 1954, in William F. Buckley Jr., ed., *Odyssey of a Friend: Whittaker Chambers' Letters to William F. Buckley, Jr., 1954–1961* (New York: Putnam, 1969), 67. Whittaker Chambers, "vapors," Duncan Norton-Taylor, ed., *Cold Friday* (New York: Random House, 1964), 7.

4. Russell Kirk, "he is a golfer," quoted in James Person, "A Portrait of Chairman Bill," *National Review,* April 29, 2010.

5. Friedrich Hayek, *The Road to Serfdom: Texts and Documents,* ed. Bruce Caldwell (Chicago: University of Chicago, 2007), 73.

6. See Jesse Curtis, "'Will the Jungle Take Over?' *National Review* and the Defense of Western Civilization in the Era of Civil Rights and African Decolonization," *Journal of American Studies,* May 9, 2018, https://doi.org/10.1017/S0021875818000488 (the original *National Review* editorials were published August 24, 1957, and April 23, 1960). Borstelmann, *Cold War and the Color Line,* 46.

7. See McGeorge Bundy, "The Attack on Yale," *The Atlantic,* November 1951, 50.

8. F. Scott Fitzgerald, *Tender Is the Night* (New York: Scribner, 1995), 61–62. See Russell Kirk, *The Conservative Mind: From Burke to Santayana* (Chicago: Regnery, 1953).

9. See Barry Goldwater, *The Conscience of a Conservative* (Shepherdsville, KT: Victor Publishing Company, 1960); and Edmund Gibbon, *The Decline and Fall of the Roman Empire* (New York: Dutton, 1974).

10. James Burnham, *The Suicide of the West: An Essay on the Meaning and Destiny of Liberalism* (New Rochelle, NY: Arlington House, 1964), 160, 258, 19, 257, 15.

11. Burnham, *Suicide of the West,* 17.

12. Burnham, *Suicide of the West,* 26, 172, 109, 59, 97, 129.

13. Burnham, *Suicide of the West,* 189, 200, 201.

14. Burnham, *Suicide of the West,* 184–185, 288, 179.

15. Burnham, *Suicide of the West,* 260, 258, 273, 236.

16. Burnham, *Suicide of the West,* 130, 255, 277.

17. On Richard Nixon serving William F. Buckley Jr. South African brandy (in June 1968), see John Judis, *William F. Buckley, Jr.: Patron Saint of the Conservatives* (New York: Simon & Schuster, 1988), 280.

18. See Norman Podhoretz, *Breaking Ranks: A Political Memoir* (New York: Harper & Row, 1979).

19. See Vaclav Havel, *The Power of the Powerless: Citizens against the State in Central-Eastern Europe,* ed. Steven Lukes (New York: Routledge, 1985). See Adam Michnik, *The Church and the Left,* trans. David Ost (Chicago: University of Chicago Press, 1993).

20. Ronald Reagan, "Remarks at the Brandenburg Gate" (speech), June 12, 1987, https://www.americanrhetoric.com/speeches/ronaldreaganbrandenburggate.htm.

21. Reagan, "Remarks at the Brandenburg Gate" (speech), June 12, 1987, https://www.americanrhetoric.com/speeches/ronaldreaganbrandenburggate.htm.

22. Matthew Jacobsen, *Roots Too: White Ethnic Revival in Post–Civil Rights America* (Cambridge, MA: Harvard University Press, 2006), 228.

23. See Paul Gilroy, *The Black Atlantic: Modernity and Double-Consciousness* (Cambridge, MA: Harvard University Press, 1993).

24. See Marshall G. S. Hodgson, *The Venture of Islam: Conscience and History in a World Civilization* (Chicago: University of Chicago Press, 1974).

25. See Gayatri Spivak, "Can the Subaltern Speak?" in Cary Nelson and Lawrence Grossberg, eds., *Marxism and the Interpretation of Culture* (London: Macmillan, 1988), 25.

26. See Tzvetan Todorov, *The Conquest of America: The Question of the Other,* trans. Richard Howard (New York: Harper & Row, 1984).

27. Levine, *Opening of the American Mind,* 64. Frederic L. Cheyette, "truncated and provincial," quoted in Levine, *Opening of the American Mind,* 64. William King, "I know Professors," quoted in Herbert Lindenberger, *The History in Literature: On Value, Genre, Institutions* (New York: Columbia University Press, 1990). William King, "the acknowledgment," quoted in Levine, *Opening of the American Mind,* 70. William Bennett, "defend the West," quoted in Levine, *Opening of the American Mind,* 68.

28. See Dinesh D'Souza, *Illiberal Education: The Politics of Race and Sex on Campus* (New York: Free Press, 1991), and Chancellor Williams, *The Destruction of Black Civilization: Great Issues of a Race from 4500 B.C. to 2000 A.D.* (Chicago: Third World Press, 1987). Ta-Nehisi Coates, *Between the World and Me* (New York: Spiegel and Grau, 2015), 43, 53.

29. Bloom, *Closing of the American Mind,* 36, 281, 52, 256. On the publishing success of *The Closing of the American Mind,* see Levine, *Opening of the American Mind,* 6.

30. Bloom, *Closing of the American Mind,* 322, 320, 321, 380, 256.

31. Bloom, *Closing of the American Mind,* 312, 79, 382.

32. See Francis Fukuyama, "The End of History?" *National Interest,* no. 16 (Summer 1989): 3–18.

33. On the CIA and Nelson Mandela, see Borstelmann, *Cold War and the Color Line,* 156.

34. Fukuyama, *End of History,* 323, 48.

35. Fukuyama, *End of History,* xiii, 7, 48.

36. Fukuyama, *End of History,* 18.

37. Fukuyama, *End of History,* 45.

CHAPTER SIX: THE POST–COLUMBIAN REPUBLIC, 1992–2016

1. McNeill, *Pursuit of Truth,* 133, 136.

2. William McNeill, "Debunking Columbus," *New York Times,* October 7, 1990. See Kirkpatrick Sale, *The Conquest of Paradise: Christopher Columbus and the Columbian Legacy* (New York: Knopf, 1990); see Jan Carew, *Rape of Paradise: Columbus and the Birth of Racism in the Americas* (New York: A&B Publishers, 1994).

3. Jon Sanchez, "while Columbus," quoted in Jacobson, *Roots Too,* 340. National Council of Churches, "for the descendants," quoted in Muccigrosso, *Celebrating the New World,* x.

4. Francis Fukuyama, *The End of History and the Last Man* (New York: Free Press, 1992), 338, 339.

5. Dwight D. Eisenhower, *Waging Peace, 1956–1961: The White House Years* (New York: Doubleday, 1965), 658.

6. George H. W. Bush, "A Europe Whole and Free: Remarks to the Citizens in Mainz" (speech), May 31, 1989, https://usa.usembassy.de/etexts/ga6-89 0531.htm.

7. Bill Clinton, "an America that will not coddle," quoted in James Mann, *The Obamians: The Struggle Inside the White House to Redefine American Power* (New York: Viking, 2012), 33.

8. See Philip Zelikow and Condoleezza Rice, *Germany Unified and Europe Transformed: A Study in Statecraft* (Cambridge, MA: Harvard University Press, 1995).

9. Warren Christopher, *Chances of a Lifetime* (New York: Scribner's, 2011), 274. Madeleine Albright thesis cited in Michael Dobbs, *Madeleine Albright: A Twentieth-Century Odyssey* (New York: Henry Holt, 1999), 153; Madeleine

Albright, "broad-based coalitions," quoted in Dobbs, *Madeleine Albright*, 350; on photos in Secretary Albright's office, see Dobbs, *Madeleine Albright*, 401

10. See Thomas L. Friedman, *The Lexus and the Olive Tree: Understanding Globalization* (New York: Picador, 2012).

11. Robert Kaplan, "lifelong Democrat," in "Looking the World in the Eye," *Atlantic Monthly*, December 2001, https://www.theatlantic.com/magazine /archive/2001/12/looking-the-world-in-the-eye/302354/.

12. Samuel Huntington, *The Clash of Civilizations and the Remaking of World Order* (New York: Simon & Schuster, 1996), 13, 20, 19, 28.

13. Huntington, *Clash of Civilizations*, 42, 46.

14. Huntington, *Clash of Civilizations*, 51, 33, 55.

15. Huntington, *Clash of Civilizations*, 131, 183.

16. Huntington, *Clash of Civilizations*, 65, 83, 58.

17. Huntington, *Clash of Civilizations*, 303, 305, 321.

18. Huntington, *Clash of Civilizations*, 306, 307, 318, 308.

19. See Francis Fukuyama, *America at the Crossroads: Democracy, Power, and the Neoconservative Legacy* (New Haven, CT: Yale University Press, 2006).

20. Edward Said, *Orientalism* (New York: Vintage Books, 2003), xix.

21. Heinrich August Winkler, *Geschichte des Westens. Von den Anfaengen in der Antike bis zum 20. Jahrhundert* (Munich: Beck, 2016), 13 [author's translation]. See Samuel Huntington and Lawrence E. Harrison, eds., *Culture Matters: How Values Shape Human Progress* (New York: Basic Books, 2000). See Bernard Lewis, *What Went Wrong? Western Impact and Middle East Response* (New York: Oxford University Press, 2002).

22. George W. Bush, Second Inaugural Address, January 20, 2005, https:// www.npr.org/templates/story/story.php?storyId=4460172.

23. Joschka Fischer, "I am not convinced," quoted in Kate Connolly, "I Am Not Convinced, Fischer Tells Rumsfeld," *The Telegraph* (London), February 10, 2003. See Jürgen Habermas, *The Divided West*, trans. Ciaran Cronin (Cambridge: Polity, 2006).

24. On the 2003 State Department Office of Policy Planning memo, "Why NATO Should Invite Russia to Join," see Angela Stent, *The Limits of Partnership: US-Russian Relations in the Twenty-First Century* (Princeton, NJ: Princeton University Press, 2014), 75.

25. See Robert Kagan, *Of Paradise and Power: America and Europe in the New World Order* (New York: Knopf, 2003).

26. Derek Chollet, *The Long Game: How Obama Defied Washington and Redefined America's Role in the World* (New York: PublicAffairs, 2016), 33.

27. "Ideas in Western Literature" from David Remnick, *The Bridge: The Life and Rise of Barack Obama* (New York: Knopf, 2010), 76. Barack Obama, "flake," quoted in Remnick, *The Bridge*, 133.

28. Barack Obama, "legacy of colonialism," quoted in Chollet, *Long Game*, 67; Barack Obama, "point fingers," quoted in Ibrahim Sundiata, "Obama, African Americans, and Africans," in Heywood, Blakely, Stith, and Yesnowitz, eds., *African Americans in US Foreign Policy*, 207; Barack Obama, "strong institutions," quoted in Chollet, *Long Game*, 66.

29. Chollet, *Long Game*, xiv. See Jeane Kirkpatrick, *Making War to Keep Peace: Trials and Errors in American Foreign Policy from Kuwait to Bagdad* (New York: Harper, 2008).

30. Chollet, *Long Game*, 135. Ben Rhodes, *The World as It Is: A Memoir of the Obama White House* (New York: Random House, 2018), 64.

31. Rhodes, *World as It Is*, 18–19. See Samantha Power, "*A Problem from Hell*": *America and the Age of Genocide* (New York: Basic Books, 2002).

32. See Hedley Bull, *The Anarchical Society: A Study of Order in World Politics* (New York: Columbia University Press, 1977), 16; Hedley Bull *The Expansion of International Society* (New York: Oxford University Press, 1984); and Hedley Bull, *Justice in International Relations* (Waterloo, Ontario: University of Waterloo, 1984). William Burns, *The Back Channel: A Memoir of American Diplomacy and the Case for Its Renewal* (New York: Random House, 2019), 20.

33. See John Ikenberry, *Liberal Order and Imperial Ambition: Essays on American Power and World Politics* (Malden, MA: Polity, 2006); and *Liberal Leviathan: The Origins, Crisis, and Transformation of the American World Order* (Princeton, NJ: Princeton University Press, 2011).

34. G. John Ikenberry, "Democracy, Institutions, and American Restraint," in *America Unrivaled: The Future of the Balance of Power* (Ithaca, NY: Cornell University Press, 2002), 215. Michael McFaul, *From Cold War to Hot Peace: An American Ambassador in Putin's Russia* (New York: Houghton Mifflin, 2018), 220. Rhodes, *World as It Is*, 48.

35. See Hua Hsu, "The End of White America?" *The Atlantic*, January/February 2009.

36. Hillary Clinton, *Hard Choices* (New York: Simon & Schuster, 2014), 561, 567, 568.

37. See Anne-Marie Slaughter, John Ikenberry, Thomas J. Knock, and Tony Smith, eds., *The Crisis of American Foreign Policy: Wilsonianism in the Twenty-first Century* (Princeton, NJ: Princeton University Press, 2008). Anne-Marie Slaughter, "A large part," quoted in an interview with Alan Johnson, in Alan Johnson, ed., *Global Politics After 9/11: The Demokratiya Interviews* (London: Foreign Policy Centre, 2008), 131.

38. Rhodes, *World as It Is*, 53. On attitudes toward the United States in 2016, see Richard Wike, Jacob Poushter, and Hani Zainulbhai, "As Obama Years Draw to a Close, President and US Seen Favorably in Europe and Asia," Pew Research Center, 2017, https://www.pewresearch.org/global/2016/06/29/as-obama-years-draw-to-close-president-and-u-s-seen-favorably-in-europe-and-asia/.

39. Rhodes, *World as It Is,* 267. Chollet, *Long Game,* 170. Rhodes, *World as It Is,* 230. On Mustafa Nayyem and Francis Fukuyama, see Joshua Yaffa, "Reforming Ukraine After the Revolutions," *The New Yorker,* August 29, 2016, https://www.newyorker.com/magazine/2016/09/05/reforming-ukraine-after -maidan.

40. Douglas Brinkley, *Tour of Duty: John Kerry and the Vietnam War* (New York: William Morrow, 2004), 61, 62.

41. Rhodes, *World as It Is,* 149.

42. Rhodes, *World as It Is,* 91.

43. "Getting to Denmark," in Francis Fukuyama, *The Origins of Political Order: From Prehuman Times to the French Revolution* (New York. Farrar, Straus & Giroux, 2011), 25.

44. For a transcript of Donald Trump foreign-policy speech, delivered on April 27, 2016, see https://www.nytimes.com/2016/04/28/us/politics /transcript-trump-foreign-policy.html.

45. See Patrick Buchanan, *The Great Betrayal: How American Sovereignty and Social Justice Are Being Sacrificed to the Gods of the Global Economy* (Boston: Little, Brown, 1998); *A Republic, Not an Empire: Reclaiming America's Destiny* (Washington, DC: Regnery, 1999); *Where the Right Went Wrong: How Neoconservatives Subverted the Reagan Revolution and Hijacked the Bush Presidency* (New York: Thomas Dunne, 2004); and *Suicide of a Superpower: Will America Survive to 2025?* (New York: Thomas Dunne, 2011).

46. Pat Buchanan, *The Death of the West: How Dying Populations and Immigrant Invasions Imperil Our Country and Civilization* (New York: Thomas Dunne, 2002), 228, 6, 9, 150, 208, 223, 229.

47. Buchanan, *Death of the West,* 4, 209, 10, 163.

48. Buchanan, *Death of the West,* 240.

49. Charles Lindbergh, "another barrier," quoted in Painter, *History of White People,* 349.

Conclusion

1. Angela Merkel, "I offer the next President," quoted in Carol Giacomo, "Angela Merkel's Message to Trump," *New York Times,* November 9, 2016, https://www.nytimes.com/interactive/projects/cp/opinion/election-night -2016/angela-merkels-warning-to-trump.

2. David Cornstein, "with academic freedom," quoted in Griff Witte, "Soros-Funded University Says It Has Been Kicked Out of Hungary as an Autocrat Tightens His Grip," *Washington Post,* December 3, 2018, https://www .washingtonpost.com/world/soros-founded-university-says-it-has-been -kicked-out-of-hungary-as-an-autocrat-tightens-his-grip/2018/12/03/26bd fc28-f6ed-11e8-8d64-4e79db33382f_story.html?utm_term=.f867ac7c4d50.

3. See Charles Kupchan, *No One's World: The West, the Rising Rest, and the Coming Global Turn* (New York: Oxford University Press, 2012); and Fareed Zakaria, *The Post-American World* (New York: W. W. Norton, 2008).

4. See Dipesh Chakrabarty, *Provincializing Europe: Postcolonial Thought and Historical Difference* (Princeton, NJ: Princeton University Press, 2000).

5. Edmund Gibbon, *The Decline and Fall of the Roman Empire* (New York: Dutton, 1974), 120.

6. Thomas Jefferson, "were not to be joined," quoted in Fulvio Lenzo, "Jefferson: Architecture and Democracy," in *Jefferson and Palladio: Constructing a New World,* ed. Guido Beltramini and Fulvio Lenzo (Milan: Officinia Libraria, 2015), 43–44.

7. James Baldwin, "If we are going," quoted in Kathleen M. Kendrick, *The Official Guide to the Smithsonian National African American History and Culture Museum* (Washington, DC: Smithsonian Books, 2017), 12.

8. Langston Hughes, "I, Too" in *The Collected Poems of Langston Hughes,* ed. Arnold Rampersad and David Roessel (New York: Knopf, 1998).

9. Barack Obama, "is a monument," quoted in Kendrick, *Official Guide to the Smithsonian National African American History and Culture Museum,* 5.

10. Laura Bush, "Side by side," quoted in Kendrick, *Official Guide to the Smithsonian National African American History and Culture Museum,* 24.

Index

[[Index TK]]

Michael Kimmage is a professor of history at the Catholic University of America and a fellow at the German Marshall Fund. From 2014 to 2016, he served on the secretary's policy planning staff at the US Department of State. He specializes in international relations and in the history of the United States, Europe, Russia and the Soviet Union. He is the author of two books, *The Conservative Turn: Lionel Trilling, Whittaker Chambers and the Lessons of Anti-Communism* and *In History's Grip: Philip Roth's Newark Trilogy*. He has written for the *New York Times Book Review, Washington Post, Frankfurter Allgemeine Zeitung, Foreign Affairs* and the *New Republic*. He lives with his wife and two daughters in Washington, DC.